Cheatham County Tennessee

WILLS AND INVENTORIES

Volume A

1856–1871

WPA RECORDS

Heritage Books
2024

HERITAGE BOOKS

AN IMPRINT OF HERITAGE BOOKS, INC.

Books, CDs, and more—Worldwide

For our listing of thousands of titles see our website
at
www.HeritageBooks.com

A Facsimile Reprint
Published 2024 by
HERITAGE BOOKS, INC.
Publishing Division
5810 Ruatan Street
Berwyn Heights, MD 20740

May 25, 1938

— Publisher's Notice —

In reprints such as this, it is often not possible to remove blemishes from the original. We feel the contents of this book warrant its reissue despite these blemishes and hope you will agree and read it with pleasure.

International Standard Book Number
Paperbound: 978-0-7884-9069-9

TENNESSEE

RECORDS OF CHEATHAM COUNTY

WILLS & INVENTORIES VOL. A
1856 - 1871

HISTORICAL RECORDS PROJECT
OFFICIAL PROJECT NO. 165-44-3-115

COPIED UNDER WORK'S PROGRESS ADMINISTRATION

MRS. JOHN TROTWOOD MOORE
STATE LIBRARIAN & ARCHIVIST, SPONSOR

MRS. ELIZABETH D. COPPEDGE
DIRECTOR OF WOMEN'S & PROFESSIONAL PROJECTS

MRS. PENELOPE JOHNSON ALLEN
STATE SUPERVISOR

MISS MATILDA A. PORTER
SUPERVISOR SECOND DISTRICT

COPIED BY
MRS. EDNA HUNTER

TYPED BY
1856 -1860
MRS. FRANKIE BEERMAN
APR. 29, 1937

1860 - 1871
MRS. VIOLET PERRY

MAY 25, 1938.

WPA RECORDS

The WPA Records are, for the most part, carbon copies of the original that was typed on onion skin paper during the Depression. Since these records were typed on poor machines by people who did not type well either and read by persons not always sure of the older handwritten material, the results are often less that perfect.

We have made every attempt to make as good a copy as can be made from these older papers. Sometimes there are water stains and burned edges around the paper.. This is the results of a fire at the home of one of the workers, Mrs. Penelope Allen, who was over most of the project.

The WPA Records are now very scattered between the State Archives, various Public and Private Libraries and other collections. Some day, there is a hope that all of these can be collected and stored in one place. In spite of their many mistakes and problems, these are still the most complete collection of Tennessee records found anywhere.

CHEATHAM COUNTY

WILLS & INVENTORIES VOL. A.
1856 - 1871

ORIGINAL INDEX

Note: Page numbers in this index refer to those of the original volume from which this copy was made. These numbers are carried in the body of the manuscript within parentheses, as; (p 124)

A

B

J

ERRATA

(Note 1. The page numbers for ERRATA refer to the pages of the original volume, and are to be found enclosed between parentheses throughout the body of the manuscript.)

(Note 2. Where paragraphs or instruments covering half a page, or more, have been omitted, an additional page has been inserted immediately after the one in error, as: page 102 is followed by page 102a, which contains the omitted items. This correction is not to be confused with entries for ERRATA. Shorter ommissions are to be found under ERRATA.)

(p 10) Should be Pritchard
(p 14) Should be Michalson
(p 54) Should be Hollis
(p 63) Should be Thomas
(p 77) Should be Fagleman
(p 115) Should be S. Walker
(p 131) Should be Tensley
(p 174) Should be Purson

(See Errata for corrections)

CHEATHAM COUNTY

WILLS & INVENTORIES VOL. A
1856-1875

(p1) Last Will and Testament of JOHN HUNT, deceased.

I John Hunt do make and publish this as my last will and testament, hereby making null and void all other wills by me at any time made.

First I direct that my funeral expenses and all my just debts be paid out of any money that I may have at my death, or that May first come into the hands of my executors

Secondly, I give to my wife Elizabeth H. Hunt during her widowhood, or life, my boys Henry and Mack and my Woman Jane and my girls Gustavia and Kitty my tract of land allmy household and kitchen furniture, farming tools and stock of all kinds, at the Marriage or death of my Wife Elizabeth, the above named property to be sold by my executor and divided as I may hereafter direct, that is to say the proceeds to be equally divided between my children after making all equal with the advancement already made and charged to each of them. I charge my daughter Polly P. Ryan, with four hundred and ten dollars, I Charge My daughter Eliza W. Wilson with five hundred and ninety dollars. I Charge my daughter Dicy Ann Shaw with five hundred and five dollars, I charge my daughter Elizabeth S. Gatewood with seven hundred and ninety two dollars.

Thirdly, I give to my daughter Narcissa C. My slaves. Sally Dick and Anna, and my horse Charley to be valued to her at My death by two disinterested persons.

Fourthly, I give to my son James B. My boys Marcelle and Strickland, and my horse, Porter, to be valued to him at my death by two disinterested persons.

Fifthly, I leave to My daughter Dicy Ann Shaw My girl Lucy during her life, to be valued to her at my death, and at the death of My daughter Dicy Ann the girl Lucy and her increase to be sold and the proceeds to be equally divided between the Children of my daughter Dicy Ann.

Sixthly, It is my will that at My death that all my Notes and accounts be Collected and the proceeds With all the Money on hand be equally divided between My wife Elizabeth H. and all My children.

Seventhly, I direct that My wife Elizabeth H. have power and authority to sell or dispose of any stock or other perishable property for the use and support of the family.

And lastly I do hereby Nominate My wife Elizabeth H. Hunt, and My Nephew J. W. Hunt, my executrix and executor to this my last will. In Witness where unto I have set my hand and Affixed my seal this the second day of July 1855.

Signed and acknowledged in our presence.

Test:

N. J. Alley John Hunt (SEAL)

S. J. Alley

(p2) Cheatham County July term 1856.

State of Tennessee, Cheatham County. To JAMES W. HUNT and E. H. HUNT citizen of Cheatham County.

It appearing to the Court that John Hunt has died le aving a written will, in which you are appointed executor and executors which has been duly proven in Open Court, and you having given bond and qualified according to law, and it having bean ordered by the said Court that letters testamentory issue to you.

These are therefore to empower you the said J. W. Hunt and E. H. Hunt to enter upon the execution of the said will and take into your possession all the property and to make to the next Court a perfect inventory thereof and make due Collection of all debts and after paying all the just demands against the testator and settling up the business of said estate, according to law. You will pay over and deliver the property and effects, that may remain in your hands and to do all other things that may be required according to the provision of the said will and the laws of the land.

Witness W. W. Williams, Clerk at office the 7th, day of July 1856 and the 80th year of American Independence.

W. W. Williams, Clerk

The following is an inventory of the property belonging to the estate of John Bledsoe, deceased, as reported by the administrator Samuel A. Thompson.

Accounts

1 Account on E. W. Goodrich ---------------- 1.15
1 Account on W. R. Hutton ---------------- 1.00 2.15

Land

1 Tract of land Containing 37 Acres

Slaves

1 Woman aged 22 years
1 Child aged 3 years

A list of property sold a sale price and Co 26th July 1856.

Purchasers Named	Property sold		
B. F. Hannah	1 Wooden lathe	2.00	
B. F. Hannah	2 plains	.80	
B. F. Hannah	1 Plain and Square	.40	
B. F. Hannah	1 Square and guage	.20	
B. F. Hannah	3 Chisels	.25	
B. F. Hannah	1 hand saw	.60	
B. F. Hannah	1 iron laythe	5.00	
B. F. Hannah	1 work bench	.50	10.45
B. F. Hannah	1 work bench	.70	12.60
B. F. Hannah	1 box sundries	.25	12.60

(p3)

B. F. Hannah	1 " "	.25
B. F. Hannah	1 bow saw	.12
B. F. Hannah	1 lot Machine Cards	.15
B. F. Hannah	1 lot Machine Timber	.75
B. F. Hannah	1 Vice	2.40
B. F. Hannah	1 anvil and bellows	1.00
B. F. Hannah	1 sledge hammer	.25
B. F. Hannah	1 drill and ladle	.40
B. F. Hannah	1 pair shears	.50
B. F. Hannah	1 Chisel amd file	.20
B. F. Hannah	1 Iron	.30
B. F. Hannah	1 Machine	.15
B. F. Hannah	1 stock and dies	2.10

B. F. Hannah	2 Yearling 2m 8m	4.55	
B.F. Hannah	Hire Negro at $2 pr.Mth	4.80	
Louesa Bledsoe	1 brace and bit	.60	
Louesa Bledsoe	1 hatchet	.05	
Louisa Bledsoe	1 sideboard	1.00	
Louise Bledsoe	1 lot leather	1.10	
Louisa Bledsoe	1 lot hoop iron	.05	
Louisa Bledsoe	1 pea patch	.50	
Louisa Bledsoe	1 White face Cow	5.50	
Louisa Bledsoe	1 screw driver	.05	
William Biggers	1 Fore Plain	.50	
William Woodward	1 Terrant saw	.75	
Moses Jones	1 roll wire	.15	
Moses Jones	3 pin saws	.20	
W. D. Henry	1 peice rolled iron	.35	
W. L. Clark	2 Machines	.40	
Joseph Hannah	1 Clock	.80	
J. B. Hannah	1 pair last	.25	
Joseph Mays	1 Statue Book	.60	43.62

The Commissioner appointed by Court yo lay off and set apart to Louisa Bledsoe, widow of John Bledsoe deceased, one years provisions for her and her family from the death of her said husband, made the following report, which was submitted to Court and approved.

We the undersigned freeholders of Cheatham County, after being duly sworn have proceeded to set apart to Louisa Bledsoe widow of John Bledsoe, deceased so much of the crop and provisions on hand as will be in our opinion to support her and her family one year from the death of her said husband, we set apart to her fro said purposes the following Articles (to wit) 1500 pounds of pork, 10 headsof stock hogs, 2 Cows (p 4) and calves, 60 barrels of Corn, 1000 bundles of fodder, 500 bundles of oats, all the poultry on hand, 3 bed steads and furniture, 1 cupboard and all the Cupboard Ware, 11 Chairs, 1 dinner table all the Cooking utensils, 3 Water Vessels or pails, 1 Wash tub, 1 Was Kettle, 1 loom and gear, 1 plow, 1 set of geer, 1 Weed hoe, 1 grub hoe, 1 Chipping Axe, 150 pounds of sugar, 10 Gallons of Mollasses, 75 pounds of Coffee, 50 pounds pict Cotton, 20 lbs. Wool, 2 sack Salt, 2 barrels flour, one dollars worth of Spice pepper and ginger, 5 lbs Rice all the potatoes she now has growing , 1 Coffee Mill, one fire shovel, one pair dog irons, one hundred and fifty dollars in Cash for Contingent expenses

Henry M. Hutton (SEAL)
Leonard Burnett (SEAL)
Joseph Mays (SEAL)

The following is an inventory of the estate of John Hunt, deceased as reported and sworn to by James W. Hunt executor of the will of said testator the amount of which she holds a life estate in.

One tract of land 625 Acres
One Negro Man Named Henry
One Negro Man Named Mack
One Negro Woman Named Jane
One Negro Woman Named Gustavia
One Negro Girl Named Kitty

Three beds, bedsteads and furniture
Two beds and ticks.
8 Chairs, 3 Tables, 1 Cupboard, 4 head of horses, 9 head of Cattle, 21 heads of sheep, 19 heads of hogs, 1Clock, 1 Spinning Wheel, 1 Real, 1 desk and bookcase, 1 Candle stand, 1 small bereau, 1 fan Mill, 1 half bushel, 1 pair of steel yards, (p 5) 1 Cutting Knife, 1 lot of books, 1 Yoke of oxens,
The above specified Articles is a true inventory as per will of John Hunt, deceased of which a receipt has been executed to me as one the executors.

James W. Hunt, executor of John Hunt, deceased

An inventory of property willed to James B. Hunt. Narcissus C. Hunt and Dicy A Shaw by John Hunt deceased and vlaued to them by Commissioner appointed by Cheatham County Court.

To James B. Hunt

1 Negro Man Named Marcelle	$925.00
1 Negro boy Named Strickland	925.00
	$1900.00

1 House Porter died before delivered

To Narcissa C. Hunter

1 Negro boy Named Dick	$800.00
1 Negro Girl Named Sally	425.00
1 Negro Girl Named Anna	337.50
1 Horse	80.00
	$1642.50

To Dicy A. Shaw.

1 Negro girl Named Lucy	$725.00

The above specified property has been delivered and recipts taken for the same.

E. H. Hunt and J. W. Hunt Executors of John W. Hunt, deceased.

An inventory of Cash, Notes, and Accounts on hand.

Cash in bank Notes	$531.60
Cash in gold and Coin	366.45
Gold which is Base Coin	2.50
Cash in silver Coin	25.55
	$923.00

1 Note on Wilson and Wall, due 25th December 1854 for	$70.00
1 Note on Harris Dowlen due 7th January 1856 for	275.00
1 Note on G. W. Shaw due 18th of February 1855 for	100.00
2 Hhds. Tobacco sold by W. S. McClure	132.15
	$577.15

Amount received for bacon	$80.00
Amount received from G.W. Hunt for which there was No Acct.	7.10
1 Account on Lorenzo Fox	3.12
1 Account on James Walker	2.56
	$92.78

$1592.93

(p 6)   On Account of the amount of the sale of the personal property of John Hunt deceased at his late residence in Cheatham County after having advertised According to law.
Amounts brought over.   1592.93

Articles sold	Purchaser Named		
16 Barrels 1 bul Corn	A. L. Fortune	156	25.27
10 Barrels Corn	A. H. Williams	150	15.00
10 Barrels Corn	A. H. Williams	151	15.10
10 Barrels Corn	A. H. Williams	151	15.10
10 Barels Corn	A. H. Williams	153½	15.35
10 Barrels Corn	A. H. Williams	155½	15.55
10 Barrels Corn	A. H. Williams	157½	15.75
10 Barrels Corn	A. H. Williams	158½	15.85
10 Barrels Corn	A. H. Williams	158	15.80
19 Barrels Corn 33/4 bu	A. H. Williams	158	31.19
1 side saddle	N. C. Hunt		8.00
1 Mans saddle	James Rauls		7.50
1 Lime seive	James Moore		.45

Whole Amount of Cash, Notes accounts and sale property   211.01
John Hunt, deceased   1803.94

The foregoing is a full and perfect account of the sale, of all the property of the estate of John Hunt, deceased directed by his Will to be sold Notes with good securities, due twelve Months after date was taken from the purchasers, September 27th 1856.

E. H. and J. W. Hunt, executors of John Hunt, deceased.
Sworn to in Open Court
W. W. Williams, Clerk

The following is an inventory of the personal property belonging to the estate of John Berry, deceased, as reported and sworn to by Thomas W. Whitfield, administrator of said estate.

Slaves, Eliza aged about 50 years Boss aged about 55 years, Jenny aged about 34 years, G neva aged about 39 Years, Gorden aged about 26 years, Mingo aged about 18 years, Patience aged about 14 years, Sterling aged about 13 years, Barbary aged about 13 years, John aged about 24 years, Isabella aged about 20 years, Susan aged about 20 years, Betsy aged about 3 years, and Henry seven Months old.

(p 7) Cash on hand at the time of his death. $1012.10 1012.10
A list of Notes supposed to be good.

One Note on George Mays due August 2nd 1854 for	14.00
1 Note on George Green due July 26th 1856 for	400.00
1 Note on George Greer due May 22nd 1856 for	235.00
1 Note on D. J. Allen due Aug.14th 1856 for	35.90
1 Note on A. Jones and J.S. Prichard Due Dec.25 1856 for	55.00
1 Note on J. H. Allen and Lawson Allen due Feb. 6th 1856 for	400.00
1 Note on W. J. Anderson due 25th Dec.1857 for	80.00
1 Note on J. R. Anderson due May 13th 1856 for	28.35

1 Note on A. H. Mitchell due March 22nd 1856 for 50.00
1 Note on W. J. Johnson due Jan.1 1857 for 110.00
1 Note on J. R. Anderson due April 28 1856 for 385.10 1793.35
1 Note on Turner Davis due 25th December 1856 for 49.20
1 Note on J. C. Anderson due January 17 1855 for 360.00
1 Note on A.J. Keys and B. B. Beech due 25th Dec.
1856 36.00
1 Note on J. S. Pritch due July 29, 1856 240.00
1 Note on A. H. Mitchell due Jan 21st 1848 5.00
1 Note on Turner Davis due August 21st 1855 3.15
1 Note on M. D. Yromey due 25th Dec.1854 22.50
1 Note on M. D. Yromey due 25th Dec. 1855 17.50
1 Note on Caldwell Vanleer and Co. due Dec.25th
1856 472.50
Y. Bridges obligation for his interest in the
estate of the Alexanders 600.00
1 Note on B. B. Berry due Jan. 25th 1855 for 138.60 1946.45
1 Receipt on W. Jones for a Note on D. J. Allen
due 8th February 1856 89.25
1 Note on J. C. Anderson due January 12th 1856 9.22
1 Note on S. P. Hildreth and Mary Hildreth due
February 1st, 1856 for 285.00
383.47

Notes supposed Not to be good
1 Note on N.B. Dreen due Aug.30th 1854 for 4.71
1 Note on James Tally due Dec. 12th 1848 for 16.35
1 Note on Park Campbell and Co. due Jan.22nd 1847 85.00
106.06

A list of accounts supposed to be good.
1 account Isaic Ivy due 25th Dec. 1856 11.25
1 Account on Annis Knight due 25th Dec. 1856 5.35
1 account on J. C. Anderson due 25th Dec. 1856 10.05
1 account on George Mays due 25th Dec. 1856 9.90
1 account on James Davis due 25th Dec. 1856 4.70
1 account on Wilson Ivey due 25th Dec. 1856 6.15
1 account on Willie MacFerson due 25th Dec.1856 3.95
1 account on James T. Davis due 25th Dec. 1856 8.75
1 account on Joseph MacFerson due 25th Dec. 1856 1.80
62.40

5303.83

(p 8)
1 account on Turner Davis due 25th Dec, 1856 9.95
1 " " Thomas Sellers " " " " 2.10
1 " " D. J. Alley " " " " 6.10
1 " " Green McFerson
1 " " W. J. Linton " " " " 2.65
1 " " A. Allison " " " " 1.95
1 " " J. F. Mays " " " " .70
1 " " James Smith " " " " 1.80
1 " " N. J. Moss " " " " 2.80
1 " " T. Davis " " " " .70
1 " " W. G. Smith " " " " 1.00
1 " " William Perkins" " " " .50
1 " " John McFerson " " " " 1.00
33.95

1	account on J. Keyes due 25th Dec. 1856	32.50	
1	" " Washington Mcferson	.60	
1	" " Thomas Jones	.20	
1	" " William Alexander	2.20	
1	" " J. H. Allen	8.50	
1	" " W. G. Davis	6.15	
1	" " L. Alexander	1.50	
1	" " Edward Alexander	.20	
		9.45	
1	" " Jessee Harrison	.35	
1	" " the estate of N. Knight for	35.00	
1	" " " " " " " "	15.00	
			111.65

A list of Accounts that are doubtful

1	account on Jack Ham due		38.76	
1	" " James Porter	1854	11.75	
1	" " " "	1854	2.35	
1	" " " "	1853	5.45	
1	" " Mrs Raines	1855	4.50	
1	" " M. B. Drew	1854	.60	
1	" " W. Forchand	1855	1.60	
1	" " John Oglee	1855	2.55	
1	" " Mrs Raines	1855	12.50	
1	" " Joseph Kennedy	1856	2.40	
1	" " Lewis Byrd	1856	.20	
1	" " David Alexander		4.70	
1	" " Lyn Loflaw		.50	
1	" " G. W. Brown		4.00	
1	" " John Hane		2.25	
1	" " A. Kermida		.22	
1	" " J. Raines		3.40	
1	" " J. Byrd		.85	
1	" " W. J. Davis		2.80	
				101.38

(p 9) Account of sale of property belonging to the estate of George Berry, deceased.

Purchaser Named	Purchaser Named
William Whitfield	Annis Berry
Annis Berry	Annis Berry
Annis Berry	Annis Berry
Annis Berry	D. J. Allen
D. J. Allen	William Herrin
James Smith	D. J. Allen
James Smith	Lewis Byrd
Annis Berry	William Herrin
A. Allison	Annis Berry
John S. Pritchard	Annis Berry
Isaic Ivey	Isaic Denioss

Articles sold	$ ¢	$ ¢
1 Clock	$ .25	
1 Bureau	7.00	
1 Bed and furniture	5.00	
1 Looking glass	.75	
3 Pitchers	.10	
1 Bed and furniture	5.00	

1 Bed and furniture	5.00	
1 Lot of Books	.20	
1 Lot of Books	.05	
1 Lot of Books	.05	
1 Lot of Books	.05	23.45
1 Lot of Books	.10	
1 Lot of Books	.05	
1 Bureau	2.25	
1 small table	.25	
1 Folding table	2.00	
1 Folding table	.30	
1 sugar chest	.50	
1 shot gun	1.85	
1 Lot of Iron	5.00	
1 Drill	.75	
1 Crow bar	1.25	

Annis Berry	James Smith
Isaic Ivey	Isaic Ivey
John S. Pritchard	John S. Pritchard
John S. Pritchard	Oscar Charlton
James L. Smith	Reuben White
Reuben White	John S. Pritchard
J. S. Smith	J. S. Pritchard
J. S. Pritchard	Reuben White
J. S. Pritchard	Samuel Ogle
J. S. Pritchard	John S. Pritchard
John S. Pritchard	Isaic Demoss
Annis Berry	A. Smith
Annis Berry	Johnson Vaughn

1 Log Chain	2.40	
1 Harrow and hoe	.50	
1 Bar Shear Plow	.85	18.05
1 Dimond Plow	.10	
1 Dimond Plow	.65	
1 Dimond Plow	.40	
1 Dimond Plow	1.50	
1 Pick	1.05	
2 Grub hoes	.75	
3 Axes	.20	
7 Axes	.35	
3 grass blades	.10	
2 Hoes	.10	
1 Bar shear Plow	.50	
1 Bar Shear Plow	.60	
1 Hassel saw	.10	
1 Broad Axe	.30	
1 drawing knife	.35	
1 auger and chisel	.20	7.25
		48.25

(p 10)

1 Auger and Iron Square	.35
1 single tree and hoe	.05
1 Cross Cut saw	2.85
1 Cross Cut saw	.50
1 Sythe blade	.30
1 Sythe blade	.25

John S. Pritchard	Thomas J. Allison
John S. Pritchard	John S. Pritchard
Isaic Ivy	B. F. Pritchard
Annis Berry	J. L. Smith
Annis Berry	Thomas W. Whitfield
Annis Berry	Annis Berry
Annis Berry	Thomas W. Whitfield
John S. Pritvhard	D. J. Allen
William Herrin	Isaic Ivy
D. Alexander	James L. Smith
John S. Pritchard	Reuben White
Annis Berry	Thomas J. Sellers
Thomas W. Whitfield	D. J. Allen

1 Lot of geer	1.10	
1 Lot of geer	.50	
1 Lot of geer	.50	
1 spinning Machine	11.25	
1 spinning Machine	5.25	
1 spinning Wheel	.10	
1 spinning Wheel	.05	
1 Loom	.50	
1 Loom	5.25	
2 Bell Cows and bells	2.00	
1 White face Cow	1.00	
1 black steer	2.00	
1 White Cow and Calf	12.25	
1 White Mealey Cow and Calf	7.20	
1 brindle Cow and Calf	6.10	
1 red Cow and Calf	8.75	
1 red Cow and Calf	8.00	
1 red spotted heifer	9.10	
1 black Yearling	3.20	
1 White face Yearling	1.70	72.45
1 White face Cow and Calf	10.00	
1 pided heifer	1.00	
1 sow and 5 pigs	5.25	
1 black sow and four pigs	4.00	
1 spotted sow and nine pigs	7.25	
1 black sow and 1 pig	5.00	

George W. Brown	David Alexander
Thomas W. Whitfield	G. W. Hogan
G. W. Hogan	Isaic Alexander
Z. Denney	James Davis
Joseph Allen	
(p 11)	Henry Ferbes
Henry Halstead	F. Glass
W.W. Johnson	W. W. Johnson
James Tarkington	Reuben White
Richard Berry Sr.	John A. Wilkins
J. A. Wilkins	J. A. Wilkins
J. A. Wilkins	J. A. Wilkins
D. J. Allen	William Gower
William Gower	William Gower

1 spotted sow and pigs	11.00
5 first choice shoats	10.00

7 second choice shoats	11.25	
10 second choice sheep	12.00	
10 third choice sheep	10.75	
9 remainder shepp 1.30	11.70	
1 brown horse	51.00	
1 bay horse Mule	128.00	
1 dark bay Mule	140.00	508.20
1 bay Mare Mule	90.00	648.85
(p 11)		
12 year old Mule	113.00	
1 bay Mare Mule	87.50	
1 sucking Mule short tail	60.50	
1 sucking Mule long tail	66.50	
1 bay Mare	70.00	
1 Jack ass	114.00	
1 red steer	22.25	
5 first choice Pork hogs	61.25	
5 second choice pork hogs	58,50	
5 third choice pork hogs	54.00	
5 fourth choice pork hogs	36.50	
5 fifth choice pork hogs	40.00	
5 sixth choice pork hogs	34.00	
5 seventh choice pork hogs	32.50	
5 eights choice pork hogs	30.50	
5 ninth choice pork hogs	28.50	

William Gower	William Gower
Not sold	Reuben White
John Ogle	George W. Hogan
G. W. Hogan	G.W. Hogan
James McCarvey	James Knight
George W. Brown	G.W. Brown
G. W. Brown	Branch B. Beech
Richard Berry	D. T. Thomson
Daniel Harrison	Annis Berry
Annis Berry	Eliza Berry

5 tenth Choice pork hogs	29.00	
8 remainder	40.00	889.00
6 shares in the Richland turn pike		
1 Ox Chart	2.50	
10 barrels Corn 1.76	17.60	
10 barrels Corn 1.71	17.10	
10 barrels Corn 1.72	17.20	
10 barrels Corn 1.80	18.00	
10 barrels Corn 1.78	17.80	
18 barrels Corn 1.74	31.32	
10 barrels Corn 1.71	17.10	
10 barrels Corn 1.72	17.20	
10 barrels Corn 1.78	17.80	
4½ barrels Corn 1.65	7.48	
1 lot of refuse Corn	5.00	
1 stack of oats	6.60	
1 stack of oats	6.00	
2 stack of Hay	3.50	
1 buggy	50.00	
1 gray Mare	125.00	377.20
		1915.05

The above is an inventory and account of sale of all the goods and Chattel rights and Credits of the estate of John Berry which have come into My hands or to the hands of any other person to My Knowledge this the 5th day of January 1857.

Sworn to in Open Court

Test:
W. W. Williams, Clerk Thomas W. Whitfield, Administrator

(p 12) We the undersigned freeholders of Cheatham County after being duly sworn have proceeded to set apart to Annis Berry, widow of John Berry, deceased, so much of the stock and provisions on hand as will be sufficient in our opinion to support her and her family one year from the death of her said husband.

We set apart to her for said purpose the following articles to wit, One gray Mare, one Sorrel blaze faced Mare, three Cows and Calves, twenty five head of stock hogs, ten head of sheep, one Yoke of Oxen, one Wagon, twenty hundred pounds of pork, one Crib of Corn supposed to be one hundred barrels, one thousand bundles of fodder, one stack of oats, all the poultry on hand, thirty bushels of Wheat, three sacks of salt, two hundred pounds of sugar, one hundred pounds of Coffee, fifty pounds of picked Cotton, twenty gallons of Molasses, three pounds of pepper, two pounds of spice, one pound of gigger three pounds of soda, fifteen pounds of rice, two plows, two sets of gear, twenty five pounds of bar iron, one grub hoe, two weeding hoes, one iron wedge, one Chopping Axe, six Chairs one bureau, one press, all the cupboard Ware all the Cooking utensils, one wash kettle all the water vessels, one hundred pounds of soap, one dining table, all the dryed fruit on hand one hundred dollars in Cash, three beds and furniture.

Henry M. Hutton (SEAL)
James M. Dunn (SEAL)
Joel F. Mays (SEAL)

The following is a list of the personal property of E. L. Stewart, deceased, sold March the 5th 1857 at his late residence.

Names of purchaser	Articles sold		
Widow	1 Cupboard	.50	
Widow	1 small table	.25	
Widow	1 Clock	.10	
A. W. Stewart	6 Chairs	2.50	
Widow	1 dressing table	.50	
Widow	1 lot of books	.50	
Widow	1 bed and furniture	1.00	
Widow	35 lbs.of Coffee	1.75	
Widow	1 half barrel sugar	1.75	
Widow	1 lot sweet potatoes	.25	
W. L. Gower	500 lbs.bacon 8	40.00	
W. L. Gower	500 lbs.bacon	40.00	
W. H. Oliver	234 lbs.old 415 New 7 1/6	56.40	145.50

(p 13)

Widow	1 lot Joles	.20
W. D. Gleaves	2 barrels lard 415 lbs.	

	$8\frac{1}{4}$	34.23 3/4	
W. G.Smith	1 lot old irons	1.50	
James Lenox	1 shovel & fork	2.20	
Chris Shivers	1 saw set	1.15	
W. G. Gunter	1 brace and bit	1.10	
Widow	1 lot tools	1.00	
Church Rasberry	1 Chisel and Mallet	.50	
Isaic Eatherly	10 barrow teeth	1.00	
Joseph Crance	1 lot tools	1.65	
William Walker	1 lot of old iron	.35	
Widow	1 lots of irons	.05	
Church Rasberry	1 square & hatchet	1.00	
Widow	1 iron Wedge	.10	
M. B. Stewart	1 Crow bar	2.80	
D. S. Binkley	2 Froes	.70	
William Stewart	2 iron Wedges	.80	
W. G. Gunter	2 " "	1.15	
W. L. Gower	3 " "	.85	
D. E. Barton	1 foot adjuster	1.50	
Jefferson Morris	3 New plains	3.80	
M. B. Stewart	1 hand saw &Auger	1.65	
James Crance	1 long Auger	.35	
William Stewart	2 " "	.70	
Thompson Herron	2 large Augers	1.35	
D. E. Barton	1 steel square	1.25	
G. W. Highland	1 spade	.75	
Charles Symes	1 stone pick	.50	
W. C. Smith	1 iron Mole board	.20	
Anthony Swift	1 hand saw	.30	
W. A. Hunter	2 Cutting knives	.50	
Burgess Shearon	1 " "	.30	
Charles Symes	1 mowing blade	.80	
M. B. Stewart	1 Sythe	1.05	
T. C. Carney	1 Cross Cut saw	6.50	
James Lenox	1 stak pole digger	1.00	
Isaic Eatherly	1 patent Axe	.85	
Frank Balthrop	1 " "	1.20	
W. C.Smith	3 old Axes	.35	
W. Miles	2 " "	.30	
James Walker	1 " "	.10	
M. B. Stewart	1 " "	.35	
Jesse Shearon	2 " "	.25	
D. S. Binkley	3 " "	.45	
D.E. Barton	1 lard barrel	.75	
E. F. Carney	1 lot large Nails	1.25	
			50.68
			226.18

(p 14) To Amount brought over $226.18

Purchaser Named	Articles sold	
Henry R. Felts	1 pair steel yards	.25
G. Green	Hoops and hinges	.45
Granville Nisholson*	1 pair gear	1.00
W. H. Oliver	Trot line & hook	1.40
Frank Balthrop	1 hoop for fishing	.15
A. J. Teasley	1 iron rod	1.00
A. F. Carney	1 lot old iron	2.10

A. F. Carney	1 lot old iron	.90
G. W. McCurley	2 Anker plows	1.00
G. W. McCurley	1 piece of iron	.50
G. W. McCurley	1 steamboat anchpr	1.75
Shelby Stewart	1 plow	3.40
Albert Smith	1 plow	3.25
Isham Harris	1 Bull Tongue	1.00
Widow	1 Davis plow	.25
William Stewart	1 Plow	3.10
William Stewart	1 Plow	.15
Zach Shearon	1 Doris Plow	2.00
Widow	1 Sythe	.50
Jesse Shearon	1 Sythe	1.25
D. T. Binkley	1 store Jug	.25
A. F. Carney	1 Grindstone	4.00
Joseph Krantz	1 shovel	.25
Widow	1 small gray Mare	25.00
Widow	1 bay Mare	15.00
John Turner	1 bay Mare	150.00
W. W. Stuart	1 bay Mule	100.00
Anthony Swift	1 Rone filly	80.00
A. H. Famber	1 sorrel Mare	30.00
A. Boyte	1 black Colt	40.00
T. S.Carney	10 barrels Corn 2.10	21.00
A. T. Carney	lo barrels Corn 2.05	20.50
A. T. Carney	Remainder 5Bbls.1.95	9.75
Wm. Pinson	1 Yoke Oxen	71.50
J. J. Connell	1 Yoke Oxen	28.00
Jefferson Morris	1 Cart & Bed	31.50
E. S. Gleaves	1 Log Chain	2.95
Widow	1 Red Cow	1.00
L. J. Perdue	1 Cow & Calf	11.25
L. J. Perdue	1 Black Steer	15.00
L. J. Perdue	1 Dun Steer	7.75
Jas. Crance	1 Black Steer	9.30
L. J. Perdue	1 Muley Steer	7.00
John Shivers	2 Young Steers	27.00
		733.40
		959.58
(p 15)		959.58
W. Gunter	1 red Cow	12.50
John Hudgens	1 black faced heifer	9.75
L. J. Perdue	1 brindle heifer	6.25
L. J. Perdue	1 white steer	5.25
L. J. Perdue	1 red yearling	5.25
L. J. Perdue	1 black Colt	1.25
Wash Stewart	1765 bundles of oats 1¼	22.06
L. J. Perdue	1 Large Male Hog	8.00
L. J. Perdue	5 first Choice hogs	31.00
L. J. Perdue	5 Second " "	25.00
L. J. Perdue	5 third " "	21.00
L. J. Perdue	10 fourth " "	40.00
W. H. Stewart	10 fifth " "	25.00
L. J. Perdue	10 Sixth " "	15.00
James L. Perdue	Remainder H	11.75
W. D. Wall	5 sacks Salt 2.35	11.75
Edward Sullivan	3 " " 2.30	6.90

Wm. Stewart	5 Sacks Salt 2.15		10,75
Ben Smith	5 " "		10.75
Jonathon Sanders	1 lot of Plank		3.00
A. F. Carney	1 lot of cabbeams		1.05
A. F. Carney	1 lot of barrels		2.00
W. H. Oliver	1 Justing Seive		2.00
Newton Sanders	1 Jig		.50
A. F. Carney	1 barrel tar		2.30
M.B. Stewart	1 Canoe		5.15
W. H. Oliver	1 skiff		10.00
Guilford Speights	304 Cords Wood	1.66	504.64
Guilford Speights	215 " "	1.02	219.30
Jack Perdue	93½ " "	.80	74.80
A. F. Carney	115 " "	.65	74.75
Guilford Speights	29 " "	.66	19.14
Guilford Speights	259½ " "	1.50	389.25
M. B. Stewart	1 Wood boat		240.00
Guilford Speights	1 Wood boat		150.00
Jonathon Sanders	10 Acres land 3.30		33.00
John Stewart	13 " "		20.80
John Stewart	1 sack salt		2.15
John Stewart	1 lamp		1.50
	$2034.54		
	2994.12		

(p 16) A. Lowe and R. H. Reding came into Court and were qualified according to law and upon oath testify that the following is a true purport of the direction given in these presents by Mrs Martha Raules, deceased in her last sickness at her late residence, and also that the same was Commited to writing within the time prescribed by law.

We the undersigned were present on the 26th day of February last, and were called on by Mrs Martha J. Raules, to witness the dispositiin she wished to make in relation to her property in her last sickness at her dwelling house which was as follows, (Viz) she wished (using her own language) Hamilton Williams, or some other suitable Man to to administer on the estate to sell the land, and divide the proceeds equally, among her Children, the stock and all other out property to be divided in like Manner.

The disposition of house hold furniture was arranged with her husband the first Certifeir heard a portion of the Conversation to this purport, between said Raules and his wife.

May 4th, 1857

Alex Lowe
R. H. Reading

The following is an Inventory of the goods and effects of Martha J. Raules, deceased as returned upon oath by James Raules, her Administrator, sold at her late residende on the 27th day of April 1857.

Articles Sold	Purchaser Named	
1 Spinning Wheel	B. F. Binkley	1.15
1 Spinning Wheel	John D. Huffman	.25

1 Barrel and Irons	J. W. Crockett	.30
2 Single tree and Clevice	A. L. Fortune	.25
3 hoes and Axes	James Walker	.05
1 Stove & Cooking utensils	Thomas Perry	1.50
Waffle Irons	J. W. Crockett	.35
1 Reflectar	A. L. Fortune	.10
1 pot and hooks	Thomas Perry	.40
1 Oven and lid	James Walker	.25
1 pot hook 7 2 lids	Thomas Perry	.60
1 Wash pan & bowl	John D. Huffman	.15
1 Loom	Randall Felts	3.25
1 barrel soap grease	J. W. Crockett	.15
1 bell and Collar	James Moore	.10
1 600 Sleigh	William Dowlen	.40
1 500 Sleigh	Ben Williams	.30
1 500 Sleigh	Rândle Felts	.70
		10.25
(p 17) Amount brought over		$10.25
2 pair harness	Randle Felts	.35
1 Kitchen Table	J. W. Crockett	.20
1 Cupboard	John D. Huffman	1.30
1 8 day Clock	James Moore	.50
3 Stone Jars	A. Walker	.20
1 pair tong & poker	J. W. Crockett	.70
8 dinner plates	J. W. Crockett	.30
2 small dishes	J. W. Crockett	.05
Cups, dish & bowls	Henry Perry	.50
1 dish	J. W. Crockett	.15
5 Chairs	James Walker	.60
4 Chairs	A. L. Fortune	.45
1 Clock real	William Walker	.25
1 Split Basket	A. L. Fortune	.10
1 bed stead	Harris Dowlen	.50
2 small bedsteads	Jane Fortune	.25
1 small bedsteads	J. W. Crockett	.05
1 press	Jane Fortune	.25
1 breakfast table	J. W. Crockett	3.75
1 grind stone	J. W. Crockett	.85
1 Milch Cow	Jane Fortune	10.00
1 Yearling	Harris Dowlen	3.10
2 sows 8 shoats	Thomas Hudgens	7.80
1 Yoke Oxen	C. A. Hudgens	45.50
1 set plow geer	Harris Dowlen	1.00
1 Cutting knife	J. J. Bradley	3.00
2 Barrels and Hogsheads	A. L. Fortune	.25
1 side saddle	Isac England	.10
1 pot rack	J. W. Crockett	.50
1 pair balance	A. Walker	.20
4 head sheep	A. L. Fortune	3.00
1 Wheel sold after sale		.20
Amount of Inventory		$96.20

(p 18) I Elizabeth Woodson being very weak of body but of disposing mind do hereby make this My last Willand testament hereby revoking all other wills by me at any time made.

First, I direct that My debts and funeral expenses be paid by My executors as early as practiable out of any Money

I May be possessed of or that May Come into his hands.
Secondly, I give to My son P. H. Woodson a Negro Man named Meredith to be by him freely enjoyed.
Thirdly, I give to My daughter Henretta D. Lowe a Negro girl named Joanna and her increase to be for the sole and seperate use of My said daughter during her life and at her death to go to her Children equally share and share alike.
Fourthly, I give to my daughter Joamed B. Williams one hundred
Fifthly, I give to My son James G. Woodson one hundred and twenty five dollars.
Sixthly, I give to My grand Children Thomas A. Woodson, Walter S. Woodson, Marr P. Woodson, Children of My son Peter H. Woodson and to his infant daughter Not Named the sum of fifty dollars each to be placed in the hands of their father for their benefit and if either dies before reaching 21 years of age, his or her share so dying to go to the surviving ones.
Seventhly, I give to My grand daughter, the infant daughter Not Named of My son P. H. Woodson My large bed and furniture.
Eightly, I give to my daughter in law, Wilmuth S. Woodson forty five dollars to be by her used as she thinks proper.
Ninthly, I direct that My executor pay to the following Negroes ten dollars each Viz, to Big Maria, Harriet, Joanna and little Maria and Meredith for their Kind attention to me for years passed.
Tenthly, should it so happen that the will Not be enough of My estate, to pay all the Money legacies herein bequeathed. I direct that the same be paid pro rata each receiving their prOportion.
11th, I direct that the residue of My estate or a sufficiency thereof be used by My executor to assist My sons Howell,H. Woodson and James G. Woodson in paying off the Notes they owe to My son Peter H. Woodson the one (p 19) on James G. Woodson being for about $106.00 besides interest and the one on Howell H. Woodson being for about $80.00 besides interest, assisting them so far as the principal respectively of said Notes is Concerned what I Mean is should there be sufficient residue of My estate after paying off fully all the legacies herein bequeathed to assist My said sons so Much respectively as the sums of the principal of said Notes. I wish the same to be done by My executor.

I nominate and appoint My son Peter H. Woodson as executor to My will in testamentry whereof. I do to this My will set My hand and seal this the 5th day of March 1857

Elizabeth H. Woodson (SEAL)

Signed sealed and published in our presence and we have subscribed our names in the presence of the testator and of each other this the 5th day of March 1857.
Test:
John E. Garner
B. W. Bradley
H. E. Hyde

JOHN M. LOVELL Will.

In the name of God Amen. I John M. Lovell of Davidson County and State of Tennessee being in a Common state of health both of body and Mind, but reasouing that is appointed for all men ever to die, do now Make and ordain this My last Will and

Testament in Manner and form following. (to wit) and first of all I give My soul to God that gave it hoping that he will raise it at the last day to live with him in heaven and My body to be buried where and in what Manner My wife and executor May think proper and for the disposal of My wordly goods that it pleased God to bless, and endow me with.

Item, I give to my Wife Susannah Lovell furing her Natural life all My land I Claim where I now live for her to live on and to rent any part of the same she May think best to support herself and family but Not to dispose of by sale. I also give to her all My household and kitchen furniture with all My stock of every Kind or as Much as she is willing to Keep and all Corn fodder and oats with all bacon lard or Meat of any kind that May be on hand at My death, and if there is More of any of the above Named articles than she is willing to keep for My executor to sell them at public sale on a reasonable credit and when the Money is Collected keep it on interest until the settlement of My estate.

I also give to her My Negro Woman Marye (p 20) with all her Children she now has or may have with all Moneys or Notes for money or Accounts that I May there have for her to use to maintain herself and family, except those of any or our own children which may be kept till settlement of my estate. I give to My son William H. Lovell his heirs & Co. all the lands I now Claim where I now live which is 209 acres which is to be his after the death of My Wife as I have left it to her during her life the land is valued at three hundred dollars as part of his legacy of My estate.

Item, I give to My son B. P. Lovell, by deed the land where he now lives valued by me at two hundred and seventy five dollars and as he has paid to me part of that valuation in Money and I wish him to be paid back at the settlement of estate sixty dollars.

Item, having given to My son C. G. Lovell the land where he lives by deed the land valued by me at $325 dollarsand as I have received in Money part of said valuation I desire he should be paid back fifty dollars at the settlement of My estate.

Item, I have also given to My son John M. Lovell the land where he now lives valued by me at $300 dollars, as part of his legacy of My estate.

Item, It is My will and desire that after the death of My Wife that all my Negro property, which is Mary and her Children, all she now has or May have until that time be equally divided by Valuation between My five Children or their heirs to wit, William H. Lovell, Benjamin P. Lovell, Charles G. Lovell, John H. Lovell and Nancy L. House, I desire that My Children all being of age to act for themselves, shall (p 20) choose the values.

Item, I give to the heirs of Emily J. Hollis if then living to Milinda F. Rosse ten dollars and Isaic H. Hollis ten dollars and tis my desire that after the death of My wife that all the property that May be on hand that is not already disposed of to be sold on a credit of twelve Months and if any Money is on hand or to be Collected and when all is Collected pay the above bequests already Made then it My desire that Nancy L. House or heirs be paid two hundred dollars if there be that Much and if any over to be equally divided between My five Children before Named.

I hereby appoint My son Benjamin P. Lovell and My son Charles G. Lovell, executors, to this My last will and testament hopin equal Justice will be done.

I hereunto subscribe My Name this twelvth day of June 1852.

John M. Lovell (SEAL)

E. S. Hooper
G. I. Hooper

(p 21) State of Tennessee, Davidson County, May Term.

A paper writing purporting to be the last will and testament of JOHN M. LOVELL was produced in Open Court for probate and proved thus E. L. Hooper and George J. Hooper the subscribing witnesses thereto being first duly sworn, depose and say that they be came such in the presence of the said J. M. Lovell, deceased, and at his request and in the presence of each other and that they truly beleive he was of sound and disposing Mind and Memory at the time of executing the same ordered that said paper writing be admitted to record as such last will and testament of the said John M. Lovell, deceased.

The following report of the sale of the Negroes belonging to the estate of John Bledsoe, deceased was Made upon Oath by Samuel A. Thompson, administrator and Commissioner sold on the 4th day of October 1856 upon a Credit of twelve Months for which Notes and good security was taken. W. D. Hutton being the highest bidder William H. Scott and Thomas M. Dunn his secutities.

Name of Negroes sold	Purchaser
1 Woman Named Caroline and her Child Jesse	William D. Hutton $1206.00

An Inventory of the sale of the slaves belonging to the estate of Harris Dowlen, deceased sold on the 7th day of January 1857.

Name of Negroes Sold	Name of Purchaser	
1 Negro boy Andrew	M.V. & Harris Dowlen	1562.50
1 Negro Woman Nancy	Martin Frey	930.00
1 Negro Woman Susanny	Sarah Dowlen	500.00
L Negro boy David	Harris Dowlen	796.00
1 Negro Woman Ester	Sarah Dowlen	2.00
		3790.50

(p 22) The following is 2nd inventory of the personal estate of Harris Dowlen, deceased Made by John Dowlen, Administrator & C.

Articles sold	Names of Purchaser	
1 stack of oats	J. D. Mays	11.50
10 Barrels Corn 1.95	J. D. Mays	19.50
5 barrels Corn 1.50		
1 lot Keg Timber	W. W. Graham	2.94
1 dining Table	Sarah Dowlen	.05
1 pair and irons	Sarah Dowlen	.25
		34.24

MARTHA J. RAWLS Sale of Land.

An account of sale of the lands belonging to the heirs of Martha J. Rawles, deceased at her late residence in Cheatham County after advertising according to law, the tract contains 82½ acres, was bid in by B. L. Williams at $12.30 cents per acre that being the highest and best bid for said land the order of payments.

Cash paid in hand	40.00
One Note due twelve Months after date with interest from date	242.91 3/4
One Note due two years after date, with interest from date	242.91 3/4
One Note due three years after date, with interest from date	242.91 3/4
One Note due four years after date, with interest from date	242.91 3/4
Amount land sold for 1 3/4	1011.67
acres land more than sold on day	21.52
Sold on the 26th of September	1033.19
1857 according to a decree of	21.52
the County Court of Cheatham County	1054.71

the above amount of land over its Amount sold 1 3/4 acreContains a true and perfect account of the sale of said lands, Sept. 26th 1857.

Sworn to before Me October 5th 1857
W. W. Williams, Clerk
J. W. Hunt,
Special Commissioner

SIM HUNTS heirs sale of land.

An account of sale of the lands belonging to the heirs of Sim Hunt, deceased sold by W. W. Williams, Clerk and Commissioner, sold on the 31st day of August 1857.

Cash paid in hand	25.00
One Note twelve Months after date, without interest	333.75
One Note 24 Months after date, without interest	333.75
	$692.50

I W. W. Williams do hereby Certify that the foregoing is a true account of the sale of the land belonging to the heirs of Sim Hunt, deceased.
John L. Harris being the highest and best bidder, Notes and good securities have been taken for the same.

W. W. Williams,
Clerk and Commissioner

(p 23) Dower of SARAH DOWLEN.

We the undersigned was appointed by the County Court of Cheatham County at the February term 1857 being unconnected with the parties either by affinity or Connanguinity disinterested having been summoned and duly sworn by the County Surveyor of said County as a Jury to allot and set off to Sarah Dowlen her dower out of the real estate of Harris Dowlen, her deceased husband, after having duly considered and fully understood the whole Matter, do hereby assign to the Sarah Dowlen, for her dower the following described lands with the erection and improvements thereon (to wit) a tract of land in the County of Cheatham on the waters of Sycamore Creek Containing thirty Nine and three quarters acre, and bounded as follows, begining at a stake in the center of the lane, thence North sixty four degrees, West one hundred and forty poles to a stake, hickory Marked as a pointer, thence east thirty eight poles to a stake, thence North forty degrees east thirty eight poles to a White oak, thence North sixty one degrees east, thirty poles to a Sycamore thence South twenty degrees east sixteen poles to a small black gum thence South twenty two degrees West one hundred poles to the beginning, stake in said lane which in our opinion constitutes one third of the real estate of the said Harris Dowlen, deceased.

Given under our hands and Seals this 3rd day of March 1857.

James W. Hunt (SEAL)
A. H. Willimas (SEAL)
G. W. McQuary (SEAL)

Dower of EVALINE STEWART.

We the undersigned was appointed by the County Court of Cheatham County at its March term 1857, being unconnected with the parties either by affinity or Contanguniity and entirely disinterested, have been summoned and duly sworn by the County Surveyor of said Cheatham County, as a Jury to allot and set off to Eveline Stewart her dower out of the real estate of Edward Stewart, her deceased husband, after having duly considered and fully understood the whole Matter do hereby assign to the said Evaline Stewart, for her dower the following described land with the erections and improvement thereon, to wit, a tract of land lying in the County of Cheatham on the waters of Sycamore Creek Containing one hundred and forty Nine and 3/4 Acres and bounded as follows, Beginning at a White oak in the East boundary line of the original tract which this is a part of the same 243 poles from the river to the beginning (p 24) White oak thence West 68 poles to a beech thence North 77½° W. 45 poles to a stake hickory Marked as pointers, thence North 231 poles to a stake Hickory White oak and beech Marked as pointers, thence East 103½ poles to a small sugar tree and two beeches, thence South 240 poles, to the beginning, White oak which in our opinion Constitutes one third at the real estate of the said Edward Stewart, deceased.

Given under our hands and seals this 4th day of March 1857.

Charles Symes (SEAL)
B. H. Gibbs (SEAL)
Gardner Green (SEAL)

We the undersigned was appointed by the County Court of Cheatham County, at its October term 1857, being unconnected with parties either by affinity or Comanagunity and entirley disinterested having been summoned and duly sworn by the County Surveyor of said County as a Jury to allot and set off to Rebecca Sanders her dower out of real estate of Daniel Sanders, her deceased husband after having duly considered and fully understood the whole Matter, do hereby assign to the said Rebecca Saunders for her dower the following describ-ed land with the erection and imporvements, thereon (to wit) a tract of land in the County of Cheatham on the waters of Sycamore Creek Containing sixty five acres and bounded as follows. (to wit) beginning at a stake on the Nashville road by the way of Sycamore Mills thence North fifty three poles to a White oak, thence east twenty eight to a poplar thence North Sixty poles to a stake in the field thence West forty three poles to a stake, thence South twenty poles to a stake, thence west eighty five poles to a stake and pointers, thence South ninety three poles to a stake at the Mouth of the lane, thence Easr one hundred to the beginning which in our opinion Constitute one third of the real estate of the said Daniel Sanders, deceased given under out hands and seals this October 20th 1857.

Wash Wall (SEAL)
A. J. Teasley (SEAL)
Raules Maxey (SEAL)

EVALINE STEWARTS years provision.

We the undersigned free holders of Cheatham County after being duly sworn have proceeded to set apart to Evaline Stewart widow of Edward Stewart, deceased so much of the Crop stock and provision on hand as will be sufficient in our opinion to support her and her family one year from the death of her said husband. We set apart to her for said purposes the following articles (to wit) 70 barrels of Corn, 2000 pounds of bacon, 1 barrel of (p 25) lard, 2 barrels of salt, 1 barrel of sugar, 100 pounds of Coffee, 50 lbs. of picked Cotton, 40 bushels of wheat, 15 gallons Molasses, 2 pounds of pepper, 1 lb. spice, 2 lbs of ginger, 3 lbs of soda, 20 lbs of rice, 200 lbs of soap, three bed steads and furniture, two Cows and Calves, One dozen Knives and forks, one dozen plates all the dishes all the cupboard ware, all the Cooking utensils, 1 dining table, 2 tablecloths, 1 dozen Chairs, one saft, 1 wash bowl and pitcher, 1 wash Kettle, 2 Wash tubs, 1 Chopping Axe, 1 spinning wheel, 1 Pair Cotton Cards, 1 Crib, 1 Mule horse and yoke of Oxens 1,2 horse wagon and harness, 2 plows, 2 hoes, 1 cutting Knife, 1 set plow, geer, 1 mans saddle, 1 ladies saddle, 2 bridles, 2 stacks of oats, 2 stack of fodder, poultry on hand, 10 stock hogs, 15 stock hogs, 2 bushels Irish potatoes, 2 bushels sweet potatoes.

Given under our hands and seals this 21st day of February 1857.

B. J. Barnes (SEAL)
W. H. Stewart (SEAL)
Wash Wall (SEAL)

WILLIAM SIMMONS Heirs Sale of land.

On Account of sale od the land belonging to the heirs of William Simmons, deceased sold by W. W. Williams Clerk and Commissioner sold on the 1st day of September 1857.

Cash paid in hand	16.00
One Note twelve Months after date without interest	119.50
One Note twenty four Months after date	

Without Interest 119.50
255.00

I Willie W. Williams, Clerk and Commissioner do hereby Certify that the above is a full true and perfect account of the sale of the lands belonging to the heirs of William Simmons, deceased Notes and good security havd been taken.

W. W. Williams,
Clerk and Commissioner

Division of the Negroes of J. M. LOVELL, deceased.

We the heirs of John M. Lovell deceased, have this day had a division of the Negroes belonging to the estate of the said John M. Lovell, deceased, according to his will the following is the allotments Made on the 22 day of October 1867.

W. H. Lovell, gets Mary and Hugh valued at twelve hundred and fifty dollars.

B. P. Lovell, Evaline and California valued at twelve hundred and fifty dollars.

C. G. Lovell, Judy Ann and Tom valued at twelve hundred dollars.

Nancy L. Hows, gets Martha Jane valued at one thousand dollars.

(p 26) John H. Lovell gets Jacob valued at nine hundred and fifty dollars.

W. H. Lovell, B. P. Lovell and C. G. Lovell, has paid to Nancy L. Hows and John H. Lovell in Money so as to Make each ones share eleven hundred and thirty dollars.
We the above Named heirs do agree to and are satisfied with the above division of said Negroes given under our hands and seals the day and Year above written.

Test:
W. B. Lee
Isaic Russell

W. H. Lovell (SEAL)
B. P. Lovell (SEAL)
C. G. Lovell (SEAL)
Nancy L. Haws (SEAL)
J. H. Lovell (SEAL)

State of Tennessee, Cheatham County.

Personally appeared before me Willie W. Williams, Clerk of the County Court of said County W. B. Lee and Isaic Russell subscribing Witnesses to the within division of the Negroes of John M. Lovell, deceased and upon oath say that they are personally acquainted with W. H. Lovell, C. S. Lovell, Nancy L. Haws and J. H. Lovell and that they signed and acknowledged the within divisiin to be their acts and deeds for the purposes therein Contained. Given under My hand at of this 2nd day November 1857.

W. W. Williams, Clerk

John M. Lovells, act sale, sold, on the 20th day of October 1857 by C. G. Lovell, Executor

Purchaser Named	Articles sold	$ ¢
W. H. Lovell	1 bedstead & Sundry household	44.15
B. P. Lovell	1 bed & furniture Sundry artic	158.50
C. G. Lovell	Sundry household	20.30
Nancy L. Haws	1 bed & furniture	9.25
J. H. Lovell	1 bed & Bacon & Lard	15.90
W. H. Lovell	50 head hogs & some corn	300.50

Jerann Abernathy	4 head of Cattle	14.00
Alex Work	1 Sorrel Mare	105.00
James Work	1 Cow & Sow & pigs	22.45
George W. Dozier	2 Steers	17.00
W. J. Wyatt	1 Cow and Calf	13.25
Owen & Hamilton	1 Lot of Corn	82.50
B. P. Lovell	1 Bay filly	75.00
J. H. Lovell	1 Lot of potatoes &leather	7.65
C. G. Lovell	1 Bay Mare	45.00
E. C. Allen	2 harness & singletrees	2.15
		832.60

(p 27) Amount of Inventory brought over	832.60
Notes belonging to the Estate of J. M. Lovell with interest to the 20th day of Oct. 1857	
1 Note on R. Hows	29.50
1 Note on C. G. Lovell	33.37
1 Note on J. H. Lovell	44.50
1 Note on W. H. Lovell	64.00
1 Note on B. P. Lovell	103.26
1 Note on C. C. Hooper	67.00
1 account on E. C. Allen not due	30.00
Cash on hand	97.10
Whole Amount of inventory Claims and Cash	1301.33

State of Tennessee, Cheatham County.

Personally appeared before me WILLIE W. WILLIAMS, Clerk of the County Court of said County, C. G. Lovell, Executor of the last will and testament of J. M. Lovell, deceased and Made oath that the within inventory a full true and perfect inventory of all the effects of J. M. Lovell, deceased, that Came into his hands as executor of said estate, sworn to before Me this 2nd day of November 1857.

C. G. Lovell, Executor

Attest:
W. W. Williams, Clerk

Will of CHARLES SYMES, deceased.

In the Name of God Amen, I Charles Symes of the County of Cheatham and State of Tennessee on the Seventh day of October in the year of Our Lord one thousand eight hundred and fifty seven, being of sound Mind and disposing Memory do Make and ordain this instrument to be My last will and testament forever revoking all others. I do hereby appoint My brother in law and trustworthy friend, Abram Stevens, and My beloved Wife Emaline Symes to be my Executor to Carry into effect, this My last will and desire in relation to My property and earthly affairs it is My will and desire that ample provision be Made out of My property for the Maintainance of My beloved wife during her Nat ural lifetime, and for the Maintainance and education of My children and for that purpose My Executor aforesaid and they are hereby authorized and required to sell or not to sell as in their judgement and discretion May seem most condusive to the just interest of My legal heirs all or any portion of My property within real, personal or mixed, it is My will and desire after paying My funeral expences and all My just debts, of which there are but few and but one og Much Magnitude that (p 28) My M ney and property of every king, sort and description real personal and Mixed be equally divided among all My beloved Children, share and share alike, and My beloved Wife, Emaline shall receive two shares or a sum equal to twice the amount which may be received by one of my Children.

It is further My will and desire that My Martal remains be deposited in the family burying ground or Cemetery belonging to My good friend Benjamin C. Robertson in testamentory whereof. I have hereunto subscribed My Name and fixed My seal in the presence of William G. Anderson and H. G. Shaw, on the day above written.

Attest:
William G. Anderson
Henry J. Shaw   Charles Symes (SEAL)

Inventory of T. and R. Durard, Deceased as returned by G. C. Binkley, Administrator on the 7th day of December 1857, on the 29th Aug. 1857.

Articles Sold	Purchaser Named	
1 Tub & Churn	Henry Myers	.60
1 pair fire dogs & Tongs	William Myers	.25
1 Oven & Hooks	J. W. Haines	.35
1 skillet & Stove Kettle	James Rose	.55
1 shovel	Nat Farmer	1.20
1 pot & rack	James Rose	.55
1 smoothing Iron	James Rose	.55
1 small pot & lid	Henry Myers	2.00
1 table & tray	James Rose	.55
1 bucket & Barrel	Henry Myers	.15
1 Coffee pot	William Farmer	.15
Scissors & pinchers	John Bradley	.20
1 set cup & saucers	William Rose	.35
1 pitcher & Sundrys	John Bradley	.55
1 set plates	Henry Myers	.70
1 Bible	Nat Farmer	.15
1 Cupboard	William Rose	4.00
1 spinning Wheel	Henry Myers	1.70
1 Slay	William Turentine	.25
1 Clock and Glass	James Harris	1.00
5 Chairs	G. W. Felts	2.05
1 Cow & Calf	E. Dunn	15.00
1 Sheep	William Rose	1.00
1 Loom	William Rose	.10
4 Chickens	Sam Richardson	.35
(p 29)		
2 sheets & Table Cloths	William Farmer	.50
1 bed & Clothing	John Bess	12.00
1 bedstead	John Bess	5.50
1 Bed and Stead	Elizabeth Rose	3.00
1 lot plank	William Rose	.50
1 Slay	William Rose	.10
		55.90

Amount of Claim belonging to the estate of T. and R. Durard, deceased.

1 Note on	William Rediker for	.45
1 Claim on	B. F. Binkley	1.00
1 Claim on	Henry Myers for Chairs	.70
1 Claim on	H. H. Binkley	.25
1 Claim on	William Rose	.10
1 Claim on	Nancy Farmer	.50
1 Claim on	Nancy Farmer	1.50
		4.50
1 Bond on	A. H. Binkley for 50 bbls.	

of corn to be paid by 60.40
installments pf five barrels per year for ten years.
1 Claim on An Binkley for rent 6.00
1 N te on An Binkley due 15 day of October 1858 17.20
1 N8te on G. Gullen 15 interesr 6 yrs. 6.80
Inventory of the sale of a tract of land belonging to the estate of Timothy Durard sold on the 15th of October 1857, sold upon a Credit of one and two years and was bought by G. W. Binkley
1 Note due on the 15th day of October 1858 for 259.50
1 Note due on the 15th day of October 1859, for amount land sold for 259.50
$519.00

On account of sale of a tract if land belonging to the heirs of L. L. Read, deceased sold by W. W. Williams, Clerk of the County Court of Cheatham, on the 7th of January 1858 upon a Credit of twelve Months except Cash enough to pay charges The said land was bid off by W. H. Stuart for L. J. Perdue at the sum of fifteen hundred and thirty three dollars and twenty five Cents.
Received in Cash 33.25
Receiver L. J. Pardue and W. H. Stuart
Note twelve Months after date for 1500.00
1533.25

(p 30) An inventory of the estate of E. H. Woodson, deceased as rendered by P. H. Woodson, Executor of said deceased on the 28th day of November 1857.
1 Note on Joseph Wilson due February 17th 1853 for 4.50
1 Note on Dr. A. Lowe due January 10th 1852 for 100.00
With a Credit of five dollars and thirty four Cents given on the 13th day of February 1857
L Note on Dr. A. Lowe for one hundred dollars due the 5th day of December 1855 100.00
1 Note on Moses Fontain due the 25th day of March for 100.00
1 Note on A. H. Williams due on the 9th day of April 1856 for 125.00
1 Note on John D. Dismukes due January 1, 1857 for 116.66
58 Bushels of Wheat at $700 40.60
28 Pork Hogs for Mays & Co. 190.00
Cash left on hand 77.65

Will of JOHN R. TULOSS
State of Tennessee, Cheatham County.
I John R. Tuloss calling to mind the uncertainty of human life and being desirous of settling My wordly affairs in a Manner More satisfactory to Myself than are the provisions of

law do make and publish this My last will and testament hereby revoking all others by me at any time Made.

Item first, It is my will and desire that My executor herein after appointed pay all my just debts out of the property I may have.

Item second, After the payment of My debts it is My Will and desire that all the residue of My estate both real and personal be for the use and benefit of My beloved Wife Elizabeth Tuloss during her Natural life to be used by her in such Manner as she May Choose either by hiring out the Negroes and renting the land or by repairing either species of property in her possession and occuping with the privilege to her at her discretion appropating the (p 31) proceeds as she may think proper.

Item third, it is My will and desire that at the death of My beloved wife Elizabeth Tuloss that all my estate both real and personal of every description shall go into the possession of Joseph Kellum as trustee of My daughter Mary S. Neal and her children he giving bond and security for his faithful performance of the duty herein enjoined on him as trustee My will and desire is for the said Kellum as Trustee to Manage or have Managed said estate in any way he May think best for the benefit and interest of Benjamin D. Neal his Wife Mary S. Neal and his Children and the said Joseph Kellum shall have full power and privilege to buy sell and Convey any species of property that he May think best so to do for the interest of the said Benjamin D. Neal, Mary S. Neal and her Children as trustee and shall take the title to all newly acquired property in his own name as Trustee and shall Manage all of said estate as May seem just and right for the interest of the said Benjamin D. Neal, Mary S. Neal and her Children as long as she May live with the said Benjamin D. Neal but in case the said Mary S. Neal and her husband B. D. Neal should seperate I then desire tha t the whole proceeds arising from the use of the property in the hands of the Trustee be for the benefit of the said Mary S. Neal and her Children, a nd the said B. D. Neal shall be excluded are in Case Mary S. Neals should die and the said Benjamin D. Neal should Marry again My will and desire for all My estate so given into the hands of Joseph Kellum as trustee shall be equally divided between the Children of My daughter Mary S. Neal it is furthermore My will and desire that all My grand Children shall have a good education and desire the said trustee to have them educated out of the property so given into his hands as trustee and it is furthermore My will and desire that the said tru stee shall assist My wife in settling up My estate and also in Manageing her affairs and that he be allowed a reasonable Compensation for all his services so rendered as trustee, I further direct and desire that My Negroes shall not be taken out (p 32) of Cheatham, Williamson and Davidson Counties during the life of My beloved Wife or by the trustee after her death I furthermore desire that My beloved wife shall Not take Benjamin D. Neal and his family to live with her and in Case she does do it, I desire all the personal property heretofore given to her to be given into the hands of My trustee Joseph Kellum, and I further direct and desire that in Case My beloved Wife Elizabeth Tuloss should Marry again that the personal property so given her shall be subject to the Controles of My Trustee and I hereby appoint My beloved Wife Elizabeth Tuloss My Executrix of this My last will and testament and having full Confidence in her prudence and integerity. I desire that she May be qualified and perform the duties of said office within being requested to give security. My desire in regard to My Negroes being Kept in the Counties above Named in Case they should be sold but in regard to those being hired out I have no perference or limits in testamentory, whereof I have hereunto set My Name and Affixed My seal this 3rd day of August 1857, signed sealed and delivered in the presence of us.

Witness: John R. Tuloss (SEAL)
James M. Dunn
Henry Kellum

ELIZABETH BEARDEN Dower.

The undersigned being unconnected with the parties either by Conmanginity or affinity and entirely disinterested having been summoned and duly sworn by the Sheriff of Cheatham County as a Jury to allot and set off to Elizabeth Bearden her dower out of the real estate of H. Bearden, deceased after having duly considered and fully understood the whole Matter do hereby assign to the said Elizabeth Bearden for her dower the following described land with the erections and improvements thereon to wit, A tract of land in the County of Cheatham on the waters of Dry Fork Creek District No 7, Containing 49 acres and 23 poles and bounded as follows beginning at a stake and pointers in J. S. Majors North boundary line being North 3 degrees West one hundred and four (p 33) poles to a thicket thence last 20 poles near a pair of Bars thence North 3 degrees West 28 poles to a large Sycamore on the bank of a Creek thence South 60 degrees east thirty poles to a dogwood, thence east with said Creek 26 Poles to a beech thence South ten degrees east 58 poles to a red oak, th ence South 80 degrees West 20 poles to a Dry branch on a hollow thence South 5 degrees east 56 poles to J. S. Majors line, thence with said line 62 poles to the beginning which in our opinion Constitutes one third of the real estate of the said H. Bearden, deceased given under our hands and seals this the 20th day of January 1858.

W. Clifton (SEAL)
J. H. Williams (SEAL)

ELIZABETH BEARDEN Years Provisions.

We the undersigned free holders of Cheatham County after being duly sworn have proceeded to set apart to Mrs Elizabeth Bearden, widow of Haywood Bearden, deceased so much of the Crop and provisions on hand as will be sufficient in our opinion to support her and her family one year from the death of her said husband.

We set apart to her for said purpose the following articles 6 Pork Hogs supposed to Make about 1000 pounds, 50 pounds of lard, 40 barrels of Corn or all in two Cribs supposed to be equivilent to about 40 barrels of Merchantable Corn, 14 bushels of wheat, 125 pounds of sugar, 50 pounds of Coffee, 15 gallons of Molasses or half barrel, 1 barrel of salt, $5 Cash to buy loaf sugar, pepper, spice, ginger, & C.

We also set apart to her the following articles the same being on hand and by the laws of the State exempt from execution 2 Bed Steads and furniture Necessary for the same 1 Cow and 1 dozen Knives and forks, 1 doz. plates, 1 dish all the spoons, 1 Bread Tray. 1 Coffee Pot, 1 doz, Cups and Saucers, 1 dininf Table, 2 Table Cloths, 1 doz. Chairs, 1 Bureau, 1 Press, 1 large Pot, 1 Tub, 1 Chopping Axe, 1 spinning Wheel, 1 Pair Cotton Cards all the Cooking utensils, 1 sifter, 1 Cradle, 1 Mare, 1 Ox Cart, Yoke ring and steeple, 1 Log Chain, 2 Plows, 2 hoes, 1 set Plow Geer, 1 saddle, 1 Bridle, 500 Bundles of oats, 500 Bundles of Fodder all the Poultry, 10 head of stock, Hogs, 1 Bible, 1 Loom and Geer.

Given under our hands this 14th day of December 1857

James H. Williams (SEAL)
William Clifton (SEAL)

(p 34) An account of the sale of the personal property of Agnes Jones, deceased. Sold by John W. Teasley, administrator on the 28th day of December 1857 on a Credit of twelve Months.

Articles Sold	Purchaser Names	
1 Yearling	E. H. Nicholson	2.55
1 Cow	Dempse Hunter	9.25
1 Tub	E. H. Nicholson	.30
1 oven	E. T. Clifton	.50
1 oven and Lid	William Walker	.90
1 Large Pot	E. H. Nicholson	1.45
2 head of Sheep	E. H. Nicholson	1.00
1 Jar	W. W. Williams	.20
2 Dishes	W. K. Hollis	.30
2 Bowls	E. H. Nicholson	.20
4 Tablespoons	E. H. Nicholson	.25
4 Plates	E. H. Nicholson	.05
1 Pitcher	H. R. Felts	.25
1 Pitcher	W. W. Walker	.30
1 Dish Pan	E. H. Nicholson	.10
1 Peggin	E. H. Nicholson	.45
1 Basket	Henry W. Turner	.20
1 Reel	Eli Harris	.90
1 Pair Cards	E. H. Nicholson	.45
1 Wheel	E. H. Nicholson	1.60
1 Bed and Clothing	Eli Harris	23.75
1 Bed stead	Eli Harris	5.90
1 Chair	E. T. Clifton	.25
6 Chairs	E. H. Nicholson	3.40
1 Chest	B. Nicholson	6.60
1 Pail	E. H. Nicholson	.50
1 Smoothing Iron	E. H. Nicholson	.55
		$62.15

Amount of Cash on hand
Amount of Cash left on hand by Agnes Jones 327.85 327.85

Amount of Notes, Accounts & C.
1 Note on Granville Nicholson Due the 8th day of January 1853 for and interest Collected 93.89 126.28
1 Note on E. H. Nicholson due July 21st 1856 for and interest on sum Collected 40.00 46.00

1 Note on R. H. Knox due April 26th 1852 (illegible) with a Credit of three dollars February 1854 10.00 10.20
1 Note on W. K. Hollis due the 15th day September 1856 for interest Collected 20.00 22.95
1 Note on Alsey Jones due the 9th Dec. 1842
for 21.00 41.67
$637.10
(p 35) 1 Note on Alsey Jones Due January the 4th 1855
for and interest Collected 8.00 8.96
1 Note on D. W. and William McFadden due February 29th 1852
for 25.00 31.30
1 Note on John S. Majors due the 1st day of January 1858
for hire Sam 143.55 143.55
820.91

The foregoing inventory of the goods and Chattels rights and credits of the estate of Agnes Jones, deceased was sworn to before Me by John W. Teasley, administrator of said estate.

W. W. Williams, Clerk

Inventory of the estate of Charles Symes, deceased 490½ Acres of land, Slaves 1 Man Alex aged 60, 1 Man William aged 40, 1 Man George aged 32, 1 Boy Fria aged 18, Stock, 3 Horses, 1 Mare and Colt, 1 Mule, 1 Yoke of Steers, old r Cows and Calves, 2 small steer beefs, 4 two year old heifers, 41 Pork Hogs, 30 Shoats, 7 Sows and Pigs, 1 steer Cart old, 5 Plows, 2 Bull Tongues, 1 Coulter, 300 Barrels Corn, 1400 Bundles of Fodder small stack of oats, 1 Cooking Stove, 1 large Kettle, 1 gold watch.
Household furniture, 5 Beds, 6 and Lounge, 1 Bureau, 1 safe, 1 sideboard, 1 Wardrobe, 1 Crib, 1 doz. split bottom Chairs, 3 rocking Chairs, 1 Dresser Table, 2 small Tables, 2 Wash Stands, 4 feather Beds, 3 shuck Matresses, 1 Carpet New, 1 Carpet old, 1 Large Mirror, 2 small looking glasses, 1 dozen silver tea spoons, ½ doz silver tablespoons, ½ doz each Large and small Common spoons, 1 Clock, 1 Lot various Carpenters Tools, 2 Saddles, Shot gun and rifles, 1 Lot Cups and Saucers and plates, 1 Castor and Table, Cutlery, 1 large Pot, 1 small Kettle, 2 Cords of Wood.

(p 36) Amount of Claim due the estate of Charles Symes, deceased that came into the hands of his executors.
1 Claim on Church Rasberry due for 4.15
1 Claim on E. S. Stewart, dec. due for 76.00
1 Claim on Jo Krantz due for 6.65
1 Claim on A. H. Williams Due for 84.35
1 Claim on R. C. McNairy and Co. due for 25.00
1 Claim on W. D. Wall due for 2.53
1 Claim on F. Balthrop due for 2.85 (Total) $201.53

The above is a Correct inventory of the property and effects of Charles Symes, deceased sworn to before me the 1st day of February 1858

Emaline A. Symes, Exex.
A. Stevens, Exr. of
Charles Symes, deceased
Sworn to before me W. W. Williams, Clerk

Inventory of the estate of Mrs Elizabeth H. Woodson, deceased Made by Peter H. Woodson Executor to the Will of said deceased, anaccount of sale of property

Articles sold	Purchaser Named		
455 Bundles Oats	Thomas J. Shaw	$1\frac{1}{4}$	5.69
410 " "	B. Moore	$1\frac{1}{4}$	5.13
450 " "	N. Morris	$1\frac{1}{4}$	5.62
450 " "	H. Dowlen	$128\frac{1}{4}$	5.76
350 " "	M. A. Fountaine	128	4.48
455 " "	N. Morris	$128\frac{1}{4}$	5.82
428 " "	M. A. Fountaine	$128\frac{1}{2}$	5.50
450 " "	W. Dowlen	128	5.76
275 Bundles Fodder	J. J. Bradley	100	2.75
275 " "	J. J. Bradley	100	2.75
162 " "	W. M. Colman	100	1.62
300 " "	M. C. Oran	100	3.00
2 Doz Chickens	P. H. Woodson	100	2.00
1 sack Salt	P. H. Woodson		2.00
1 " "	P. H. Woodson		2.00
1 " "	P. H. Woodson		1.85
(p 37)			
52 Barrels Corn	A. H. Williams	150	78.00
6 " "	A. L. Fortune	150	9.00
7 Bushesl Corn	James Rawles		2.00
5 Barrels damaged Corn	Thomas J. Shaw	$75\frac{1}{2}$	3.92
12 " " "	A. Dickerson	70	8.40
1 Pen Shucks	Parrish		2.70
1 " "	Parrish		3.00
2342 Tobacco	W. Crouch	5.50	128.81
8 Bushels Irish Potatoes &			
2 Barrels Damaged Corn	P. H. Woodson		3.80
Accounts			
One account on Dr. R. H. Reading			2.80
One account on M. P. Frey			1.00

An account of the sale of a tract of land belonging to the heirs of David Sanders, deceased sold by W. W. Williams, Clerk of the County Court of Cheatham County by a decree of said County Court on the 3rd day of February 1858 upon a credit of twelve Months and purchased by John Sanders for the sum 1230.00 1230.00

Credits or Charges		
For printed fees as per receipts		6.00
By State Tax		3.50
By Commissioner for selling & C.	21.30	30.80
Net Proceeds		1199.20

An account of a sale of a sale of a Negro Boy, Sam belonging to the heirs of Agnes Jones, deceased sold by W. W. Williams, Clerk of the County Court of Cheatham County by a decree of said County Court of Cheatham County on the 2nd day of February 1858, upon a Credit of twelve Months and purchased by Isaic Frazier for the sum of $1400.00

Charges for Selling		
By Printers fees as per receipts	$6.00	
By State tax	350	
By Commissioner for selling Collecting & C.	23.00	32.50

By Bill of Cash $1367.50
.50
1367.00

(p 38) An account of the sale of personal property belonging to the estate of Daniel Sanders, dec. sold at his late residence on the 27th day of October 1857 on 12 Months Credit

Articles Sold	Purchaser Named	
1 Pot rack	R. Sanders	.15
1 Pot rack	R. Sanders	.20
1 Oven	J. S. Krantz	.50
1 Oven & Hooks	R. Sanders	.15
1 Churn	B. F. Stewart	.55
2 Augers & Nub Iron	R. Sanders	.10
3 Augers	W. W. Sanders	.10
1 Hatchet	E. Harris (B.H.)	.50
2 Hoes	Jo Krantz	.10
1 Hoes	Henry Hunter	.45
1 Shovel	J. L. Edward	.30
1 Frow	A. W. Stewart	.30
1 Ox ring & Axe	J. L. Krantz	.60
2 Pewter Basins	J. C. Weakley	.30
1 Cutting Axe	A. F. Carney	.15
1 Briar Hook	A. J. Sanders	.25
1 Singletree & Plowhoe	J. D. Stewart	.10
1 Drawing knife& Chisel	Jas. Walker	.10
1 Grind Stone	A. C. Walker	.55
1 Sythe & Cradle		
1 lot Irish Potatoes	Thomas OBrien 25¢	2.25
1 lot Sweet Potatoes	A. J. Sanders 70	3.50
a Buckets	R. Sanders	.15
1 Jar	R. S. Sanders	.15
1 Coffee Mill	R. Sanders	.25
1 Pewter Bason	R. Sanders	.10
1 Coffee Mill & C.	R. Sanders	.05
1 Coffee Nailer	R. Sanders	.10
1 Ladle & Fleshfork	R. Sanders	.10
1 pair Steelyards	R. Sanders	.10
1 set Candle Molds	R. Sanders	.10
1 Table	R. Sanders	.25
1 Dish	R. S. E. Stewart	.50
1 Bowl	R. Sanders	.10
6 Tumblers	R. Sawer	.25
1 Large Jug	Samuel Durham	.45
1 Jar Jug & C.	R. Sanders	.10
(p 39)		
1 Loom	R. S. E. Sanders	2.00
1 Shovel & Iron	R. Sanders	.10
1 Chess Board	R. Sanders	2.00
1 Looking Glass	H. W. Sanders	.20
1 Pair Dog Irons	R. Sanders	.20
1 Chest	R. Sanders	.25
1 Trunk	Sam Durham	3.00
6 lbs. Tobacco18	John Sanders	1.08
1 Canister & Powder	R. S. E. Stewart	2.00
1 Bag Shot	R. Sanders	.10
2 Smoothing Irons	R. Sanders	2.00

1 Clock	H. W. Sanders		.20
1 Pan Steelyards	R. Sanders		.20
1 lot gun flints	R. Sanders		.25
1 Rifle Gun	Sam Durham		3.00
1 Shot gun	John Sanders		1.08
1 Spinning Machine	A. J. Sanders		.10
54 lbs Seed Cotton 41/6	A. J. Teasley		.95
1 Bed stead & Clothing	R. Sanders		.10
1 Read	R. Sanders		2.00
1 Chest	H. W. Sanders		1.00
1 Flax Wheel	E. G. Hudgens		.10
1 Hatchet	A. J. Sanders		1.50
8 Slates	Sarah Smith		.50
1 slate	H.R. Felts		.50
2 slaus	R. S. E. Stewart		.50
1 slaus	John Sanders		.25
1 lot leather	Jonathan Sanders		.60
1 side upper leather	A. F. Carney		1.10
1 side sole leather	A. F. Sanders		1.75
1 kip skin	E. G. Sanders		1.70
1 Hatchet	D. Sanders		.40
1 Pair Cards	A. J. Sanders		.05
1 pair Cards	A. J. Sanders		.01
1 Life of Washington	D. Sanders		.30
1 Bible	John Sanders		.25
1 Book	R. S. E. Stewart		.10
1 Family Medicine	W. C. Sanders		1.00
1 " "	D. S. Sanders		1.00
1 Bee Gum	A. J. Sanders		.25
1 " "	A. J. Sanders		1.00
1 wheat Stand	R. Sanders		.10
10 Bushels Wheat	Thomas OBrien	65	6.50
10 " "	Thomas OBrien	65	6.50
10 " "	A. J. Sanders	69	6.90
(p 40)			
10 Bushels Wheat	Elias Harris	74	7.40
1 old Plow & Axe	John Sanders		.90
2 small Steer	James Harris		20.00
1 Pided Heifer	A. F. Carney		13.00
1 pided Ox	A. F. Sanders		19.00
7 Brindle Cow	A. F. Carney		8.50
1 Wheat stand	David Sanders		.50
10 Barrels Corn	W. J. Stewart	.125	12.50
10 Do Do	A. J. Sanders	1125	12.50
10 Do Do	Jonathan Sanders	130	13.00
10 Do Do	D. Sanders	130	13.00
10 Do Do	Thomas OBrien	126	12.60
10 Do Do	W. W. Sanders	127	12.70
14½ Barrels refuse Corn	A. J. Sanders	61	8.84
660 Bundles Oats	Thomas OBrien	1	6.00
750 Bundles Oats	W. H. Plaster		8.80
1 Chain 1	Thomas OBrien		.10
7 Sheep	R. S. E. Stewart	80	5.80
1 Fan Mill	John Sanders		5.00
2 bells,belt &Cloverseed	Nat Sanders		2.15
1 Set Geer	A. J. Sanders		.50
1 ShovelPlow	A. F. Carney		.25

1 old Plow	A. F. Carney	.25
1 Cradle	John Sanders	.50
5 first Choice Hogs	E. W. Felts	36.75
5 2 " "	H. W. Sanders	30.00
1 first Choice Sow	A. J. Sanders	5.25
1 2 " "	A. J. Sanders	5.10
1 3 " "	H. W. Sanders	4.70
3 Hogs first Choice	H.W. Sanders	6.50
3 2nd Choice Hogs	H. W. Sanders	6.50
1 Stack Oats 105	Wm. H. Plaster	7.08
1 StakkOats 100	A. J. Sanders	3.00
Tobacco	W. W. Sanders	47.70
1 Cart Bed	H. W. Sanders	.25
1 Stack Fodder 105	A. J. Sanders	315.00
		426.05

Notes Accounts Cash & C.

1 Note on J. T. Sexson due on the 8th day of August 1856 for 16 dollars 60 Cents with a Credit of Ten dollabs Dec. 20th 1856 8.00 — 800

1 Note on Nat Sanders for three dollars and 00 Cents due 7th day of May 1848 — 4.80

1 Note on David Sanders for five dollars and ten Cents due 12th day of Dec. 1857 — 8.30

$21.10

(p 41) 1 Note on W. W. Williams for twn dollars and 92 Cents, due 2nd day of May 1849 with a Credit of two dollars and 29 Cents, September 30th 1849 — 12.76

1 Note on Nab Sanders for one hundred dollars due 1st day of January 1856 — 118.00

1 Note on Nat Sanders for fifteen dollars due 31st day of December 1854 — 1860

1 Note on Susannah Durham for twenty five dollars Due 10th May 1856 — 29.50

1 Note on Jonathan Sanders for ten dollars due 9th day of December 1858 — 14.80

Cash left on hand

In Silver	165.45
In Gold	165.35
In paper	90.00
Amount brough proceeding page	21.10
	635.56

JAMES RAULES, administrator with will annexed of MARTHA J. RAWLES.

To Amount of Inventory	96.20
Credits	
By James Rawls proven Account	58.88
B. E. G. Hudgens proven Account	12.00
B. G. W. McQuary " "	2.00
By Ed Hewitt " "	7.95
Interest on same	1.40
By J. W. Morris previous Account	3.00
Interest on same	1.08
By Lowe and Reading proven account	24.75
By check for Admr. Bond	2.00
By check for letters Administration	.50
By check for Copy of same	.50

Check for recording Will	25
Check for this settlement	60
Check for recording inventory	35
	115.26
By amount paid for taxes	2.20
	117.46
Amount of debts over the Personal estate	21.26

State of Tennessee, Cheatham County Court January term 1858.

The foregoing settlement of JAMES RAWLS, administrator of the estate of MARTHA J. RAWLS, Decd. was presented in open Court examined, approved and Confirmed and ordered to be recorded and the balance of debts against said estate was ordered to be paid by James W. Hunt, special Commissioner to sell a tract of land belonging to said estate.

(p 42) An account of the sale of the personal estate, Cash Notes and accounts of HAYWOOD BEARDEN, dec. Sold by JOHN S. MAJORS, administrator on the 19th day of December 1858.

Articles Sold	Purchaser Names	
1 Bull Tongue Plow	John Fambrough	.25
2 Plows	G.W. Gossett	1.00
1 Plow	John Blankenship	.15
1 Lot Hoes	G. W. Gossett	.25
1 Do Do	R.W. Dunn	.25
1 Hoe end Frow	T. M. Thaxton	.50
1 Two Horse Plan	John Blankenship	3.40
1 lot sundries	G. W. Gossett	.15
1 set gear	John Fambrough	.30
1 Cross Cut saw	A. Gupton	5.10
1 sythe	G. W. Gossett	2.50
1 Do	John Mohom	1.50
1 Moving Blade	R. W. Dunn	.05
1 Faw Mill	Joseph Gupton	13.40
1 lot Hides	R. W. Denny	1.50
1 Chopping Axe	J. S. Stewart	1.05
1 Grind Stone	Wm. Steel	3.10
1 iron wedge	William J. Nicholson	.60
3 planes	William Cross	3.00
1 hand saw	Widow	.25
1 Do Do	R. W. Denny	.35
1 lot Tools	Widow	.10
1 auger	Wm. J. Nicholson	1.35
1 lot augers	Gid Nicholson	.25
1 lot reap hooks	John Chambliss	.05
1 lot Tools	E. W. Richmond	.25
1 Tool Chest	E. W. Richmond	1.55
1 Table	Wm. Whitworth	2.10
1 Wheel	A. R. Lewis	2.00
1 Bed	Widow	.50
1 Cupboard	Widow	2.80
1 Bed stead & C.	Jobe Bearden	22.10
1 Bed & furniture	Nancy Bearden	21.00
1 Chest	Nancy Bearden	1.00
2 water buckets	B. Frazier	.55
1 Bureau	Wm. Whitworth	18.50

1 Looking Glass	B. Frazier	2.20
1 DO Do	Widow	.25
1 Clock	Widow	1.55
1 Table	B. Frazier	2.60
1 Jug	E. Gupton	.10
(p 43)		
Jug & Lantern	John Mohom	.85
1 Rifle Gun	R. W. Dunn	8.90
1 shot gun	Sally Weakley	2.30
1 Violin	Frank Jones	6.55
1 Barrell Tobacco	James H. Wilson	108.00
5 first Choice Hogs	R. T. Gupton	62.00
5 Second " "	R. T. Gupton	54.00
4 Third " "	R. T. Gupton	23.00
10 Barrels Corn	B. Frazier	14.00
10 " "	E. W. Richmon	13.10
10 " "	Sally Weakley	13.10
10 " "	R. F azier	13.50
5 " "	David Blanks	6.50
7 1/3 " "	F. M. Thaxton	9.00
2 Acres Corn & fodder drowned	S. D. Powers	9.25
1 Lot Shucks	William Plaster	1.40
225 Bundles Fodder	William Sutton	2.75
1 Large Hog	R. T. Gupton	21.00
1100 Bundles oats 1.45	C. Parker	15.95
1 pair saddle bags	P. Jones	2.00
1 Cows Calf	Widow	1.00
1 Cow and Calf	G. A. Edwards	13.00
1 Cow	John Mohom	13.75
1 sow & pigs	John Nicholson	11.00
23 barrels of Corn	E. Gupton	28.75
1 Bay horse	John Mohom	50.00
1 Colt	G. W. Gossett	50.25
1 Yoke Oxen	John Blankenship	40.00
Hogs in the Woods	G. W. Gossett	4.25

Notes accounts Cash & C. left on hand

Amount of Cash left on hand by the deceased	66.50
1 Note on J. H. Williams Due on the -- day-- 185	110.70
1 Note on Thomas M. Williams due 9th day of March 1855	26.75
1 Note on R. H. Weakley due 3rd day of June 1856	14.55
	936.60

Sworn to before me W. W. Williams, Clerk

(p 44) An inventory of the property of the estate of JOHN R. TULLOSS, deceased Made the 3rd day of May 1858 Number of Negroes ages & C.

1 Negro Woman Named Nelly aged 40 years.
1 Negro Man Named Henry aged 40 years.
1 Negro Woman Named R becca aged 30 years.
1 Negro Man Named Gustavus aged 18 years the said Gustavus by a decree of the Circuit Court at its February term 1858.
1 Negro boy Named James aged 16 years.
1 Negro boy Named John aged 15 years.
1 Negro boy Named Hulard aged 14 years.
1 Negro Girl Named Julia aged 9 years.
1 Negro girl Named Sarah aged 10 years.

1 Negro girl Named Zelpha aged 8 years.
1 Negro girl Named Nancy aged 8 years.
1 Negro girl Named Cely aged 7 years.
1 Negro boy Named Abram aged 3 years.
1 Negro boy Named Perry aged 6 years.

Household furniture Stock & C.
3 Beds and furniture.
1 Folden Leaf Table.
1 Sugar Chest, 5 Heads of Horses.
1 Mule,
6 heads of Cattle
15 heads of Hog.
7 headsof Sheep.
2 of the horses of the above Named lot was sold by Jas. Kellom Admr. of said deceased, the first was purchased by John Hailey for $55.00
The second was also purchased by John Hailey for 71.00
The Mule was also sold by said administrator and purchased by Joseph N. Newman for 150.00
The Negro boy Named Jim was hired out to J. N. Newson at 70.00
The said administrator sod two heads of Cattle to a butcher in Nashville for $49.00 $395.00

Sworn to before me May 3rd 1858
W. W. Williams, Clerk

(p 45) An Account of the sale of the land belonging to the heirs of Thomas Perry, deceased sold by W. W. Williams, Clerk of the County Court of said County sold on the 30th day of March 1858 on a Credit of one and two years, sold in two tracts The first tract was purchased by Charles Vedder Containing 16 Acres at $7.00 per Acre $112.00
The second tract was purchased by John Perry Containing 115 Acres at $6.00 per acres $690.00
Cash received from Charles Vedder $5.00
Cash received from John Perry 17.00

112.00
690.00
802.00
22.00

An account of the sale of a tract of land belonging to the heirs of S. G. ROBERTSON, deceased sold by W. W. WILLIAMS, Clerk of the County Court of Cheatham County sold on the 6th day of May 1858 and was purchased by G. W. Gossett
The tract 95 Acres at $8.00 per acre. $760.00
Cash received from said G. W. Gossett 35.00

An inventory of the estate of THOMAS PERRY, deceased as returned by A. Boyte, administrator of said deceased on the 15th day of April 1858.

Persons Named	Articles sold	
Benjamin Smith	1 lot Geer	.90
John Perry	1 Plow	.30
A. Eatherly	1 spade and Chisel	.60
A. Teasley	1 plow and stock	.10
James Davis	1 lot plows & hoes	.50

Lewis Perry	1 Wedge & C.	.75
Ben Smith	1 Frow	.65
Mary Reed	1 Axe	.25
Joseph Krantz	1 Clevice & single Tree	.75
Ben Smith	1 Clevice & harness	.25
James Perry	1 Tub and Irons	.50
A. Eatherly	1 Brier sythe	.35
Joseph Krantz	1 oven & Hooks	.60
James Perry	1 skillet	.40
James Davis	1 Pot	.15
Lewis Perry	1 Pot	1.00
James Perry	1 Kettle	2.00
A. Eatherly	1 Grind stone	.40
Ben Smith	1 sythe,Cradle	.10
		$10.55

(p 46)

Martha Sanders	1 pair fire Irons	1.55
Martha Sanders	2 Smoothing Irons	.80
Mary Read	1 Piggin	.05
W. E. C. Gower	1 lot Shoe Tool	1.10
Lewis Perry	1 side saddle	1.00
Martha Sanders	1 Ten Trunk	.25
John Perry	1 Coffee Mill	.35
Thomas Perry	1 lot leather	2.00
Mary Read	2 Slaie	.25
Mary Read	1 Slaie	.10
Mary Read	1 Pair Harness	.60
John Perry	1 mans saddle	1.50
Martha Sanders	1 Cupboard	6.25
J. J. Forbes	1 lot Cupboard ware	.45
Lewis Perry	1 sugar box	.30
James Davis	1 tray & table	.25
Martha Sanders	1 lot Chairs	1.55
Martha Sanders	1 Bed quilt	.50
Sarah Perry	1 quilt & sheet	1.00
Lewis Perry	1 Counter pane	1.65
James Perry	1 Counter pane	.80
Lewis Perry	2 Bed quilts	2.60
Lewis Perry	4 Quilts	.80
Sam Perry	1 Bedstead	12.75
Lewis Perry	1 Bedstead	16.25
Lewis Perry	1 Rifle Gun	4.00
Mary Read	1 Cow and Calf	20.25
Mary Read	1 Meal sack	.35
Joseph Krantz	1 Heifer Yearling	2.30
Joseph Krantz	1 Oxen	1.25
R. Simmons	1 sanded saw	5.55
R. Simmons	2 Guinea Hogs	4.25
Eleas Harris	3 Hogs	6.00
Outstanding Hog Claim	John Perry	13.00
		111.65
		122.20

Cash Notes and Accounts left by Thomas Perry, deceased that came into the hands of A. Boyt, Admr. of said deceased
1 Note on R. B. Gibbs for fifteen dollars due 19th day of January 1853 and interest 15.00
Interest on same 5.00 20.00

1 Note on W. L. Gower for fifty dollars due 12th day of May 1856 with a credit of twenty dollars given the 28th day of October 1856 (Doubtful) interest on same 30.00
1 Note on Henry Harris for twenty four dollars.
(p 47) Due the 25th of December 1850 with a Credit of seventeen dollars the 4th day of February 1853, also a Credit of five dollars on the 1st day of November 1853

Interest on same		2.00
on account on James Connell for	$2.05	2.05
One account on Mary Read for	5.00	5.00
Cash left on hand		20.00
on Account one Sampson Perry		3.50
1 Note on James Perry for one dollar and 5¢ Feb. 20th 1859 due		1.05
1 Note on John and Lewis Perry for three dollars 20th Feb. 1859		3.00
Note on G. A. Sanders for		1.25
due March 1st 1858		1.25
		37.85
		$ 180.05

Inventory of the estate of HAYWOOD BEARDEN, deceased as returned by JOHN S. MAJORS administrator of said deceased Sold on the 19th day of December 1857.

Articles sold	Purchaser Names	
1 Bull Tongue plan	John Fambrough	.25
2 Plows	Geo. W. Gossett	1.00
1 Plow	John Blankenship	.15
1 lot of hoes	Geo. W. Gossett	.25
1 Do Do	R. W. Denny	.25
1 Hoe and Froe	F. M. Thaxton	.50
1 Two horse Plow	John Blankenship	3.40
1 lot Sundries	G. W. Gossett	.15
1 set geer	John Blankenship	.30
1 Cross Cut saw	A. Gupton	5.10
1 Sythe	G. W. Gossett	2.50
1 Do	John Mohon	1.50
1 Moving blade	R. W. Denny	.05
1 Fan Mill	Joseph Gupton	13.40
1 lot Hydes	R. W. Denny	1.50
1 Chopping Axe	J. S. Stewart	1.05
1 grind stone	Wm. Steel	3.10
1 iron Wedge	W. J. Nicholson	.60
3 Planes	W. Cross	3.00
1 Hand saw	Widow	.25
1 Do Do	R. W. Denny	.35
1 lot tools	Widow	.10
1 Auger	W. J. Nicholson	1.35
1 lot Augers	Gid Nicholson	.25
1 Lot Reap Hooks	John Chambliss	.05
1 Lot of Tools	E. W. Richmond	.25
1 Tool Chest	E. W. Richmond	1.55
1 Table	Wm. Whetworth	2.10
1 Wheel	A. R. Lewis	2.00
1 Bed	Widow	.50
(p 48)		
1 Cupboard	Widow	2.80

1 Bed stead & C.	Jobe Bearden	22.10
1 Bed & furniture	Nancy Bearden	21.00
1 Chest	Nancy Bearden	1.00
2 Water Buckets	B. Frazier	.55
1 Bureau	W. Whatworth	18.50
1 Looking Glass	B. Frazier	2.20
1 Do Do	Widow	.25
1 Clock	Widow	1.55
1 Table	B. Frazier	2.60
1 Jug	E. Gupton	.10
1 Jug & Lantern	John Mohon	.85
1 Rifle Gun	R.W. Denny	8.90
1 Shot Gun	Sally Weakley	2.30
1 Violin	Frank Jones	6.55
1 Barrel of Tobacco	James H. Williams	108.00
5 first Choice hogs	R. T. Gupton	62.00
5 second choice hogs	R. T. Gupton	54.00
4 third Choice hogs	R. T. Gupton	23.00
10 Barrels Corn	B. Frazier 140	14.00
10 Barrels Corn 131	E. W. Richmond	13.10
10 Do Do	Sally Weakley 135	13.50
10 Do Do	B. Frazier 135	13.50
5 Do Do	D. C. Blanks 130	6.50
7 1/5 Do Do	F. M. Thaxton 125	9.00
2 acre of Corn & fodder drowned	S. D. Power	9.25
1 Lot Shucks	Wm. Plaster	1.40
Bundles Oats 145	C. Parker	
1 Large Hog	R. T. Gupton	21.00
Bundles Fodder 100	Wm. Sutton	
1 pair saddle Bags	R. Jones	2.00
1 Cow & Calf	Widow	1.00
1 Cow & Calf	G.A. Edwards	13.00
1 Cow	John Mohon	13.75
1 sow & pigs	John Nicholson	11.00
23 Barrels Corn 125	E. Gupton	28.75
1 Bay Horse	John Mohon	50.00
1 Colt	G. W. Gossett	50.25
1 Yoke Oxen	John Blankensip	40.00
Hogs in the woods	G. W. Gossett	4.25

Amount of Notes, Accounts & C.

Cash on hand		66.50
Cash received on Note on	J. H. Williams	110.70

1 Note on T. M. Williams for 26.75 due Mar. 9th 1855 — 26.75

(p 49)

1 Note on R. H. Weakley for fourteen dollars and 55 Cents due 3rd day of June 1856 (D) — 14.55

The following is an inventory of the personal property of JAMES STEWART, deceased as Made by JAMES S. STEWART, administrator of the estate of said deceased sold at his late residence on the 26th day of April 1858.

Purchaser Named	Articles sold	
John Weakley	1 Diamond Plow	2.00
A. H. Fambrough	1 " "	1.05
John Perdue	1 " "	.50
J. C. Weakley	1 single tree & Clives	.50

A. J. Teasley	1 Diamond Plow	.25
John Perdue	1 Set Geers & Co.	.50
R. E. Stewart	3 Hoes	.60
A. H. Fambrough	1 Bell	.50
A. W. Stewart	1 Pewter Basin	.15
David Coleman	1 lot Sundries	.50
R. E. Stewart	1 Gritter & C.	.30
J. S. Stewart	1 Fan Mill	.10
J. C. Weakley	1 Pair Steelyards	.50
J. S. Stewart	6 Plow Moles	.10
J. S. Stewart	1 Vice	.25
J. S. Stewart	1 lot Iron	.10
John Perdue	1 Axe	.50
Henry Turner	1 Sheep Skin	.35
Jo Price	1 saddle	2.00
J. Fambrough	4 Boxes	.35
R. E. Stewart	1 Candle stand	1.75
Mary Morris	1 looking Glass	1.50
A. W. Stewart	1 Flax Wheel	1.00
J. S. Stewart	1 Reel	.80
Lucinda Eatherly	1 Spinning Wheel	.70
Mary Morris	1 Basket	.25
Susan Smith	1 "	.25
Lucinda Eatherly	1 "	.25
Lucinda Eatherly	1 "	.50
D. S. Stewart	1 Pair Saddle bags	.55
J. S. Stewart	1 Bed stead	.05
Susan Smith	1 Bed stead	2.00
Susan Smith	1 Bed stead & bed Clothing	11.00
Lucinda Eatherly	1 Counterpane	.80
Lucinda Eatherly	1 Bed quilt	1.35
Susan Smith	1 " "	1.50
Lucinda Eatherly	1 " "	1.00
Lucinda Eatherly	1 white Counterpane	1.00
Susan Smith	1 Bed quilt	.15
Lucinda Eatherly	1 Bed Quilt	1.60
(p 50)		
Lucinda Eatherly	3 pillow slips	.15
Lucinda Eatherly	2 Coverlids	2.60
Lucinda Eatherly	1 Counterpane	2.70
Mary Morris	1 "	2.15
Mary Morris	1 Bed spread	1.00
Lucinda Eatherly	1 Counterpane	1.00
Jo Price	1 "	1.60
Lucinda Eatherly	1 Coverlid	5.50
Mary Morris	1 Brush	.25
Susan Smith	1 "	.25
Mary Morris	1 small Waiter	.30
Susan Smith	1 umbrella	.25
R. E. Stewart	1 Book	1.50
Mary Morris	1 "	.30
R. E. Stewart	1 "	1.00
Lucinda Eatherly	1 Blanket	2.50
Jo Price	1 "	2.55
Susan Smith	1 Bureau	6.00
J. S. Stewart	1 desk	1.50
R. E. Stewart	1 Keg Copperas	.10

J. S. Stewart	3 Chairs	1.60
Mary Morris	6 Chairs	1.60
R. E. Stewart	1 sugar Chest	7.00
Thomas Miles	1 Clock	4.25
Susan Smith	1 Tin Can	.55
R. E. Stewart	1 Glass Jar	.50
Mary Morris	1 Wooden Can	.50
Mary Morris	1 Pitcher	.30
Mary Morris	1 "	.30
Lucinda Eatherly	Plates & knives & forks	1.10
Mary Morris	1 set plates	.85
Lucinda Eatherly	1 salt & pepper box	.20
Mary Morris	1 sugar Bowl	.50
Lucinda Eatherly	2 Bottles	.10
Mary Morris	4 Bottles	.25
Mary Morris	1 Plate & C.	.25
Mary Morris	Cup & Saucers	.50
Mary Morris	Plates & glasses	1.50
Lucinda Eatherly	1 dinner table	6.15
Susan Smith	1 bowl & pitcher	.10
Mary Morris	1 safe	3.00
(p 51)		
R. E. Stewart	1 Demi John	1.00
R. E. Stewart	1 Jug	.15
A. J. Teasley	1 Hatchet	1.30
A. H. Fambrough	1 Jar	1.30
Lucinda Eatherly	1 Meal sack	.40
Jo Price	1 " "	.30
John Perdue	1 " "	.35
Mary Morris	1 sifter	.10
John Perdue	1 Trey	.35
R. E. Stewart	1 Trey	.25
Lucinda Eatherly	1 Churn	1.00
J. S. Stewart	1 Jar	.30
R. E. Stewart	1 "	.45
M. Nicholson	1 "	1.00
A. H. Fambrough	1 Wooden Can	.35
Lucinda Eatherly	1 Water Bucket	.65
A. H. Fambrough	1 Piggin	.50
G. Edwards	1 Pail	.80
H. Miles	1 small kettle	.25
Susan Smith	1 Oven	.30
J. S. Stewart	1 Skillet	.45
D. Teasley	1 Boiler	2.00
J. S. Stewart	1 lot sundries	.20
John Perdue	2 pair pot hooks	.40
J. S. Stewart	1 pot	.55
R. E. Stewart	1 frying pan	.05
J. S. Stewart	1 Copper Kettle	.05
D. S. Stewart	1 Kettle & Hooks	1.55
Jonathon Fambrough	2 Barrels	.05
L. J. Perdue	1 Grindstone	.15
R. S. Stewart	1 Mortar	.05
S. M. McDaniel	3 Bdls & salt	.25
Geo. Edwards	2 lard stands	.05
J. S. Stewart	$127\frac{1}{2}$ lbs bacon $8\frac{1}{2}$	10.84
J. S. Stewart	Bacon	8.16

R. E. Stewart	Bacon	23.26
J. S. Stewart	2 Troughs	.10
J. S. Stewart	7 Head hogs	28.00
Geo. Shaw	1 sorrel Mare	80.25

(p 52)

Mamy Morris	1 dry Hyde	.52
R. E. Stewart	1 pr. dog irons	.10
R. E. Stewart	1 " " "	.10
R. E. Stewart	1 shovel	.25

Notes and accounts

1 Note on W. W. Smith for two dollars and nine cents due 21st day of January 1856 2.09
December 9th 1850 received one dollar 1.50 3.59
One Note on Charles Gent for one dollar and 93 cents due January 1849 for 1.93 1.93
1 account on John Forbes for two dollars and Ninety seven cents due in 1844 & 45 2.50
1 Note on L. J. Perdue for sixty dollars due April 30th 1856 60.00
With a Credit of twenty three dollars and 45 cents given on the 36.55 5th day of February 1857. 23.45 Credit
Interest on same 10.60
1 Note on J. S. Majors for two hundred dollars due 1st day of January 1857 200.00
Interest on same 39.00
1 account on E. J. Herrel for two dollars and 12½ cents due 1st January 1841 2.12
1 account on R. Weakley for 87½ cents due 1st day January 1845 $ 366.17
673.88

(p 53) Below is an inventory of the personal estate of W. A. Williams, deceased as returned by A. S. Williams sold at the late residence of said deceased on the 28th day of May 1858.

Purchasers Names	Articles sold	
S. C. Harris	5 sheep	5.00
Thomas Batson	harness & slaie	.25
John Daniel	Window Curtains	.25
John Wyatt	1 lot of Books	.50
Thomas Batson	1 pair balances	1.50
W. H. Minor	Barrels & C.	.40
Smith Batson	Boxes	.50
W. H. Minor	Tea Kettle & flat iron	1.75
Thomas Batson	Box & sand paper	2.00
G. W. Gossett	Quilting Frames	1.00
Jonathon Hollis	1 saddle & Bridle	11.25
Wm. Harvey	1 Horn	.75
Smith Batson	1 lot of Tools	1.50
Wm. R. Wyatt	1 lot of Bottles	.10
Wm. H. Minor	1 large Jug	.80
W. H. Minor	2 sam Jugs	2.50
W. B. Batson	1 Box & paint	2.75
W. B. Batson	1 box & Contents	.60
John Daniel	1 lot of sulphur	.30
S. C. Batson	1 sythe Blade	1.00
Daniel Waller	1 lot powder & shot	.75
Smith Batson	1 box & Contents	.20

W. B. Batson	1 table & saw	.25
W. R. Wyatt	1 Cross Cut Saw	3.25
Thomas Batson	2 shovels	1.10
F. Pack	1 Musket & C.	1.50
T. L. Fain	1 double shot Gun	10.00
Thomas Batson	1 rimlet	15.00
W. T. Crockett	1 double shot Gun	19.00
John Hagewood	1 lot barrels	.50
John Daniel	1 Tub Soap	1.00
W. F. Gray	54½ lb lard	3.81
W. F. Gray	201 lbs Bacon 8 3/4	17.58
Thomas Batson	Basket & Wasping Boxes	1.25
W. B. Batson	1 skillet & pot	.10
F. Pack	1 Oven & C.	.20
F. Pack	2 Pots	1.50
Thos. Batson	1 Churn & Oven	.30
J. H. GOssett	1 Jar Pickles	.40
W. F. Gray	1 Do Do	1.00
J. H. GOssett	1 DO Do	.30
Wm. H. Minor	6 Chairs 125 per	7.50
J. Bull	1 Rocking Chair	.60
(p 54)		
Wm. F. Gray	3 Chairs	.90
S. C. Harris	6 bushels Wheat	2.28
S. C. Harris	2 Hogshead	.25
S. C. Batson	1 Fan Mill	5.00
Daniel Walker	1 House sheep	.75
R. W. Wyatt	1 Colt	22.00
R. W. Wyatt	1 Brod Axe	.50
Wm. Harvey	1 Mare & Colt	76.00
Wm. F. Gray	1 Red Cow	10.50
S. C. Batson	1 Black Steer	7.25
Wm. H. Minor	1 Black & White heifer	6.50
Tho Ellis	fruit & eggs	.30
John Daniel	23 geese 15¢	3.45
John Daniel	7 glasses	.90
J. H. Gossett	1 Mollasses stand	.65
Smith Batson	1 lot of Bottles	.25
Thomas Batson	1 lot bottles	.25
E. Trotter	1 lot knives & forks	.70
A. Hollis*	1 " " "	.80
John Daniel	1 set plates	.20
Tho Batson	2 dishes & bowls	.75
James Phips	1 set perserve dishes	.75
Thomas Batson	1 set plates and dishes	.35
John David	3 pitchers	.75
Thos Batson	candlesticks	.15
John David	1 steel trap	.30
S. C. Batson	candle Moles	.35
S. C. Harris	3 glass Jars	1.00
R. Connell	1 lot plates	.45
John Daniel	1 set Cup & saucers	1.00
James Phips	1 Tea pot	.25
Z. H. Morgan	1 Themomter	1.00
R. Collins	1 dining table	7.00
W. B. Batson	1 Clock	10.00
Thos Batson	1 silver Watch	4.25

Thos. Batson	1 pair toys	.10
R. Mills	1 pair toys	.10
J.H. Gossett	1 pair toys	.10
Thomas Batson	1 piano fort	25.03
W. B. Batson	1 pair toys	.30
A. Hollis	1 Chest & Contents	4.40
Thomas Batson	Tobacco & C.	1.95
Thomas Batson	1 Bed & stead	15.10
Wm. B. Batson	Contents of drawer	1.50
Thos. Justice	1 Fiddle	1.75
(p 55)		
J. H. Gossett	1 Bureau	9.50
J. H. Gossett	1 safe	7.00
J. H. Gossett	1 Bed & stead	30.00
R. Conell	1 Bed & stead	21.00
Wm. R. Wyatt	1 Spbing launt	.10
R. Conell	1 Bed quilt	.50
Thos. Batson	1 Coverlid	1.75
B. Wyatt	1 Quilt	.50
John Daniel	4 Turkeys	.60
Smith Batson	22 Chickens	1.76
Z. Batson	Broom Corn	.10
Z. Batson	1 Hat & Cap	1.05
W. B. Batson	1 lot oil	2.50
Z. Batson	1 pair saddlebags	.85
Tho Baxter	115 doz oats & C.	9.20

Account Notes and Money belonging to the estate of W.A. Williams, deceased.

Cash left on hand by said deceased 42.00

Good Claims

1 Note on A. S. Williams for two hundred and sixty four dollars due the 12th day of June 1836

1 Note on James Sutton for twenty dollars due 25th day of December 1858.

1 Note on O. Tinsley for one jundred and seventy seven dollars due 1st day of January 1857.

with a credit of eight dollars and Ninety on the 9th of February 1857 8.90

One other credit of one hundred dollars on the 13th of April 1857

One other Credit of twenty dollars 2nd December 1857.

One Note on W. Carrol Jr. for four dollars and eighty five cents due 28th day of May 1858

One Jury ticket for three dollars and 20 Cents.

(p 56) Years Provisions for Mrs ELIZABETH PACK.

We the undersigned freeholders of Cheatham County after being duly sworn have proceeded to set apart to Elizabeth Pack, widow of B. D. Pack dec. so much of the Crop and provisions on hand as will be sufficient in our opinion to support her and her family one year from the death of her said husband we set apart to her for said purposes the following articles (to wit) 75 lbs of lard, all the Irish potatoes and garden vegetables on hand seventy five barrels of Corn, fifteen hundred pounds of pork, 2o bushels of wheat, 1000 bundles of fodder, 50 lbs of Coffee, 50 lbs of sugar, 15 gallon Molasses, 1 barrel salt

five dollars to buy other Necessities Twenty five dollars to pay Doctor Bills.
June 22nd 1858

G. T. Harris (SEAL)
A. W. Turner (SEAL)
J. M. Brown (SEAL)

An account of sales Made of the personal property of the estate of B. D. PACK, dec. at his late residence in Cheatham County after haveing advertised according to law.

Purchaser Names	Articles sold	
B. L. Pack	5 old Axes	.25
F. S. Pack	1 Plow	.50
S. D. Pack	2 singletrees	.50
B. L. Pack	2 large bolts	.25
B. L. Pack	1 Pick	.50
Joseph Harris	1 Spade	.55
L. D. Pack	2 Brier hooks	.25
B. S. Pack	1 Demi John	.25
Joseph Harris	1 Jug Vinegar	.55
Henry Hale	1 Crow bar	2.00
B. L. Pack	1 lot of old iron & C	1.05
B. S. Pack	1 " " sythe blades	,10
L. J. Pack	4 lap rings	
L. J. Demoss	1 pair of breast Chains	.45
L. B. Pack	1 lot Chairs	.80
Warren Jordan	1 saw Mill stiness	.50
Wm. H. Scott	1 fifth Chain	1.25
John McCaslin	1 fifth Chain	.65
B. L. Pack	1 lot hollow Ware	.25
J. L. Demoss	1 Cow Bell & Collar	6.00
L. D. Pack	2 Bells & Curry Comb	.75
J. L. Demoss	1 lot Carpenters Tools	2.25
T. A. Jackson	1 box old iron	.20
B. S. Pack	1 shelling Machine	.50
T. A. Jackson	1 spinning Machine	.25
J. L. Demoss	1 lot Wool 2 Barrels	1.10
(57 p)		
James W. Bennett	1 spinning Wheel	.10
Henry Hall	1 Cross Cut saw	7.00
J. S. Demoss	1 lot Geer & C.	.95
F. L. Pack	1 lot Geer	1.70
Wm. Bennett	1 lot Geer	.45
G. T. Harris	6 halter Chains	1.00
J. A. Stroud	1 Barrel & Millet seed	1.40
B. L. Pack	1 Box Millet seed	.10
S. D. Pack	1 Cherry Bed stead	3.05
F. L. Pack	1 plain Bed stead	.50
F. L. Pack	1 Bed & Clothing	6.00
B. L. Pack	1 Candle stand	1.50
S. D. Pack	1 Cable Rope	2.00
B. L. Pack	1 Rocking Chair	.75
L. D. Pack	1 lot Wagon Work	13.00
B. L. Pack	1 old Plow	.10
John McCaslin	1 lot Wagon Geer	1.00
Tenie Andrews	1 Copper Still & Worm	3.30
L. J. Pack	1 Copper Still	16.00

Joseph Harris	1 Mowing blade		1.00
D. E. Powell	2 Cradles		2.00
T. A. Jackson	1 Cradle		.50
Joseph Harris	1 large Kettle		5.50
B. L. Pack	1 Harrow		.25
B. L. Pack	1 small shot gun		10.00
Elizabeth Pack	1 trundle bedstead		.50
Elizabeth Pack	1 looking glass		.50
Elizabeth Pack	1 Clock		.10
Elizabeth Pack	1 Book		.10
John L. LOvell	1 Bureau		5.00
B. L. Pack	1 Case for bureau		1.15
B. L. Pack	1 Book History of U.S.		1.50
Joseph Brown	75 lb seed Cotton	3	52.25
D. E. Powell	90 " " "	2	2.47
Burgess Harris	1 Feed trough		.10
Daniel Brown	48 lb Bacon 8½		4.08
T. A. Jackson	1 lot old iron		.25
L. J. Pack	1 peice Hoop iron		.10
John McCuslin	1 Bar show plow		.80
B. L. Pack	1 Harrow		3.00
Wm. Bennett	1 Grindstone		.40
B. L. Pack	1 Plow		.80
Burgess Harris	1 pair shafts		.45
D. E. Powell	1 lot Blacksmiths tools		27.00
J. W. King	1 Buggy		18.50
(p 56)			
W. R. Gilbert	1 Two Horse Wagon		80.00
John McCaslin	2 Cans & paint		.25
L. D. Pack	10 Hogs 1st Choice		41.00
B. L. Pack	10 Hogs 2nd Choice		12.00
B. L. Pack	10 Hogs Remainder in pen		5.00
L. D. Pack	1 saw in L.J. & F.L.Packs lot		3.75
B. L. Pack	1 sow & Nine Pigs		5.60
L. D. Pack	1 black sow & pigs		4.75
B. L. Pack	1 sow & five pigs		3.35
F. S. Pack	6 hogs 1st Choice in Cot		21.00
B. L. Pack	3 black shoats		4.50
B. L. Pack	3 shoats		6.75
Daniel Brown	1 sow & pigs		3.00
B. L. Pack	1 sow & five pigs		5.75
B. L. Pack	1 sow & one Pig		2.25
L. J. Pack	All Claim to hogs in Woods		4.25
B. S. Pack	1 Young bull		5.75
Warren Jordan	1 Black Cow		8.00
Warren Jordan	1 Red heifer		5.75
J. W. King	1 large Cow & Calf		20.00
Burgess Harris	1 Heifer (Spotted)		8.75
Burgess Harris	1 old stag Steer		15.50
J. W. King	1 Dun Steer		10.00
Warren Jordan	1 Cow & Yearling		12.25
Elizabeth Pack	1 sorrel Horse		25.00
Henry Turner	1 sorrel Mule blind in one eye		77.00
W. R. Gilbert	1 sorrel Mule		87.00
Burgess Gilbert	1 Young sorrel Mule		135.00
L. D. Pack	1 Brown Mule		90.00

Peter Jackson	1 Black Filly	20.00
B. L. Pack	1 sorrel pony	31.00
Wm. H. Stewart	1 Yellow pony	35.00
John McCaslin	1 pair Mill Stones	2.00
L. D. Pack	1 Canoe	50.00
L. D. Pack	1 Jack & Bridle	5.50
Peter Jackson	1 Fan Mill	5.50
J. M. Brown	1 Sack Salt	2.05
J. M. Brown	1, " "	2.05
Geo. W. Highland	5 head of sheep 1.70	8.50
Geo. W. Highland	3 Do 1.45	4.35
Alfred Smith	1 young steer (Private)	8.00
		1023.00

(p 59) Good Claims owing B. D. PACK estate.
One Accounts on J. L. Bell due 26th Dec. 1857 Int. $142.59
.46.65
1 Account on Joe Brown, dec. proved 7th May 1858 5.25
1 Note on B. L. Pack for $100.00 due 20th Nov. 1855 with a Credit of 50.18 given 30th June 1857 65.65
One Note on L. D. Pack due March 18th 1858 for & Int. 70,00
79.18
One Note on T. A. Jackson due 1st January 1856 with interest from 1st January 1855 Interest as same 54.30 70.35
One Note on T. A. Jackson due 1st January 1859 for 100.00
105.17
One Note on W. M. Harris due 19th Dec. 1854 5.20 6.35
One Note on Wm. Harris due 4th March 1850 2.29 3.42
One Note on L. J. Perdue due when called for 90.00 91.80
One Note on Buriel Jackson Due 25th Dec. 1857 2.05 2.15
One Note on Jo Harris due 27th June 1850 5.04 10.10
One Note on JO Harris due 6th Nov. 1838 both & interest 2.75
13.60
One Note on R. A. Reavis & William Talley for $46.00 due 29th May 1857 with a Credit of $20.00May 29th 1857 and a Credit of $10 Febry 8th 1858 17.90
One Account on Rufus Furbie for rent of his farm for the year 1858 100.00 107.75
One Account on J. M. Brown for 3.50

Doubtful Claims owing B. D. PACKS Estate.
One Note on D. E. Powell due 23rd June 1857 for 10.00 10.75
One Note on Amos Robertson due 31st January 1853 for 11.00
11.00
One due bill on R. Doulton due when Called for and to be discharged in stone Mason work dated 18th Aug. 1852for 20.00
20.00
One Note on James Parr for 24.50 due 18th Aug. 1852 for $20.00
20.00
One Note on John W. Stevens for $9.50 due 27th June 1818 which has a Credit of one dollar given Feby. 15th 7.50 and also a Credit given Jany. 28th 1852 for one dollar
One Account on Cavy Prichard for 25 Cts. .25
One Account on Jackson Appleton for 40 Cents .40
One Account on Samuel T. Anderson for $1.00 1.00
One Note on S. J. and J. I. Bell for $73.00 due Oct. 12th 1839
73.00

One Account on H. T. Stringfellow shows 33.72		33.72
		895.77

(p 60) Inventory of perishable property of M. T. HALE, dec. sold at his late residence on the 27th day of May 1858

Names of Purchaser	Articles sold	
Widow	1 Work Table	3.00
Widow	1 lounge	5.00
Widow	1 small bed	5.00
Widow	1 small Table	1.50
Widow	1 Clock	3.00
Widow	1 Candle stand	.50
Widow	1 trunk	3.00
Widow	1 Bed stead & furniture	10.00
Widow	2 Beds & steads	25.00
Widow	1 wash stand	.50
Widow	1 broken set Chairs	6.00
John Shivers	1 Crib	.50
John Shivers	1 rocking Chair	1.75
Widow	1 lot picture frame	.50
Widow	1 watch	10.00
G. W. Hale	1 settee	.50
Widow	1 lot Tools	1.00
Widow	1 lot Crockery ware	3.00
Widow	1 Cooking stove	1.00
C. J. C. Shivers	300 lb Bacon 9.10	27.30
Hiram W. Lewis	378 lb Bacon 8.25	31.18
G. W. Hale	225 lb lard 7.50	16.97
Widow	1 Bell	1.00
John T. Hale	10 1st Choice Hogs	51.00
John T. Hale	10 2nd " "	50.00
R. T. Gupton	10 3rd " "	40.00
R. T. Gupton	10 4th " "	15.00
R. T. Gupton	Remainder of Hogs	10.00
R. T. Gupton	Remainder of hogs in pen	5.00
Widow	9 shotes in pen	4.00
Widow	11 hogs outside pen	5.00
Charles Vedder	1 Yoke Oxen	45.00
R. T. Gupton	2 peded steers	38.00
R. T. Gupton	2 White face steers	17.00
Warren Jordan	2 White face steers	10.00
Warren Jordan	1 Cow & Calf (Red)	11.25
W. W. Dozier	1 Black & White Cow	15.50
J. S. Parr	1 White faced heifer	12.00
Warren Jordan	1 Heifer Yearling	3.95
Warren Jordan	2 small steer Yearlings	10.00
F. M. Follis	1 Cow & Calf	15.00
(p 61)		
James B. Parkerson	1 gray horse	114.00
R. E. Stewart	1 gray Mare	103.00
E. S. Gleaves	1 sorrel Mare	50.75
E. W. Carney	1 Rone Colt	91.00
Warren Jordan	1 One year old Colt	58.00
E. S. Gleaves	1 sorrel Colt	41.00
Widow	1 sorrel Horse	50.00
Widow	1 sorrel Mare &Mule Colt	40.00
Widow	1 Bay Colt	25.00

L. W. Lovell	1-2 horse plow	2.00
Wm. Hooper	3 plows	2.30
T. J. Shaw	1 Wheel Barrow	.50
John B. Demunbra	1 Harrow	3.50
John B. Demunbra	1 Harros	4.05
E. G. Hudgens	2 Cart hubs	.10
B. F. Miles	1 Bull tongued Plow	.30
Tho. Arrington	1 Coulter old Plow & C.	.25
G. W. Hale	1 spike	.10
S. S. Speight	1 Dimon plow	2.40
Wm. Binkley	5 Cultivators	1.60
C. Smith	2 Collars	.10
J. Shivers	1 Collar	.05
R. T. Gupton	1 set tin hoops	1.05
Thos. OBrian	1 hog Chain	2.20
Thos. OBrian	1 Log Chain	3.75
John B. Demunbra	1 Large rope	3.25
John B. Demuñbra	1 " "	4.85
A. Hunter	1 Wheel barrow	.35
B. S. Miles	1 Lot hoes	.75
J. B. Demunbra	1 Crow bar	2.10
Warren Jordan	2 spades & C.	.45
J. W. Simpkins	2 Double tree	.40
S. S. Knight	2 " "	.35
J. Shivers	5 pair Harness	2.00
S. S. Knight	1 lot single trees	.85
J. T. Hooper	2 old tin irons	1.65
J. T. Hooper	1 lot old iron	.60
J. T. Hooper	1 " " "	.25
J. W. Simpkins	1 Nail drawer	1.25
G. W. Hale	3 Axes	1.00
Burel Jackson	1 Moving blade	1.00
Wesley Harris	2 iron Wedges	.65
D. S. Binkley	2 " "	.90
J. W. Simpkins	2 " "	.35
J. Perdue	2 " "	.50
R. B. Gibbs	3 Croking Chisels	.15
P62)		
Wash Hunter	3 Augers & saw	.35
G. Green	1 Corking hammer	.25
B. S. Miles	1 Axe & grub hoe	.10
S. S. Knight	1 Axe	.75
G. Green	1 shelling Machine	1.75
B. C. Robertson	1 lot iron	3.10
J. T. Hooper	1 Bar iron	2.00
B. C. Robertson	1 lot iron	.25
John B. Demunbra	1 lot iron round	6.00
John B. Demmnbra	1 " " "	10.25
B. C. Robertson	1 " " "	5.10
Asa Carney	1 " " "	.85
Wm. Cato	1 " " "	.70
J. B. Demunbra	1 " " "	1.70
D. S. Binkley	1 lot sheet iron	.60
B. C. Robertson	1 lot spikes	2.30
B. H. Gibbs	1 " "	4.75
B. C. Robertson	1 " "	5.10
P. Williams	1 Buggy	100.00

C. Vedder	1 Cow	9.25
L. J. Perdue	1 "	2.00
Wash Hunter	1 Cross Cut Saw	3.25
Warren Jordan	1 " " "	3.25
G. W. McCarley	1 old Cart	4.00
Wm. Hooper	1 Ox Cart	16.25
Tho. D. Hunter	1 Thresher	156.00
B. S. Miles	5 sacks wheat 55	5.63
N. M. Felts	10 " " 55	15.54
Jas. Crantz	10 " " 52	10.36
A. F. Carney	10 " " 53	
J. B. Demunbra	10 " " 50	9.85
Tho Obrian	10 " " 50	9.90
Wesely Harris	5 " " 51	5.25
A. F. Carney	13 Whole Amount 50	34.73
B. C. Robertson	324 lbs seed Cotton 3.05	9.88
Wm. Demunbra	10 Barrels Corn 1.45	14.50
Wm. Demunbra	10 Barrels Corn 1.40	14.00
Wm. Demunbra	10 " " 1.45	14.50
Wm. Demunbra	10 " " 1.60	16.00
Wm. Demunbra	10 " " 1.60	16.00
H. W. Lewis	10 " " 1.55	15.50
John Galleher	10 " " 1.60	16.00
Wm. Demunbra	10 " " 1.50	15.00
Wm. Demunbra	10 " " 1.50	15.00
Wm. Demunbra	10 " " 1.50	15.00
(p 63)		
Wm. Demunbra	10 " " 1.50	15.00
Wm. Demunbra	10 " " 1.50	15.00
Wm. Demunbra	10 " " 1.50	15.00
Thomas D. Hunter	10 " " 1.60	16.00
R. T. Gupton	10 Barrells Corn 1.60	16.00
John B. Demunbra	1 lot Cedar logs	8.25
Rhomas D. Hunter	1 Upper stack hay	13.00
L. J. Perdue	1 lower stack hay	9.25
G. W. Hale	101 Cards Wood 1.51	155.90
Widow	Wild hog Claim	10.00
John Galleher	5 Bdls & 3 bu Corn	8.40
		$2009.29

Notes and Accounts

One Note on Caroline Miles due Feby. 23rd 1858 for 7.15	7.60
One Note on John Galleher due 1st day of May 1858 for fifty one dollars 51.00	51.00
One Note on B. S. Miles due 1st day of Dec. 1858 for & interest 30.00	31.50
One Note on Samuel Watson due Nov. 13th 1858 with interest from date for & interest recd. 1092.16	1140.50
One Note on Tho. J. Crouch due Feb. 19th 1858 for 500.00	535.68
One Note on Abraham Edgings due 18th of March 1857 for (Doubtful) 26.60	26.60
One Note on Samuel B. Davidson due the 1st day of April 1857 for and interest 546.00	634.45
Cash left on hand 15.00	15.00
	2442.33

4451.62

Inventory of personal estate of W. T. Shepard, dec.
To Amount due him from his guardian N. J. Alley as shown by settlement with the Clerk of Robertson County Court Aug. 1st 1858 $115.36

Inventory of the personal estate of G. W. STACK, dec.
One Note on hand on Jacob Stack $100 due 25th 1852 Amounting to the present time to 134.50
One Note on hand on same for 190.00
Due Dec. 25th 1853 Amounting to the present time 244.15
578.65
20.67
599.32

The above is a true and perfect inventory of all the goods and Chattel rights and Credits of the said G. W. Stack dec. which have come to my hands possession or knowledge or the hands of any other persons for me to the best of My Knowledge and belief this Sept. 24th 1858
A. J. Bright, Administration

(p 64) Will of WILLIAM D. HUTTON, dec.

I William D. Hutton of the County of Cheatham in the State of Tennessee being weak in body but sound in Mind do Make this My last will and testament hereby revoking all others Made by me heretofore in the following Manner in the first place I desire that My funeral expence shall be paid out of the first Money that shall be received by My executor and executrix, secondly I give and bequeath to My beloved wife Virginia Hutton during her Natural life or widowhood, the Exum tract of land whereon I now live land purchased by me from Samuel Barclift, deceased, and Constituting one of the fields or portion of the field of the Exum tract also the Shelton tract of land. I also give her Negro man Charles, Negro man Jack and Negro Woman Clary and her infant Named Sarah Negro girl Lucy Ann, girl Named Mary and a boy Named Solomon . I also give her. I also give her My Yellow or Clay bank Mare and one Mule the Mule to be selected by her as she May think proper, I also desire that the Commissioner that May be appointed to lay off her years provisions will be liberal in appropriating to her an ample sufficiency of all other stock Not heretofore enumerated, household and kitchen furniture and provisions, in the event of the Marriage of My beloved wife Virginia it is My desire that she shall retain a Childs part of the Negroes and her dowery in the land. Thirdly I give and bequeath to My daughter Sallie Newsom and her Children a Negro Woman Named Bettie and her Child Named Louesa which I value at twelve hundred dollars also I give to My daughter Sallie one hundred and twenty five dollars in Cash Making the amount thus given her thirteen hundred and twenty five dollars. fourthly I desire that My sons John, Thomas and Carter shall receive out of the balance of My Negroes Not heretofore Mentioned the amount of thirteen hundred and twenty five dollars each being the amount given to My daughter Sallie Newsom, and for the services of My sons John Thomas. I give to each of them one hundred and fifty dollars More than I have given to My daughter Sallie and son Carter all the balance of My perishable property after excluding that portion alloted to My beloved wife. I desire to be sold after the payment of My debts. I desire the balance of the Money be equally divided among My four Children Sally Newsom, John, Thomas and Carter and My beloved Wife Virginia for the Convenience of timber I desire that fifty five acres of the tract of land I bought Known as the Garland tract. Fifthly I desire that all My lands exclusive of that portion alloted to My beloved Wife (p 65) shall be equally divided among My four Children before Named but that No division shall take place until the time arrives when the tract whereon My beloved wife lives shall be distributed equally between them also the balance of My Negroes, Not heretofore Mentioned shall be equally divided between My before Named Children Sally Newsom, John Thomas and Carter and as before stated what I have given to My daughter Sallie Newsom I give to her and her Children and My object in the distribution of My estate among My Children is that they shall share equally alike with the exception of one hundred and fifty dollars each. I gave to John and Thomas for their services. lastly I Constitute and appoint My beloved wife Virginia, Executrix and Affectionate brother Henry M. Hutton, Executors to this My last will and testament in testament whereof I have hereunto subscribed My Name this 21st day of July 1858.

Wm. D. Hutton

Signed in presence of:
Wm. Shearon
G. B. Forhand

In the event of Brother Henry M. Hutton being unable to attend to the duties as executor of My will and testament as specified with it is My desire and wish that James E. Newsom would supply the deficiency and act accordingly.

This July the 21st 1858

Signed in presence of:
Wm. Shearon
G. B. Forehand

William D. Hutton

I William D. Hutton being still sound in Mind and of disparging Memory, it is My Will and wish if either My sons John or Thomas or Carter shall die before they come of age, or Marry that the other two shall have the portion of property that I give to him equally divided between them this the 3rd day of August 1858 whereof I here set My hand

Wm. D. Hutton

Wm. Shearon
G. B. Forehand

(p 66) Will of TABITHA KING' dec.

I Tabitha King do Make and publish this as My last Will and testament hereby revoking and Making void all former Wills by me at any time Made.

First I direct that My funeral expenses and all My debts be paid as soon after My death as posible out of any Monies I May die possessed of or May first Come into the hands of My executor.

Secondly, I give to My grandaughter Hannah R. Osburn during her Natural life one Negro Woman Named Cloa One Negro Man Named Daniel and one other Negro boy Named Washington at the death of My grandaughter H. R. Osburn the above Named Negroes to go over to the Children of her body, should the said H. R. Osburn die without Child or Children then the above Named Negroes to go over to the Child or Children of My grandaughter Josephine T. Hudgens.

Thirdly, I give to my grandaughter Josephine T. Hudgens during her Natural life one Negro Woman Named Cyntha, one girl Named Tennessee and one boy Named James and their increase and at the death of My grandaughter Josephine T. Hudgens the above Named Negroes to go over with their increase to the Children of her body should the said Josephine T. Hudgens die without Child or Children then all the above Named Negroes with their increase go over to My grandson Benjamin L. Hudgens.

Fourthly, I give and bequeath to my Grandaughter, Josephine T. Hudgens and H. R. Osburn all my household furniture to be equally divided between them.

Fifthly, I direct that My executor sell all My stock of Horses, Cattle, hogs all My farming utensils and kitchen furniture and the proceeds to be equally divided between My three grandchildren, Benjamin L. Hudgens, Josephine T. Hudgens and Hannah R. Osburn.

Sixthly, I give and bequeath to My three grandchildren Benjamin L. Hudgens, Josephine T. Hudgens and H. R. Osburn the tract of land on which I now live to be sold or divided as they May prefer if sold the proceed to be equally divided between them, if divided to be divided according to value, equally between them.

Seventhly, I hereby nominate and appoint Willie W. Williams My Executor to this My last will and testament, in testimony whereof I have hereon to set My hand and seal this 11th day December A. D. 1856.

Tabitha King (SEAL)

Signed sealed and delivered in the presence of Elijah Hudgens and A. J. Teasley.

(p 67) An inventory of the property sold at the sale of SARAH DAVIS, dec. by THOMPSON BIGGERS, Admr. on the 29th day of Dec. 1858.

David K. Alley	9 Plates	.30
J. D. Nicholson	6 "	.70
J. D. Nicholson	1 set knives & forks	.75
Joel W. Pace	1 Pitcher	.70
Joel W. Pace	2 "	.60
J. D. Nicholson	1 Coffee Mill	.35
Joel W. Pace	2 Dishes	.30
J. D. Nicholson	1 Cream Pitcher	.20
J. W. Pace	7 glases	.55
David K. Alley	1 set Cups & saucers	.25
Isaic Alley	1 " " "	.25
Isaic Alley	1 Sugar bowl	.15
J. D. Nicholson	1 lot bottles	.15
George Davis	1 Tea tray	.15
David K. Alley	2 Stone Jars	.45
Joel W. Pace	1 pair Cards	.30
Tho Hunter	1 lard stand	1.25
Geo Davis	1 Coffee pot & C.	.55
Geo Davis	2 Trays	.05

Geo Davis	1 smoothing Iron	.40
J. D. Nicholson	1 Basket	.15
Isaic Alley	1 Axe	.65
Geo Davis	1 looking glass	.70
Isaic Alley	2 water buckets	.60
J. D. Nicholson	1 Bucket & piggin	.75
Thomas Hunter	1 Pot and Hooks	2.25
Geo Davis	1 Pot & Hooks	.95
Curtis Mohon	1 Frying pan	.50
H. R. Felts	1 Wash pan	.05
Curtis Mohon	1 small oven & hooks	.75
David K. Alley	1 Churn	.25
David K. Alley	1 skillet	1.05
Thomas Hunter	1 Reel	1.00
J. W. Pace	1 Table	1.65
R. B. Biggers	1 side saddle	14.00
Curtis Mohon	1 bridle & blanket	1.30
J. D. Nicholson	1 Cow and Calf	17.00
J. D. Nicholson	1 Chest	2.55
J. D. Nicholson	1 Bureau	12.00
D. K. Alley	1 Cupboard	7.25
D. K. Alley	6 Chairs	3.60
		77.30

(p 68) Will of THOMAS WALKER, dec.

I Thomas Walker of the County of Cheatham and State of Tennessee do this 18th day of June 1858 Make and Constitute this My last Will and Testament.

1st, I desire that a good and sufficient dower be given to My wife Elizabeth Walker.

2nd, I give to My son Richard B. Walker the tract of land on which he now lives the same that I purchased of A. W. Stewart formerly the Wilson tract.

3rd, I desire the tract of land that I purchased of James Mallory and on which I now live to be divided between My daughter Amanda M. Majors and Mauring L. Stewart in the following Manner, let on east and West line be run, starting on the lane that runs out in front of My dwelling, let the line be run due east, to Dempsey Hunters line and run so as to pass on the North side of any Clause to a portion of Wood land in the field to the right hand side of said lane, I desire that My daughter Amanda M. Majors have the land lying south of said east and West line and also the land I purchased of Abner Gupton on the South side of Racoon Creek.

And I give to My daughter Mauring L. Stewart the land lying on the North side of said east and West line and after her death said land to be equally divided among her Children with the understanding that My wife's dower be first laid off of this said Mallory tract of land this division of it is Made between My daughters.

4th, after the death of My Wife I desire daughter Amanda M. Majors shall have the dower alloted to My Wife.

5th, L give to My son, Josiah M. V. B. Walker the balance of My lands including the lands purchased of the Biggers the Alleys and Turners With the understanding that if any portion of said land be taken off to Make and My Wife's dower the same shall revert to him at her death.

6th, L give to My Wife during her Natural life the following Negroes (Viz) Roxy Ann, Mariah, Jesse and his wife Martha with her three Children., called Jesse, Jim and Edmond with their increase all except little Jesse, to be divided in four shares and that My son Richard B. have one share, My son Josiah M. V. B. have one share and My daughter Mauring L. Stewart Children have one share.

7th, I give to My son Richard the boy Named Patrick

(P 69) 8th, I give to MY daughter Amanda M. the girl Named Grace and her daughter Named Sally together with their increase .

8th, I give to My daughter Mauring L. during her Natural life the girland Named Harriett and her increase and after My daughters death said girl and her increase to be equally divided among her Children.

9th, I give to My son Joshiah M. V. B. the two Negroes Named Frank and Frosby and after the death of My wife I desire that he May have the little boy Jesse, son of old Jesse,

10th, I desire that My daughter Amanda M. have all the stock she brought home with her.

11th, I give to My son Richard B. the stock I own in the Parodise Hill and Clarksville Turn pike.

12th, I give to My grandson Thomas A. Stewart one hundred dollars.

13th, I give to My grandson John T. Walker one hundred dollars.

14th, I desire the balance of property sold and the proceeds be divided into five shares and I desire the balance of all unapprobated Money be included in these five shares and that My wife have ene share, My daughter Amanda M. have one share. My son Richard B. have one share. My son Josiah M. V. B. have one share and that My daughter Mauring L. have half a share and that the Children of My daughter Mauring L. have half a share.

15th, I desire that My executor get the Court to appoint some suitable person to take charge of the money that I have Willed to My daughter Mauring L. Children and keep the same until the Children Marry or become of age he paying such interest as the Court May think proper.

16th, I request that the Commissioners who lay off My wife's dower May include any and all such land as they May think proper but that the same shall revert to those that I have willed it at My wifes death.

17th, I Appoint and request My friend Dr. R. J. Mallory and My son Richard B. Walker to qualify and act as executor to this My last will and testament, and I request that no useful hand or stock be removed until all Necessary attention is paid to the Crop or until same together with stock be sold and divided.

And now having Materialy reflected on the contents of this My last Will and testament, I hereunto set My hand and seal.

Test:

H. Hunter — Thomas Walker (SEAL)

M. V. B. Walker

(p 70) Will of FRANK BALTHROP

I francis Balthrop do Make and publish this as My last

Will and testament hereby revoking and Making Void all other wills by Me at any time Made.
First, I direct that all My just debts be paid as soon after My death as possible out of any Monies I may die possessed of or May first come into the hands of My executor.
Secondly, I will and desire that all My Children shall share equally in My estate after accounting to My Executor for what I have already given them as heretofore Mentioned except J. Madine Balthrop heirs or Children I give them one dollar Jointly and No More of my estate whatever the Names of the above Children that I desire to share equally is as follows, after first accounting for the several amounts hereafter Mentioned, or a deduction of the same out of their share of My estate without interest. Thomas G. Balthrop, John C. Balthrop Robert Balthrop, Henry F. Balthrop, William Balthrop, Jordan R. Balthrop, Patsey Kemp, Names Children, Nancy R. Everett, Mary Norris, Lucy Ann Mose, Sarah B. Gibbs, Patsey KempNorris, Children to have share jointly or in other words all of them to have jointly as Much as one of My above Mentioned Children after accounting for twenty five dollars which I gave her in her life time (without interest) Thomas G. Balthrop has to Account for fifty dollars without interest I let him have John C. Balthrop twenty dollars without interest I let him have Elizabeth Gilmore My daughter which I Neglected Mentioning in the foregoing list if My Children I also desire her to have an equal of My estate after deducting twentyfive dollars I let her have No interest to be exacted in addition to what I have given Henry F. Balthrop, Jordan R. Balthrop and John C. Balthrop I will that they shall have a Bed and furniture each, as I have never given them one in the foregoing part where I Mentioned Robert Balthrop having an equal part of My estate, with the rest of My Children I will and desire and do hereby give that portion to said Robert Balthrop Children and do hereby appoint him guardian of said Children and require no security of the said Robert Balthrop for his performance as said guardian. I let said R. Balthrop have one hundred and ten dollars which amount said Children will have to account for, or in other words to de dedücted from their share of My estate. I hereby Nominate and appoint H. F. Balthrop and Jordan R. Balthrop My executors.

Witness (p 71) whereof I do to this My Will set My hand and seal this February 10th 1849.

F. Balthrop (SEAL)

Signed sealed and published in our presence and we have subscribed our Names in the presence of the testator This February the tenth day 1849.

Witness:
W. G. Shelton
Wm. Hooper

An inventory of the property sold by MRS E. HUNT one of the executors of JOHN HUNT, dec. as directed in said will.

Purcheser Named	Articles sold	
John Purdy		
J. Walker	1 Yoke Oxen	36.25
John Purdy	1 Cow	8.00
S. D. Powers	2 Steers	15.05

Wm. W. Felts	1 Red Cow	13.25
J. M. Frey	1 Gray Horse	22.75
James W. Hunt	1 Gray Filly	85.00
G. Nicholson	1 Bed	12.18
Ben Moore	1 Bed	11.50
Henry R. Felts	1 Spinning Wheel	.10
G. W. Shaw	3 Sheep	4.50
Wm. W. Felts	5 Sheep	5.10
John Purdy	5 Sheep	7.55
		221.23

Sworn to by James W. Hunt agent.
W. W. Williams, Clerk

Inventory of the estate of JOHN A. MASON, deceased sold on the 23rd of August 1858.

Purchaser Names	Articles sold	
E. J. Binkley	1 lot tuss Hoops	.30
T. J. Webb	1 Drawing knife	.90
John Harper	2 Drawing Knives	.75
John Harper	3 Drawing Knives	.50
John Harper	4 Drawing Knives	.80
John Harper	1 Drawing Knife	.50
John Harper	1 Drawing Knife	.75
John Harper	1 Drawing Knife	.40
John Harper	1 Chamfering knife	.25
John Harper	1 " "	.70
John Harper	1 Crow	.65
Aaron Smith	1 Chopping Axe	1.20
Aaron Smith	1 Coopers Adze	2.25
John Harper	1 Hand Saw	1.00
John Harper	1 Brace & Bit	1.10
W. W. Bennett	1 Lot Books	3.90
(p 72)		
B. H. Newman	1 Axe	.15
J. T. Webb	1 Bed stead & Cord	5.00
D. F. Binkley Jr.	1 Barrel Jointer	1.60
Wm. Demunbra	4 Chairs	1.20
A. Smith	1 Shot Gun	14.00
J. T. Webb	1 Skillet	.25
H. Turner	1 Pot	.20
John Harper	1 Hand Bar	.75
E. J. Binkley	1 lot files	.25
Wm. Demunbra	1 Lot bottles	.10
Wm. Demunbra	1 " "	.15

1 Note on Ed Furgerson for thirty two dollars & 40 Cents
Doubtful $32.40

Sworn to before me on the 1st day of Nov. 1858
W. W. Williams, Clerk

The following is a list of the articles set apart to Mrs Elizabeth Hale widow of M. T. Hale, dec. for the support of her and her family one Year from the death of her said husband as reported by Commissioners .

150 Barrels Corn on hand
50 Bushels Wheat on hand
2000 Bacon on hand
1500 Bundles fodder on hand

1000 Bundles Oats
100 pounds Coffee
200 pounds sugar
10 pounds soda
15 Bushels salt
5 pounds pepper
20 pounds rice
20 gallon Molasses
50 pounds loaf sugar
1 pound ginger
1 pound spice
100 dollars worth family Clothing
20 pounds ran Cotton on hand
1 Yoke Oxen and Cart on hand
(p 73)
1 Wagon on hand
5 Mules & Gear on hand
2 Milk Cows on hand
Pounds of soap on hand
120 pounds of laid on hand
1 Beef and tallow on hand

We being Commissioners appointed by the County Court of Cheatham County at its May term have Met and set apart for the support of the family of Matthew T. Hale, deceased the Articles stated above

Sworn to the day and year above written
Joseph Hudson
James Lenox
J. M. Lee, Commissioners

(p 74) An inventory of the estate of R. FULGHUM, dec.
A list of accounts due Fulghum and Bros. at Shelbyville Tenn.

1 Account of F. Blakemore D of trust	18.45
1 Account on William Wieene C	.85
1 Account on Will Blake & Co. C	3.10
1 Account on S. N. Titcomb Brake	.70
1 Account on J. B. Fuller Insolvent	3.80
1 Account on J. W. Wallis D of trust	63.79
1 Account on Tho. Ledbetter C	.10
1 Account on Whiteworth C.	.50
1 Account on W. B. Rayborn doubtful	2.50
1 Account on J. N. Thompson & C. D of Trust	1.10
1 Account on J. M. Elliott C	4.45
	99.34
1 Account on G. W. Thompson C.	1.65
1 Account on Bell Basket & Co Broke	6.80
1 Account on Mrs Newton C.	1.20
1 Account on James Young C.	.60
1 Account on Alx Eakin C.	4.05
1 Account on R. N. Wallace C.	10.36
1 Account on C. W. Cummery Doubtful	.15
1 Account on C. A. Fowler "	1.70
1 Account on James Dixon Sr. C.	.60
1 Account on J. T. Chilton C.	7.70
1 Account on J. Shofree C.	.25
	35.06

1 Account on Braime & Hughes C.		5.60
1 Account on Wallace & Boilin Broke		.30
1 Account on T. Lipscomb Broke		5.18
1 Account on James Cummings C.		3.75
1 Account on James Nowell Doubtful		.35
1 Account on Mrs Knight Doubtful		.10
1 Account on Thomas Trotenger C.		.35
1 Account on Knott & Ledbetter C.		65.62
1 Account on Gid McDowell, Broke		.40
1 Account on G. E. Cunningham, Doubtful		1.25
1 Account on B. C. Cowen, Sr. Doubtful		.25
		83.15
1 Account on D. W. Harrison C.		1.25
1 Account on T. G. Harlin C.		.20
1 Account on R. Matthews C.		.20
1 Account on R. P. Halborton, Broke		7.85
1 Account on V. H. Steel C.		.85
1 Account on Wm. Morton Deed of trust		.25
1 Account on Mrs E. Morgan C.		.15
1 Account on J. & W. C. Zechery C.		.25
1 Account on Miley Daniel C.		26.50
1 Account on Robert Cannon C.		.45
1 Account on Josiah Nesbit C.		.40
1 Account on S. A. Dolton Daoubtful		.90
		47.95
	220.50	

(p 75)

1 Account on Joseph Thompson C.		64.25
1 Account on Robert Buchanan C.		2.50
1 Account on Houson & Warren C.		4.20
1 Account on Young Willhort C.		.80
1 Account on William Tune C.		.30
1 Account on G. W. Cunningham C.		27.00
1 Account on J. E. Eakin C.		.50
1 Account on G. W. Buchanan C.		13.26
1 Account on T. B. Cannon C.		3.00
1 Account on J. H. Neil C.		3.15
1 Account on Thomas Burnett C.		.90
		119.91
1 Account on B. M. Tillman C.		1.20
1 Account on Jesse Crockley C.		4.00
1 Account on J. & N. Thompson & Co. C.		1.50
1 Account on J. M. Winston C.		18.40
1 Account on J. F. Calhoun C.		1.50
1 Account on Wm. Meirs C.		1.25
1 Account on R. A. Colwell C.		3.90
1 Account on G. P. Baskett C.		2.60
1 Account on T. C. Ryall C.		2.50
1 Account on John Tune C.		.60
		37.45
1 Account on R. Jones C.		6.48
1 Account on T. G. Boles, Doubtful		.75
1 Account on William Spence "		1.05
1 Account on Dr. M. McGraw C.		1.50
1 Account on Moses Marchel C.		4.40
1 Account on Thomas Burt C.		2.15
1 Account on A. J. Ellot, Broke		12.55

1 Account on J. E. Perison & Brothers C.	2.60
	31.48
1 Account on Halling & Jones C.	
1 Account on John Dolton, insolvent	1.85
1 Account on John Morgan C.	31.40
1 Account on Peter English C.	.15
1 Account on S. E. Gilliandd C.	.10
1 Account on R. W. Cowen C.	1.10
1 Account on W. Willhight C.	.10
1 Account on T. S. Clay C.	.70
1 Account on G. W. Jenigan C.	.20
1 Account on T. M. Callville C.	22.65
	58.75
	508.09
1 Account on S. M. Doolen C.	7.00
1 Account on James Wortham C.	1150
1 Account on Jacob F. Thompson C.	.70
1 Account on Green Michal C.	1.80
1 Account on R. C. Greer C.	.40
1 Account on W. P. Goodwin	.40
(p 76)	
1 Account on James Story C.	31.03
1 Account on Mrs Shepphard, Doubtful	.30
1 Account on R. D. Duny C.	16.75
1 Account on William Gosslin C.	20.35
1 Account on William Sanders C.	.40
1 Account on H. Halbert, Doubtful	5.79
1 Account on Aunitung & Co. C.	.50
1 Account on J. F. Thompson C.	.90
	87.82
1 Account on J. C. Eakin C.	2.45
1 Account on J. Armstrong C.	.75
1 Account on Joslin Whiteside & Co. C.	1.00
1 Account on W. W. Standfield, Doubtful	4.00
1 Account on William Carpenter C.	2.05
1 Account on Moorman & Spery C.	6.65
1 Account on M. D. Moorman C.	.50
1 Account on S. A. Bivens C.	4.15
1 Account on Cotton & Sharon C.	31.60
1 Account on W. G. Cowen C.	6.60
1 Account on John W. Cowen & Co. C.	4.65
1 Account on T. B. Lard & Co. C.	175
1 Account on Morgan & Maddagan C.	8.98
1 Account on F. P. McCross, Doubtful	1.00
1 Account on Dr. Barksdale C.	3.05
	78.18
1 Account on M. E. W. Dunnaway C.	.50
1 Account on P. Fay C.	2.70
1 Account on H. H. Head C.	2.00
1 Account on Robertson & Rhom, Broke	30.75
1 Account on Henry Brown C.	.25
1 Account on Thomas Halland, Broke	.90
1 Account on Henry Cooper C.	3.55
1 Account on Newell & Norton, Broke	.25
1 Account on Drony & Majors C.	.20
1 Account on A. J. Greer C.	.40
1 Account on J. B. Kent D of T	5.20

1 Account on J. H. Onsil C.	2.20
1 Account on S. B. Knott C.	81.45
1 Account on J. S. Sandder C.	.10
1 Account on J. N. Willhort C.	1.45
	131.90
1 Account on Mrs Willis Cannon, doubtful	.50
1 Account on J. W. Jones, doubtful	.50
1 Account on William Griffin, Broke	8.00
1 Account on John C. Edger C.	7.60
1 Account on Mrs L. Eakin C.	18.79
	805.99
(p 77)	
1 Account on J. W. Wallis & Co. D of trust	7.65
1 Account on J. L. Neily C.	2.35
1 Account on T. A. Bell, Broke	.40
1 Account on Sheppard & Mitchell C.	10.12
1 Account on J. H. Colwell C.	21.84
1 Account on Griffin & Thompson, broke	19.35
1 Account on J. A. Blakemore C.	3.47
1 Account on E. D. Drumgool, broke	2.30
	137.08
1 Account on Baskett & Stamp C.	6.20
1 Account on William Brown C.	1.50
1 Account on Mrs A. P. Freson C.	44.45
1 Account on Old Prebystilan Church C.	2.50
1 Account on R. B. Davidson C.	3.05
1 Account on Shafner & Woolseys C.	1.00
1 Account on G. W. Ruth C.	.25
1 Account on Mitchell & Shofner C.	33.50
1 Account on H. L. Davidson C.	2.85
1 Account on Dr. Goslin C.	1.25
1 Account on J. E. Colwell C.	.15
1 Account on W. S. Felts C.	3.05
1 Account on Titcomb & Elliott, broke	.10
1 Account on R. S. Dwiggin C.	19.05
	118.90
1 Account on T. C. Whitside C.	3.65
1 Account on John Nevins, Broke	1.50
1 Account on Granly Fletcher C.	.10
1 Account on J. M. Tromger C.	24.02
1 Account on Andrew Enion C.	5.20
1 Account on John W. Nelson, Broke	7.46
1 Account on James Ross C.	25.95
1 Account on N. & C. R. Road & Co. C.	2.55
1 Account on Colwell & Humming C.	13.16
1 Account on Newcom & Thompson, Broke	13.08
1 Account on Wilhights & Brothers C.	1.60
1 Account on W. W. Simmons C.	1.25
1 Account on William Words C.	16.45
1 Account on Robert Dennison C.	79.42
1 Account on G. & J. W. Fletcher C.	.60
1 Account on J. A. Ganaway C.	5.75
1 Account on J. Miller C.	.85
1 Account on John Sehom C.	4.75
	1273.31
1 Account on Mrs M. V. Fooleman C.	19.90
1 Account on Mrs E. A. Kincade C.	.50

1 Account on J. W. Hamlin C.	.75
1 Account on Robert Armstrong C.	3.00
(p 78)	
1 Account on C. A. Robertson, insolvent	1.35
1 Account on C. B. Ward C.	.90
1 Account on J. L. Armstrong C.	.80
1 Account on William Hoover C.	.60
1 Account on W. T. Zallecaffe C.	.35
1 Account on Dr. Whitman, Doubtful	.25
1 Account on E. A. Bobo C.	1.50
1 Account on David Morgan C.	.40
1 Account on H. B. Turnby C.	.10
1 Account on O. A. Mofly, insolvent	.25
1 Account on Z. Zechery C.	15.75
1 Account on Jesse Evans C.	3.20
1 Account on Tally & Goodrich C.	4.34
1 Account on E. Cooper C.	.25
1 Account on D. F. Jackson C.	3.00
	74.34
1 Account on Helbert & Burdell d of T.	7.84
1 Account on John Gromby	3.60
1 Account on T. S. & S. Clay C.	1.75
1 Account on D.S. Evans	1.00
1 Account on Shelbyville University C.	45.70
1 Account on S. F. Crutcher C.	.45
1 Account on Joseph Blackwell C.	2.10
1 Account on Dr. R. F. Evans C.	4.00
1 Account on J. W. Gotham C.	.30
1 Account on Jack Smith C.	.55
1 Account on Joseph Bendet, insolvent	.25
1 Account on Dromgool & Hallowburton Do	.20
1 Account on J. G. Fulghum C.	.25
1 Account on George Hutton C.	1.00
1 Account on H. Powell, insolvent	.15
1 Account on Amos Haze C.	.25
1 Account on Dr. Duvall C.	.60
1 Account on John T. Neil C.	1.20
1 Note on Hurt & Murphey C.	110.00
1 Due Bill on R. D. Dany C.	40.00
1 Note on Isaic Greer, Broke	17.71
	238.90
	1586.55

Amount due the firm of Fulghum & Bros. Shelbyville John J. Fulghum Dr to firm of Fulghum & Bros.

To Amount on sale book	286.90
To Amount drawn out Bank	226.41
To Amount advanced by R. & J. H. Fulghum	236.89
To Amount due the firm by others	2336.75
The amount due the firm at Shelbyville	2347.95

750.20
11.00
2336.75
2347.95

(p 79)

Amount due the estate at Shelbyville	2347.95
Cr.	
By Burial expense of deceased	175.00

By Bill on Fletcher	10.85
By firm debts paid by J. G. Fulghum	477.27
By insolvent debts	274.40
By Cash paid on bridge by same	40.00
By boarding 3 hands	155.00
By boarding the deceased	61.87
	1194.39
Amount due after paying debts	1153.56
Cr. by Burial expense Charged to eronious	175.00
By Bill at Fletchers	10.85
This Amount divided by two	1339.41
Amount of profits to parties	669.70
Amount due the deceased at Shelbyville	334.85
Cr. by Amount of Burial expense	185.85
Dr. to Amount of stock on hand	302.74
Amount the estate at Shelbyville	451.74
Value of the estate in Cheatham County	1669.39
Amount due estate in all	2121.13
Allowance to administrator	55.50
Balance said estate on settlement	2065.63

(p 80) Inventory of the estate of SARAH DAVIS brought from page 67. 77.30

Purchasers Names	Articles sold	
David K. Alley	1 bed & pillow	20.00
David K. Alley	1 stead, Cord & C.	3.05
David K. Alley	1 Bed & pillows	17.53
J. D. Nicholson	1 Bed stead	.45
E. G. Murphey	1 sorrel Mare	50.00
E. G. Murphey	1 Bridle	.10
J. D. Nicholson	1 sifter	.30
A. J. Bright	1 sifter	.10
William Alley	1 set Candle Moles	.05
J. D. Nicholson	1 shovel & fire irons	.75
F. A. Jones	1 sack	.15
J. D. Nicholson	1 sack	.35
		92.83
		170.13

Cash

Left on hand by deceased	130.75

Notes

1 Note on W. W. Davis due the 14th Feby. 1857 doubtful for	100.00
Interest up to time of settlement	116.75
1 Note on John D. Nicholson due 12th January 1853 for	300.00
with a Credit 13th April 1855 for	11.00
One on the 13th Feby. 1857 for	100.00
	189.00

(p 81) Commissioners report to the Widow of W. D. HUTTON

We the undersigned free holders of Cheatham County after being duly sworn have proceeded to set apart to Virginia Hutton widow of W. D. Hutton, dec. so much of the Crop and provisions on hand as Will be sufficient in our opinion to support her and her family one year from the death of her said husband, we set apart to her for said purpose the following articles to Wit, all of the household and kitchen furniture all of the Crop on the place on which she resides, with farming utensils belonging thereto five Milch Cows and Calves One beef twenty two pork hogs and the remainder of stock hogs on hand twenty three head of sheep all of the poultry, fifty dollars in Cash, four hundred pounds of bacon, one Yoke of Oxen and one Wagon.

Given under our hands and seals this 28th day of September 1858.

S. W. Adkisson (SEAL)
W. N. Thompson (SEAL)
James M. Dunn (SEAL)

We the Commissioners Make the above allowance to Virginia Hutton with the express understanding that she is to give the other Children as Much as have been given to Mrs Sarah Newson, that is as regards housekeeping.

S. W. Adkisson (SEAL)
W. N. Thompson (SEAL)
James M. Dunn (SEAL)

(p 82) An inventory of the personal estate of W. D. HUTTON deceased sold by M. M. HUTTON, Exr. on the 28th day of Sept. 1858.

Purchaser Names	Articles sold		
W. J. Cass	1 Horse Cart		8.25
W. D. Henry	1 Pair Cart Wheels		3.55
W. W. Hutton	1 Cross Cut Saw		1.00
W. T. Jones	1 lot old iron		1.30
Wm. Deal	1 lot Blacksmith Tools		7.00
W. T. Jones	1 Crow Bar		1.05
Henry Hutton Jr.	1 Do Do		1.35
James E. Newsom	1 Bar shore plow		
Wm. Deal	1 Scythe & Cradle		1.00
P. Jackson	1 Do Do		.50
James E. Newsom	2 sides sole leather		7.06
James E. Newsom	2 " " "		7.75
T. J. Rogan	2 " " "		5.19
R. Pegram	2 " " "		6.76
R. Pegram	2 " " "		7.73
S. W. Adkisson	2 " " "		6.57
Henry Knight	2 " " "		5.72
Winfield Knight	2 " " "		7.09
J. P. Pegram	2 " " "		6.50
H. T. Gower	3 " " "		13.26
P. Jackson	3 " " "		6.63
James E. Newsom	2 " " "		6.95
Wm. Deal	2 " " "		7.28
Samuel A. Thompson	2 " " "		5.92
Wilson Thompson	2 " " "		6.37
Moses Jones	9 " " "		29.50
N. Jordan	2 " " "		7.16
James E. Newsom	2 " " "		5.31
P. Jackson	2 " " "	22½	
H. W. Hutton	2 " " "		6.19
Thomas Riggin	2 " " "		6.69
Henry Kellum	2 " " "	25	5.57
Henry Hutton Jr.	2 " " "	25¼	6.56
Thomas Riggin	2 " " "	23½	
Thomas Riggin	2 " " "	23½	28.20

Thomas Riggin	2 sides sole leather	$24\frac{1}{4}$	
Thomas Riggin	2 " " "	24 3/4	8.08
Thomas Riggin	2 " " "	24	
R. Pegram	2 " " "	$24\frac{1}{2}$	5.02
Thomas Riggin	2 " " "	$24\frac{1}{4}$	13.54
J. P. Pegram	2 " " "	$24\frac{1}{2}$	5.08
(p 83)			
M. Young	2 " " "	$24\frac{1}{2}$	6.15
Thomas Riggin	2 " " "	24	10.32
Thomas Riggin	4 " " "	20	5.05
Henry Knight Sr.	5 peices sole leather	$21\frac{1}{2}$	5.16
James E. Newsom	1 lot bacon	6 3/4	131.50
Virginia Hutton	1 Gray Horse		50.00
J. W. Ray	1 Gray Horse		91.50
H. Knight	1 Young bay Mare		111.00
Thomas Jackson	1 old bay Mare		39.00
Wm. Newsom	1 sorrel Mare		51.00
Thomas Jackson	1 sucking Mule		18.00
Wm. Newsom	1 Black Mule		135.00
R. Pegram	1 Bay Mare Mule		89.00
J. M. Newsom	1 Brown horse Mule		87.00
T. McGore	1 Bay Mare Mule		75.00
James E. Newsom	1 Brown Horse Mule		65.00
James E. Newsom	1 Bay Mare Mule		71.00
Selas Sinton	1 Brown horse Mule		69.50
James E. Newsom	1 sorrel Mule		55.00
P. Jackson	1 Bay Mare Mule		106.00
James E. Newsom	1 Brown horse Mule		105.00
James E. Newsom	1 White Bull		8.50
John Hutton	1 Small red steer		7.50
R. Pegram	1 small pided heifer		3.75
L. W. Hutton	1 red Cow & Calf		8.50
W. W. Hutton	1 Black & white pided Cow		7.00
J. W. King	1 Young bay Mare		79.00
G. Hickee	1 Yoke oxen		26.00
Thos. F. Hutton	1 Dunn Cow		10.00
S. A. Thompson	1 pided steer		6.25
John T. Frazier	1 White back Cow		9.00
H. M. Hutton	1 Black Cow		13.00
S. A. Thompson	1 speckled Heifer		5.50
Virginia Hutton	1 Buggy Horse		130.00
H. M. Hutton	1 Barrel lard		20.00
H. M. Hutton	172 pounds bacon		11.62

(p 84) An inventory of the personal estate of JAMES HUDGINS, Sr. dec. sold on the 22nd day of November 1858. Thomas W. Harris, Adm.

Purchaser Names	Articles sold	
Daniel Hudgens	1 Clock	5.00
Polly Hudgens	1 Chest	.30
James Hudgens	1 Bed & furniture	10.00
Daniel Hudgens	1 Trundle bed & stead	12.10
Polly Hudgens	1 Bed & stead	4.00
James Hudgens	1 pair steelyards	1.00
Daniel Hudgens	1 Flax wheel	.80
Daniel Hudgens	1 Table	.45
Daniel Hudgens	1 Pair sheep shears	.10

Polly Hudgens	1 Cupboard	.10
Henry Harris	1 Donia Peon	2.80
Daniel Harris	1 bull tongued Plow	.65
John Hudgens	1 Diamond Plow	.80
James Hudgens	1 Bull Plow	.10
Daniel Hudgens	1 Grindstone	.25
James Hudgens	1 Lot of Gear	.75
James Gray	1 Big Pot	2.95
Polly Hudgens	1 lot Caslings	.05
Polly Hudgens	1 Pot rack & shovel	.60
James Hudgens	1 Loom	.25
Daniel Hudgens	1 box & Contents	.15
Daniel Hudgens	1 tray & sifter	.25
Daniel Hudgens	1 sythe & Cradle	.50
Polly Hudgens	1 lot Hoes	.50
Henry Harris	1 pair Cart wheels	4.00
Daniel Hudgens	2 Jars	.25
James Hudgens	1 scalding stand	.20
James Gray	1 Box	.10
Polly Hudgens	1 Tub & piggin	.90
Polly Hudgens	5 sheep	5.00
James Hudgens	5 sheep	4.00
Daniel Hudgens	Balance of sheep	3.55
Polly Hudgens	5 first Choice Hogs	9.00
James Hudgens	5 2nd do do	5.50
James Hudgens	6 3rd do do	4.00
William Walker	1 Steel trap	.05
Daniel Hudgens	1 lot sundries	.15
John Hudgens	1 Yoke Oxen	70.00
James Hudgens	1 Cow & Calf	10.15
James W. Walker	1 White Cow	10.50
Daniel Hudgens	1 Yearling	3.00
John Hudgens	1 White Yearling	3.80
(p 85)		
Thomas OBrien	1 Bell Cow	9.25
Polly Hudgens	1 lot Corn	14.25
Polly Hudgens	1 small Mare	40.85
Thomas OBrien	Hire of Negro Man Buck	12.75
Daniel Hudgens	1 lot Wool	1.25
B. W. Bradley	Hire of Sarah	3.55
Daniel Hudgens	1 stack Fodder	3.50
James Hudgens	1 lot Corn 5 barrels	10.50
Jesse Durham	3 lots Corn 15 bbls.	30.75
James Hudgens	Remainder of Corm	8.80
James Hudgens	1 lot sack	1.00
James Hudgens	1 stack Fodder	2.40
Jesse Durham	2 lots Corn, 10 Bbls.	20.50
Wm. Fortune	Remainder of Corn	
James Hudgens	1 lot of sacks	.50
R. H. Alley	1 stack fodder	5.05
John Hudgens	1 stack fodder	1.55
James Hudgens	1 stack fodder	4.05
R. H. Alley	1 small trunk	.20
James Gray	1 Horn	.15
John Hudgens	1 Hone	.80
Cr. by three hogs Claimed by Polly Hudgens		3.75

Years provision to Mrs ELIZABETH HALE, widow of M. T.

HALE, deceased until the 1st day of January 1859 for the purpose of finishing the cropCommenced to wit,

150 Barrels Corn, on hand
50 Bushels Wheat on hand
2000 Pounds of Bacon on hand
1500 Bundles on hand
1000 Bundles Oats
100 Pounds Coffee
200 Pounds sugar
10 Pounds soda
15 bushels salt
5 Pounds pepper
20 pounds rice
20 gallons Molasses
50 Pounds loaf sugar
1 Pound ginger
1 Pound spice
100 Dollars worth of Family Clothing
(p 86)
20 Pounds ran Cotton, on hand
1 Yoke Oxen and Ox Cart on hand
1 Wagon, on hand
5 Mules and geer on hand
2 Milk Cows, on hand
 Pounds of soap, on hand
2 Tin stands 120 pounds of lard on hand
1 Beef and tallow on hand

We being Commissioners appointed by the County Court of Cheatham County at their May term have Met and set apart for the support of the family of Matthew T. Hale, dec. until the 1st of January 1859 such articles as stated above.

Sworn to and subscribed the day and year above written

Joseph Hudson (SEAL)
James Lenox
James M. Lee, Com.

(p 87) Settlement of J. W. & E. H. Hunt, Exc. of John Hunt dec.

To amount of Cash left on hand	923.00
One N te on Wall & Wilson Dec. 25, 1854 for	70.00
Interest on same	4.20
One Note on H. Dowlen	275.00
One Note on G. W. Shaw	100.00
To Hogheads of Tobacco	132.15
Amount received for bacon	80.00
One Account on G. W. Hunt	7.10
One Account on L. Fox	3.12
One Account on James Walker	2.56
Amount of the sale of property	211.01
	1808.14

Credits

By G. W. McQuary receipt surveying	1.00
J. Vanrocking proven act	4.85
N. Morris act for hauling Tob.	7.35
G. W. Bells proven act	1.75
James Ryan proven act	14.91
Tax receipt 1857	38.11

E. G. Hudgens proven act	13.30
R. J. Mallory proven act	29.50
James Walker proven act	2.00
E. G. Murphey crying receipt property	1.50
W. H. Morris proven act	6.30
H. Dowlen affidavit	75.00
E. G. Murphey tax receipt 1856	15.75
James Walker proven act	6.75
To Clerk for qualifying Executor	3.96
James B. Hunt receipt for his portion Tobacco	25.20
Amount of Judgement G. W. Shaw	28.86
Cost of suit	1.45
To Clerk for taking and recording a refunding bond	3.00
For recovering 15 receipt	1.50
To Clerk for this settlement recording same & C.	2.05
Allowance to Executor	200.00
Amount due heirs	1324.05

(p 88) Settlement of THOMAS W. WHITFIELD, Administrator of the estate of JOHN BERRY, deceased.

Thomas W. Whitfield administrator of John Berry, dec. Dr.	
To Amount of first inventory	77465.86
To amount of interest received by administrator	542.45
To one Claim on Green McPherson Not retained in 1st Inventory	125.00
To one Claim on G. W. Brown Not in first inventory	20.00
Interest in same	.90
To one Claim on G. G. Mays	15.00
To one Claim on David Alexander	12.00
To one on Turner Davis	8.00
To one on Isaic Ivy	10.00
To one on W. G. Davis	9.00
To the rent of land 1857	124.00
" " " " " 1858	125.00
To dividen Turn Pike stock 1856	78.00
" " " " " "	24.00
To one act on G. Hogan	5.00
To one act on J. T. Davis	10.00
	8514.21
Cr.	
By invoices	771.64
By widows receipts	149.75
By East & Shane receipt advice	65.00
By John Ham proven act	39.96
By B. D. Clift proven act	7.50
By State & County Tax 1857	26.95
By Sloans receipt for tomb stone	22.00
By David Alexander proven act	29.55
By D. J. Allen proven act	17.10
By W. G. Anderson proven act	347.80
By E. C. Cooks proven act	5.10
By Foster & Cooks proven act	3.10
By John R. Anderson proven act	37.90
By M. B. Dunn proven act	9.06
By M. B. Dunn proven act	3.92
By A. Allison act	15.22
By James Williams	28.50

By D. H. Walton Receipt	2.00
By Ezra Holstead	2.00
By D. H. Walton proven act	.50
By W. S. Smith proven act	4.01
By J. H. Farley proven act	3.17
By W. B. Inman proven act	17.95
(p 89)	
To W. B. Inman proven act	4.10
G. W. McQuary Surveyor	2.50
Johnson & Vaugh Receipt	14.20
J. S. Dillinmunty Receipt	2.50
M. Burnes receipt	4.08
W. Knights Note	37.39
J. A. Keys proven act	113.00
Daniel Harrison act	9.25
Copy of deed	1.00
Tax receipt 1858	5.11
Commissioner lay dower & C.	2.00
Amount allowed administrator	275.00
Clerks fee for bond	2.00
Letters of administration	.50
Copy of same	.50
order to lay off dower	.25
Recording petition dower & C.	1.60
Recording inventory	2.50
State Tax	3.50
Order to lay off provision	.25
Making & Recording settlement	5.00
Recording & Refunding bonds	4.00
	2008.29
Amount to be distributed	6505.92
Jany. 6, 1859	

An Account of sale Made of the personal property of the estate of TABITHA KING, dec. at her late residence in Cheatham County after having advertised according to law.

1 Barrel Cotton 35	E. G. Murphey	.70
1 Bell	Wm. Smith	.40
1 saddle	John Shivers	.60
1 small Bell	A. J. Teasley	.35
1 Cross Cut saw	Tho Hudgens	3.10
1 lot Augers saw	J. Chandon	.50
1 saddle	Dan Hudgens	.25
1 Tin bucket & C.	J. Chandon	.50
1 skillet & rack	J. H. Harper	.85
1 spinning wheel	Janey Binkley	2.50
1 side upper leather	A. J. Teasley	1.85
1 spinning wheel	H. R. Felts	.50
1 Ox Cart	A. L. Fortune	17.75
1 large Kettle	Thos. Pace	1.70
1 Loom	Benjamin Smith	1.60
(p 90)		
1 sythe & Cradle	J. J. Wilson	.40
1 set Geer	B. H. Shearon	.75
1 set Geer	J. W. Walker	.30
5 Bushels Wheat 54	E. T. Herron	3.70
Balance wheat 10 bu 50	E. G. Murphey	5.00

1 lot Rye 3 bu. 40	W. J. Jackson	1.20
1 lot salt	W. Owen	.40
1 " "	W. Owen	.30
1 lard stand	W. Owens	.30
1 pen shucks	R. H. Reading	4.25
1 log Chain	J. Harper	1.30
1 Dorris Plow	E. G. Hudgens	1.00
1 Dorris Plow	E. Harris	.50
1 Bull tongued plow	E. G. Hudgens	.65
1 " " "	E. G. Hudgens	.25
1 single tree & Clevice	E. G. Hudgens	.25
1 iron Wedge	E. G. Hudgens	.20
1 grub hoe	E. G. Hudgens	.20
1 lot Corn 10 Barrels 179	E. Sullivan	17.90
1 " " 10 " 186	E. Sullivan	18.60
1 " " 10 " 180	E. Sullivan	18.00
1 " " 175	R. H. Alley	17.50
Remainder of Corn 17-165	J. Binkley	28.05
5 first Choice hogs	H. Dowlin	26.75
6 second " "	H. Dowlin	26.50
6 third " "	James Harris	9.20
6 fourth " "	E. G. Murphey	5.00
1 Kip Skin	E. G. Murphey	1.50
1 side upper leather	A. J. Teasley	2.50
1 pair candle Moles	Ben Smith	.40
1 Pewter basin	E. G. Hudgens	.50
1 Smoothing Iron	J. Chandon	.20
1 set Harness 8 slaie	Wm. Walker	.55
1 Jar	J. W. Walker	.25
1 Demi John	James Walker	.60
1 Churn	A. Walker	.15
1 Flax Wheel	E. G. Hudgens	1.00
1 Reel	B. F. Walker	1.20
1 Bay Mare	Stephens Bobbitt	30.50
1 sand horse	E. G. Murphey	33.00
1 Bay Mare	W. L. Bradley	105.50
1 stack fodder	J. D. Dismukes	5.30
1 stack fodder	J. D. Dismukes	5.50
1 " "	H. Simmons	5.00
1 old steer	A. E. Lovel	12.25
(p 91)		
1 Yoke steer	J. W. Pace	55.00
1 Heifer	Daniel Gleen	12.00
1 White Cow	Daniel Gleen	10.00
1 first Choice Yearling	Elias Harris	14.00
1 second " "	Thomas J. Shaw	4.00
1 White Heifer	Daniel Gleen	5.75
1 lot Tobacco	J. W. Walker	10.00
4 Hogs	Cash	4.25
		548.10

Notes and Accounts Not good

One Note on James Walker due 1st January 1859	10.00	
with a Credit of	2.49	7.51
One account on Thomas W. Osburn due 1st January 1858	52.00	
One due bill on J. L. Hudgens due 13th January 1836 for	27.00	

With a Credit Jan. 11th 1837	25.00	
Amount principal due on said Note	2.00	
One Note on J. L. Krantz due 16th Feb. 1837	146.64	
Credits		
January 28th 1840	5.75	
Nov. 30th 1841	12.12	
May 1st 1847	2.00	
" " "	10.50	30.37
Amount principal on said Note		116.27
and one Note on J. L. Hudgens due 1st August 1844		176.00

The foregoing is a full and perfect account of the sales of all the property of the estate of Tabitha King, dec. directed by law to be sold 31st Oct. 1858

J. W. Hunt, Administrator
With the Will annexed
Amount of estate $1059.61

(p 92) Second inventory of the sale of the personal property of the estate of M. T. HALE, dec. sold on the 28th day of December 1858

Purchaser Names	Articles sold	
Mrs A. E. Hale	1 Plow	1.00
Do Do	1 Do	1.00
Do Do	1 Do	1.00
Do Do	1 Do	1.00
Do Do	1 sythe & Cradle	.50
Do Do	1 big sorrel Mule	150.00
Do Do	1 Mouse Colored Mule	130.00
J. C. Newland	1 Brown Mule	135.00
Mrs A. E. Hale	1 Young MUle	10.00
Thos. N. Hooper	20 Bushels Wheat 67½	13.50
Thos. N. Hooper	20 " " 67	13.40
Thos. N. Hooper	20 " " 66	13.20
Thos. N. Hooper	20 " " 68	13.60
Thos. N. Hooper	All the Wheat 67	6.70
Thos. N. Hooper	10 Barrels Corn 2.56	25.60
Thos. N. Hooper	10 " " 2.50	25.00
Thos. N. Hooper	10 " " 2.50	25.00
Thos. N. Hooper	10 " " 2.51	25.10
Thos. N. Hooper	10 " " 2.50	25.00
James Lenox	Remainder of Corn 2.49	
Mrs A. E. Hale	1 Yoke Oxen & Cart	25.00
James Lenox	40 Bbls. 23.40 ac.Corn249	100.92
Thos. N. Hooper	13 Bushels Wheat .67	8.71

(p 93) Inventory of THOMAS WALKER estate as sold on Dec. 8th 1858.

Purchasers Names	Articles sold	
Widow	1 Kettle	2.00
Do	1 pot & irons	.50
Do	1 brass Kettle	.50
Do	1 Tray	.25
R. J. Mallory	1 lot pint Cans	.40
Widow	1 Pot	1.50
M. V. B. Walker	1 Oven & lid	1.00

M. V. B. Walker	1 Pot & Hook	.50
Granville Nicholson	1 Tea Kettle & 2 irons	.70
Widow	1 Reflector	1.50
M. V. B. Walker	1 Pair Steelyard	3.75
M. V. B. Walker	1 Bucket & Jar	.10
Henry Felts	1 lot leather	.87
Nathan Morris	1 side leather	1.80
M. V. B. Walker	1 spinning wheel	1.00
Widow	Loom real & Machine	5.00
R. J. Mallory	1 stove	8.50
M. V. B. Walker	1 lot old barrels	.50
M. V. B. Walker	1 Grind stone	.75
J. J. Wilson	200 lb bacon 7½	15.00
J. D. Tucker	1 lot shoulders 3	
Widow	1 Clock	5.00
John W. Perdue	1 lot toys	.80
Amand Majors	1 Flax Hackel	.50
R. J. Mallory	1 small table	.30
G. Nicholson	1 Castor	.85
M. V. B. Walker	5 Glasses	.25
J. W. Perdue	2 glass stands	.35
J. W. Perdue	2 Candle sticks	.35
A. Jones	1 Lot B ooks	.60
W. Pace	1 " "	.85
Widow	1 Water Can	.75
Do	1 sugar Chest	4.00
M. V. B. Walker	1 Bed & stead	45.00
M. V. B. Walker	1 small bed & stead	11.50
Wm. Randale	1 Bed & stead	43.00
Widow	Shovel tongs & poker	1.00
Widow	1 Buggy & harness	50.00
M. V. B. Walker	2 Grubbing Hoes	.75
Greenville Nicholson	4 weeding hoes	.50

(Note: Page 94 is left blank)

(p 95) To Amount of first inventory of the estate of E. L. STEWART, dec. brought from page 13,14 & 15 2994.12

Amount of 2nd Inventory	
1 Account on Phillip Ball	2.50
One Account W. A. Couch	30.00
1 Account on W. Stewart	15.00
Balance on Note on Jesse Chandown	6.60
1 Note on C. Rasberry for	60.56
Credit with	1.50
G. W. Speght Note	31.00
Credit on same	11.50
Cash received for rent of land on Harpeth 12.00	146.66
1 Note on Ross & Barton for hire of Negro	131.69
Amount of just inventories	3272.47
1 Account on E. Rasberry for	83.93
1 Account on A. W. Stewart & Co.	30.00
1 Account on A. W. Stewart	10.00
1 Note on W. Morris due 25th Dec. 56 (Bad)	70.00
1 Note on Simon Morris due Sept. 1st 56	25.00
1 Note on G. M. Perdue due 23rd Dec 1857	200.00
1 Account on D. G. Murphey for	13.75

1 Account on L. J. Perdue		16.50
Cash received from Speight for Wood		47.50
Cash received from Rasberry		16.00
1 Account on James Perry		2.75
Cash received from Speight for Wood		7.50
1 Note on Rasberry for rent of house	6.00	528.93
		3801.40
1 account on W. Duke (bad)		15.00
		3816.40

Cr.

By Amount plead out of date by A. W. Stewart	40.00
By Washington Morris Note, bad	70.00
By Clerk for last settlement	1.00
By his Note to W. H. Oliver	394.00
By Charles Symes proven act	76.00
By G. M. Perdue proven act	25.50
By G. M. Perdue proven act	7.50
By G. M. Perdue proven act	4.50
By G. M. Perdue proven act	13.50
By James Shores proven act	4.75
	639.05

(p 96) I JOHN J. HOOPER do Make and publish this My last Will and testament hereby revoking and MakingVoid all other Wills by me at any time made, first I direct that My funeral expenses and all My debts be paid as soon after My death as possible out of any Money that I May die possessed of or May first come into the hands of My executor.

Secondly, I give and bequeath to My Wife Mildred R. Hooper the use of all My real and personal estate during her life if she should remain single if she should Marry it is My will and request that My real estate should be divided upon her Marriage as hereinafter directed, and that My personal estate should be divided between My wife and Children so as to Make their share in My real and personal estate equal. Should My wife Not Marry I give and bequeath at her death to My son Hiram V. Hooper all My land within the following boundaries beginning at the rock spring house in Dr. A. Lowe line running up the Spring road in the direction of the house to a White oak at or near the Mouth of a lane leading eastwardly in the direction of Harris Dowlen, running with and through the Center of the lane east to Harris Dowlen boundary line, thence North to a black oak My corner in Harris Dowlen line thence West 74 poles to two small dogwoods, thence North 37 poles to a post oak and poplar thence West 22 poles to a black oak standing in a sink, thence Continuing said Course until it strikes the line of the land Conveyed to My daughter Virginia Nye thence with her line to Dr. A. Lowe's line thence with Dr. Lowes line to the beginning I give and bequeath to My son Robert L. C. Hooper all the lands within the following bounds beginning at the Rock Springs house, and South of the land given above to My son Hiram.

I give and bequeath all the remaining portion of My land lying North of the land given to My son Hiram, to My daughter Indinia J. Wilkins for her life to have and to hold the same to her sole and seperate use free from the debts and Contracts of her husband during her life, and after her death to go to her Children.

I give and bequeath to My daughter Sarah D. Hooper such portion of My personal estate, as shall Make her share in My whole estate equal to My other Children and the remainder of My personal property to be divided between My children as to Make their share in My real and personal estate. My land given to My children by deed or will is to be valued at the time it is finally divided by disinterested Commissioners for the purpose of Making the shares of My whole estate equal.

I authorize and empower My wife to give to such of My Children as she May deem proper at any time a Negro slave or slaves to be valued by disinterested Commissioners and to be taken by the Child to whom it is given at its Valuation as so Much of its share of My estate but the (p 97) slaves given Must not exceed in value including other property given to said Child its share of My estate.

I do hereby constitute and appoint My son Hiram A. Hooper My executor and do authorize and empower him to Manage My estate for the use and benefit of My wife and to Carry out all the other Provisions of this will.

The land above bequeathed to Indinia J. Wilkins. I here give to Hiram V. Hooper in trust for Indinia J. Wilkins with full power in him to dispose of the land or timber thereon and invest the proceeds in other property for her benefit if he should deem it for her interest.

John J. Hooper (SEAL)

Signed in presence of:
William Weatherford
Saml. Watson

Will of JOHN C. H. WEAKLEY.

I John C. H. Weakley do Make and publish this as My last will and testament. First I direct that My funeral expense and all of My debts be paid as soon after My death as possible out of any Money I May die possessed of or May first Come into the hand sof My executor.

Secondly, I give and bequeath to My wife Elizabeth Weakley all of My Horses Cattle, hogs and sheep all My Corn, fodder, oats, bacon, and lard all of My household and kitchen furniture and also My two wagons and all My farming utensils of every description for the use of the family, to have during her widowhood or Natural life, also the tract of land on which I now live and purchased by Myself John H. C. Weakley and My son John C. Weakley of David and George Stack to have during her widowhood or Natural life for the benefit of the family and at her death to go to My son John C. Weakley.

Thirdly, I will and bequeath to My daughter Fredonia, Nancy, Martha and Midora Weakley, the same that My daughter Susan E. Page has received when they marry or leave the family

Fourthly, I will and bequeath to My son Francis Williams and Samuel the same that My son Jas. T. Weakley has received.

Fifthly, I will and bequeath to My daughter Susan E. Page one dollar. Sixthly, I will and bequeath to My son Frankly T. Weakley, one dollar.

Seventhly, I will and bequeath to My son James T. Weakley one dollar.

Eightly, I will and bequeath tha t My son John C. Weakley at the death of My Wife Elizabeth Weakley have all the balance that May be left, lastly I do hereby Nominate and appoint My son John C. Weakley, My executor.

In witness whereof I do to this My Will, set my hand and seal, February 1st 1859

J. C. H. Weakley (SEAL)

Test:
D. W. Stack
J. B. Walton

(p 98) Will of THOMAS J. THORNTON.

I Thomas J. Thornton of the County of Cheatham and State of Tennessee being Weak in body but of sound Mind and perfect Memory do Make and publish this My last will and testament. I first desire that My soul return to God who gave it and My body to be decently buried. I also direct and deliver that all My just debts and funeral expenses shall be paid out of any Money Notes or accounts that I May leave or out of any personal property that MY Executor herein Named and My beloved Wife May think just. I then give and bequeath to My beloved Wife Mary Thornton all My land household and Kitchen furniture farming utensils, stock of all kinds together with all My real estate and personal property of every description during her Natural life, and in case the personal property will not pay My debts or in Case My executor and My wife thinks it best and prefers selling a part of My land instead of the personal property to pay My debts, I do hereby authorize and empower My executor to sell the land that he thinks best by giving the Notice that the law requires without any order of Court upon such terms as he May think best and in Case the land sold brings More than will satisfy My debts, I direct and desire that the residue shall be used by My beloved wife for the support and best interests of the family. I also charge My son John M. Thornton the sum of twenty five dollars for boarding self and wife. I also charge to My son Henry S. Thornton seventy five dollars for one bay Mare. I furthermore direct and desire that at the death of My beloved wife Mary Thornton that all My estate real and personal of every description shall be sold and the proceeds equally divided between My beloved Children share and share alike. I do further Nominate and appoint James M. Dunn My sole executor of this My last Will and testament as witness My hand and seal this January 1st 1859.

Thomas J. Thornton (SEAL)

Test:
J. M. Bagwell
Jno. M. Thornton

Will of B. L. PACK.

I B.L. Pack do Make and publish this as My last Will and testament hereby revoking and annuling all other wills by me at any time Made.

First, I direct that My funeral expenses and all My debts be paid as soon after My death as possible out of any Money that I may die possessed of or May first Come into the hands of My executor.

Item two, I give and bequeath to My beloved Wife Frances J. Pack during her Natural life or widowhood and if the said Frances J. Pack should Marry at any time I desire that the following property to be equally divided between all of My heirs which she Frances J. Pack is to get in hand at My death, I leave My residence and as Much of My farm as he May (p 99) think proper to raise My family of Children to My Widow, also all the household and kitchen furniture and farming utensild, two heads of horses, four Milch Cows, one Wagon and one Yoke of Oxens the Corn and fodder, twelve hundred pounds of bacon. Item 3rd. I desire for My executor to sell My girl Bettie and buy another young girl out of the proceeds and if it is Not enough take other Money out of the proceeds of My estate to the amount of nine hundred dollars the said new purchased slave to remain in the family. I also desire that My boys George and Isam remain in the family until they are twenty one years of age then I desire for them to be hired out until My youngest Child Comes of age, and If said b boys become unruly to be hired out a younger age. Item 4th I desire that all My above Mentioned property be sold and equally divided when My Youngest Child comes of age, all My real estate and perishable property and if My widow is single to draw and equal share when My youngest Child Comes of age. Item 5th, And if My said widow gets Married before My Youngest Child Comes of age I desire for My executor or my Children guardian to take possession of all My above Mentioned property for the special benefit for My Children.

Item 6th, For the endustry of My son R. M. Pack I give him one sorrel Colt and My shot gun extra. Item 7th, I give to My son L. Pack one brown filly extra. Item 8th, I desire that C. J. Lovell shall be My Executor to execute My Will. I also desire said Lovell or S. W. Adkisson to act as guardian for My Children.

In Witness whereof I do to this Will set my hand and seal this 10th day of February in the year of our Lord 1859

B. L. Pack (SEAL)

Attest:
G. W. Duke
J. S. Collier

I wish the 3rd Item in My Will to be altered for My executor to sell My girl Betty, either privately or publicly as he thinks best, and the proceeds Not to be invested in any other Negro but to be kept for the use of My heirs.

This February 21st 1859.

Signed in presence of
G. T. Harris
W. F. Speight

B. L.Pack (SEAL)

(p 100) G. W. HIGHLAND Administrator of E. L. STEWART Settlement Amount of Inventory brought from Page 95 3816.40

By Amount of vouchers brought from Page 95	639.05
By J. Morris Proven Act	5.20
" E. C. Yates " "	3.75
" S. Morris " "	14.50
" J. J. Hunter " "	27.43
" G. M. Perdue " "	68.85
Amount said A. W. Stewart & Co.	70.90

Note to W. Johnson, admr.	152.25
W. D. Gleaves, Receipt	2.00
J. Chandown proven act	13.42
Shaw and Hall " "	1.00
G. W. Speight " "	11.50
N. J. Shaws " "	5.00
G. M. Perdue " "	29.50
Balance on J. Harris Note	47.44
Note to G. W. Highland, Gua.	158.19
Note to W. S. Weakley	14.07
Wm. Stewart proven act	19.50
J. G. Smith " "	35.00
G. M. Speight " "	42.20
W. Johnson, Adm. proven act	15.00
A. J. Sanders " "	12.16
Note to W. D. Gleaves Note	30.35
G. W. McQuary receipt	3.00
G. Green Receipt	1.00
A. N. Strouds receipt	2.00
Note J. Morris	22.20
Note J. Ryan	76.43
Tax receipt 1858	6.64
Tax receipt 1857	9.69
David Sanders proven act	2.75
Jo Krantz " "	10.50
W. G. Gunter " "	5.00
N. J. Sanders " "	33.00
L. J. Perdue " "	49.26
Church Rasberry " "	45.57
	1610.33
Clerk for bond	2.00
Letters of Administration	.50
Copy of same	.50
Order to lay off dower	.25
	3.25
	1613.58

(p 101)

Inventory Brought up	3816.40
Amount of Credits brought up	1613.58
Copy order to lay off dower	.25
Order ro lay off years provision	.25
Copy of same	.25
Recording Inventory	1.00
Order Confirming report dower	.25
Order " " provision	.25
For Making settlement	2.67
Orders Confirming settlement and recording	.56
Attorneys fee	15.00
Amt allowed Administrator for settling said estate	175.00
Amount due on settlement	2007.34

P. H. WOODSON, Adm. of E. H. WOODSON dettlement Made on the 5th day of March 1859.

Amount of Notes, Money & C.	842.02
Amount of inventory of property	312.23
Cr.	
By 1 Slab for grave	25.50

James for Negro Clothing	8.75
Cotton Cloth for Negro Clothing	3.65
Domestic for Negro Clothing	1.31
Thread and buttons for same	.25
Paid Walker threshing wheat	5.07
Shoes for Negroes	15.05
Paid for hauling Tobacco	7.00
Curtis George for Coffin	22.00
J. &. M. Gower Act	20.18
Cheatham Watson & Co. Act	4.43
R. H. Reading Medical Act	23.50
Clerk Fee	5.75
W. E. Felts proven act	2.15
Lynch & Bracy act	30.00
Shaw & Bro act	5.20
J. E. Gower Counsel	5.00
A. Lawes Medical Act	12.55
Amount allowed Exr.	35.00
Clerk for this settlement	2.00
Amount due after paying all debts	919.21
Legacies bequeathed	
James G. Woodson Receipt	195.00
J. B. Williams receipt	100.00
(p 102)	
P. H. Woodson Exr. Settlement	10.00
Legacy to Mariah James	100.00
H. D. Lowe	45.00
W. S. Woodson	10.00
Meradith	10.00
Harriet	10.00
Mariah Woodson	10.00
Joannan Lowe	10.00
H. H. Woodson	85.17
James G. Woodson	106.00
Amount Willed to P. H. Woodson Children	200.00
Amount due after paying all debts and legacies	108.74

(p 103) And Account of the sale of the property belonging to the estate of E. G. MURPHEY, déc. sold by JOHN W. SHAW, Adm. on the 22nd of Febryary 1859.

Articles sold	Purchaser Named	
1 sythe & Cradle	W. J. Jackson	.15
1 " "	James J. Wilson	.45
1 lot of tools	M. C. Orman	.25
1 lot of Tools	M. C. Orman	.25
1 3in Auger	James J. Wilson	.75
1 " "	H. C. Pace	.45
1 saw & square	John Felts	.10
3 plains	E. F. Felts	1.00
1 Hand saw	Lewis Lowe	2.00
1 Cross Cut saw	James R. Drake	6.25
1 lot of Nails	Wm. Gossett	.45
1 Cot	G. W. Murphey	.50
3 boxes & saddle	H. R. Felts	.10
1 Foot Adz	G. W. Murphey	.80
1 drawing Axe	A. Adkins	.35
1 Broad Axe	H. R. Felts	4.75

1 half bushell of iron	G. W. Murphey	.55
1 lot of Trumpery	H. R. Felts	.10
1 lot of Halter Chains	E. L. Williams	.10
1 lot Breast Chains	E. L. Williams	.75
1 lot old horse shoes	D. G. Allen	.10
1 lot New Horse shoes	E. L. Williams	1.00
1 Bell	W. J. Jackson	.25
2 Single trees	L. J. Inman	.15
2 " "	Rob McCormack	.50
2 " "	" "	1.50
1 Chopping Axe	Widow	.25
1 " "	Wm. Durham	.10
1 " "	S. H. Bracey	.10
1 pair steelyards	R. M. McCounell	.65
1 Plain & Grindstone	John Shivers	.50
1 spinning Wheel	James Darden	.70
1 Flax Wheel	F. Crotzer	.25
1 lot of sash	J. C. Linch	.40
1 Wheel	Widow	.10
1 lot brick Moles & sash	J. J. Woodson	.30
1 lantern	Widow	.10
1 Jug & Coffee Pot	Newson Harris	.50
1 Jug Vinegar	Widow	.25
1 Jug Vinegar	U. S. Stack	.40
1 lot Paint	T. J. Shaw	1.00
1 Keg White lead	B. F. King	2.50
(p 104)		
1 Can oil	Thos. J. Shaw	.25
2 Cans turpentine	Thos. J. Shaw	.10
1 Box & Glass	W. F. Crotzer	.50
1 " "	H. H. Harris	.10
1 " "	W. Hawkins	.10
1 saddle bags	J. C. Lynch	.25
1 saddle	Henry Harris	.25
1 Mans saddle	S. H. Bracey	3.25
1 lot Bridles	J. B. Basford	.10
1 Grind stone	M. D. L. Willimas	8.75
6 gal Molasses	Thomas W. Hunter	3.60
1 Barrel Flour	Lewis Lowe	6.65
1 " "	S. H. Bracey	7.00
1 " "	J. W. Pace	7.05
1 Cook stove	B. F. King	12.00
1 Milk Jar	W. Durham	.80
1 Can & skillet	E. A. Whealer	.20
1 Pot	Widow	.75
1 Pail and Peggin	Widow	.75
1 Pan	Widow	.25
1 Large Pot & Oven	W. A. Fleming	.50
1 skillet	G. W. Murphey	35.00
1 Hand Axe	Wm. Gossett	.50
1 Water Cart & barrel	Allen Hunter	8.75
1 " " "	D. G. Allen	.30
1 lot Weatherboarding	G. W. Shaw	4.50
300 ft at Mill	" " "	3.00
1 lot shingles	E. L. Williams	6.65
1 " "	" " "	3.75
1 Ox Cart	G. F. Ellis	15.75

1 Iron Wedge	W. J. Gossett	.65
1 " "	" " "	.45
1 spade	Widow	.25
1 Froe	J. H. Pace	1.20
2 Weeding hoes	Widow	1.00
3 shovels	R. M. McCormack	.20
1 stone hammer	Henry Hunter	1.10
1 Crow bar	J. T. Morgan	1.00
1 Digger	G. W. Murphey	.35
1 Muttock	N. Morris	1.00
1 Grub hoe	H. R. Felts	.70
1 pair stretchers	G. W. Murphey	2.00
1 shov el Plow	G. H. Ellis	1.50
2 Tongue Plows	P. Nalley	.50
(p 105)		
2 Diamond Plows	P. Nally	3.12
1 Buggy & Harness	Thomas Shaw	190.00
6 Chairs	P. Nally	3.25
1 small Chair	M. V. B. Walker	.25
8 Chairs	J. W. Pace	.30
1 lot of Ware	Widow	3.00
1 Press	Widow	4.00
2 Books	Cash	.25
2 Books	W. T. Pace	.35
2 Books	M. V. B. Walker	.50
1 Bedstead	Widow	10.00
1 Chest	Widow	.25
2 Bedsteads	J. B. Basford	.10
1 Table	Widow	.50
1 sugar chest	T. Hunter	5.00
1 Table	A. F. Ellis	3.00
1 secretary	W. A. Shaw	9.30
1 Rule	B. F. King	.25
1 Walnut Table	J. J. Woodson	.95
3 razors	J. J. Albright	1.65
1 Razor	M. D. L. Williams	1.20
2 Razor strops	P. Nally	.25
1 Razor Strop	M. D. L. Williams	1.00
1 Pair sheep shears	Henry Hunter	.25
1 Walnut secretary	M. V. B. Walker	15.75
1 pair Horse flannels	William Durham	.30
1 sugar Chest	William Durham	3.25
1 Pair saddle bags	Widow	.50
1 Trunk	Widow	1.00
1 side board	Widow	3.00
1 lot Tablecloths	Widow	.75
1 Clock	G. W. Hunter	9.00
1 Wardrobe	Demps Hunter	15.00
1 small bedstead	Widow	.50
487 pounds Flour	Newsom Harris	16.68
122½ Do Do	Wm. Durham	4.16
1 side saddle	Widow	5.00
1 Mans saddle	E. W. Murphey	.25
1 Chest	B. F. King	.75
1 Bedsteads	P. Nally	1.00
1 Bowl & saucers	D. W. Stack	.20
3 Plates	D. W. Stack	.10

1 Bowl	Wm. Durham	.10
1 Dish	D. W. Stack	.45
(p 106)		
2 Dishes	P. Nally	.65
1 Dish	D. W. Stack	.55
1 Castor	D. W. Stack	.35
1 pitcher	M. V. B. Walker	.40
1 Molasses stand	P. Nally	.35
3 Tumblers	D. W. Stack	.30
1 Lot Tin Ware	Widow	.25
2 flat irons	Widow	.40
2 Do Do	M. V. B. Walker	.50
1 lot Ware	Widow	.25
1 Jar	Widow	.25
1 skillet	Widow	.10
1 Bucket	Widow	.25
2 Candlestick	Widow	.05
2 boxes & brands	E. A. Wheeler	1.00
1 Meat Mill	J. E. Turner 10	12.25
100 lb bacon	T. Watson 10½	10.50
652 lb Bulk Pork	D. Rhinehart 10 3/4	70.09
27½ lbs Beef	P. W. Randolph 8	2.20
1 Lot salt	J. W. Pace	1.50
1 Pair Steelyards	Allen Hunter	3.50
1000 New Rails	G. W. Shaw	9.62
1000 New Rails	G. W. Shaw	9.63
2228 New rails	G. W. Shaw	22.28
1 lot timber	A. H. Williams	5.00
1 lever watch	G. W. Murphey	25.25
1 Buggy whip	M. V. B. Walker	.85
1 Yoke Oxen	Widow	35.00
5 first Choice hogs	Jack Perdue	14.25
5 second Choice hogs	Jack Perdue	12.25
9 fourth Choice hogs	Jack Perdue	14.62
5 third Choice hogs	Pack Perdue	11.25
1 Young Ox	Felix Northington	16.00
1 Heifer	Clay Murphey	4.00
1 Fan Mill	E. L. Williams	17.50
1 Double Tree	Allen Teasley	.60
2 Clevices & Geer	Wm. Darden	1.75
1 set Geer	R. M. McCormack	1.35
1 lot shucks	D. W. Stack	25.25
1 lot tinery	J. Elliott	.25
1 sorrel horse	B. F. King	48.00
1 Bay horse	B. Smith	135.00
1 Brown Mare	Widow	50.00
1Bay Horse	Wm. Durham	77.00
1 Bay Mare	Wm. Woodruff	101.00
(p 107)		
1 Bay Filly	H. C. Pace	72.25
1 Bay Horse colt	G. W. Murphey	76.00
1 Bay horse Colt	W. J. Gossett	65.00
1 Mule Colt	G. H. Whitehead	54.25
Bailey hired until 10th Apr.	M. D. L. Williams	26.15
Ben hired until 10th Apr.	John Majors	30.00
		$1555.40

Cash left on hand

Bank of America Clarksville Broke 35.00

Exchange Bank Broke	3.00
Bank of Empire State Broke	1.00
Bank of Charlotte N. C. 5 per Cent des	20.00
Central Bank Alabama 5 " " "	20.00
Bank of Tennessee	302.00
Planters Bank	140.00
Northen Bank of Kentucky	10.00
Bank of Kentucky	5.00
Bank of Middle Tennessee	5.00
Bank of Knoxville	20.00
Silver	64.00
	625.00

A list of Accounts

These Accounts several of them are for loaned Money and some of them out of date, and some insolvent. I Cannot say how Many of them will be Collected.

One Account on Unah Murff June 11th 1858.	2.15
One Account on Jonathan Hollis (bad) June 11,1858	.50
One Account on W. H. C. Murphey (bad) July 11,1858	2.00
One Account on B. F. Binkley 1858	2.00
One Account on Wyatt Shearon 1858	2.00
One Account on Hardy Pace 1858	2.25
One Account on Wm. Sterry (bad) 1858	.60
One Account on H. R. Felts 1857 & 58	8.90
One Account on H. W. Turner 1858	12.68
One Account on E. L. Williams 1858	23.60
One Account on W. J. Gossett 1858	13.85
One Account on J. J. Basford 1858	2.40
One Account on Edward Tucker 1858	9.48
One Account on J. B. Basford 1858	3.45
" " " R. J. Mallory 1858	22.10
" " " P. W. Rudolph "	13.81
" " " W. B. Link "	4.87
" " " H. C. Pace "	6.30
" " " E. Clifton "	2.28
	$135.22

(p 108)

One Account on John Stack 1850	2.87
One " " J. Weakley "	5.00
" " " Mrs Martha Pace 1850	3.75
" " " Sarah Stewart 1851	7.00
" " " T. J. Muers (bad) 1851	8.00
" " " George Head "	7.00
" " " W. L. Brown (bad) 1855	10.00
" " " J. W. Smith July 20,1855	5.00
" " " L. H. Sawyer 1856	10.00
" " " A. J. Bright "	10.00
W. B. Ross Account "	10.00
One Account on Mrs Dye "	20.00
One Account on Abner Edwards 1857	17.00
" " " F. Crotzer "	10.00
" " " Green Smith "	20.00
One Account on J. D. Nicholson 1857	
" " " B. F. Stewart "	14.00
M. D. L. Williams	7.00
One Account on Unah Murff 1856	3.20

One Account on H. Bearden 1857 40.50
" " " R. J. Mallory 1857 & 1858 25.90
One Order from W. T. Pace on R. J. Mallory 1858 50.00
Notes supposed to be good
One Note on D. Brown, J. C. Burney and A. Felts due Sept. 13th 1859 for 15.00
One Note on A. J. Rhinehart, G. W. Pace and S. D. Power due 13th Sept. 1859 7.50
One Note on E. H. Williams, W. J. Gossett and P. T. Williams due 13th Sept. 1859 for 120.00
One Note on G. W. Basford, D. W. Stack and W. J. Gossett due 13th Sept. 1859 for 24.00
One Note on D. W. Stack, A. Hunter and J. D. Nicholson due Sept. 13,1859 32.50
One Note on J. R. Jennett, Abner Hunter and J. D. Nicholson due Sept. 13th1859 7.50
One Note on J. D. Jenkins, W. J. King and J. D. Nicholson due Sept. 13th 1859 for 77.25
One Note on J. W. Simpkins, Thomas Hunter and G. M. Perdue due Sept. 13th 1859 97.00
One Note on M. D. L. Williams, A. H. Williams Thomas A. Owen due Sept. 13th 1859 205.46
One Note on G. W. Pace, R. L. King, A. J. Rhinehart due 13th Sept. 1859 20.40
One Note on E. L. William, P. T. Williams and J. S. Williams due Sept. 13th,1859 196.75
(p 109)
One Noteon W. Durham, H. W. Turner, T. W. Hunter due 13th Sept. 1859 5.50
One Note on J. F. Cummins, D. Marr and G. D. Cummins due Sept. 13th 1859 466.25
One Note on G. Nicholson & A. H. Nicholson due Sept. 13th 1859 4.35
One Note on R. T. Gupton, Jo Gupton and G. W. Pace 30.00
One Note on W. H. Stewart, R. J. Mallory and J. C. Weakley due Sept. 13th 1859 120.00
One Note on J. H. Pace, J. D. Nicholson, D. Council due Sept. 13, 1859 5.55
One Note on F. Taylor, J. B. Taylor and J. D. Nicholson due Sept. 13,1859 27.70
One Note on G. W. McCarley, D. Council and A. W. Stewart due Sept. 13th, 1859 25.50
One Note on C. C. Perker, J. B. Cross, J. D. Nicholson due Sept. 13, 1859 for 35.85
One Note on W. H. Plaster, J. C. Weakley, W. D. Weakley due Sept. 13th 1859 100.75
One Note on R. H. Weakley, G. W. Gossett, J. S. Majors due Sept. 13th 1859 5.00
One Note on D. Council, J. D. Nicholson, James H. Pace due Sept. 13,1859 10.00
One Note on J. B. Cross, E. N. Gupton, C.C. Parker due Sept. 13th 1859 for 18.40
One Note on Thomas A. Owen, M. D. L. Williams, R. H. Fambrough due Sept. 13th 1859 7.50
One Note on R. J. Mallory, B. F. King, B. L. King due Sept. 13th 1859 for 101.08
One Note on W. S. Weakley due 25th Dec.1858 150.00

One Note on L. Fox due 1st April 1859 22.50
One Note on E. F. Miles, B. H. Gibbs, R.B. Gibbs due 22nd January 1859 75.00
One Note on M. D. L. Williams due 30th Dec.1857 60.75
One Note on J. D. Nicholson due 25th Dec. 1858 47.00
One Note on U. Murff due 11th April 1857 5.40
One Note on B. F. King due 8th January 1859 20.00
One Note on C. E. Peacher, P. Peacher due 1st January 1859 560.00
One Note on C. E. Peacher due 1st Jan.1859 51.25
One Note on Thomas A. Basford due 27th Aug.1858 140.00
One Note on David Sanders and J. Sanders Due Feb. 3, 1858 for 30.00
One Note on R. J. Mallory due 31st of May 1858 175.00
One Note on M. V. B. Walker due 17th July 1858 60.00
One Note on S. D. Powers due Aug. 25,1858 10.00
One Note on R. King due Sept.25,1859 75.00
One Note on G. W. Murphey due 25th Dec.1858 120.00
One Note on A. J. Bright due 4th Aug. 1859 75.00
One Note on J. W. Cross, W. B. Cross, C. C. Parker due 10 April 1859 250.00
One Note on G. W. Gossett due 19th April 1858 100.00
One Note on Thomas W. Hunter due 11 Oct. 1858 6.98
One Note on Wm. Read due 11th Nov.1859 150.00
One Note on W. J. Gossett due April 21st 1858 75.00
One Note on A. Lowe due 29th April 1858 57.18
One Note on T. Watson due 6th July 1858 6.59
One Note on Nathan Morris due 3 February 1858 160.00
One Note on C. E. Peacher, P. Peacher, J. Darden due 1st January 1858 for 500.00
One Note on A. H. Williams due March 11,1858 700.00
Credit Oct. 9th,1858 130.50
" " 30 " 5.55
136.05

363.95
(p 110)
One Note on W. T. Pace due 29th March 1858, 101.00, Credited 6th July 1858, 10.00, Credited 28th Dec. 1858, 50.00, 60.00
40.00
One Note on A. J. Bright due 1st March 1855 52.00
Credit July 5-57 15.00
Credit July 14-57 40.00 55.00
One Note on W. Durham due 22 June 1858 15.60
Credit 10th Decr. 1858 10.00
One Note on R. S. Demunbra due 22 January 1858 31.20
Credit July 5th- 58 15.60

Bad and doubtful Notes

One Note on Henry Harris due 4th January 1858 3.85
One Note on A. Eatherley due 2nd July 1852 8.00
Credit February 1st 1858 5.00 3.00
One Note on S. S. Mays due 28th Oct. 1858 21.80
One Note on W. K. Hollis due 20th Sept.1858 35.00
One Note on B. F. Pace due 1st Sept. 1858 75.00
One Note on Daniel Hudgens due 1st Oct.1856 4.00
One Note on J. E. Turner due 1st April 1857 60.00
Credit March 29-58 36.60
Credit June 16-58 3.00

Credit July 7-58	22.61
	59.21.79
One Note on J. R. Miles due 13 March 1858	25.00
One Note on J. R. Miles due 5th Feb. 1859	143.38
One Note on J. R. Miles due 5th Feb. 1860	143.38
One Note on J. H. Pritchett due May 27 for	468.62
Credit 9th March 57	25.00
By Invoice as shown by Stuart 1869 43.69	424.93
Officers Receipts	
G. W. Gossett receipt due 24th January 1857 for	
Note on L. J. Perdue for	759.40
Due 1st March 1858	
Credit 29th May 58	200.00
" 13th Jany. 59	100.00
" " " "	17.40
317.40 442.00 442.00	

J. J. Wilson receipt Jany. 10th 1859 for one Note on J. M. Cross, W. B. Cross, C C. Parker, J. B. Cross and G. W. McCarley due 10th January 1859 250.00
Wm. Demunbra Receipt 1st Nov. 1858 for a Note on Glover and Bedwell due 9th Aug. 1857 for 625.00
B. F. Paces receipt due 30th Dec. 1858 for a Note on S. D. Power and H. C. Pace due 27th May 1858. Ins from 1st January 1858 7.55 1820.88

(p 111) Inventory of the estate of J. H. C. WEAKLEY, dec. sold by W. J. GOSSETT on the 19th day of March 1859.

Names of Purchaser	Articles sold	
S. D. Power	1 Jointer	.25
S. D. Power	1 Cross & Champing Knife	.15
W. S. Stack	1 Saw & Cross	.10
S. D. Power	1 Hand Axe	.25
Ben Elliott	3 Drawing knives	.20
M. H. Pace	2 Do Do	.15
J. R. Eliott	1 Grind stone	.50
Jo Alley	3 Han saws	.05
G. W. Stack	1 square & C.	.10
J. C. Weakley	21 Flour barrels	10.50
Thos. Majors	1 Plow	.30
S. Lee	1 Wagon	2.65
J. T. Weakley	1 Cow& Calf	12.25
S. D. Power	1 Heifer	6.00
S. D. Power	1 Do	3.00
J. B. Walton	6 Hogs	5.00
J. B. Reeks	5 Do	5.25
G. W. Stack	1 Mule	36.00
J. C. Weakley	1 Do	62.00
John Basford	1 Pair Geer	1.50
W. C. Weakley	1 Gun	13.00
J. R. Elliott	Note for	100.00

An inventory of the estate of B. L. PACK, dec. sold by C. G. LOVELL, Exr. onthe 19th day of March 1859.

R. M. Crumpler	1 Yoke Oxen	18.00
B. F. Crumpler	1 Yoke Young Oxen	10.50
F. J. Pack	1 Cow & Yearling	10.00

W. Jackson	1 Heifer	8.00
Tho. J. Pack	2 Young Steers	20.00
W. Jackson	2 " "	7.00
G. W. Duke	1 sow & pigs	6.00
Tilman Harris	1 Hog	2.25
G. W. Duke	6 Hogs	10.00
R. M. Crumpler	500 lbs bacon	43.75
F. J. Pack	606 lbs bacon	48.15
L. D. Pack	320 lbs lard	28.80
J. W. Bennett	Rent of land	35.00
J. Harris	1 Bull	5.00
F. L. Pack	1 Kettle	1.00
L. D. Pack	1 Negro Woman Betty	500.00
		753.45

(p 112) Inventories of Notes belonging to B.L.PACK, dec.

1 Note on G. W. Duke	10.00
1 Note on J.W. Bennett	22.00
1 Note on L. J. Pack	45.00
1 Note on G. W. Duke	600.00
1 Note on L. J. Pack	35.00
1 Note on F. L. Pack	416.66
1 Note on S. Cortz (not good)	2.50
	2084.61

(p 113) Will of R. B. WALKER, deceased.

I Richard B. Walker desire that My property be disposed of after My death in the following Manner. I desire that My Wife Sophronia Walker shall have all My estate as long as she lives or until she Marries at either of which occurences. I desire My property shall be disposed of in the following Manner, if she Marries before My two Children, Amanda , Elizabeth and Martha Ann, Margaret, become of age, then all My estate in her possession to be divided between My two above Named Children, if she dies before My Children Marry or become of age the property to be divided between My two Children. I desire when My Children become of age or Marry that there be an equal division between them and My Wife. I desire that My executor and pay all My debts the Money remaining after that I desire him to keep for the benefit of My Wife and Children as they May need it for their education and support. I desire that My executor pay lawful interest on said Money while in his hands. I desire that My friend James Frazier act as My executor. I acknowledge the above as My last Will and testament.

Test;
H. C. Pace R. B. Walker
M. V. B. Walker

(p 114) Inventory of the personal estate of R. B. WALKER, dec. sold on the 2nd day of April 1859.

Names	Articles sold	
W. Durham	1 Coulter	3.00
M. V. B. Walker	1 Cultivator	.75
T. Biggers	1 Double Plow	5.00
T. Bigger	1 Cast Plow	.10
M. V. B. Walker	1 Cast Plow	3.00

J. Hunter	1 lot Plow	.50
S. Walker	1 lot irons & C.	.65
G. W. Gossett	1 Axe	.55
J. Woodson	1 skillet	.45
S.Walker	1 skillet & lid	.10
M. V. B. Walker	2 Barrels	1.50
S. Walker	1 set geer	1.00
S. Walker	1 pair Harness	.10
R. J. Mallory	1 pair Harness & C.	.20
R. J. Mallory	100 lbs bacon	9.00
R. J. Mallory	100 lbs bacon	8.50
R. J. Mallory	100 lbs bacon	8.00
G. W. Murphey	100 lbs bacon	7.25
G. W. Murphey	191 lbs bacon	12.41
S. Walker	2 lard stands.	1.00
S. Walker	smoothing iron & C.	.50
S. Walker	Bottles & C.	.15
G. W. Gossett	1 set bunch plains	1.10
T. Biggers	1 hand saw	.80
A. Hunter	1 Chisel	.50
M. V. B. Walker	Auger	.35
W. Durham	1 Auger	.20
H. C. Pace	2 iron Wedges	.50
M. V. B. Walker	3 iron Wedges	.75
G. W. Gossett	1 oil stove	.10
S. Walker	Table & Contents	1.00
S. Walker	1 Water Can	.50
S. Walker	1 lot Chairs	.50
M. V. B. Walker	2 Gal. Jugs	.25
M. V. B. Walker	1 Gal. Jug	.15
S. Walker	sundries	.10
S. Walker	1 dish pan & C.	.30
W. Durham	1 Buggs Tongue	3.50
S. Walker	1 Hatchet	.10
S. Walker	1 ladies saddle	.25
S. Walker	1 brown filly	50.00
R. D. Mosely	1 Black Mule	150.00
G. W. Gossett	1 gray Mule	130.00
	Total	403.56

(p. 115)

S. Walker	1 grindstone	1.50
John Albright	3 Cow Hides	2.00
S. Walker	1 Yoke Oxen	30.00
T. W. Hunter	1 White back Cow	15.50
S. Walker	1 White face Cow	8.00
H. C. Pace	1 Red Cow	11.25
G. W. Murphey	1 spotted yearling	7.25
S. Walker	4 sows & pigs	8.00
W. Durham	1 stock hog	4.75
H. C. Pace	5 1st Choice hogs	12.00
B. F. King	5 2nd " "	10.75
B. F. King	3 Choice hogs	9.05
H. C. Pace	4 " "	4.00
E. L. Williams	1 side upper leather	2.10
J. Humphrey	1 " " "	1.70
E. Walker	1 pair saddle bags	.50
S. Walker	1 Clock	2.50

S. Walker	1 safe	2.50
W. Durham	1 trundle bed	11.00
S. Walker	1 large bed & stead	8.00
S. Walker	1 spinning Machine	1.25
B. F. King	5 bu Potatoes	1.50
H. Hagewood	5 " "	2.00
D. Council	5 " "	1.55
G. W. Gossett	5 " "	1.65
S. Durham	Remainder 16½ bu 30	4.95
S. Walker	1 woman & 3 Children by mo.	00.00
R. D. Mosely	1 Man Patrick 11 per Mo.	
*	for balance year	50.00
		$ 618.81

Notes

L note on R. D. Mosely due 16th Dec. 1858 for		85.65
Interest on same		149.81
1 Note on R. D. Mosely due 20th Nov.1859 with		
interest fromthe 20 Nov. 1858 for		90.00
Interest on same 2.25		92.25
1 Note of hand on M. V. B. Walker due the 24th		
Dec. 1858 for		40.00
Interest on same .60		40.60
1 Due Bill on M. V. B. Walker due 29th Nov.1858 for		20.00
Interest on same .30		
(p 116)		
1 Note on M. V. B. Walker due Aug. 8th 1858 for		256.25
With a Credit Oct. 25,1858		125.00
Balance of said Note		131.25
Interest on same		7.12
		138.37
1 Note on H. W. Turner due 1st March 1859 for		50.00
With a Credit Aug. 10,1858		9.00
Balance on said Note		41.00
Interest on same		.20
		41.20
1 Note on Augustus Bearden due 28th Dec.1858 for		5.00
Interest on same .07		5.07
1 due bill on R. J. Mallory, Exr. of T. Walker due		
when Collected from Cheatham Watson and Hudson		
for	151.00	151.00
1 Note on J. D. Nicholson due the 5th day of		
March 1858		105.00
With a Credit 25th Dec. 1858		40.00
Balance on said Note		65.00
Interest in same		4.22
		69.25
Cash on hand		84.00
		$ 488.86

Accounts 1856

1 Act on S. D. Powers 2.06		2.06
1 Account on R. T. Gupton 1.83		1.38
1 Act on Hunter due 1858 7.95		7.95
1 Account on Isaic Jennett 1858	8.50	8.50
1 " " J. D. Nicholson "	3.35	3.35
1 " " W. B. Cross "	5.50	5.50
1 " " James Murphey "	5.70	5.70
1 " " T. Walker "	17.51	17.51

1 Account on J. M. Cross 1858		1.00	1.00
1 " " R. King	1857,1858	2.60	2.60
1 " " A. W. Stewart 1856		5.00	5.00
1 " " M. V. B. Walker 1858		9.75	9.75
1 " " Elizabeth Walker 1858		2.20	2.20
1 " " B. F. Pace	1857	1.00	1.00
1 " " R. J. Mallory 1859		15.05	15.05
1 " " M. V. B. Walker 1859		7.50	7.50
1 Note on W. W. Davis due 26th May 1847 for			3.00
With a Credit Aug. 26,1850 for			1.77
Balance on said Note		1.23	1.23
1 Note on F. A. James due 27th day of August 1858 for			5.00
(p 117)			
1 Note on T. J. Walker due 24th January 1855 for			70.70
Interest on same			
1 Note on affadavit for Note on R. E. Marlow from J. M.			
Gibbs last for due Mar.1852			65.00
With a Credit 1852			10.00
Balance on said Note			55.00
Interest on same			
1 Note on C. M. Humphreys due 25th Dec.1857 for			77.50
Interest on same		5.42	82.92
1 Note on Jonathan Fambrough due Aug.20th 1857 for			33.00
With a Credit Mar. 24,1858			20.00
Balance on saaid Note			13.00
Interest on same		3.09	16.09
1 Note on A. Caines due 28th May 1857 for 3.80			3.80
3 receipts on G. A. Woodson for Crop of tobacco			
Amounting all to 4896 lbs at 6¼ Cents			306.00
			1984.79

(p 118) THOMAS PACE Will.

In the Name of God Amen I Thomas Pace of the State of Tennessee, Robertson County, Civil district No 14 being in My proper Mind and reason do Make this My last Will and testament, to Wit,

1st I desire that a part of My perishable property be sold enough to pay My funeral expenses, and all other just debts that I owe.

2nd. I give unto My wife Martha Halloway, the land and place where I now live with all the purtaneances thereunto belonging with all the balance of effect, after paying all demands against me, during her Natural life of widowhood for the purpose of raising My Children but should she die or Marry again I will that My land with all the other property there on hand, be sold at public sale, and the proceeds be equally divided between My wife and Children.

3rd. I leave Granville Nicholson My executor whereunto I set My hand and seal this 9th day of March 1850.

Thomas Pace (SEAL)

James J. Wilson
Joel W. Pace

Settlement of JOHN W. TEASLEY Administrator of A. JONES, dec. 1859.

To Amount of inventory

Cr.

By Shaw and Bros.provent Acct. 7.10

By Shaw and Wall proven Acct.	2.75
By E. G. Hudgens Acct. Coffin	16.00
By R. J. Mallory proven Acct.	18.50
By Tax receipt 1858	4.09
By A. H. Nicholson receipt	101.00
By Clerk for bond	2.00
By Clerk Letters Admr.	.50
By Copy of same	.50
Recording Inventory	.25
Allowance to Admr.	40.00
By McFadden proven Acct	10.00
By 6 refunding Bonds	3.00
Making settlement and recording same	.75
	206.44
Amount due Legates	614.47
Clerks fee	4.00
	610.47

The foregoing settlement was presented to the Court, read examined, approved and Confirmed in all things
W. W. Williams, Clerk

(p 119) And inventory and account of sale of the personal estate of F. BALTHROP, dec. sold Dec. 10th 1858.

Articles sold	Name of purchaser	
1 Plain	L. D. Pack	.50
1 Lot Plows	Wm. Shearon	1.00
2 Axes	James Gillmore	.50
1 lot Plows	A. N. Stroud	1.75
3 Axes	James Gillmore	.50
1 Band & Chains	A. Hunter	.25
1 spinning Wheel	Wm. Demunbra	1.00
3 Weeding Hoes	W. H. Oliver	.30
2 Do Do	L. D. Pack	.35
2 Grub hoes	James Gillmore	.10
1 Weeding Hoe	James Gillmore	.25
1 lot Bacon 256 lb 5¢	B. H. Gibbs	12.80
1 Bbl. lard 265 lbs 5¢	R. H. McCllend	13.15
2 Bbls Salt	A. Boyd	4.20
1 Set Geer	F. A. Harris	.10
1 lot Geer	B. H. Gibbs	.50
1 Poll Axe	A. Puckett	.60
2 Meal Bags	James Gillmore	.60
1 steel hand Mill	J. Gillmore	2.00
1 Froe & C.	B. S. Miles	.30
1 lot old irons	James Gillmore	.15
1 Cutting Knife	John Shivers	.85
1 Cross Cut Saw	F. A. Harris	2.00
1 set Crockery ware	B. H. Gibbs	1.00
1 drawing Table	Stephens Lee	1.50
1 Keg sugar	Thos. Balthrop	1.85
1 small Table	Albert Smith	1.25
1 Candle stand	B. H. Gibbs	.25
2 Patent applie reports	James Gillmore	.15
1 Bible	B. S. Miles	.10
2 Jugs & C.	W. H. Oliver	.25
1 Reel	B. H. Gibbs	.50
1 Press	Elias Harris	4.50
3 Jugs	Tho. Balthrop	.25

1 Hatchet	B. H. Gibbs	1.20
1 Bed stead & C.	S. W. Martin	23.50
1 Bed stead & C.	S. W. Green	36.00
1 Bed stead & C.	Gordon Green	15.50
1 Double Bbl. Shot Gun	J. C. Balthrop	10.10
1 Rocking Chair	B. H. Gibbs	3.30
1 lot Chairs	John C. Curtis	1.50
(p 120)		
1 Sugar Chest	S. W. Green	3.50
1 Clock	F. A. Harris	.40
2 Barrels	Wm. Shearon	.10
1 gimlet & C.	Wm. Shearon	.25
1 Churn	J. Turner	1.00
1 Jar	Thos. Balthrop	.30
1 Jar	John Shivers	.30
1 Jar	John Shivers	.20
1 stone pitcher	E. F. Cullum	.25
1 Stone Jar	John Shivers	.35
1 Spice Morton	F. A. Harris	.90
1 Bell	A. Hunter	1.00
1 side sole leather	S. W. Green	3.25
1 Pair shoes	J. B. Demunbra	2.35
1 umbrella	B. S. Miles	1.00
1 pair Compasses	J. C. Balthrop	.45
1 Bag Peas	J. B. Demunbra	1.75
1 Crow bar & Axe	J. B. Demunbra	1.25
2 Basket Onions	John Shivers	1.25
50 Barrels Corn 217½	A. H. Williams	108.25
50 Barrels Corn 212½	A. H. Williams	106.25
50 Barrels Corn 2.10	A. H. Williams	106.00
Remainder of Corn 2.10	A. H. Williams Llb.113,2	238.10
1000 Bundles 1 5/8	G. W. McKerley	16.25
1 stack fodder 1 3/4	L. J. Perdue 1606	28.10
2 stack fodder 1/3/4	L. J. Perdue	
1 Pin shuck	L. J. Perdue	6.00
1 Other pin shuck	John Henry	5.00
1 lot shucks	W. H. Oliver	10.25
500 Bundles fodder		10.00
Remainder of stock		
that John G. Curtis bought	L. J. Perdue	20.29
1 stock fodder damaged	L. J. Perdue	33.20
1 Yoke Oxen	James Gillmore	42.00
1 Other Yoke Oxen	W. Demunbra	40.00
1 Black & 3 Yearling	J. B. Demunbra	22.00
1 Red Cow & 2 Yearling	B. H. Gibbs	17.00
1 spotted Cow & Calf	John G. Curtis	10.00
1 Red Cow	B. H. Gibbs	10.00
1 B ull	J. B. Demunbra	7.50
1 speckled heifer	Stephens Lee	15.00
2 small steers	R. Weakley	15.00
1 steer	John Henry	6.90
1 white pided heifer	J. B. Demunbra	5.00
2 sows & pigs	Wm. Shearon	10.25
1 Ox Cart	G. W. McCarley	15.50
(p 121)		
5 Pork Hogs 1st Choice	John Shivers	50.25
5 Pork Hogs 2nd Choice	John Shivers	42.00
5 Pork Hogs 3rd Choice	John C. Curtis	37.00

5 Pork Hogs 4th choice	J. M. Connell	26.00
8 small Pork Hogs	S. W. Green	15.00
1 Sorrel Horse	B. H. Gibbs	140.00
1 Other Sorrel Horse	R. B. Gibbs	100.00
1 old blaze face Horse	B. B. Everett	26.00
4 Stock hogs	B. S. Miles	22.00
Wild hog Claim	B. H. Gibbs	5.00
12 head stock hogs	G. M. Perdue	26.50
1 Half Bushel	J. Stewart	.95
1 Tub	A. Smith	.85
1 Grid Iron & tea Kettle	B. H. Gibbs	.75
1 Pot rack	J. Gillmore	.35
1 lot ovens & C.	A. Smith	3.25
1 old Ox Cart	J. W. Simpkins	7.60
1 Canoe	J. W. Simpkins	1.00
1 Grind stone	Stephens Lee	1.05
1 Pot	S. G. Green	.60
1 Mans saddle	Thos. G. Balthrop	1.00
1 Canoe	J. B. Demunbra	1.00
1 Chair	J. G. Curtis	.35
1 pair dog Irons	E. Miles	.30
		1580.00

A list of Notes Money & C. left on hand.

1 Note on Wm. Shearon dated Oct. 8th 1858 (D)	17.40
Interest on same	1.04
1 Note on Joseph Forbes Aug.15th 1857 for	20.00
Interest on same from Oct.15 to April 19th 1858 in all 8M 4d	.81
	20.81
Cr. by Cash April 19th 1858 (D) 10.10	10.81
Interest on same	.64
1 Note on R. B. Gibbs dated Dec.2,1857 due April 1st 1858 (D) for	95.00
Interest on same	5.70
1 Note on A. B. Gibbs dated April 28,1857 (D) for	146.00
Interested	21.90
1 Note on B. H. Gibbs due Janry.3,1857 (D) for	100.00
Interest on same from January 3,1857 to Aug.3,1858	3.50
	163.50
	20.35
	83.15
	4.98
	386.62

7 Mo. Credit by Cash Aug. 3/58
Interest on same
(p 122)
1 Note on G. Green dated Feb. 17th 1858 (D) for40.00 Int.3.60
1 Note on Smith Gleaves dated Oct.4th to Nov.4th 54 in all
1 Mo. & 2 days .67
125.67

Nov. 6th 1854 Cr. By Cash	100.00
Interest	1.54
1 Note on G. W. Miles dated July 18th 1857 (D) for	7.62
Interest on same	.90
1 Note on B. H. and R. B. Gibbs dated Sept.16th 1854 for	200.00

Interest on same to January 17th 1856 1 year and 9 Months			21.03
			221.03
Jany. 17,1856 Cr. by Cash		200.00	21.03
Interest on same		52	
1 Note on G. W. Miles due July 4th 1857 for (D)		20.00	
Interest on same		18.00	
1 Note on Joseph Krantz due Feb. 7,1859	10.19		
Cash left on hand	39.45		
		730.14	

The foregoing inventory and account of sale of the estate of F. Balthrop is Correct to the lest of My belief.
Sworn to this 3rd day of January 1859.
Amount Notes Cash etc. 730.14

(p 123) GEORGE C. BINKLEY, Administrator of T. DURARD,Dr.

To Amount sale of land	
Note due 15th Oct. 1858	519.00
1 Note on A. N. Binkley due on the 15th Oct.1858	17.20
Interest on same	.25
	536.45
Cr.	
By A. N. Binkley Note	74.00
By A. N. Binkley	17.76
By A. N. Binkley	8.88
By A. N. Binkley	2.96
By E. J. Binkley receipt	1.00
Jacob Mayo Note	59.20
A. Rose Note	16.89
Cheatham Watson & Co.	48.55
G. C. Binkley,Guardian J. Morris	35.00
Amount (D.C.) Clerks Copy Adm.settlement	1.25
Check for Bond	.25
Check for this settlement	1.25
Amount allowed Adm.	15.00
Amount due legates	253.96

An inventory and account of sale of the personal effects of BENJAMIN P. LOVELL, dec. Aug. 12th 1859.

Property sold	Names of purchaser	
1 set blacksmith Tools	G. W. Allen	6.00
1 Grindstone	James Reggan	1.25
1 Cross Cut saw	J. N. Dozier	5.25
1 Bull tongued Plow	Ab Vick	.50
1 Mowing blade & C.	James Reggins	1.30
3 Plows	D. R. Lovell	.10
1 Froe	D. R. Lovell	.55
1 set plow geer	Widow	.25
1 set Bench plains & C.	Dr. R. Lovell	3.40
3 Augers	S. S. Knight	.50
Sash Plain & C. & C.	D. R. Lovell	3.80
1 hot Chisels	D. Knight	.60
1 set Chisel & Tool Chest	D. R. Lovell	1.75
1 side board & Chest	Widow	.50
1 Table	A. Worke	.70
1 sugar Chest	Miss Lovell	.25
1 Clock	Widow	1.00
Encoyclopedia	A Work	2.50

1 Mule	A Work	80.00
	D. R. Lowell	15.00
	Widow	35.00
	B. W. Davison	10.00
	Widow	10.00
		70.00
		180.70

(p 124) State of Tennessee, Cheatham County.
I do hereby Certify an Oath that the foregoing inventory and account of sale of the personal effects of Benjamin P. Lovell, dec. to the best of My belief.
This the 12th day of August A. D. 1859.
W. G. Shelton
Administrator of Ben P. Lovell, deceased

A list of the property sold at the sale of Cassey Shores deceased Aug. 16th 1859.

Names of purchasers	Articles sold	
A. W. Stewart	1 Plow & single tree	2.60
Tho. Bell	2 " " "	.40
W. H. Pace	1 Weeding Hoe	.80
Henry Harris	2 Grub Hoes	.35
W. Owen	1 Chopping Axe	.55
Tho Bell	1 Axe	1.00
W. Owens	1 Do	.65
H. R. Felts	1 Basket	.10
John Perdue	1 Do	.30
Thomas Taylor	1 Do	.15
John Perdue	1 half Bushel	.35
W. T. Pace	2 smoothing Irons	.65
W. H. Stewart	1 Keg & Washboard	.50
Alexander Walker	1 Wedge	.35
Henry Hunter	1 Pad lock	.20
Thomas Bell	1 Hammer & Quart Pot	.15
M. V. B. Walker	3 Gimblets	.35
Thomas Shores	1 Brush & Draw Knife	.10
John Perdue	1 Pair Geer	1.10
W. Owens	1 Do Do	.25
Jo Pace	1 Wash Tub	1.25
John Perdue	1 Do Do	1.70
A. W. Stewart	1 Barrel & Cauter	.25
Jesse Shearon	1 Reed	.40
James Hunter	1 Spinning Wheel	.95
Jesse Shearon	1 Bedstead & Card	.55
Jo Pace	1 Tray & sifter	.50
Jo Pace	1 Tablecloth	4.00
(p 125)		
N. Sanders	1 stew Pot	.25
N. Sanders	1 Kettle	.50
J. Shearon	1 Oven	.10
N. Sanders	1 skillet & lid	.50
Jesse Shearon	1 Baker	.10
Wash Owen	1 Tea Kettle	.55
W. H. Pace	1 shaving kettle	.10
N. Sanders	1 Churn	.20
Jesse Shearon	1 skillet & lid	.15

John Perdue	1 Cedar Can	.75
W. H. Pace	1 Peggin	.20
Harris Nicholson	1 Peggin	.25
Hesse Shearon	1 Water bucket	.30
Thos. McDaniel	1 Loom & Geer	.65
W. H. Pace	1 Pot rack	.45
N. Sanders	1 fire shovel	.10
Jack Perdue	2 Meal sacks	.65
J. D. Stewart	1 side saddle	2.25
J. W. Perdue	1 Bridle & Martingale	1.50
N. Sanders	1 set plates	.40
Wm. Pace	1 set plates	
John Perdue	1 set Cups & saucers	.15
John Perdue	1 set Cups & saucers	.50
Jesse Shearon	1 set Tumblers	.60
Henry Felts	1 set Knives & forks	.45
W. T. Pace	1 dish Bean Pot	.50
Wm. Pace	1 dish & 2 Bowl	.30
J. W. Perdue	2 pitchers	.35
J. W. Perdue	1 lot Tin	.70
H. R. Felts	1 Coffee Mill	.25
W. H. Stewart	1 Jug	.25
W. H. Pace	1 Box	.20
J. W. Perdue	2 Pair shears	.60
W. T. Pace	1 umbrella	1.00
Tho Shores	½ rifle gun	7.50
W. T. Pace	1 Bed	18.50
N. Sanders	1 Bed	5.00
Wm. McFadden	1 Bed & stead	16.00
Mrs Pace	1 Chest	.50
N. Sanders	1 Clock	.25
Wm. Stewart	1 safe	7.25
John Perdue	1 Counterpane	.85
John Perdue	1 Bed Quilt	1.25
John Perdue	1 Bed Quilt	1.00
Wm. McFadden	1 Bed Quilt	2.40
(p 126)		
James Pace	1 Counterpane	1.25
G. W. Shores	1 Do	1.00
John Perdue	1 Bed Quilt	1.25
Wm. McFadden	1 Do Do	2.00
Wm. McFadden	1 Do Do	2.00
John Perdue	1 Do Do	1.30
Jack Perdue	1 Do Do	1.05
Wm. McFadden	2 Do Do	1.00
Wm. Pace	3 Chairs	.40
A. Walker	1 set Chairs	3.96
M. V. B. Walker	1 barrel Corn	4.80
M. V. B. Walker	1 Do Do	5.00
N. Sanders	1 Do Do	5.00
Robert King	1 Do Do	5.00
H. W. Turner	Remainder Do	1.40
H. W. Turner	51 lbs Bacon 10¢	5.10
M. V. Walker	52 lbs Bacon 10¼	5.33
H. W. Turner	45 " " 12	5.40
Abner Hunter	1 keg lard	.75
G. W. Murphey	1 lard Barrel	.25

G. W. Murpheyn	1 Barrel Salt	2.55
W. Durham	½ Barrel salt	1.10
Benjamin Stewart	½ Ox Cart	10.75
G. W. Murphey	1 lot fodder	.90
Henry Hunter	1 Brown Mare	80.00
Thomas Shaw	1 Colt	60.00
J. H. Adkins	1 Black Mare	66.50
Thomas Shaw	1 Cow & Calf	17.25
Thomas Perdue	1 Steer	8.50
Harris Nicholsom	5 1st Choice Hogs	16.00
J. H. Pace	5 2nd " "	13.00
N. Sanders	5 3rd " "	12.00
J. J. Woodson	6 4th " "	7.00
John Perdue	10 Geese	1.00
Amount of sale of Corn field		136.18
		$ 587.89

W. T. PACE, executor of THOMAS PACE.

1 Note on E. T. Clifton	15.00
1 " 2 James Hunter	6.60
Account on hands	
1 account on E. T. Clifton	10.00
1 Do " E. P. Morris	3.55
1 Do " Julia Clifton	10.00

(p 127) A list of property sold at the sale of JAMES SHORES, dec. Aug. 16th 1859.

Purchasers Names	Articles sold	
John Albright	1 pair steelyards	.35
W. H. Pace	1 ring and steeple	.45
A. W. Stewart	1 razor strop & C.	.60
Henry Hunter	2 Brushes	.60
Henry Harris	1 Man saddle	3.00
Thomas Shores	½ Rifle Gun	7.50
Henry Hunter	1 Sythe	1.85
Ben Stewart	½ Ox Cart	10.75
Amount of his share of Corn sold		68.09
		$ 93.19

Last will and testament of ABNER GUPTON, dec.

I Abner Gupton do Make and publish this as My last Will and testament hereby revoking and making void all other Wills by Me any time Made.

First, I direct that My funeral expenses and all My debts be paid as soon after My death as possible out of any Monies that I May die possessed of May first come into the hands of My executor.

Secondly, If my Wife Judith Gupton should survive Me in life My estate all is to stay in one Common stock in her charge till her death, and after the death of us both I want it divided in seven equal shares and distributed as follows.

1st Unto the heirs of Mary Hunter My daughter. I Will one seventh share and I appoint Mary Hunter Mu daughter their executor to keep the said share and its increase together, till her death and after her death to be divided among them.

2nd Unto the heirs of Sarah Perdue My daughter. I will one seventh share and I appoint Sarah Perdue and John Perdue her

husband their executor and executrix to Keep the said Shawy and its increase together till the death of Sarah Pardue. My daughter, and after her death to be equally divided amongst her heirs.
3, Unto the lawfull begotten of James Gupton, My son I will one seventh share, and I appoint James Gupton. My son their executor to keep the said James Gupton My son and after his death the said Share and its increase to his lawful begotten heirs.
4th, Unto Abner Gupton My son I leave one seventh share to have and to hold , during his life time and its increase (p 128) and after his death the said Abner Gupton My son I want it divided as stated in the other shares and appoint Robert T. Gupton his executor, to act for the said Abner Gupton, My son.
5th, Unto Judith Gupton, My daughter I leave one seventh share to have and to hold during her life time and if the said Judith Gupton My daughter should Marry and have heirs at her death, the said Judith Gupton My daughter the said seventh share to be equally divided among them.
6th, Unto the lawful heirs of Robert T. Gupton My son I will one seventh share the said share is to be kept together and its increase till the death of My son Robert Gupton and after his death to be equally divided among all his lawful begotten heirs and I appoint R; T. Gupton My son their executor.
7th, Unto the lawful begotten heir of Elizabeth Hale, My dayghter, I will one seventh share the said share its increase till the death of Elizabeth Hale My daughter and after her death to be equally divided amongst all her children that she May leave, And I appoint Matthew T.Hale and Elizabeth Hale, their exeuctors and executrix And further if any of My Child-ren should die without one heir the share or shares they draw for their children is to be divided amongst them My children that has heirs as stated.
Lastly I do hereby Nominate and appoint James and Robert T. Gupton My executors to Comply with My above Name distribution In Witness whereof I do to this My will set My hand and seal This 5th day of April 1841.

Test: Abner Gupton (SEAL)
Joseph Gupton
his
Joshua X Stroud
mark

Signed sealed and published in our presence and we have subscribed our Names hereto in the presence of the Testator this the 5th day of April 1841.

(p 129) I ABNER GUPTON do Make and publish this as My last will and testament hereby revoking and Making void all other wills by me at any time Made.
First, I direct My funeral expense and all My debts be paid as soon after My death as possible out of any Money that I May first come into the hand s of My executor.
Second, I give and bequeath to My Wife Martha A. Gupton all the property that she was entitled to in her former husband estate Samuel A. Powers, to have and to hold the same as her distributive part of My estate.

And thirdly that the balance Of my estate personal and real be divided in seven eqaal shares unto the body heirs of Mary Hunter My daughter one of said shares to be kept together until the death of Mary Hunter and My daughter as Trustee to the same without giving secubity unto the lawful begotten heirs of James Gupton. I give another said shares the same to be kept together until the said James J. Guptonsdeath then to his children as above Named and I appoint James J. Gupton My son as trustee to Manage said share without security unto the heirs of the body. If Sarah Pardue My daughter to have another of said shares the same to be kept together during her life time during the life time of My daughter Sarah Pardue and at her death to be equally divided amongst her children and I appoint Sarah Perdue and her husband as Trustee to the same without secubity and another of said shares to Abner Gupton My sons lawfully begotten heirs to be kept together during his life time and at his death to be equally divided amongst his lawful begotten children and I appoint 66------ as Trustee unto the same.
Unto the heirs of the body of Judith Dozier, My daughter I give another of said shares to be kept together during the life time of Judith Dozier, and at her death to be equally divided amongst her children and I appoint Judith Dozier and her husband as Trustees to the same without security.
Unto the lawful begotten heirs of Robert T. Gupton, My son I will another of said shares to be kept together during the life time of R. T. Gupton My sona nd after his death to be equally divided amongst the Children as above Named. And I appoint R. T. Gupton My son as Trustee to the same without security.
Unto the bodily heirs of Elizabeth Hale, I give another of said shares to be kept together till the death of My daughter Elizabeth Hqle (p 130) then to be equally divided amongst her Children and I appoint Elizabeth Hale and her husband Trustee to the same without security, But if any of My Children should die leaving No children then said share of shares to be equally divided amongst the balance of My Children, as above pointed out I do hereby Nominate and appoint ------ My executor.

In witness whereof I do to this My will set My hand and seal This -- day of -- 18 --

Abner Gupton (SEAL)

Signed sealed and published in our presence and we have subscribed our Names hereto in the presence of the Testator the day of -- 184--

Jan. 11th 1858.

Whereas I have been informed that some years ago My deaf and dumb son ABNER GUPTON was Married to one Jane Batts without My Knowledge or Consent, and since said Marriage up to the death of My son Abner which took place some two years ago and up to his death and since the said Jane has had sevaral children some of which I learn is now living, and for reasons best known to Myself. I Make this My wish will and desire. I willunto the said Jane and her children twenty five Acres of land including the place shw now lives on runing back to Pool line and run so as to take half the spring, and this all her said children is to have in My estate after My death that I

May die seized and possessed of in any shape form or fashion in land or equity.

Given under My hand and seal.

Abner Gupton (SEAL)

I have this day Made this My wish will and desire that that portion of My estate that My son ROBERT GUPTON would be entitled to after My death should be the longest liver I want it drawn off and set apart and it is to remain in Common stock during the said R. T. Guptons life time and it is after his death to be equally divided amongst his heirs as the law directs. I appoint the said R. T. Gupton, My son Trustee, to take Charge of said portion and Manage it for his said Children as he May think best, and he is Not bound to security for said portion in any way whatever, and he is to take from the proceeds of said portion a sufficient amount to support himself on anually he May Need it.

Given under My hands and seal this the -- of -- 1858

Abner Gupton

(p 131) Settlement of A. S. WILLIAMS, Adm. of W. A. WILLIAMS.

To amount of inventory	839.49
Cr.	
By W. C. Callison proven act.	5.00
" O. Teasley proven act.	5.00
" W. Frazier Note	48.25
" W. B. Batson Note	19.11
" W. B. Batson proven act.	23.97
" James McCauley proven act.	18.00
" B. R. Miller proven act.	22.40
" Tax receipt 1848	.51
Tax receipt on his property	12.50
R. Wyatt proven act.	22.26
Atty. fee	25.00
W. H. Minors proven act.	18.81
Tax receipt 1859	4.09
Tax on land present year	2.00
S. C. Bates proven act.	22.15
A. J. Brights fees	10.75
E. J. Minors receipt	3.00
Henny Bulls proven act.	1.20
Tho. L. Justice proven act.	61.42
Hagewood and Jones Note	23.19
W. Hagy Notes	45.75
John Colliers proven act.	26.80
Hagewood and Jones proven act.	81.50
George Eleazer proven act.	145.50
A. S. Williams proven act.	15.60
Smith Batson Note	286.00
Smith Batson "	8.79
Shot Gun taken by S. M. Roberts	10.00
Clerks fee for bond & C.	3.00
Recording inventory	.74
Certifying Executor	.25
Recording refunding bond	.50
Allowance to Admrs.	45.00
Clerk for this settlement	2.00
	1010.04

Amount over assets ,170.55

(p 132) Inventory of the personal estate of H. W. HANNAH, sold on the 15 August 1859 at his late residence in said County.

Names of purchasers	Articles sold	
S. N. Hannah	1 diamond Plow	3.00
N. B. Mayo	1 " "	4.25
Thomas Deal	1 " "	1.75
H. V. Thompson	1 Bull Tongue plow	.50
Thomas M. Dunn	1 Peacock Plow	.75
Moses Jones	1 spade	.65
James P. Clark	1 Wedge & hoe	.40
James P. Clark	1 log Chain	1.50
John P. Pegram	1 half bushel	.65
S. N. Hannah	1 sythe & Cradle	1.15
Wm. Yates	1 hand saw	1.20
N. B. Mays	2 Augers	.50
H. L. Clark	,1 drawing Knife	.90
S. N. Hannah	1 pr. Harness & Collar	.80
Wm. Yates	1 shot Gun	1.45
John Haley	1 Rifle Gun	6.00
W. T. Jones	1 pair last	.45
Thomas Deal	1 set shoe tools	.85
Franklin Jones	1 razor hone & strop	1.05
Martha A. Hannah	2 Books	.50
William Jones	1 Slate	.10
James P. Clark	1 lot growing Corn	50.50
Moses Jones	5 first Choice hogs	4.25
James P. Clark	5 second " "	3.00
James P. Clark	5 third " "	1.90
James P. Clark	the remainder 20 Cts each	1.80
S. N. Hannah	1 Bay horse	41.00
John H. Hutton	1 Bay Horse	101.00
William Yates	1 Cow	5.25
Sam A. Thompson	1 saddle	6.50
John A. Clark	1 Fiddle	3.50
Martha A. Hannah	1 Trunk	1.25
S. N. Hannah	1 Axe	1.00
James H. Baker	1 Axe	.30
Moses Jones	2 Beef Hydes in tan Not sold	3.10
George Randall	1 lot Cord wood	2.00
		254.85

Notes and accounts

1 Note on S. A. Thompson good due 19 May 1858 for	7.70
One account on G. W. Hannah good	7.70
One Account on M. A. Hannah good	2.00
One account on H. Whitfield doubtful	5.00
One account on H. M. Hutton	3.25
One account on B. F. Hannah, a minor	1.00
	27.05

(p 133) Amount of property sold by A. Stewart and E. A. SYMES, Exr. of CHARLES SYMES, deceased as directed in his Will.

One house to A. Boyt April 4	50.00
13 Cord wood	26.00
299 lbs ham	23.92

50 lbs ham	5.00
996 lbs sides 7½	74.70
1 steer	5.75
1108 48/56 Bushels Corn 42½	471.26
683 lbs lard 10	68.30
Cash of J. L. Krantz for rent	15.00
184 Cord wood 1.50	276.00
17 Cord wood	34.00
Balance of Krantz	54.50
56 Cord wood	81.50
18 lbs Bacon	2.00
Cash from J. B. Demunbra	10.00
512 lbs Bacon to Hale	51.25
Cash from Church Rasberry	60.00
W. H. Oliver & A. Smith, Note due 11th Dec.1859	25.00
John Perdue & G. W. McCarley Note due 11th Dec 1859	10.00
John Perdue & W. H. Stewart	30.30
A. Smith & W. H. Oliver	25.00
W. H. Stewart & Z. Shearon	85.00
Jo Krantz & H. Boyt Due January 1st 1860	95.00
J. B. Demunbra & James Lenox Due Dec 25th 1859	340.00
J. B. Demunbra account	22.28
Interest received on Cash loaned	18.00
Premium on gold	19.00
Cash received from Brinkley Ex.	48.97
Credits	2027.73

(p 134) Settlement of JOHN SANDERS, Adm. od D. SANDERS, deceased.

John Sanders Adm. of D. Sander, dec.

Dr. 1061.61

To Amount of Inventory

By L. J. Perdues proven act.	9.05
" Shaw & Walls " "	15.99
" R. Maxey " "	2.65
" W. W. Walker " "	2.15
" A.J. Sanders " "	25.00
" A. J. Teasleys " "	2.00
" E. G. Hudgens " "	6.00
" W. B. Hooper & Son "	2.15
" W. W. Sanders " "	26.00
" G. W. McQuary " "	6.00
" E. G. Hudgens " "	2.34
" Henry Maxeys " "	3.50
" H. J. Shaws " "	59.75
Money paid for sugar and Coffee	19.15
Allowance to Admr.	50.00
Letters Administration	.50
Copy of same	.50
Taking bond	2.00
Order to Pay off years provisions	.25
Copy of same	.25
Order Confirming same	.25
Recording Report Comp	.25
Order to lay off dower	.25
Copy of same	.25
Order Confirming same	.25

Recording Report	.25
Recording inventory	.77
Making this settlement	1.00
Order Confirming the same	.25
	239.35
Amount due Legates on settlement	822.26

(p 135) Settlement of G. C. BINKLEY, Admr. of R. DURARD.

George C. Binkley, Admr. of R. Durard, deceased Dr.

To Amount of Inventory	60.40
One Claim on Gullege	6.80
10 Barrels Corn on obligation	15.00
	82.20
Cr.	
By Claim on Gullege on insolvent	6.80
Cheatham Watson & Co. act.	4.80
D. C. Day proven act.	4.50
A. N. Binkley proven act.	2.35
W. M. Rose proven act.	4.00
Mary Myers " "	.50
Henry Myers " "	3.30
E.L. Darrow " "	2.10
W. H. Blankenship Act	2.00
E.L. Darrow Clerk at sale	.50
Allowance to Admr.	5.00
E. J. Binkley receipt	1.00
	36.85
Dr.	45.35
One Note on A. N. Binkley	30.00
Amount received from	75.35
Andersons estate	91.55
Amount due distributes on settlement	166.90
By W. L. Hollis act.	5.85
	161.15

Settlement of THOMPSON BIGGERS, Administrator S. DAVIS

Thompson Biggers, administrator of Sarah Davis, dec.

To amount of inventory on page 67	77.30
To amount of inventory on page 80	529.33
Amount of inventory	606.63
Cr.	
By J. D. Nicholson proven act.	27.32
" E. N. Gupton Coffin	9.00
" Thompson Biggers proven act.	2.93
" Shaw & Brothers " "	4.08
" Thompson Biggers " "	50.00
Allowance to Admr.	25.00
Clerk for Bond	2.00
Letters of Administration and Copy of same	1.00
Recording Inventory	.30
Making settlement and receiving same	.75
Recording and refunding bonds	3.00
	125.38
Amount due distributes	481.25

(p 136) Inventory of the personal property of JACOB BELL, deceased sold by STERLING WALKER, Administrator on the 5th day of October 1859.

Articles sold	Purchaser Names	
1 lot iron	L. Fox	.90
2 Axes	R. Murphey	.15
1 Axe	J. Stack	.10
1 shovel	W. T. Morris	.10
1 spade	E. Simmons	.55
1 lot hoes	John Shores	.25
1 Do Do	James Walker	.15
1 Do Do	W. Hawkins	.10
1 Adze	James Hunt	.15
1 lot irons	J. L. Harris	.35
1 lot Bells	J. L. Harris	.05
1 Do Do	R. Murphey	.20
1 Do Do	R. Fort	.25
1 Auger & Harness	L. Fox	.45
1 Chisel	J. Shivers	.20
1 round shave	R. Lane	.10
1 Hand saw	J.Walker	.15
1 Hand saw	John Walker	.20
1 Do Do	E. D. Allen	.10
1 Bell	W. H. Stewart	.10
1 lot Chains	Jo Shearon	.15
1 lot irons	J. J. Wilson	.30
1 Do Do	G. Nicholson	.20
1 Auger & C.	R. Lane	.40
1 Do	R. Lane	.20
1 Broad Axe	R. Pennington	1.00
1 Hatchet	J. H. Wilson	.10
1 Plane	James Walker	.20
1 Do	James Walker	.25
2 Augers	W. Parris	.25
1 tray & seive	J. M. Cormack	.65
1 Brier hook	R. Head	.50
1 pair Moles	B. Moon	1.05
2 pitchers	J. Bradley	.85
1 Table	R. Head	.35
1 Counterpane	Thos. A. Owen	1.15
1 Do	Thompson Herron	.40
1 Quilt	R. Lane	.85
1 Tablecloths	R. Paschall	.25
1 sheet	Thomas M. Parrish	.45
1 Do	G. Dickerson	.85
		14.80

(p 137)

1 pair Blankets	W. J. Gossett	.60
1 Counterpane	W. Hawkins	.45
1 Quilt	Thomas A. Owen	.80
1 Bed & C.	G. Dickson	16.00
1 Bed & C.	W. H. Head	13.05
1 Bed & C.	J. Parrish	13.00
1 Bed & C.	Jacob Stack	13.00
1 Bed & C.	W. Dodd	12.25
1 Bed stead	J. Parrish	3.25
1 Bag Cotton	N. J. Alley	1.00
1 saddle & Bridle	B. Paschall	2.50
1 Dip Net	G. W. Murphey	1.00

1 Bed stead	J. Mc.McCormack	4.50
1 Bed stead	J. McCormack	5.05
1 Press	J. McCormack	10.60
1 watch	N. J. Alley	5.10
1 shot gun	D. Hudgens	4.25
1 shot gun	W. Hudgens	4.26
1 shot gun	W. J. Gossett	7.00
1 Tray	G. Dickerson	.10
1 grind stone	Z. Owen	.75
1 set wagon Harness	J. Shivers	6.50
1 pair harness	B. Pasdhall	.25
1 set gear	W. Elliott	.55
1 Cut saw	Z. Owen	2.05
1 Wheat Fan	J. McCormack	6.90
9 Bushel & 1 peck Wheat	Jesse Durham	8.32
10 " 3 " "	Jesse Durham	9.57
18 " Wheat	M. D. L. Williams	13.14
1 Lot Plank	A. Dickerson	2.00
1 stack Fodder	A. E. Lovell	1.90
1 Do Do	G. W. Hawkins	3.30
1 Do Do	B. J. Stack	3.80
1 Do Oats	William Shearon	4.25
1 Do Do	Jacob Stack	4.05
1 Do Do	A. E. Lovel	3.75
1 Do Do	B. J. Stack	1.60
5 Barrels Corn	R. Lane	20.25
5 " "	A. E. Lovel	17.50
5 " "	R. Lane	17.00
1 stack fodder	B. J. Stack	3.00
100 pounds Bacon	J. Stack	13.25
50 lbs bacon	J. Stack	6.25
75 lbs Soap	J. D. Dismukes	1.97
25 pounds soap	John J. Hudgens	.62
(p 138)		
1 Gray Horse	Wm. Bennett	5.25
1 Bay Mare	R. Paschall	9.00
1 Bay Horse	J. McCormack	55.50
1 Bay Mare	G. W. Murphey	73.50
1 Cow & Calf	Gid Lowe	15.50
1 Cow & Calf	Gid Lowe	14.25
1 Heifer	W. B. Woodruff	10.00
5 Head of Hogs	J. McCormack	24.25
5 Do Do	J. Z. Hudgens	21.00
5 Do Do	J. Shivers	13.00
5 Do Do	W. H. H. Stack	7.00
5 Do Do	W. H. H. Stack	6.00
5 Do Do	D. Alley	5.00
5 Do Do	A. E. Lovell	4.75
8 Chairs	J. McCormack	5.60
1 Pistol	Jacob Stack	.50
1 set Tablespoons	B. F. Pace	.15
1 Water bucket	P. H. Woodson	.20
1 Do Do	B. Paschall	.10
1 Do Do	E. T. Harris	.10
1 Loom	J. McCormack	.25
2 Bowls	N. Morris	.30
1 lot earthenware	J. Pilant	.15

1 lot earthenware	N. Morris	.15
1 " "	N. Morris	.10
1 set Knives & forks	W. Hawkins	.75
2 blowing horns	N. Morris	.80
2 pair Cards	Jack Harris	.25
1 lot Vials	J. Benson	.20
1 Testament	A. J. Teasley	.55
1 Bible	J. Shivers	.25
1 Bible	J. Z. Hudgens	1.40
1 Table	G. W. Dickerson	1.50
1 lot leather	W. Dodd	.35
1 lot leather	John Benson	3.95
1 pair saddle bags	J. Shivers	.75
1 side saddle	R. Head	.50
1 Box & Contents	C. Dickerson	.60
1 pair fire irons	J. McCormack	1.50
1 Trunk	J. Walker	1.45
1 Case bottles	W. H. Stewart	2.20
1 lot shoe tools	J. McCormack	.75
2 smoothing Irons	Do	.50
1 Pot	Do	.65
1 Oven & lid	Do	.50
(p 139)		
Frying Pan	J. McCormack	.35
1 Kettle	Do	3.00
1 Pot	Do	1.05
1 skillet	Do	.10
1 Pot	Do	.05
1 skillet & lid	Shivers	.35
1 Pot	J. McCormack	1.10
2 Drawing Knives	J. Shearon	.25
1 saddle	Ben Walker	.10
1 Pair Steelyards	J. McCormack	1.25
1 Wedge	R. Lane	.40
1 Do	R. Lane	.35
1 lot Plows	J. Walk	.05
1 Mattock	R. Lane	.75
1 Mattock	W. H. Stuart	.50
1 Collar	J. D. Dismukes	.50
1 lot Irons	A. J. Teasley	.25
1 plow & singletree	J. Z. Hudgens	.15
1 Plow	J. D. Dismukes	3.80
1 Plow	A. Walker	2.50
1 Seive	D. Fort	.80
1 Keg	J. Benson	.10
1 half bushel	Ben Walker	.20
1 Flax Wheel	E. Sullivan	.20
1 Tray	E. Clifton	.50
1 Tray	J. Shivers	.25
1 Wheel & Cards	J. Z. Hudgens	.90
1 Wheel	W. Parrish	.80
2 Meal Bags	J. Walker	.35
2 Meal Bags	J. Z. Hudgens	.35
1 spinning Wheel	J. McCormack	2.05
1 pair wool Cards	J. McCormack	.15
1 sythe & Cradle	Jas. Walker	1.05
1 Do Do	E. T. Herron	.10

1 Jar	W. H. Head	.40
1 Jar	B. W. Bradley	.60
1 Pitcher	J. A. Farmer	.55
1 Jug	W. Parrish	.20
1 Jug	A. Walker	.10
1 lot slates	H. Nicholson	.25
1 set Geer	John Bradley	.85
1 set Geer	J. A. Farmer	.50
Cash left on hand		277.45
		871.55

(p 140) In the Name of God Amen.

I NARCISSA C. SMITH HUNT of the County of Cheatham and State of Tennessee do Make this My last will and Testament as follows,

I bequeath to My Mother Elizabeth Hunt My Negro boy Dick during his life and then to be equally divided among his heirs also My Negro girl Sally to My Sister Elizabeth Sarah Gatweood during her life time and then to be disposed of as she May see fit. Also My Negro girl Anna to My sister Eliza W. Wilson during her life time and then to My Brother James Byran Hunt of his heirs after him. Also My saddle horse to be sold and the amount appropriated to the schooling of My Sister Dicy A. Shaws Children.

I give my trunk to My Neice Narcissa Shaw, My saddle to Mattie D. Byran and what Money I have on hand to the payment of of My debts and if any remains to be equally divided among My brothers and sisters. My braclets. I give one to Eliza Heritgage Gatewood and the other to Narcissa Shaw My breastpin to My Sister Elizabeth Gatewood provided this last testament to be as above Mentioned after My debts and all paid.

This 26th day of August in the year ofour Lord 1859.

Attest: Narcissa Cy Hunt

E. Charlton, Test

L. C. Byran, Test

(p 141) THOMAS W. WHITFIELD, Administrator of JOHN BERRY, deceased.

To Amount Collected on Bridges obligation reported in settlement as being insolvent	600.00		
Interest on same	100.00		
		700.00	
By Attorneys fee Collecting same		150.00	
Clarks fee in Davidson County		14.25	
Amount tax Railroad		10.87	
Amount State & County Tax		2.25	
Error on W. W. Benny Note		60.00	
		102.37	
Amount to be divided in addition to first settlement			597.63

Inventory of the sale of the personal estate of CASA SHAW, deceased sold on the 28th day of November 1859 by A. HUNTER, Administrator one third of the same belongs to JAMES SHORES.

N. Sanders 5 barrels Corn 2.55		12.75
D. G. Teasley 5 Barrels of Corn	2.35	11.75
R. J. Mallory 10 " "		35.00

R. J. Mallory 5 Barrels Corn		18.00
G. W. Murphey 10 " "		34.00
B. Nicholson 5 " "	3.50	17.50
B. J. Stack 5 " "		16.50
B. J. Stack 4 " "		9.80
N. Sanders Picking fields		2.10
John Pool 1 lot shucks		2.10
R. J. Mallory 1 lot shucks		2.50
R. J. Mallory 1 lot shucks		2.65
G. W. McCarley 1 lot shucks		1.75
N. Sanders 8 bushels potatoes	31	2.48
N. Sanders 1 Pot		.30
		204.28

One third of the Amount belongs to the estate of James Shores, dec. 68.09
Amount belonging to the Estate of Mrs Shores 68.09
136.19

(p 142) 2nd. Inventory if the sale of the property belonging to the estate of JACOB BELL, deceased sold by STERLING WALKER, Administrator of the estate of said deceased on the 28th day of November 1859.

E. Clifton	15 Barrels Corn		61.75
James Moore	10 " "		41.00
Thomas Bracey	30 " "		117.00
S. Bobbitt	5 " "		19.75
R. H. Alley	15 " "		57.25
J. J. Alley	5 " "		19.00
N. J. Alley			00.00
N. Morris	1 pen shucks		6.10
L. Fox	1 " "		6.55
Henry Stotzz	1 stack fodder		4.10
James Walker	1 pen shucks		5.25
Eli Harris	1 Yoke Oxen		39.00
J. J. Wilson	1 Waggon		35.00
Willis Hyde	1 Cutting Knife		1.10
H. Hudgens	129 Bundles fodder		2.29
L. Fox	1 stack fodder		4.00
J. J. Alley	1 stack fodder		1.10
S. N. Bracey	Hire boy Jim per Mo	4.00	18.00
George Bell	" " Parker	1.20	3.60
M. D. L. Williams	" girl Mary	1.00	3.40
M. C. Orman	" " Mariah	2.50	7.50
T. A. Basford	1 Stack fodder		6.00
L. Bobbitt	1 " "		4.40
W. A. Fortune	1 " "		4.00
James Walker	1 " "		3.30
Thos. A. Basford	1 " "		4.00
	1 " "		3.55
	1 " "		5.00
	1 " "		6.10
	1 " "		6.00
H. Williams			46.25
D. G. Allen	1 stack fodder		3.00
Jenner Grady	Wheat Straw		2.00
			539.94

(p 143) A list of articles sold belonging to the estate of ABNER GUPTON, deceased On the 17th day of October 1859 it being the amount of all the personal estate that came into the hands of R. T. GUPTON Executor.

Articles sold	Purchasers Names	
1 sorrel Mare	W. B. Stewart	102.00
1 Black Mare	James H. Gupton	41.00
1 Mare & Colt	Mrs M. H. Gupton	58.00
1 sorrel Mare	J. D. Nicholson	7.25
1 sorrel Mare & Colt	Mrs M. H. Gupton	13.50
1 Yoke Young Oxen	J. H. Gupton	33.00
1 White Cow	Mrs W. H. Gupton	16.50
1 Muly Cow & Calf	H. C. Pace	11.25
1 Red Cow & Calf	Mrs Mary Hunter	15.00
1 spotted Cow & Calf	Mrs M. H. Gupton	13.50
1 Cow & Calf	J. J. Williamson	16.25
1 Black Cow & Calf	J. Bell Jr.	10.00
1 Bull Cow & Calf	J. S. Major	16.25
1 speckle Heifer	J. S. Major	11.00
1 White face heifer	J. S. Major	8.10
1 Ox Cart	Mrs M. H. Gupton	5.50
1 large Kettle	Allen Hunter	3.50
1 Grind stone	R. M. McCormack	.15
1 Bed stead & Cord	Abner Hunter	4.30
1 Trundle bed stead	A. J. Thorn	.50
1 Bed stead	H. R. Poole	2.00
1 low bed stead	M. V. B . Walker	.60
3 diamond plows	Barney Frazier	1.55
1 Double plow	Barney Frazier	1.90
2 Diamond plow	Barney Frazier	.35
1 Flax Wheel	Mrs M. H. Gupton	.25
1 lot old Copper	G. W. Hale	.60
1 set Plow geer	John Comperry	.70
1 set Breeching	Mrs M. H. Gupton	.35
5 single trees & harness	En Gupton	.50
1 Double Tree	Barney Frazier	1.05
1 lot Weeding hoes	Barney Frazier	.10
1 small Mare	Melvin Wall	88.00
1 Grubbing Hoe	Barney Frazier	.85
1 Grubbing Hoe	M. V. B. Walker	.60
1 Do Do	Barney Frazier	.25
1 pair dog Irons	A. Hunter	1.70
1 Vice	R. McCormack	2.10
1 lot Tool	H. P. Pool	.50
1 Ring & Steeple	Barney Frazier	.30
1 Plane & Chair	H. V. Pool	.25
1 Large Chest	E. N. Gupton	.10
(p 144)		
1 Rifle gun	Thos. D. Hunter	9.50
4 Bed Matts	Mrs M. H. Gupton	1.30
1 Bed stead	George Davis	1.40
1 lot Trumpery	H. R. Pool	1.70
1 stone Churn	Mary Hunter	.05
1 stone Jar	Mrs Gupton	.05
2 dishes	Abner Hunter	.15
1 lot Table Ware	Mrs M. H. Gupton	.25
1 Table	Mrs M. H. Gupton	.05

1 Grid iron	Mrs Mary Hunter	.05
1 Baker	Mrs Mary Hunter	.05
2 Pot rack	Mrs M. H. Gupton	.10
1 small Kettle	Mrs Mary Hunter	.75
1 large Kettle	Barney Frazier	2.75
1 large Pot	John Weakley	1.20
1 Oven	Barney Frazier	.25
1 skillet & lid	Barney Frazier	.25
1 small Pot	Moody Page	.25
1 stew kettle	Barney Frazier	.15
1 Tea Kettle	Moody Page	.20
1 lot old irons	Barney Frazier	.10
1 loom	J. C. Hale	2.00
1 Tin Box	J. D. Nicholson	.35
1 small bell	G. W. Hale	.55
1 lot Trumpery	J. D. Nicholson	.10
1 Cupboard	John Smith	3.00
1 Clock Reel	Barney Frazier	.65
1 Coffee Mill	P. J. Williams	.10
1 pitcher & Jar	Mrs J. Dozier	.25
1 Iron Tea spoons	Geo. Davis	.10
1 pitcher	Mrs Elizabeth Hale	.25
1 pitcher & Goblet	Mrs M. H. Gupton	.25
2 decanters	Mrs E. Hale	.25
1 sugar bowl	Mrs Mary Hunter	.10
1 Tin Box	Mrs E. Hale	.05
2 pitchers & C.	Mrs M. H. Gupton	.25
1 lot Bottles	E. N. Gupton	.25
1 Bell	Mary Hunter	.05
1 Jar	Mrs M. H. Gupton	.20
1 silver watch	Griffin Langford	.35
1 steelyard	Barney Frazier	2.00
1 stone pitcher	Mrs Mary Hunter	.15
1 large dish	Griffin Langford	.35
1 Demijohn	Wm. McFadden	1.10
1 Jug Molasses	James H. Gupton	.75
1 Hand bellows	John Smith	.25
1 Clock & Case	Griffin Langford	.30
(p 145)		
1 Clock	Barney Frazier	1.25
1 N. R. Case Clock	James Pardue	1.00
1 Clock	Barney Frazier	.10
1 side board	Mary Hunter	8.50
1 Book Case	Jas. H. Gupton	12.00
1 Clothes press	John D. Nicholson	12.00
1 small Book Case	E. N. Gupton	1.30
1 Bureau	Joseph Perdue	4.00
1 Chest	J. H. Gupton	5.00
1 Bed 1 st Choice	Barney Frazier	17.00
1 " 2 nd "	Barney Frazier	15.00
1 " 3 rd "	J. M. Comperry	14.00
1 " 4 th "	Mrs M. H. Gupton	6.00
1 " 5 th "	Mrs M. H. Gupton	5.00
1 Bed 6 & 7 Choice	Mrs M. H. Gupton	4.00
2 Clocks & Cases	Mrs M. H. Gupton	.25
1 Corner Cupboard	J. C. Perdue	2.25
1 lot Queensware	Mrs E. Hale	.10

1 looking glass	Mrs M. H. Gupton	.05
1 pair Waffle irons	Mrs E. Hale	.10
1 Bedstead	Mrs M. H. Gupton	1.75
1 lot pitchers	Abner Hunter	.25
1 shot gun	G. W. Hale	9.00
2 pair Tongs	Mary Hunter	.10
1 Trunk & frame	John M. Batts	1.00
2 dimijohn	Abner Hunter	.50
1 lot Chairs	Mrs M. H. Gupton	.50
1 Slate	W. H. Pace	.05
1 sythe blade	J. H. Gupton	.25
1 saddle & Tablr	Nemrod Gupton	3.00
1 Trunk	James H. Gupton	6.00
1 lot rags	Mrs M. H. Gupton	.35
1 lock screws & C.	Mrs M. H. Gupton	.75
1 Turn saw	J. B. Allsbrook	.60
1 oil stove	Robert King	.50
1 rocking Chair	Mrs M. H. Gupton	.10
1 Couch shell	J. T. MOrgan	.45
2 sheep bells	Cooper Gupton	.10
1 Trunk & frame	E. N. Gupton	1.05
1 lot shoemake tools	Mrs M. H. Gupton	.25
1 peice upper leather	John Comperry	.30
2 old family bibles	Mrs M. H. Gupton	.50
1 Book	S. D. Power	.10
1 lot Books	Mrs M. H. Gupton	.10
45 lbs pict Cotton	Mrs M. H. Gupton	2.60
(p 146)		
1 Book	S. D. Powers	.10
1 lot Tallow	Mrs Mary Hunter	.25
1 lot tallow & bucket	Mrs M. H. Gupton	.60
1 Tin box	Mrs M. H. Gupton	.10
1 old Trunk		
1 Carpet Bag		
1 lot Soap		
1 lot old bacon		
1 Cow Bell		
1 cutting Knife		
1 CuttingKnife		
Cash left on hand		
In par funds		4877.15
Exchange Bank		20.00
Bank of Claborn		5.00

An inventory of the estate of NARCISSA C. HUNT, dec.

1 slave Dick aged 15 years	
1 slave Sally aged 13 years	
1 slave Anna aged 7 years	
1 Trunk	
1 saddle	
1 lot of Jewelry all of which is specially devised	
1 Horse	100.00
1 account on A. H. William due 15th Sept. 1858	112.30
1 Note on W. Gatewood due 1st 1860	20.00

Sworn to before me Feb. 6, 1860

J. W. Hunt, Administrator

With the will annexed.

W. W. Williams, Clerk

(p 147) An inventory of the property belonging to the estate of C. SYMES, deceased sold on the 24th day of December 1859. CHARLES M. STUART, Guardian

Articles sold	Purchaser Named	
1 Pick	A. Smith	.35
2 single trees	Jo Krantz	.30
1 log Chain	W. H. Oliver	.40
1 pair Chains	G. W. McCarley	.50
2 pair Chains	A. Carney	.55
1 apir Chains	J. L. C. Adams	.15
1 frow	W. H. Oliver	.25
2 Wedges	G. W. McCarley	.20
2 Wedges	Geo. Bell	.25
2 Wedges	W. H. Stewart	.25
1 Axe	L. J. Perdue	.25
1 Axe	G. W. McCarley	.55
2 Axes	L. J. Perdue	.25
1 Hay fork	Thomas Obrien	.25
1 pair harness & Chains	G. W. McCarley	1.40
1 Cradle	G. W. McCarley	1.05
1 Hand saw	Tho Bell	.70
1 apir Irons	Ralph Shivers	.25
1 Vice	Wm. Stewart	.75
1 Bedstead	Wm. Blankenship	1.50
1 Cross Cut saw	E. Simmons	.50
1 Cross Cut saw	D. Saiger	5.75
1 Mowing blade	A. Carney	.25
1 Mowing blade	Wm. Stewart	.40
1 Mowing blade	A. Carney	.25
1 grind stone	G. W. McCarley	.30
1 straw Cutter	A. Carley	.60
1 spinning wheel	W. H. Oliver	2.20
1 Harrow	James Lenox	.25
1 Plow	James Lenox	.25
1 Plow	James Lenox	.25
1 Plow	Thomas Bell	1.85
1 Plow	Wm. Gent	.70
1 Plow	Wm. Gent	.25
1 raw Hide	Wm. Gent	.25
1 Kettle & hooks	A. Carney	2.25
1 Pot	A. Carney	1.30
1 Oven	W. H. Oliver	1.80
1 Oven	Jo Krantz	.25
1 Cooking stove	N. Smith	10.50
1 Table	James Lenox	1.80
1 stine Hammer	Jo Krantz	.35
1 sow & pigs	Jack Gent	2.00
(p 148)		
1 Cow & Calf	Gid Lowe	4.00
1 Cow & Calf	Gid Lowe	4.25
1 Calf	Gid Lowe	.50
1 Cow	Gid Lowe	9.50
1 side board	Wm. Binkley	30.00
1 Bureau	A. Carney	13.50
1 Bed stead	A. Carney	7.50
1 safe	Jessie Simmons	5.00
1 Bureau	A. Carney	
1 Lounge	G. W. McCarley	6.75

1 Crib	Wm. Binkley	4.50
1 Bedstead	Jesse Chandowen	3.00
1 Bedstead	W. H. Stewart	1.50
1 Bedstead	S. D. Page	3.25
1 Bedstead	Jesse Chandowen	3.00
40 Barrels Corn	G. W. Hale	140.00
1 pin shucks	Thos. OBrien	7.25
1 sheller	Wm. Binkley	1.00
1 Top stack	Thos. OBrien	5.00
5 Hogs	J. B. Demunbra	20.75
5 Hogs	J. B. Demunbra	13.75
5 Hogs	Ralph Shivers	10.25
5 Hogs	J. B. Demunbra	7.25
7 Hogs	J. B. Demunbra	5.25
1 Negro Elec hired	H. Porter	150.25
		497.45

Sworn to before me Jan. 20th 1860
W. W. Williams, Clerk

A list of property of SARAH WEAKLEYS sold by JOHN S. MAJORS, administrator on the 25th February 1860.

1 lot Barrels	James Thaxton	.10
1 grindstone	James B. Cain	2.60
1 Bed bedstead & furniture	Eliza Cain	25.00
1 Press	Eliza Cain	12.00
1 Folding Table	Eliza Cain	3.20
1 lot Cushings	A. Bearden	.25

Notes

1 Note on John S. Majors for five hundred dollars due 13th day of December 1857 — 500.00

1 Note on J. B. Cain for thirty five dollars due 25th Dec. 1859 — 35.00

1 Note on A. Bearden for thirteen dollars and thirty five Cents due Feb. 3rd 1859

Sworn to before Me
W. W. Williams, Clerk

(p 149) Amount returned by JOHN W. SHAW, administrator of E. G. MURPHEY, deceased Not Charged on the book of deceased.

1859		
Mar 2	Amount received of M.S. Draughon C & M	20.40
Mar 5	" " W. C. Pinson, on acct.	7.39
" "	" " R. Bobo Tax receipt	3.95
" "	" " James Mallory Cast	
	Dan Hudgens	.50
" "	Amount received of John H. Shephard	
" "	judgements in favor of Stephens Watson & Cost	28.28
" "	Amount paid G. W. Whitehead	10.00
" "	Amount received from E. L. Williams Oct.1859	6.48
Mar 22	Amount of Cost from W. J. Gossett	.50
May 5	Amount of Judgement & Cost against W. Bryant	
	for H. W. Turner	79.00
Apr 11	Amount J. J. Wilson Act 168 lb Bacon	13.44
	In stock 220 lbs Bacon	11.00
June 3	Cost of Warrant on B. D. Dye	
" 23	Amount of Judgement against W. Slayden	6.30
" "	Amount received from W. W. Williams S.C.	170.87

June 23	Amount of loaned Money from Jesse Shearon on Note	36.05
"	R. J. Mallory 141 poplar Trees $1	141.00
	Amouht received from Chancery Clerk Davidson County	4.00
	Amount paid by Sam Rosson on acct.	.25
	Amount paid by H. R. Felts on acct.	.22
	Amount of act on E. R. Clifton March 23rd	1.50
	Amount of act on Thomas Pace, dec.	.12
	Amount of Judgement against J. H. Majors for G. W. Murphey	26.60
	Amount of Cost on execution Jones & Cross	2.65
	Amount of cost paid by H. W. Turner	3.50
	Amount paid by Henry Harris	.35
	Amount paid by G. W. Gossett for Sutton Claim Sept. 21st 1857	50.00
	Amount of cost paid by Has. W. Hunt	1.00
	Amount of cost paid by J. J. Wilson	2.00
	Amount paid by A. J. Bright for flour	2.25
	Amount received from Cheatham County Ex office	30.00
	Amount paid by R. King	1.00
	Amount paid by B. F. Binkley	2.00
	Chancery Clerk at Clarksville	.65
	Amount received from H. Maxey	2.35

(p 150) Settlement of N. J. ALLEY, Admr. of the estate of W. S. SHEPHARD, dec. Jan. 24, 1860.

N. J. Alley, admr. of the estate of W. S. Shephard Dr.

To Amount due him as guardian as shown by settlement with Clerk of the County Court of Robertson County 115.36

Cr.

By Martha Shepard act	15.00
" H. J. Shows proven act	39.08
" E. T. Herron proven act	8.50
" E. G. Hudgens proven act	6.15
" Shaw and Brothers proven act	2.35
" Allowance to administrator	10.00
" Clerk for bond	2.00
" Letters of administration	.50
Copy of same	.50
For this settlement and recording same .50	80.54
Amount due on settlement	30.78

Settlement of JOHN S. MAJORS Administration of the estate of HAYWOOD BEARDEN , dec. Made on the 6th day of January 1860 .

John S. Jamors, Admr. of the estate of H. Bearden, deceased

To Amount of inventory

Cr.

By G. A. Edwards proven act	42.72
" W. E. Clifton froven act	1.65
" G. W. Gossetts receipt	6.00
" H. C. Paces act	6.25
" H. J. Shaws proven act	82.37
" H. Lyle Tax receipt 1856	5.25
" L. Watts proven act	4.30
" John Hunters proven act	10.07

By George Eleazer proven act	13.20
" G. H. Akins proven act	5.93
" H. C. Paces proven act	18.10
" A. Bearden proven act	118.42
" H. C. Paces proven act	24.65
" Tax receipt 1858	5.04
" Clerk for bond	2.00
" Letters administration	.50
" Copy of Sames	.50
" Recording inventory	.53
Order lay off years provision	.25
For Copy of same	.25
	347.98

(p 151)

For recording Rept Commissioners	.25
" Order confirming same	.25
Order to lay of dower	.25
Copy of same	.25
Recording report and Commissioner	.25
Order Confirming the same	.25
Recording four Confirming bonds	2.00
Allowance to Administrator	30.00
Clerk for settlement & rec'd same	1.47
Henry Naney proven act	8.75
D. C. Blanks proven act	2.02
G. A. Edwards for Coffin for Child	10.00
	403.72
Balance due	532.88
Cr. by Thomas M. Williams Note insolvent	26.75
Cr. by R. H. Weakleys Note insolvent 14.55	41.30
Amount due legatees on settlement	491.58
Cr. by Cash paid for groceries for widow	28.95
Amount due Legatees	462.63

An inventory of the personal estate of J. L. BELL, dec. Died 9th Feb. 1860.

Cash on hand	7430.00
A Bill on Phillips & Son of Considerate due 6 Months from date	3000.00

From some unsettled act other small accounts, will be due the estate, heirships in Montgomery Bells estate

List of Negroes belonging to the estate.

Names	ages	Names	ages
Sally	4	Abe	10
Harry	1	Malinda	8
Bob	60	Elizah	28
Mary	53	Miles	32
Mulacha	21	Elizah	6
Jacob	19	Grace	14
Jeff	8	Melinda	12
Luke	35	Murrah	10
Sally	20	William	32
Malachi	18	Milly	32
Jeff	16	Alexander	10
Jane	12	Polly	8
Asberry	14	William	6

(p 152)

Names	Ages	Names	Ages
Alferd	4	Anthony	60
Doctor	45	Dave	50
Green	42	Jacob	55
Peter	55	Elijah	48
John	55	Fred	18
Harry	50	Ceely	53
John	35	Charity	9
Berry	70	Meredith	34
Harty	55	John	42
Zechriah	38	Amy	15
Elias	36	Lizzie	13
Esther	7	Judith	60
Reuben	70	Asberry	58
Betsey	55	Letilda	55
Levisa	35	Jim	40
Wesley	36	Green	28
Reuben	26	Malissa	18
Elizah	18	Elizah	3
Huntock	16	Letita	2
Columbus	12	Lewis	55
Thomas	10	Squire	22
Jane	8	Lewis	18
Catherine	6	John	16
Charlie	4	Altemo	10
Matthew	2	Billy	60
Judith	32	Polly	55
Lily	14	Wesely	50
Allen	15	Wash	48
Jack	7	Anderson	28
Matilda	5	Charles	24
Ben	60	John	22
Lily	46	Benny	20
Penny	16	George	18
Betsey	11	Charley	17
Harry	69	Jackson	38
Henry	40	Sam	25
Clay	30	Alfred	23
Sophia	19	Cambridge	21
Mary	17	Daniel	55
Andrew	15	Dick	70
Annie	45	Jere	55
Willis	45	Anthony	25
Sam	43	Ben	40
Hiram	24	Lewis	53
Moses	22	Sue	70

(p 153)

Names	Ages	Names	Ages
Browley	90	Leander	45
Austin	43	Tom	55
Redin	18	Elias	26
Alfred	36	Jim	40
Jim	3		

Total Slaves No 125

List of other property of J? L. BELL, deceased

Mules 82 Horses 6 Cattle 114 Sheep 75
Hogs & Pigs 68 Yoke Oxen 11 Goats 11 Plows 16

Hoes 14 Carts 6 One horse Cart 1 Wagon 9 Barrouch 1
Buggy 1 Pairs of harness 70 Blacksmith Tools 2
Set furnace tools 1 Set fork tools 1 Set Wagon Make tools 1
Slides 3 Collum shovels 26 Mattock 20 Axes 12
Stacks Fodder 6 Stacks hay 4 Barrels Corn 800
Bushels Millet seed 130 Pounds bacon 10,000 Heating stoves 2
Dining Table 1 A lot of kitchen furniture
At the Worley furnace
A lot of pig Metal at Worley Furnace perhaps 20 Tons

The above is a true and oerfect inventory of all the goods and chattel rights and Credits of the said J. L. Bell deceased which have come to My hands possession or Knowledge or hands of any other persons for Me to the best of My Knowledge and belief. This 29th day of March 1860

N. C. Stockard
Adm. of J. L. Bell, dec.

Sworn to before Me April 2, 1860
W. W. Williams, Clerk

(p 154) Account of the sale of the property of M. D. L. WILLIAMS, deceased on the 17th day of March 1860, sold by H. E. HYDE, administrator.

L. B. Harris	1 Avery plow	5.00
I. J. Wilson	1 Do Do	4.00
J. D. Nicholson	1 Dorris plow	.50
Jack Stack	1 grind stone	6.75
G. Nicholson	1 lot harness	.40
G. Nicholson	1 " "	.25
W. T. Pace	2 pair stretchers	.65
J. E. Turner	1 Chain & stretcher	1.80
Willis Hyde	1 " "	3.75
Willis Hyde	1 " "	3.50
S. H. Bracey	1 shave Collar	1.00
A. H. Walker	1 lot ploughs	.25
S. H. Bracey	1 large plow	2.50
S. H. Bracey	1 Do Do	.55
B. Paschael	1 Grub hoe	.62
S. H. Bracey	1 shovel & hoe	.35
J. Z. Hudgens	1 shovel	.35
John Stack	1 Cross Cut saw	8.75
G. B. Ellis	1 Cross Cut saw	3.70
P. I. Nally	1 Pistol	1.00
H. Head	1 waggon line	1.30
W. Hawkins	1 pair steelyards	2.30
S. H. Bracey	1 set Wagon geer	4.00
G. Nisholson	1 Do Do Do	2.75
J. W. Shearon	1 lot bridles	.60
G. Nicholson	1 set front geer	3.35
D. H. Felts	1 set Do Do	2.50
J. J. Wilson	1 plow point	.30
T. B. Harris	1 plow point	.30
B. Paschall	1 lot Chains	1.35
G. F. Ellis	1 Bell	.50
R. Head	1 Bell	.50
Thos. Owen	1 Plain	1.50
B. Shearon	1 shovel & double tree	.45
Hugh Head	1 lot Chains	2.00

B. L. Williams	1 plow point	.10
W. C. Nichols		
B. L. Williams		
L. Fox		
G. F. Ellis	3 draw Knives	1.25
Widow	1 Hand Axe	1.00
J. B. Hunt	1 Do Do	1.00
D. H. Felts	2 draw Knives	.85
Geo. Basford	1 Croze & Howell	.90
(p 155)		
Widow	1 Draw Knife	.50
Joshia Winters	3 pair Compassesses	.35
L. Fox	1 square	.50
Henry W. Turner	12 in Auger	1.10
E. C. Herron	1 Draw knife	.65
L. G. Inman	2 Augers	.60
J. Walker	1 draw knife	.20
J. N. Bennett	2 draw Knives	.55
W. J. Jackson	1 saw set	.45
S. Bobbit	1 Knife	.40
J. Stack	2 sythe blades	.20
D. S. Adams	1 Knife	.30
Ben Stack	1 Croze & C.	.25
D. S. Adams	1 Adze	.30
J. Walker	1 pair Croze plain	.25
E. S. Williams	2 Adz	.60
R. Murphey	Do	.10
W. Nichols	1 lot irons	.20
W. Byran	1 saw set & C.	.50
W. Byran	1 Brace & bit	.90
Wm. Darden	1 lot Chisels	.90
H. Harris	1 Bell	.10
W. Byran	1 lot irons	.15
P. Love	1 hand saw	.25
Wm. Darden	1 hand saw	.30
P. I. Nolly	1 buck saw	.50
J. Walker	1 Jointer	.85
N. Walker	1 Jointer	1.00
R. L. Angford	1 Wagon & whip	.30
Widow	1 sheet	.15
John Hudgens	1 Wedge	.25
P. I. Nolly	1 Wet stone	.25
J. Walker	1 Fan Mill	13.00
J. Walker	1 Work bench	.25
R. Langford	1 stack Wry	12.00
Pat Williams & Co.	1 stack oats	34.25
Pat Williams & Co.	1 stack fodder	4.25
L. Fox	680 Bundles Oats	17.00
B. Stack	1 lot shucks	5.00
R. J. Mallory	5 Barrels Corn $4	20.00
Irad Morgan	5 Barrels Corn 3.80	19.00
Ed Clifton	5 " " 3.75	18.75
John Stack	1 Waggon saddle	3.35
G. W. Murphey	1 Waggon	40.00
Wm. Darden	1 pair stretcher	2.05
J. J. Wilson	1 Chain	.35
(p 156)		
George Basford	1 lot Corn	1.63

John Stack	1 lot Corn	1.30
W. Byran	1 stave Machine	.50
L. J. Inman	1 lot hoops & c.	.15
Geo. Basford 2760	staves 20¢	5.52
Geo. Basford	sow & pigs	2.00
Widow	sow & 2 pigs	6.00
W. Stroud	580 Headings 20	5.52
P. A. Williams	sow & 4 pigs	5.75
W. T. Pace	1 sow and pigs	6.60
Widow	1 Gray Mare	20.00
M. W. Hunter	1 Bay Horse	50.00
Widow	1 Trundle bed	1.00
Widow	1 Clock	.50
B. F. Pace	6 Chairs	5.60
Widow	1 Dress table	.50
L. Fox	1 shot gun	8.50
J. J. Bradley	1 drawing table	5.00
Widow	1 safe	1.25
G. Wilson	1 hand saw	1.60
Widow	1 Table	.10
D. S. Adams	1 Raw Hyde	.25
D. S. Adams	1 Powder flask	.20
H. Smith	1 Oxen	1.25
Widow	1 half bushel	.80
Widow	3 sheep	1.00
Widow	1 pair scales	.50
Widow	1 pair fire dogs	1.00
Widow	2 baskets	.25
S. H. Bracey	2 single trees	.10
C. C. Williams	1 Axe	.75
W. Byran	Oats35	.15
R. Langford	1 Feed trough	.50

Sworn to before Me May 7th 1860
W. W. Williams, Clerk

(p 157) Inventory of the Notes Accounts & C. of the estate of M. D. L. WILLIAMS, deceased rendered by H. E. HYDE, administrator.

1 Note on R. W. Johnson for four hundred four Months after date and dated the 5th day of Dec. 1859 payable to the order of J. B. Kellebrew at the Northen Bank of Tennessee	400.00
Dec. 5th 1859 Credit one hundred and forty dollars	140.00
Balance due on said Note	260.00
Interest on same	
1 Note on E. S. Hickunmth and W. H. Farmer due two Months after date and dated 6th day of February 1860 for	300.00
1 other Note on E. S. Hickunuth and W. H. Farmer due 6th April 1860 for	300.00
Interest on same	
One Note on Isach Winters due 25th July 1859 for	7.40
Interest on same	
1 account on Willis C. Nichols due 1859	4.00
1 account on Willis C. Nichols	3.75

Settlement of A. BOYTE, Administrator of the estate of THOMAS PERRY, deceased Made on the 15th April 1860 Confirmed on the 7th day of May 1860

A. Boyt, Administrator of the estate of Thos. Perry, deceased.

To Amount of inventory	180.05
Contra	
L. J. Perdue proven act	4.00
E. L. Darrow proven act	2.05
Chas. Vedder receipt	1.00
Tax receipt 1858	1.40
Ennis Hooper receipt	1.60
Thos. J. Shaw proven act	9.60
H. J. Shaws proven act	2.80
James Connell for Coffin	5.90
G. W. Felts proven act	1.00
Henry Harris proven act	2.27
W. L. Gower receipt Clerk at sale	1.00
G. W. McQuary Surveyor	6.00
Recording Deed	1.00
Conveying Chain	1.00
Conveying Chain	.50
A. Boyte proven act	8.00
Allowance to administrator	15.00
Clerks fee	4.80
	68.92
Amount due legatees	111.13

(p 158) JAMES S. STEWART, administrator of the estate of JAMES STEWART Dr.

To Amount of inventory	
Contra	
By G. W. Rasberry for waiting on deceased	10.50
J. G. Smith for Coffin	15.00
Advertising insolvent	1.60
Shrouding	6.50
Allowance to administrator	40.00
Clerk for bond	2.00
Letters fo administration	.50
Copy of same	.50
Recording Inventory	1.30
Filing suggestions for insolvency	.50
7 Claims filed 10	.70
For schedule available assets	.50
Stating an act porata	.55
For recording same	.25
Order of Court Confirming settlement	.25
Order to pay Money into Court	.50
Cost paid in suit against W. W. Smith	1.75
Claims against W. W. Smith, In	3.59
Claim against Chas. Gent	1.93
Claim against E. J. Hunt In	2.12
Claim against R. H. Weakley In	.87
Making settlement	1.00
Claim on Susan Smith In	22.20
Amount of estate	559.47

The assets pf the Estate of JAMES STEWART, deceased is 559.47

Claim filed against it	1262.97

pays c44.3m on the dollar

Creditor names	amt Claims	Amt Received
R. M. Patton adm	1175.55	520.77
James E. Justice	6.00	2.68
L. J. Perdue	31.54	13.79
H. J. Shaw	2.30	1.02
H. J. Shaw	35.65	15.97
R. J. Mallory	8.12	3.60
G. W. McCarley	3.70	1.64
	1262.86	559.47

(p 159) A list of the property sold of B. L. PACK, deceased sold on the 7th April 1860

J. W. Simpkins	1 Yoke Oxens	102.50
Francis Pack	1 Bay Horse	138.00
Francis Pack	Hire of Negro boy	18.00
L. P. Pack	1 Harrow	2.00
Wm. Bennett	Rent of land above the ditch	50.00
Wm. Bennett	Rent of land below ditch	42.00
		352.00

Inventory of the property of R. D. FELTS, deceased sold by H. DOWLEN, adm on the ------ 1860

1 Candle stand	Nancy Felts	2.00
1 Book of religon	Nancy M. Felts	.50
2 books Eastern World	Nancy M. Felts	2.00
1 Book Volume	Nancy M. Felts	1.00
1 Clock	Nancy M. Felts	1.50
1 Cross Cut saw	Nancy M. Felts	2.00
1 Frow & Plow	Nancy M. Felts	.10
1 Grind stone	Nancy M. Felts	.50
5 Head sheep	Nancy M. Felts	5.00
6 Head sheep	H. H. Binkley	6.00
1 plow & horse	John Bennett	5.00
1 shovel plow	N. M. Felts	.10
1 pair Chains & harness	N. M. Felts	.50
Cash received from W. W. Felts		.50
		26.70

(p 160) Inventory of the estate of SAM W. GREEN, deceased

1 Note on Caroline Miles for	6.00
Credit for 345	2.75
1 Note on G. W. Miles due	5.00
1 Note on A. Pucket due	9.38
1 Note on W. H. Harris due	2.60
1 Note on John G. Green due 23rd January 1860	110.00
1 Note on G. Green due for	81.50

April 7th 1860

Sworn to April 7th 1860

W. W. Williams, Clerk

Will of THOMAS A. BASFORD, Dec. Cheatham County Tenn.

In the Name of God Amen.

I Thomas A. Basford being of sound Mind and disposing Memory do hereby Make My last will and Testament revoking all

others.
First, I give to My wife Eliza W. Basfordqand My son Thomas I. Basford the tract of land on which I live with all its appertances and so much of the tract of land which I bought of Kinchen Basford as lies West of the field Now Cleared on the same with one sorrel horse and one black colt. With all My cattle, but one white Cow and also three beds with their furniture and two bedsteads and Bureau with the balance of the household and kitchen furniture and ten head of sheep and one spinning wheel and farming utensils all of which they are to have and to hold forever unless My widow should again Marry, then said lands to revert in to to My son Thomas J. Basford.
Secondly, I give to My daughter Marina Ann, Mary J. and Rebecca Ann Basford the remainder of the tract of land that I bought of Kinchen Basford and the balance of My perishable property after all My just debts are paid this 17th day of April 1860.

his
Thomas A. X Basford
mark

Attest:
M. Ramey
W. J. Gossett
B. F. Wilson
T. J. Harris

(p 161) The last will and Testament of MARTHA A. HARRIS of Cheatham County and State of T nnessee.

I Martha Harris, considering the uncertainty of this Mortal life, and being of sound mind and Memory so Make and publish this My last will and testament IN Manner and form following (that is to say)
First, I Want My debts and burial expenses paid, and lastly as to the rest and residue, and remainder of My real and personal estate goods and chattels of what kind and Nature forever I wish sold on a twelve Months credit and the proceeds arising from said sale. I wish equally divided between My seven Children (To Wit) My daughters Lucinda, Minerva and Catherine W. Harris My four sons Isaic N. Etherid, Edwin C. and Hamilton P. Harris.
I hereby appoint sole executor of this My last will and testament My brother Plumer Williams and R. J. Stringfellow hereby revoking all former wills by me Made.

In Writing whereof I hereunto set My hand and seal this 18th day of June in the year of our Lord One thousand eight hundred and fifty six 1856

Martha A. Harris (SEAL)

The within instrument consisting of one sheet was now here subscribed by Martha A. Harris the testator in the presence of each of us and was at the same time declared by her last will and testament and we at her request signed our Names hereto as attesting witnesses. June 18th 1856

B. C. Robertson
Burgess Harris

(p 162) Settlement of G. W. HIGHLAND, adm. of M. T. HALE, deceased Dr.

To Amount 1st inventory or sale	2009.29
To Amount 2nd Inventory or sale	775.23
To Amount of Cash & Notes on hand	2442.33
	5226.85
Contra	
W. W. Williams receipt	1.00
W. G. Shelton receipt	5.00
F. A. Harris	2.00
Greenville Institute	65.00
Jo Hudson proven act	12.50
E. A. Hale receipt	143.50
W. W. Williams receipt Cost	8.00
John Hooper proven act	16.25
W. Binkley proven act	14.00
Tho. J. Crouch receipt	16.00
J. C. Hales proven act	8.05
E. A. Hales receipt	345.31
B. F. Binkley receipt	1.00
G. W. McQuary receipt	3.00
J. C. Johnson Atty. Receipt	15.00
B. C. Robertson Account	11.48
Thomas J. Shaw Med Bill	10.00
J. V. Johnson Atty. bill	20.00
Josh Brown proven act	27.68
Cary Pritchett act	3.00
D. A. Wilkins proven act	43.60
J. A. Shearon receipt	1.00
G. W. Dozier proven act	1.50
W. H. Stewart Receipt	5.00
McKevin & Bailey	95.00
J. T. Darden M. Bill	20.00
Tax Receipt 1858	18.11
Insolvent Note	36.60
Allowance to Administrator	225.00
Cost laying off dower	8.30
Cash dividing slaves	8.30
Cost laying off year provision	6.05
Bond	2.00
Letters of administration & Copy	1.00
Recording Inventory	1.60
Order Confirming settlement	.25
Recording Bonds & Receipt	4.50
(p 163)	
2 years provisions	6.05
Settlement	1.60
J. J. Hentons proven act	2.06
Bal allowed admr.	25.00
Amount paid out by adm.	1230.29
Amount due the heirs	3996.56

Settlement of R. J. STRINGFELLOW, Adm. B. D. PACK.

R. J. Stringfellow adm. of B. D. Pack	Dr.
To Amount Inventory	1023.00
" Amount 2nd Inventory	23.40
" Amount Accounts	895.77
" Amounts Collected Not Charged	100.72
	2042.89

Contra

By J. C. Swiney proven act	1.00
" J. M. Brown " "	2.40
" D. C. Jones " "	23.85
" L. J. Pack " "	,9.00
" A. N. Strouds " "	2.00
" Perdue and Shearon proven act	15.60
" J. H. Fulghum proven act	9.40
" Thos. A. Jackson proven act	12.95
" J. J. Hinton proven act	19.40
" William Harris Note	13.27
" R. J. Stringfellow act	10.00
" Peter Jackson proven act	8.00
" D. Pernell proven act	5.75
" Thomas C. Morris Act	10.00
" R. H. Reeves proven act	8.46
" W. J. Osburn proven act	5.15
" A. D. Nicks	2.55
" Bon Howel act	2.00
" Cheatham County Tax	16.92
" W. B. Joslin Stayer	7.50
" E. S. Axum Note	17.10
" G. W. Brown receipt	1.00
" L. D. Packs account & Receipt	79.18
" W. H. Stuart	10.00
" L. D. Perdue paid tax	20.55
" A. P. Nicks act & receipt	10.76
" Daniel Brown	.85
" Elizabeth Packs act	40.00
" Joseph Harris act & receipt	11.50
(p 164)	
Stanfield Halley proven act	9.50
George M. Perdue act	25.75
R. J. Stringfellow Note	75.45
J. M. Larkin	3.00
W. J. Carter Act	62.80
W. J. Carter act	75.43
Henry Stewart	2.00
Thomas A. Jackson	2.00
H. T. Stringfellow act	30.00
J. M. Brown act	3.25
Bond	3.00
Recording Invenotry	1.50
Order to lay off dower	.25
Copy of same	.25
Recording commissioners report	.25
Order Confirming same	.25
Order to lay off provisions	.25
Copy of same	.25
Commissioners report	.25
Order Commissioners same	.25
Recording receipts and bonds	3.50
Recording receipts	.25
Allowance to administrator	100.00
Jo Brown Claim insolvent	5.25
H. T. Strigfellow	33.72
John W. Stevens	9.50

Sam Anderson	1.00
J. L. & John J. Bell	73.00
Amos Robertson	11.00
J. Appleton	1.40
Cary Pritchett	.25
James Parr	24.50
R. Dalton	20.00
	956.13
Amount due him	1086.70

(p 165) A list of the property sold by W. J. GOSSETT, Administrator of the estate of THO H. BASFORD, dec. on the 14 June 1860.

G. W. Basford	1 Brown Mare	45.00
B. M. Jordan	1 Wagon	50.50
J. A. Williams	12 sheep	13.50
B. M. Jordan	1 Bed	5.50
Joseph Kelly	1 set of	.65
G. W. Basford	1 Cow	17.00
M. J. Basford	1 side saddle	1.10
B. F. Basfor	1 box shoe tools	2.70
L. J. Basford 10 3/4 lb Wool		2.35
J. J. Wilson 1 receipt on J. J. Wilson		3.75
R. J. Mallory 1 Due Bill		1.85
J. J. Wilson	1 pair steelyards	.90
Sowrn to before Me July 2nd 1860		144.80

W. W. Williams, Clerk

Inventory of the personal estate of NANCY FRAZIER, deceased made by G. W. GOSSETT, Adm. on the 1st day of June 1860

Cash received from W. W. Williams his share of the slaves sold by order of the County Court of Cheatham	200.00
Amount received from John S. Majors Adm. her share of the personal estate	92.52
	292.52

Sworn to before Me June 1st 1860
W. W. Williams, Clerk

(p 166) Will of J. J. WOODSON State of Tennessee, Cheatham County.

I Joseph Woodson of the County aforesaid and rational do devise that My property be disposed of in the following way and Manner to Wit,

1st, I will that all My debts be paid out of My effects.

2nd, I will all My hand and effects remaining after paying all My debts against Me to My wife Martha Woodson to have and to hold, for the Mutual benefit of her and our Children during her Natural life and at her death to be equally divided between our Children.

3rd, I hereby invest My wife with the power to sell or dispose of this land at any time she May think proper and Make good the title to same.

4th, I further More appoint My wife My sole executrix to this My last will and Testament and that No bond or security be required of her for the execution of said will.

I Joseph Woodson in the presence of these Witnesses acknowledge this my last will and Testament revoking all others.
Signed 20th June 1860

J. J. Woodson (SEAL)

Nathan Morris
R. J. Mallory
J. J. Wilson

Will of G. W. DUKE

I, G. W. Duke do make and publish this as My last Will and Testament hereby revoking and Making Null and Void all other Wills by me at any time Made.
1st, I direct that My funeral expense and just debts be paid as soon after My death as possible out of any Monies that I may die possessed of or May first Come into the hands of My Wife.
2nd, I give and bequeath to My Wife Roda Ann all My household (p 167) and kitchen furniture also all of My stock consisting of Mules, Cattle and hogs and wagon and Buggie also all of the Money Notes and accounts that I May die possessed of and that she take the Money and purchase a tract of land such as she mau think Will suit her consulting her best friend as respects the purchase of the land for the use of her and My Children, Viz, Martha Ann, Erevina, Anner and Thoda Anne until My said Child Roda Anne arrives at the age of twenty one years and then the tract of land so purchased by My wife together with all the household and kitchen furniture stock and everything in possession or belonging to My wife to be sold on a Credit of twelve Months and the proceeds arising therefrom to be equally divided between My wife Rhoda Anne and My five Children Robert, Green Martha Anne Erevina Anna and Roda Anne.
This June 6th 1860.

Witness: G. W. Duke (SEAL)
R. J. Stringfellow
G. T. Harris

Inventory of the personal estate of J. G. SMITH, deceased sold by B. J. BARNES, on the 26th day of June 1860.

Purchaser Names	Articles sold	
H. C. Pace	1 Frow	.25
Tho. B 11	1 lot Trumpery	.30
John C. Weakley	1 lot Augers & C.	.50
Jonathan Smith	1 Cross Cut saw	.75
John T. Hooper	1 Barrel & C.	.60
Wash Smith	1 saddle	2.00
Jonathan Smith	1 Axe & C.	.35
Jonathan Fambrough	1 Grindstone	1.00
Jonathan Smith	1 sythe & Cradle	2.05
John Feilder	1 pair Geer	.25
Alwin Edwards	1 shovel	.50
J. L. Perdue	1 Kettle	1.10
Jonathan Smith	1 skillet & lid	.35
W. D. Weakley	1 oven & lid	.50
W. D. Weakley	1 pickle stand	.10
John Feilder	1 lard stand	.10
W. C. Perdue	1 Box	1.25
Mary Smith	1 lot shingles	.25

Wash Smith	1 lot Cooper tools	7.00
W. J. Stewart	1 lot tools	2.75
Wash Smith	1 pair saddle bags	1.50
Wash Smith	1 lantern	.55
W. H. Plaster	1 Jug	.35
Jonathan Snith	1 lot books	.55
A. Walker	1 lot books	.30
Mary Smith	1 Book	.35
Thomas Miles	1 Book	.25
John Feilder	2 Books	.35
Mary Smith	1 Clock	.50
Mary Smith	1 Chest	2.00
Mary Smith	1 Bed & stead	5.00

Continued on page 172

(p 168) Martha Harris, deceased

E. Harris	2 pair Hooks & C.	.50
E. Harris	1 Oven & 2 skillets	1.00
E. Harris	1 Tea Kettle & C.	1.00
E. Harris	1 pot & dish	.50
E. Harris	1 oven gridiron & C	.75
E. Harris	2 Flat irons	.60
E. Harris	1 Oven	.25
E. Harris	1 lrage Kettle	1.00
E. Harris	1 lot tin Ware	.50
E. Harris	1 large skillet	.75
E. Harris	1 lamp	.15
E. Harris	1 lot Cooper Ware	2.00
E. Harris	1 Bread sythe	.25
T. J. Pack	1 Mowing blade	.60
E. Harris	1 sythe & cradle	2.50
E. Harris	1 lot stone ware	.40
E. Harris	1 spinning wheel	1.00
E. Harris	1 spinning whell	2.00
E. Harris	1 Loom & geer	1.00
E. Harris	Warping Bars & C.	.25
Jo Harris	1 lot scrap Iron	1.00
E. Harris	2 iron Wedges & C	1.00
E. Harris	3 Axes	2.00
Mr. Burke	1 lot Carpenters tools	2.00
James Howell	3 old plows	.25
E. Harris	3 spades & C	1.00
E. Harris	1 log Chain	1.00
E. Harris	1 log Chain	2.00
E. Harris	2 plows & C	1.20
L. J. Pack	2 plows	2.50
E. Harris	1 Plow	3.20
E. Harris	2 plows	.20
E. Harris	1 Briar hook	.25
E. Harris	3 weeding hoes	.40
E. Harris	2 grubbing hoes	.75
E. Harris	1 pair geer	1.00
E. Harris	1 pair geer	1.50
E. Harris	1 pair geer	1.60
E. Harris	1 pair geer	1.00
E. Harris	1 Bridle	.70
E. Harris	1 Bridle	.75
E. Harris	1 Fan Mill	2.00

E. Harris	1 Measuring Tub & C.	.75.
E. Harris	1 Ox Cart & C	9.00
(p 169)		
E. Harris	1 wagon & bed	70.00
E. Harris	1 Yoke Oxen	63.00
E. Harris	1 stack Fodder	4.00
E. Harris	1 stack oats	14.50
E. Harris	1 Do Do	13.00
E. Harris	1 Do Do	8.00
E. Harris	1 lot oats	.50
E. Harris	1 Cow & Calf	15.00
E. Harris	1 Cow & Calf	14.00
E. Harris	1 Cow & Calf	16.00
E. Harris	1 Cow & Calf	17.00
F. L. Pack	1 white faced steer	9.50
A. Smith	1 Cow & Calf	14.00
L. D. Pack	1 Bell & Collar	2.10
L. D. Pack	1 Heifer	8.75
L. D. Pack	1 red steer	17.25
L. D. Pack	1 red steer	17.25
L. D. Pack	1 white faced steer	8.00
L. D. Pack	1 white rump heifer	13.75
L. D. Pack	1 Yearling	8.25
L. D. Pack	1 Black Bull	5.10
L. D. Pack	1 Dunn Bull	4.00
L. D. Pack	1 white heifer	4.25
L. D. Pack	1 brindle heifer	3.25
L. D. Pack	1 short tail bull	10.75
E. Harris	1 Cow	20.00
Jo Harris	1 black Cow	13.50
E. Harris	8 head hog	23.25
E. Harris	8 head hogs	59.50
J. N. Harris	3 sows & 20 pigs	35.50
J.N. Harris	1 sorrel Mule	100.00
E. Harris	1 Brown Mule	100.00
E. Harris	1 Gray Mule	145.50
J. N. Harris	1 Bay Mule	19.25
J. N. Harris	1 sorrell filly	91.00
J. N. Harris	1 sorrell filly	91.00
E. Harris	1 Brown filly	61.00
Lucinda Harris	1 Bay Horse	125.00
Minerva Harris	1 Bay Mare & Colt	100.00
E. Harris	26 Head sheep 205	53.50
E. Harris	7 lambs 155	10.85
Brunel Jackson	10 head sheep 150	15.00
James Howell	11 head sheep 140	15.40
J. N. Harris	200 lb bacon sides 18 3/4	37.50
J. W. Harris	238 lb Bacon sides 16	16.08
J. W. Harris	200 lb showlders 12½	25.00
(p 170)		
J. N. Harris	81 lbs shoulders 14½	11.75
J. N. Harris	152 lbs Ham 12 3/4	19.38
J. N. Harris	50 lbs lard 13 3/4	6.87
J. N. Harris	50 lbs lard 12 3/4	6.38
J. N. Harris	100 lbs lard 12½	12.50
J. N. Harris	2 lard stands	.50
J. N. Harris	1 lard stand	.10

J. N. Harris	1 Barrel	.40
J. N. Harris	100 lbs seed Cotton	3.00
Jas. Harris	1 old Cutting knife	.05
Wm. Tally	22½ Bu wheat 140	31.50
J. N. Harris	36 " " 155	55.80
J. N. Harris	34 lbs wool 35	11.90
J. N. Harris	1 Table	.15
J. N. Harris	1 Bed stead & Clothing	17.25
J. N. Harris	1 lounge	2.00
J. N. Harris	1 Book case	4.00
J. N. Harris	1 Bure au & Cloth	8.25
Lucinda Harris	1 looking glass	1.00
J. N. Harris	1 small table	1.00
Minerva Harris	1 Bed stead & Clothing	13.00
Lucinda Harris	1 Clock	.50
Catherine Harris	1 pair & Irons	.75
Minerva Harris	1 pair & irons	.75
Minerva Harris	1 table & Cloth	5.00
Minerva Harris	1 Candle stand	.10
Minerva Harris	1 Cupboard	5.00
Minerva Harris	1 bed stead & Clothing	17.50
Minerva Harris	1 Reel	.25
Minerva Harris	1 bed stead & Clothing	19.25
Minerva Harris	1 bed stead & Clothing	16.00
Minerva Harris	1 Chest	.25
Minerva Harris	1 Table	1.75
J. N. Harris	1 looking glass	.10
J. N. Harris	9 Chairs 70	6.30
J. N. Harris	1 lot China ware	.80
Miberva Harris	3 set plates 30	.90
Minerva Harris	3 pitchers	1.00
Minerva Harris	1 lot glass ware	1.05
Minerva Harris	1 set knives & fork	1.55
Minerva Harris	1 Brass Kettle	1.50
J. N. Harris	1 grind stone	1.55
Minerva Harris	1 wash stand	.05
Lucinda Harris	1 Bible	.25
Lucinda Harris	1 lot books	.25
(p 171)		
Minerva Harris	4 Books	.30
Minerva Harris	42 head geese 10	4.20
Minerva Harris	1 lot poultry	1.10
Minerva Harris	1 stone Jar & C	.30
J. N? Harris	2 sheep	2.00
J. N. Harris	116 lbs sugar 10	11.60
J. N. Harris	84 lbs Coffee	13.44
J. N. Harris	2 Bushels Salt 45	.90
J. N. Harris	2 sides upper leather 12	4.00
E. Harris	1¼ Bu Millet seed	1.87
E. Harris	2 Barrels Corn 3.75	75.00
E. Harris	20 Bushels rubbage Corn 40	8.00
E. Harris	3164 lbs Hay	31.64
E. G. Sears prâvate sale	4 Head Beef Cattle	75.80
Cash left on hand		387.00

One Note on Tho. Pawk & D. C. Jones due the 1st day of November 1860 with interest from dates dated on the 17th March 1860 for 20.00

One Note on Joseph Harris due on the 3rd day of March 1860 for 40.00
One Note on L. J. Perdue due on the 1st day of January 1861 for 161.00
One account on A. P. Nicks for balance on Corn sold to him by Martha Harris before her death 95.00

Sworn to before me on the 6th day of August 1860
W. W. Williams, Clerk

(p 172) Amount brot from page 167

Mary Smith		
Wash Smith	1 Bedstead	10.00
Mary Smith	1 watch	5.00
James H. Williams	1 lot of old lumber	.50
M. M. Chamblis	1 work bench	1.00
W. D. Weakley	1 trunk	.40
A. J. Pardue	4 sheep	5.40
A. J. Perdue	5 sheep	5.00
J.L. Perdue	1 small bull	4.00
J. H. Williams	1 heifer	4.00
J. H. Williams	1 white heifer	11.30
Mary Smith	1 spotted heifer	7.00
J. Fambrough	1 Bull	9.25
William Smith	1 Cow & Calf	14.00
L. L. Read	1 Bay Mare	135.00
W. C. Perdue	1 Horse Mule	110.00
W. H. Stewart	1 Mare Mule	51.00
J. H. Williams	1 lot lumber	5.96
J. T. Hooper	1 lot posts	.85
J. T. Hooper	1 lot Cherry lumber	5.50
J. T. Hooper	1 lot Walnut lumber	24.38
Wm. McFadden	1 pile lime	.55
H. C. Pace	1 lot shingles	10.98
John T. Hooper	1 log wagon	3.50
Wash Smith	1 lot twist hoops	.10
M. M. Chambliss	1 lot " "	.25
M. M. Chambliss	1 lot barrels	49.00
Wash Smith	2 Jointers	.10
Wash Smith	1 lot staves	2.50
Jonathan Smith	5 Bushels wheat	4.80
W. J. Stewart	5 " "	4/50
WashSmith	1 lot hoop poles	.10
Wash Smith	1 side upper leather	1.20
		525.95

Inventory of THO. M. and E. A. HALE, Administrstor of S. P. HALE' deceased.

Cash received from G. W. Highland, administrator of M. T. Hale, deceased 666.09
Credit by difference in his lot of Negroes, Amount Cash 566.09
3 Slaves Woman 45, Boy 20 Child 3 Months
(p 173) Accounts

One Account on G. A. Edwards (B) 9.63
One Account on Isaic Hollis (N) 3.00
One Account on R. W. Denny (B) 10.00
One Account on A. Edwards (G) 10.05

One Account on D. C. Clark bal (G)	10.00
One Account on Wm. Mayfield (B)	12.47
One Account on Wm. Robertson (B)	8.00
One Account on G. A. Edwards (B)	3.00
One Account on H. H. Shaw (GO	6.50
One Account on L. J. Perdue (G)	2.00
One Account on J. W. Smith (D)	38.37
One County Claim	20.00
One County Claim	4.50

A list of the property sold by W. J. GOSSETT, administrator if THOMAS A. BASFORD, deceased on the 17th Aug.1860

Purchasers Names	Articles sold	
Jacob Stack	1 Coulter & plough	.10
M. A. Bryne	1 lot old ploughs	.10
M. A. Bruce	1 lot Geer	.55
M. A. Bruce	1 plow	.35
M. A. Bruce	1 two horse plow	.30
E. W. Basford	1 Bed & furniture	10.00
E. W. Basford	1 Bed & furniture	9.20
P. W. Randolph	3 Bed quilts	2.55
E. W. Basford	1 Clock	2.00
E. W. Basford	1 Chest	1.10
M. J. Basford	1 spinning wheel	.75
M. Raney	1 Bed stead	.80
E. W. Basford	1 Heifer	4.00
E. W. Basford	1 Cow & Calf	5.00
E. W. Basford	1 Filly	10.00
E. W. Basford	5 sheep	7.10
J. S. Williams	1 pot	.55
M. Raney	1 Oven	.25
M. Raney	1 Kettle	2.00
E. W. Basford	1 Kettle	.50
J. I. Wilson	1 double tree	.55
E. W. Basford	1 sugar chest	.20
M. J. Basford	1 trunk	.10

Sworn to before Me Sept. 3rd 1860.
W. W. Williams, Clerk

(P 174) Amount of property sold by B. J. BARNES, administrator of P. H. WEAKLEY, deceased Aug. 25th 1860.

Purchasers Names	Articles sold	
Clobe Snaders	3 Books	.40
H. P. Poole	1 lot Bottles	.05
A. J. Teasley	1 Brush & C	.10
H. P. Poole	1 Jug	.05
George Shores	1 Razor & strop	1.00
D. L. Stewart	1 Bridle & saddle	6.10
John J. Fambrough	1 Pistol	4.25
J. J. Everett	1 Trunk	2.00
One Account on J. J. Everett		2.00
One Note on A. Furson due 24th April 1860 for		75.00
Cash on hand		4.20

Inventory of the personal estate of JOSEPH WILLIS, deceased sold January 4th 1860 by E. S. GLEAVES, administrator

Purchasers Names Articles sold

C. D. Lawrence	1 Grub Hoe	.70
R. H. Reding	1 lard stand	2.00
Harris Dowlen	1 Basket onions	.40
R. H. Reding	1 hand saw & hatchet	1.35
James W. Harris	1 Drawing knife	.75
R. H. Reding	1 square	.50
R. H. Reding	1 Curry Comb & brush	.50
R. H. Reding	1 lot Books	5.00
R. H. Reding	1 Bed stead	4.00
Thomas Tine	1 Tub & Onions	.50
R. H. Reding	1 Hilling Hoe	.65
Geo. W. Hunt	1 Rake	.30
Geo. W. Hunt	1 spade	.70
Henry Harris	2 Axes & C	.10
R. H. Reding	1 Plow	.50
Thomas Tine	3 Barrels	.10
Daniel Mosier	4 Barrels	.15
R. H. Reding	1 Barrel & Vinegar	1.00
R. H. Reding	1 Cutting knife	1.00
Mrs Willis	1 Buggy & Harness½	20.00
Henry Harris	1 Doz Goards	.10
R. H. Reding	1 lamp	.20

(p 175)

Amount brought up	40.50
Notes and Accounts	
One Note on L. E. Gleaves due 24th Feb, 1858 for	300.00
One Note on I. Kelly due Sept. 1st 1858 Interest	69.50
For	261.00
One Note on Nancy Byran due 25th December 1855 Int.	52.36
For	250.00
With a Credit of 100.00 Aug. 31st 1858 100.00	150.00
One Note on Nancy Byran due 24th Dec. 1854 for	225.00
Interest	64.90
With a Credit of 100.00 May 16th 1856	100.00
With a Credit of 75.00 Aug. 1st 1856 75.00 175.00	50.00
Interest	36.56
One Note on A. L. P. Green due Oct. 27th 1859 for	12.50
One draft ot Check on Missionary Society of M. E. Church South for $37.50 due Nine Months from date and dated Oct. 28th 1858 37.50 Interest 1.65	
One other draft or Check on M. E. Church South due twelve Months after date and dated Oct. 28th 1858 for	37.50
	1113.97

(p 176) JOSEPH KELLUM of J. R. TULLOS.

To Amount of Inventory	395.00
Contra	
Note to W. H. Shelton	470.73
Note to W. H. Shelton	560.62
Note to Moses Jones	31.05
Note to William Ellison	13.35
Note to William Ellison	.20
Note to J. M. Bagwell	11.70
Tax receipt 1859	13.35
Country & Law	42/40
Single and Moss Proven Account	22.36

Mrs Tullis cash paid her	35.00
Mrs Tullis cash paid her	18.50
J. P. Pegram Note	7.45
John Haley proven account	10.38
J. E. Cruchelor Note	45.23
John A. Clarks proven account	4.25
Henry Thorntons Note	10.30
Wm. Greers proven account	3.00
W. D. Hunters proven account	3.75
John A. Clarks proven account	20.65
Clerks receipt	6.25
Tax receipt 1858	14.06
Wm. Henry Note	4.22
W. T. Wagnan proven account	.85
Thos. M. Dunn proven account	1.50
Joseph Kellums Note	16.41
J. M. Bagwell	18.92
J. M. Bagwell	19.00
Mrs Tullos proven account	60.00
R. Pegram proven account	7.40
Moses Jones Note	6.17
Clerk for settlement	1.69
Recording receipt	.25
Allowance to administrator	150.00
Amount paid out	1662.94
Amount of Inventory off	395.00
Amount paid out over receipts	1267.94

(p 177) Will of THOMAS W. HARRIS, deceased

I Thomas W.Harris hereby declare this to be My last will and testament hereby revoking and Making void all former will by me at any time made.

First, I direct that My debts and funeral expenses be paid as soon as practicable out of any effects that I May die possessed of or May first come into the hands of My executor.

Secondly, I direct that all My property effects and estate of every kind and discription within the same be real personal or mixed be divided among all My Children in such Manner as to Make them equal If any Child of Mine has property settled on him or her or them from any other source than from Me. I wish it expressley understood that in that Case said Child or Children is to receive from estate only sufficient property to Make them worth in all enough to Amount to an equal Childs part of My estate Counting all that said Child or Children May have or ever derived from every source.

Lastly, I hereby sonstitute My son in law Sterling Walker My Executor to this My will.

This the 13th dau of October 1860

T. W. Harris (SEAL)

Signed sealed and acknowledged in our presence and we have subscrobed our Names hereto in the presence of each other and of the Testator, and at his request.

This October 13th 1860

P. H. Woodson
Levi Binkley

(p 178) Will of NEWSOM B. MAYS
State of Tennessee, Cheatham County.
I Newsom B. Mays being efflicted in body but of sound Mind and perfect Memory do make and publish this M_ last will and testament.
I first desire My soul to return to God who gave it and my body to be decently buried by the side of my beloved wife.
I then direct and desire that all My just debts and funeral expenses to be paid out of any Money I may leave on hand or due.
Then I give and bequeath unto My beloved brother Joseph Mays all My MOney Notes and accounts and everything I am legally entitled to in any way whatever either real or personal during his Natural life and at his death to My beloved Mother Eliza Mays if she id living and at her death I desire it all be divided equally between all My brothers and sisters as witness My hand and seal this 30th dayof Nov. 1860.
Test: N. B. Mays (SEAL)
James M. Dunn
J. M. Bagwell

One account of the sale Made of the estate of JAMES H. SMITH. deceased at his late residence in Cheatham County Tennessee after having advertised according to law.
Walter S. Smith to three hundred and forty six acres of land known as the home tract for 1140.00
James T. Mays to one hundred and seventeen acres of land Known as the Dillinghunty tract for $500.00
Nathan G. Smith to seventy three acres of land Known as the Shelton tract, sold by a quit Claim for 150.00
Nathan G. Smith to one tract of land Known as the free state tract containing fifty two acres for 55.00
The foregoing is a full and perfect account of the sale of the land of James H. Smith deceased (p 179) shown by the accompaning survey Marked "A" and Made part of this schedule by will to be sold notes with good secutity is taken at twelve and twenty four Months from date from the purchaser.
This 20th day of December 1860
Lucy Smith, Executor
Washington G. Smith, Executor

Settlement of W. G. SHELTON, administrator and S. C. of F. BALTHROP, deceased.
To amount inventories and sale Land and Negroes 14,947.16
Contra

By Smith Camp & Co proven act	5.50
" E. G. Eastman proven act	3.00
" B. H. Gibbs " "	26.50
" B. H. & R. B. Gibbs "	12.40
" W. Demunbra Receipt	2.50
" B. H. Gibbs "	5.75
" F. A. Harris "	10.00
" E. S. Gleaves "	.75
" G. W. McQuary "	10.00
" James G. Smith	27.00
" Willie W. Williams	6.28
" W. W. Williams "	8.50

CHEATHAM COUNTY

WILLS & INVENTORIES VOL A
1856 - 1871

(p 179) Cheatham County Wills and Inventories 1861.
Shown by the accompanying Survey marked A. and made part of this schedule by will to be sold, notes with good security is taken at twelve and twenty four months from date from the purchase.
This 20th day of December 1860
Lucy Smith Exr.
Washington G. Smith Exr.

Settlement of W.G. Shelton Adm.
& SC. of F. Balthrop dec.
To Amount Inventories & Sale, hand and negroes. $14,947.16

Contra.

By Smith Camp & Co.	proven acct	$5.50
By E.G. Eastman	" "	3.00
By B.H. Gibbs	" "	26.50
By B.H. & R.B. Gibbs	" "	12.40
By W. Demunbrane Receipt	Receipt	2.50
By B.H. Gibbs	"	5.75
By F.A. Harris	"	110.00
By E.S. Gleaves	"	75
By G.W. McQuary	"	10.00
By James G. Smith	"	27.00
By Willie W. Williams	"	6.28
By W.W. Williams	"	8.50
By J.J. Hinton	"	6.05
By G.M. Perdue	"	83.74
By R.J. Mallory	"	28.00
By Thos. G. Balthrop	"	50.00
By W.B. Hooper & son	"	9.83
By A.W. Stewart	"	15.00
By L.J. Perdue	"	7.36
Allowance to Adm. & Com.		423.67
Order & Judgement		75
Bill cost		40
Copying Bill cost		40
Spa to answer		75
Recording answer bonds		5.50
Recording and receipts		1.00
Making and recording Settlement		1.50
Filing Cause & order on same		50
H.C. Pace act & B. Miles Ins.		33.40
R.M. Ray. atty fee & Bal. H.C. Pace act.		28.72
		847.28
Amount due in settlements		14,099.86

(p 180) Settlement of James W. Hunt Admr. of J. King dec.
To Amount inventory 1,059.61

Contra.

By H.J. Shaw	Proven Acct	$58.35
By H.J. Shaw	"	275.79
By H?J. Shaw	Note	13.53
By H.J. Shaw		26.36
By W.W. Williams	Act.	3.66
By Thos. E Hudgens	Proven Acct	6.50
By W.L. Bradley		5.75
By Shaw & Wall		5.83
By E. Simmons	Proven acct	3.00
By James Walker		18.55
Tax 1859		1.28
Cheatham Watson & Co.		11.25
W.W. Williams		4.30
Thomas & Shaw adm.		5.15
J.W. Shaw adm.		1.50
Cash paid in case of Thos. W. Osborn	Cost	1.40
Balance on R.H. Allsys note		7.50
Thos. W. Osborn Insolvent		52.00
Jno. L. Hudgens out county		2.00
Jno. L. Hudgens, out county		176.00
Allowance to Administrator		60.00
Bonds and Receipts		1.75
Making and Recording Settlement		1.50
Order confirming Settlement		25
Amount due legatees		311.57
		748.10

Settlement of R.J. Mallory Exr. of Thomas Walker dec.

To Amount of Inventory. Dr.		3,518.16

Contra.

By Brown & Crotzer	Proven Acct.	26.72
By J.J. Hintons	Proven Acct	3.33
By W.W. Walker	"	10.97
By J.O. Hunter	"	98.39
By Shaw & Brothers	"	39.69
H.C. Pace	"	30.33
R.J. Mallory	"	131.00
H.R. Felts	"	2.65
J. Frazier Admr	Receipt	17.50
B.L. Williams	Proven Acct	1.50
James E. Justice	"	1.45
A.W. Stewart	"	24.50
(p 181) Amount of Inventory Brot up		3518.16

		597.01
Thomas A. Basford	Proven Acct	4.25
W.A. Morris	"	7.20
Alsey Jones	"	4.90
Tax Receipt 1858		25.20
Allen Hunter	"	1.00
G.A. Edwards	"	48.42
A.J. Teasley	"	19.00
E.L. Williams	"	25.25
H.J. Shaw	Note	100.00

Cash paid for Groceries		$51.30
J.W. Face	Proven Acct	1.00
I.A. Adkins	"	3.15
1 Barrel Flour		5.60
Allowance to Administrator		200.00
E.L. Williams	Com. & Surveyor	5.00
James H. Williams	Com. 2 da.	2.00
N. Morris	Com. 2 da.	2.00
R.T. Gupton	2 da.	2.00
Clerks Fee		15.20
W. Walker	Bad	26.35
W.B. Holland	"	3.25
Thomas Master		23.70
Z. Durham		69.00
H.P. Pool		47.35
		1289.13
Amount due heirs on settlement		2229.03

3rd Inventory of Sterling Walker admr of Jacob Bell dec. and hire of negroes from 10 March to 25th Dec. 1861

Mariah, woman W. C. Orman $9\frac{1}{2}$ months--$6.00	$57.00
Jim Boy, W.J. Gossett	83.12
Mary, Girl H. Dowlen	30.87
Parker, G.W. Bell	9.50
Thomas R. Bell	95
5 Barrels rent corn from Souel	20.00
5 Barrels rent corn from Morris & Mo.	17.50
1 Clifton	2.20
G.W. Bell	20.00
	241.14

(p 182) An account of sale of the property of Thos. W. Harris dec. Sold by Sterling Walker Exr. Nov. 26th 1860.

Articles	Purchasers names.	
1 plow & double tree	W.H. Stewart	$3.25
1 plow	A. Walker	1.75
1 tongue plow	N.H. Stewart	25
1 tongue plow	W.H. Stewart	30
1 Dimond plow	J.H. Harper	05
1 carey plow	A? H. Binkley	10
1 Tongue plow	E.T. Harris	1.00
1 " "	G.E. Harris	35
1 Do Do	A. Walker	4.00
1 Do Do	G.E. Harris	3.85
1 Do Do	W.H. Stewart	4.00
1 Do Do	G.W. Harris	4.00
1 collar	W.L. Hudgens	50
1 lot traces	G.W. Felts	25
1 grub hoe	G.E. Harris	25
1 Do Do	Harris Nicholson	25
2 Do Do	Ben Smith	65
1 Do Do	G.E. Harris	25
2 Do Do	Burgess Harris	25
2 Do Do	James Harris	40
2 Do Do	W.L. Hudgens	25

2 Do Do	N.H. Binkley	$0.35
1 Briar Hook	H.H. Binkley	.25
3 Axes	A.H. Walker	.10
1 saw &C	N.N. Binkley	.05
1 mat hoe	Thomas Bell	.50
1 shovell	G.E. Harris	.85
1 Do	W.L. Hudgens	.15
1 pair Steelyards	Henry Harris	.15
1 Do Do	N.N. Binkley	.20
1 lot trumpery	N.N. Binkley	.15
1-5 quarter auger	W.L. Hudgens	.25
1 inch Auger	J.W. Shearon	.20
1 lot Trumpery	N.N. Binkley	.05
2 Chissels	H.H. Binkley	.30
1 lot Irons	A.H. Walker	.05
1 Rench & hatchet	W.L. Hudgens	.25
1 Draw knife	Thomas Bell	.10
1 Frou	J.E. Turner	.10
2 Iron Wedges	J.W. Walker	.60
2 Do Do	W.L. Hudgens	.70
1 lot iron	James Walker	.20

(p 183) Amount brot up

1 Lot Trumpery &C	N.N. Binkley	.10
1 Hand Axe	A.E. Souel	1.05
1 Trowel	James Walker	.25
1 Tongue plow	A. Walker	.05
2 cart tyre	A.E. Souel	2.00
2 plow points	G.E. HARRIS	.20
2 Do Do	A. Walker	.20
2 Do Do	Jno. Bell	.20
2 Do Do	James Walker	.20
1 Do Do	W.H. Stewart	.10
1 Bar & Hoe	N.N. Binkley	.20
1 large kettle	W.A. Stuart	8.00
1 lot Geer	J.R. Binkley	.60
1 Lor Geer	G.E. Harris	.45
1 Lot Geer	W.H. Stuart	.80
1 collar Harness &c	W.L. Hudgens	.40
1 collar Harness &C	Burgess Harris	1.10
1 back band	G.E. Harris	.10
1 cutting knife	G.E. Harris	1.50
1 Scythe & Cradle	G.E. Harris	.25
1 Do Do	G.E. Harris	.75
1 Do Do	A. Walker	2.00
1 Do Do	B. Harris	1.00
1 mans saddle	Burgess Harris	2.00
1 mans saddle	Dan Kimbrough	1.00
1 lot corn 10 bbls. at $4.00	G.E. Harris	40.00
10 Barrels corn $4.00	Van Walker	40.00
10 Barrels corn $4.00	A. Walker	40.00
10 Barrels Corn 3.75	Burgess Harris	37.75
5 Barrels corn $3.95	W.L. Gower	19.75
5 Barrels corn $4.00	A. Walker	20.00
5 Barrels corn $3.90	A. Walker	19.50
5 Barrels corn 3.80	C.D. Hudgens	19.00
5 Barrels corn 3.80	W.D. Fortune	19.00

10 Barrels corn $4.20	A. Dickson	42.00
22½ Bushels corn $4.25	G.W. Harris	16.35
1 Pen shucks	Dan Gleen	8.15
1 Do Do	N. Morris	7.10
1 Do Do	T. O'Brien	6.50
1 Do Do	Thos. O'Brien	4.20
1 Lot fodder	James Harris	6.94
2 Stacks fodder	Burgess Harris	5.37
3 stacks fodder	G.E. Harris	4.50
4 stacks fodder	W. Sterry	5.02
5 stacks fodder	Allen Binkley	5.10
(p 184)		
7 stacks fodder	Thos. O'Brien	4.20
8 stacks fodder	G.E. Harris	5.00
9 stacks fodder	Thos. O'Brien	5.26
10 stacks fodder	J.A. Hudson	5.77
300 bundles fodder	George White	4.05
1 Lot Flax	L. Fox	,10
Fodder in the loft	I.N. Hudson	3.91
Oats by the bundle 2 5/8	T. Binkley	57.09
2 stacks 2 7/8	T. Binkley	49.97
3 Do 23/4	Thos. Walker	57.33
4 Do $3.00	G.E. Harris	54.00
5 Do 2 7/8	Thos. O'Brien	59.00
6 Do $3.00	Burgess Harris	60.57
Old oats 1 ¾	N. Farmer	22.66
2 stacks old oats	John S. Harris	22.66
1 Large hog	Thos. Harris	23.50
5 first choice Pork hogs	S. Watson	73.50
5 second " " "	W. McFadden	81.50
5 third " " "	James Harris	72.50
5 fourth " " "	G.W. Maxey	72.00
5 fifth " " "	William Sterry	58.00
5 sixth " " "	A.H. Nicholson	50.00
5 seventh " " "	John Shivers	57.00
5 eighth " " "	Daniel Mosier	46.50
5 ninth " " "	D. Krantz	39.00
5 sold 3 time	J.W. Walker	26.66
1 Grind Stone	W.H. Stuart	2.25
1 Do Do	J.W. Shearon	.50
1 cutting knife	I.L. Harris	.35
1 Chopping Axe	A.E. Souel	. 60
1 " "	G.W. Harris	.35
1 " "	G.W. Harris	.35
1 " "	A.E. Souel	.75
1 Scythe cradle	N.N. Binkley	.10
5 first choice shoats	W.L. Hudgens	18.00
5 2nd " "	J.J. Forbes	17.20
5 3rd " "	N.D. Farmer	11.50
5 4th " "	J.E. Morrow	11.00
5 5th " "	J.E. Morrow	9.25
5 6th " "	J.E. Morrow	8.00
5 7th " "	J.E. Morrow	8.75
6 Remainder	W. Cagle	18.60
Cut corn by the row, 1 row	Jack Ramer	.50
" " " " " 2 row	R.F. Patton	1.00
5 Rows 76	C.A. Hudgens	3.75
2 Rows 75	R.F. Patton	1.00
[illegible]		

(p 185) Amount brot up --------------------		
1 sow & 7 pigs		
1 sow & 6 pigs	J.L. Perdue	$15.50
Red sow & pigs	J.T. Perdue	12.25
1 sow & 4 pigs	G.E. Harris	8.50
1 sow & pigs	R.P. Patton	5.00
1 sow & pigs	Thomas Harris	8.25
1 sow & pigs	W. Cagle	8.00
1 Sow & pigs	W. Cagle	8.00
1 sow & pigs	N.N. Binkley	6.75
1 sow & pigs	N.N. Binkley	10.00
1 muly steer	N. Farmer	13.00
1 Red steer	J.S. Hudgens	11.00
1 red & white cow	Thomas Walker	10.25
1 Brindle cow	Thomas Walker	13.00
1 red cow	Elisha Smith	8.50
1 cow and calf	W.T. Pace	8.00
1 steer	E.J. Binkley	7.50
1 muly cow & calf	Thomas Bell	9.00
1 white and red heifer	H.H. Hudgens	7.50
1 muly heifer	Henry Simmons	3.50
1 Pided Bull	Henry Simmons	3.00
1 white face	Thomas Walker	2.50
1 white face cow	E.J. Binkley	6.00
1 muly bull	E.J. Binkley	7.00
1 muly cow	George White	10.00
1 muly white cow	E.J. Binkley	7.50
1 black cow & calf	James Walker	10.00
1 spotted cow	E.J. Binkley	7.50
1 red yearling	E.J. Binkley	3.50
5 sheep	W.T. Morris	9.50
5 sheep	W.T. Morris	10.00
5 sheep	W.J. Gossett	8.00
5 sheep	W.J. Gossett	8.25
5 sheep	Daniel Glenn	8.25
5 Sheep	J.D. Dismukes	7.75
5 sheep	H.H. Hudgens	7.00
5 sheep	E. Sullivan	6.25
5 sheep	E. Sullivan	6.00
5 sheep	D. Glenn	6.00
5 sheep	G.B. Nicholson	6.00
Remainder	J.Z. Hudgens	6.00
1 Lot tobacco	J.J. Hudgens	30.25
1 hdh Tobacco	R.F. Patton	32.00
1 lot loose tobacco	R.F. Patton	3.00
(p 186) Amount brot up		
1 yoke Oxen	W. Stuart	45.00
1 yoke Oxen	Henry Harris	20.00
1 yoke Oxen	R. Moore	60.00
1 ox cart	J.B. Harris	20.50
1 hog chain	B.W. Bradley	1.10
1 Ox Cart	G.E. Harris	18.00
1 Black colt	G.W. Murphey	30.00
1 sorrel colt	W.A. Stuart	21.00
1 yellow colt	G.E. Harris	29.00
1 mule	W.H. Stuart	65.00

1 Brown mule	Jno. W. Shaw	$40.00
1 Black Horse	W. Mediker	3.00
1 sorrel Horse	I.F. Underwood	5.00
1 Brown Horse	A. Walker	37.00
1 Clay blued mare	D. Mosier	32.00
1 Bay Mare	A. Walker	27.00
1 Clay bank mare	Burgess Harris	200.00
1 Bridle	Harris Dowlen	3.05
1 clay bank horse	ThomasHarris	157.00
1 Brown Mule	Pat Morrison	110.00
1 Lot Rye	C. Vedder	16.43
1 Lot Rye	G.W. Shaw	10.50
1 Lot Rye	T. Binkley	18.00
1 Flax Wheel	Henry Myers	.25
1 Barrel Grass seed	J.D. Dismukes	.20
1 Barrel Grass seed	J.D. Dismukes	.50
1 lot clover seed	J.W. Shearon	2.50
2 Bags seed	A.F. Carney	1.10
1 Barrel salt	Thomas Walker	3.75
1 Barrel Salt	James Harris	4.21
1 Barrel	J.E. Turner	1.00
1 Barrel Salt	J.D. Dismukes	4.60
1 Barrel empty	I.H. Pentecost	.45
1 Barrel Salt	J.H. Woodson	4.28
1 spinning wheel	A. Walker	1.95
1 Reel	A. Walker	1.15
1 new wheel	E.L. Darrow	4.25
1 new wheel	Martha Hudgens	3.50
1 Seive	A.J. Teasley	.20
Kettle	Jno. Pentecost	2.30
1 pot	B. Pace	.25
1 oven and skillet	W.H. Stewart	2.35
1 oven	H.H. Hudgens	.30
2 skillets	H.H. Hudgens	.50
1 pot	W.H. Pentecost	1.00
(p 187) Amount brot up		
Sundries		
1 Tin bucket	H.H. Binkley	.60
1 Tin Bucket	H. Myers	.40
1 milk piggin	H. Myers	.25
Sundries	H. Myers	.40
1 Bucket	John H. Pentecost	.45
1 Table	E.T. Herron	.40
1 Bucket	H. Myers	.55
1 Bucket	H. Myers	.35
Sundries	R.F. Patton	.65
1 cross cut saw	R.F. Patton	2.65
1 Table	H. Myers	3.65
1 old spinning wheel	A.H. Walker	.10
1 Pot rack	John H. Pentecost	.70
1 Piggin	W. Rose	.25
1 Pail	C. Dickinson	1.10
1 Table	J.R. Binkley	.25
1 hot sash	J.L. Harris	.70
1 loom & geer	J.H. Pentecost	2.50
1 small bedstead	H. Myers	.15
1 hot plank	J.D. Dismukes	10.17
1 hot flooring	H.H. Hudgens	4.00

Remainder	H.H. Hudgens	14.25
1 Lot Plank	G.C. Binkley	6.69
1 Lot flooring	Levi Binkley	5.74
1 wheat fan	J.W. Walker	12.00
1 lot wheat	J. Stack	22.50
Remainder	D. Hudgens	27.00
1 Lot Lard	J. Stack	2.40
1 Barrel Lard	J. Stack	.25
2 stands lard	Thomas Walker	1.55
1 Barrel vinegar	Robert Head	1.60
1 Lot barrels	Daniel Hudgens	1.00
2 sands	J.F. Underwood	.65
1 lot salt & barrels	D. Hudgens	1.00
Soap Trough	J.D. Dismukes	.35
1 Kettle	E.Y. Herron	.25
1 Lot sheep skins	A.W. Seuel	1.20
1 Lot Tar	F.H. Woodson	.35
1 Keg nails	J.W. Walker	.70
1 Barrel	R. Knox	.35
1 Lot cotton	H. Myers	.60
Half Bushel	G.E. Harris	.55
1 Lot onions	T. O'Brien	1.00
(p 188) Amount brot up		
1 Bag seed cotton	J.J. Forbes	.10
1 Flax Wheel	R. Head	.25
1 Lot nails	Thomas Walker	1.15
1 Lot Tallow	E.G. Hudgens	5.00
1 Lot Geese	Nathan Morris	5.50
10 Bushels Turnips	J.D. Demumbra	2.00
10 Bushels Turnips	E.L. Darrow	1.50
10 Bushels Turnips	H.H. Binkley	1.60
10 Bushels Turnips	Henry Myers	1.50
10 Bushels Turnips	J.D. Dismukes	1.30
10 Bushels Turnips	Asea Binkley	1.00
1 Lot potatoes	Ged E Harris	2.00
The Remainder	Ged E. Harris	5.87
1 Lot wool	H. Myers	1.80
10 lbs. wool	John Stack	5.00
8 lbs wool	John J. Forbes	3.60
20 lbs. wool	J.J. Forbes	9.00
Remainder	A.J. Harris	2.25
10 Lbs. wool rolls	E.L. Darrow	5.50
10 lbs wool rolls	T. O'Brien	6.50
10 lbs wool rolls	W.L. Gower	6.25
10 lbs wool rolls	E.L. Darrow	5.90
10 lbs wool rolls	David	6.00
35 lbs wool	J.J. Forbes	17.85
10 lbs feathers	R. Head	3.65
10 lbs feathers	G. Hawkins	3.80
10 lbs feathers	D. Hudgens	4.40
16½ lbs. Feathers	W. Sterry	6.60
1 Keg Copperas	W. Sterry	.50
1 Keg Sulphur	R. Head	.30
15 lbs. wool rolls	W.H. Stuart	9.15
5 lbs wool rolls	G.W. Harris	3.00
1 Side upper leather	J. Ramer	.80
1 " " "	J.H. Harper	1.95

1 Side upper Leather	J.W. Shearon	$2.30
1 " " "	Asia Binkley	2.55
1 " " "	J.H. Harper	2.35
1 " " "	J.H. Harper	2.60
1 " " "	R. Head	1.75
1 " " "	A. Walker	2.25
Remenant	J.W. Shearon	.45
1 Side sole leather	John H. Harper	2.87
1 " " "	James Hudgens	1.00
1 " " "	J.W. Shearon	4.45
(p 189) Amount brot up		
1 Lot cut Jeans	W. Read	2.64
5 yds domestic	John Z. Hudgens	1.12
6 " "	W. Read	.44
11 " "	James Walker	.91
30 " "	A.H. Binkley	3.00
36 " "	G.W. Harris	3.42
36½ " "	James Walker	3.47
10½ " "	Nan Binkley	1.32
1 side upper leather	John H. Harper	2.55
1 sheet	P.H. Woodson	1.20
1 Bale yarn	G.C. Binkley	2.65
16 twist C Yarn	John H. Pentecost	1.70
1 Lot barrels	Thos. Bell	.10
1 Lot Piggins &C	John Z. Hudgens	.35
Renmanent Dom.	W.L. Hudgens	.10
1 Box	Dan Hudgens	.25
1 Jug & Turpentine	B.G. Bradley	.25
1 Jug & Oil	B.F. Binkley	.25
1 Box	W.L. Hudgens	.25
1 Bag cotton	W.L. Hudgens	.15
1 Stone Jar	D. Hudgens	.60
1 Stone crock	Ben Pace	.15
1 Jug	Ben Pace	.15
1 Locking Glass	W.L. Hudgens	.05
Knives & Forks	John H. Harper	1.00
Do Do	James Hudgens	.30
2 Butcher knives	W.H. H. Gent	.50
2 " "	E.T. Henson	.60
1 set cups & Saucers	Nancy Harris	.30
1 set Plates	Delila Walker	.20
1 " "	N.N. Binkley	.30
1 Dish	H.I. Gower	.50
1 "	N.N. Binkley	.25
1 "	W.L. Hudgens	.25
1 "	John Pentecost	.20
1 Salt Set	John Pentecost	.20
1 Tea spoon	Thos. G. Hudgens	.15
2 cream Pat	R.F. Patton	.20
2 B. Knives	G.E. Harris	.40
2 " "	James Harris	.40
1 Bottle Turpentine	R. Head	.25
1 Dish	Delila Walker	.25
1 Dish	W.H. Stewart	.56
2 Bowls	J.F. Underwood	.20
Cups & Saucers	James Hudgens	.15
(p 190) Amount brot up		
1 Jar &C	Delilah Walker	.10

1 Door Lock	A.M. Binkley	.50
1 Door Lock	B.H. Shearron	.16
1 Lot sundries	R. Head	.10
1 lot sundries	James Harris	.75
Chewing Tobacco	William Cagles	.10
1 sundries	James Hudgens	.30
1 DO	James W. Walker	.10
1 nail keg	B.S. Bradley	.15
1 Lot sundries	W.L. Hudgens	.10
1 Lot sundries	James W. Walker	.10
1 Lot sundries	Thomas Bell	.10
1 set tablespoons	R. Head	.25
1 Box Buttons	A. Walker	.40
1 set teaspoons	M. Harris	.25
1 set knives and forks	Delila Walker	1.55
1 Lot sundries	J.C. Hudgens	.15
1 Stone Jar	John Bradley	.30
1 Lot sundries	Dan Hudgens	.10
1 Jug	Burgess Harris	.05
1 Loaf Sugar	R.F. Patton	.15
1 pair sheep shears	Mary McLaughlin	.55
1 Lot Sundries	W.L. Hudgens	.30
1 Lot sundries	I.G. Harris	.35
1 " "	W.L. Hudgens	.10
1 Razor Strop	I.F. Underwood	.15
1 " "	I.W. Shearon	.20
1 Jug	B.H. Shearon	.40
1 Lot sundries	James Hudgens	.10
1 Jug	Henry Harris	.10
1 Jug	Wash Gent	.10
1 Bag shot	Jno. Bradley	1.05
Window Lights	Jo Krantz	.10
1 Jar	I.W. Shearon	1.35
1 Jar	W.L. Hudgens	.10
1 Lot starch	Henry Harris	.10
1 Lot sundries	John Bradley	.10
1 Tea Pot	M.P. Frey	.55
1 Lot sundries	Joe Krantz	.15
34 lbs peppers	R.F. Patton	2.74
1 Lot books	James Hudgens	.05
1 Table	W.W. Read	3.00
1 Bottle Whiskey	W.S. Bradley	.55
1 Speer	John Bradley	.25
1 Lot Staies	Thomas Walker	.45
(p 191) Amount brot up		
1 pair cards	[illegible]	[illegible]
1 map	W.L. Hudgens	.75
1 Trunk	Burgess Harris	.20
1 Looking glass	W.H. Stuart	1.05
1 Dress Table	James Walker	2.00
1 Chest	Robert Head	3.85
1 pair saddle bags	B.H. Shearon	1.50
1 Table cloth	W.M. Read	.15
2 wash Pans	R. Head	.25
2 Table cloths	Thos. Bell	.20
2 " "	J.I. Forbes	.15

1 Umbrella	R. Head	.25
1 Large chest	John J. Pentecost	1.00
1 Cradle	R. Head	.10
1 Rifle gun	G.C. Binkley	1.00
1 Rifle Gun	B.F. Binkley	.10
1 shot gun	James Harris	3.00
1 Press	Delila Walker	13.00
1 Lot dry peaches	C.A. Hudgens	2.75
1 Lot apples	Asia Binkley	.95
1 Lot peaches	John Pentecost	.35
2 Bed qilts	Wm. Cagle	.60
1 Bed and clothing	Cad Harris	19.00
1 Bed and clothing	Delila Walker	19.00
1 " "	Thomas Harris	24.00
1 " "	Ben Pace	20.00
1 " "	M. Harris	23.50
1 " "	John Z. Hudgens	5.00
1 " "	W.L. Hudgens	15.50
1 " "	Heri Harris	14.00
1 " "	W.L. Hudgens	12.00
1 Jug and oil	B.F. Binkley	.25
1 Well Bucket	John Bradley	.60
1 Lot clover seed	E.T. Herron	1.15
1 Bed stead	Cad Harris	4.75
1 " "	Delila Harris	4.25
1 " "	Delila Walk er	5.12
1 " "	W.L. Hudgens	3.00
1 Brass candle	Delila Walker	.20
1 Bed Stead	ElishaSmith	6.50
1 " "	James Walker	.50
1 " "	J.W. Shearon	1.75
1 " "	J.F. Underwood	.75
1 " "	JamesWalker	.25
1 Lot red pepper	B.C. Bradley	.10
(p 192) Amount Brot up		
1 Clock	Cad E. Harris	.50
1 "	R.F. Patton	1.25
1 Cupboard	W.H. Stewart	10.50
1 Bureau	James Harris	4.75
1 Counterpans	Delila Walker	1.00
1 Do	J.L. Forbes	.25
1 "	A. Walker	.70
1 Bed Quilt	Dan Hudgens	.62
1 " "	Mary McLaughlin	1.35
1 Counterpane	Mary McLaughlin	.85
1 "	Mary McLaughlin	2.00
1 Water Bucket	James Harris	.40
1 Pair Cart wheels	James Walker	1.25
1 Briar Hook	Cad E. Harris	.05
1 Weeding hoe	G.C. Binkley	.40
1 Lot hoes	W.H. Morris	.30
1 Smothing	B.F. Binkley	1.00
1 Lot sundries	W.L. Hudgens	.25
1 Water keg	Cad E. Harris	.25
6 chairs	Burgess Harris	2.75
6 "	D. Glenn	1.50
6 "	W.L. Hudgens	2.00
1 Lot shingles	M.P. Frey	2.15

1 Raw hide	Joe Krantz	.55
1 Raw Hide	Joe Krantz	.50
29 chickens	Dan Glenn	2.90
1 pair fire irons	B.H. Shearon	1.10
1 pair fire irons	John Pentecost	1.25
1 Lot red pepper	D. Glenn	.30
1 Rope	B.F. Hinkley	.50
1 Side saddle	Wm. Simpson	2.00
1 " "	J.L. Forbes	1.00
56 Apple Cons	G. McLaughlin	5.60
56 Apple Cons	G. McLaughlin	7.00
50 Heads Cabbage	R.F. Patton	2.50
½ Pen Wheat straw	Henry Harris	1.00
1 Pen " "	Dan Hudgens	1.00

Hire of negroes until 25 Dec. 1860

Boy, Aesop	Levi Binkley	7.00
" Tilman	Thos. Walker	8.25
" Nelson	B.F. Binkley	5.50
" Albert	G.W. Harris	7.00
Girl, Chena	John Bradley	2.00
" Rachel	G. Miles	1.25
" Bill	Jo Shearon	1.00

(p 193) Amount brot up

Girl, Martha	Nancy Harris	.25
" Winny	Nancy Harris	.05
" Sarah	William Read	.25
1 Cupboard	B.F. Binkley	.50
2 sheets	G.W. McLaughlin	.25
1 sheet	Rosanna Walker	.15
1 sheet	Nancy Harris	.15
1 sheet	Dan Hudgens	.10
1 Bed Frill	WT. Pace	.25
1 Bed Frill	Delila Walker	.25
Rent of hands	Thos. Harris	1.00
550 Bundles Oats	James Watts	15.12
11 lbs. wool rolls	James Watts	6.05
26 lbs. coarse wool	James Watts	11.05
150 bundles	James Watts	3.00
Damaged Rye	James Watts	1.00
1 Lot corn	William Gower	12.75
1 " "	Turner Binkley	1.26
1 " "	William Sterry	14.00
1 Lot sugar	James Harris	6.69
1 Wheat sheet	Jo Krantz	.55
1 Wheat stand	Cad E. Harris	.15
1 Olivis	Cad E. Harris	.05
1 Lot bacon	Cad E. Harris	9.75
1 Lot shingles	James Binkley	21.60
1 Lot Plank	John Bradley	3.46
L lot Plank	Levi Binkley	5.25
Rent of land	Thomas Harris	71.00
" "	Thomas Harris	19.00
" "	Thomas Harris	23.00
" "	Thomas Harris	17.00

Rent of land	Thomas Harris	25.00
Sale wheat Patch	James Harris	.40
Boy, Aesop	Abner Bedwell	141.00
Boy, Tilman	Thomas Walker	133.00
" Nelson	William Shearon	137.00
" Albert	A.F. Carney	86.00
Girl, Ritter	Harris Williams	52.00
" Martha	Thos. Bell	17.25
" Winnie	John Shivers	5.00
" Laura	James Harris	4.00
Woman, Chana	Burgess Harris	30.00
" Rachel	Cad Harris	30.00

(p 194) Amt. brpt up

1 Shoat	S. Walker	2.00
1030 feet Plank	G.S. Binkley	6.69
Cash left on hand		451.19
240 bundles Rye	Daniel Glenn	4.20
Irish potatoes	Cad E. Harris	5.37
1 Lot Rye	S. Walker	9.62
1013 Bundle oats	G.W. Harris	17.72
One negro. Keef at the lowest bidder by the month for the year 1860 - $60 to James Harris.		5.00

Accounts on the Book

1 account on	A. Lowe	19.30
1 " "	Henry Harris	1.00
1 " "	H. Dowlen	11.25
1 " "	Len Morris	18.50
1 " "	R.D. Felts	4.00
1 " "	A.L. Fortune	10.37
1 " "	E.J. Binkley	9.00
1 " "	Harris Williams	21.50
1 " "	Jesse Shearon	4.20
1 " "	W. Gatewood	2.60
1 " "	E. Simpson	22.90
1 " "	Dan Hudgens	9.52
L " "	D.J. Walker	2.12
1 " "	D.B. Williams	13.12
1 " "	David Mosier	1.20
1 " "	R.H. Riding	64.80
1 " "	A.E. Souel	4.00
all very doubtful		
1 account on	J.A. Hudson	1.55
1 " "	S. Walker	7.60
1 " "	Thos. Walker	1.25

(p 195) An account of notes, all very doubtful that came into my hands Nov. 26th 1860 as Exr. of Thomas W. Harris decd. (S Walker)

1 note on B.W. Bradley due 3rd June 1858	125.00
1 " " Cheatham Watson & Co. due April 10 1860	127.81
1 " " A. Lowe due 1st July 1859	118.45
With a credit Mar. 5th 1860	16.42
One note on A. Lowe due 13th June 1860	45.00
One note on H. Dowlen & Henry Dowlen with interest from date due 24th June 1857 payable to Sarah Harris & Thomas Harris for	392.00
with a credit Oct. 18th 1858	180.00
One note on Harris Williams due 13th Apr. 1860 for	12.19

1 Note on G.H. Lowe and Delana Lowe due 25th Dec. 186- for 65.00
1 Note on William Sterry due 12th Nov. 1859 9.37
1 Note on J.D. Walker due 16th Feb. 1860 13.75
1 note on L. Fox due 13th Mar 1860 for 11.60
1 Note on J.D. Walker due 16th Feb. 1860 5.00
Interest on same
1 Note on H. Carney & J. Carney due 25th June 1860 110.00
Interest on same
One note on Thos. J. Felts & Elias Harrisdue 26th June 1859 90.00
1 Note on A.E. Soual due 2nd June 1859 20.00
Interest on same
1 Note on J. Carney & Asa Carney due 25th Decr. 1859 78.75
Interest on same
1 Note on James Perry & B.H. Gibbs due 25th Feb. 1860 110.00
Interest on same
1 Note on H. Carney & A.F. Carney due 7th June 1860 100.00
1 Note on Harris Williams due 12th day of Sept. 1858 125.00
Interest on same
1 Note on H. Williams due 22nd Sept. 1859 for 125.00
One note on H.H. Binkley & E.J. Binkley due 1st Jany 1860 714.28
Interest on same
With the following credits to wit
Feb. 14th 1860 412.78
Sept. 12th 1860 187.48
1 Note on Sterling Walker due 25th Jany 1859 50.00
Interest on same
1 Note on Harris Williams due 25 March 1859 61.30
Interest on same
1 Note on A.B. Gibbs due 30th Decr. 1860 for 735.00
Interest on same

(p 196)
1 Note on E.B. & B.H. Gibbs due 30th Dec. 1860 240.48
Interest on same
1 note on J.D. Dismukes due 31st Dec. 1859 223.59
Interest on same
1 Note on James Watts due 3rd January 1858 225.59
Interest on same1 note on J. Simpkins & E. Harris due 26th Feb. 1859-33.00
1 Note on Sam Watson due 25th June 1859 300.00
1 Note of A.F. & H.B. Carney due 1st May 1861 300.00
Interest on same
1 Note of A.F. & E.B. Carney due 1st of 1861 254.35
Interest on same
1 Note on A. Gowe due 15th Nov. 1859 67.75
Interest on same
1 Note on A. Gowe due 15th Jan 1860 985.47
Interest on same
1 Note on S. Watson due 11th Oct. 1860 656.25
Interest on same
1 Note on C. Vedder due 21st Jan. 1859 100.00
Interest on same
1 Note on Cheatham Watson & Co. due 5th Oct. 1860 52.36
Interest on same
1 Note on Eli Harris due 19 Jan. 1860 96.00
Interest on same
1 Note on H. Dowlen due 15th June 1860 283.41

Interest on same	
1 Note on H. Dowlen due March 9, 1860	$250.00
Interest on same	
1 Note on H. Dowlen due 23rd Jany. 1860	351.60
Interest on same	
1 Note on H. Dowlen due 9th Sept. 1859	7.58
Interest on same	
1 Note on H. Dowlen due 1st of July 1859	54.96
Interest on same	
1 Note on Thomas O'Brien & S. Watson due 1st Feb. 1859	779.57
Interest on same	
1 Note on Jno. Dowlen due 21st Jan. 1860	227.50
Interest on same	
1 Note on Elias Harris due 6th Dec. 1859	35.00
Interest on same	
1 Note on A.C. Soucl due 2 January 1860	33.03
Interest on same	
1 Note of B.H. Newman & B.F. Binkley, May 7th, 60	18.00
Interest on same	
1 Note on E.P. Morris & L. Fox due April 1861	16.00
Interest on same	
(p 197)	
1 note on B.W. Bradley due 13th Oct. 1855	300.00
Cr. May 26th 1856	100.00
Feb. 9th 1857	70.00
1 Note on Isham R. Felts due 6th May 1860	20.00
Interest on same	
1 note on Z. Owen due 20th Jan. 1860	55.00
Interest on same	
1 note on S.G. Williams & H. Harris due 15th April 1860	12.50
1 Due bill on F. Williams due 15th May 1850	25.00
Interest on same	
1 note on AH. Williams due 29th Jan. 1860	36.00
Interest on same	
1 note on W.B.C. Cower due Mar. 6 1860	25.69
Interest on same	
1 Note on John Shivers due 13 Jan. 1860	3.73
Interest on same	
1 Note on A.Rose due 9th Oct 1860	14.75
Interest on same	
1 Note on B.F. Binkley due April 17, 1860	17.10
Interest on same	
1 note on Joseph Harris due 24th Feb. 1860	500.00
Interest on same	
1 Note on B.F. Binkley & W. Goodwin due 29th Feb. 60	20.80
Interest on same	
1 Order on C.D. Lawrence due 6th Jan. 1860	10.57
Interest on same	
1 order on C.D. Lawrence d e April 11. 1860	27.57
Interest on same	
1 order on B.F. Binkley due April 22, 1860	5.00
Interest on same	
1 note on W. Farmer due 2 Jany. 1861	107.16
Interest on same	
1 note on E.L. Darrow due 2 May 1858	40.00
Interest on same	

1 note on W. Rose due 25th Jany. 1860	$25.00
Interest on same	
1 Note on H. Dowlen & H. Williams due 15 June 1860	25.08
Interest on same	
1 Note on W. Stewart due Mar. 4 1853	20.00
Cr.	
June 15 1856	2.50
Jany. 5 1859	5.00
July 5, 1856	1.50
1 note on R.W. Felts due 25th Dec. 1854	45.00
Sept. 10, 1857	25.00

(p 190)

1 note on Jesse Chandown due 21st Jany. 1857 with credits	
Interest on same	
1 Note on W.Cowor due 25th Dec. 1855	15.00
May 3rd 1858 Cr. by	12.50
Interest on same	
1 Note on J.A. Rose due 1st Jany. 1851	5.08
Interest on same	
1 Note on W.A. Henderson due 24th Decr. 1857	7.50
Interest on same	
1 note on John Krentz due Feb. 5. 1858	45.97
Interest on same	
1 note on S.A. Richardson due April 6. 1860	25.70
Interest on same	
1 note on J. Reed due 11th April 1857	20.40
Interest on same	
1 Note on J. Durham & B.W. Bradley due 8th March 1852	12.79
Interest on same	
1 note on R.H. McCormick due 28th Sept. 1851	2.05
Interest on same	
1 Note on H.W. Lewis due 7th April 1860	37.33
Interest on same	
1 Note on J.R. Binkley due 27th Apr. 1860	8.00
Interest on same	
1 Note on R.H. Reading due 5th Oct. 1859	200.00
Interest on same	
1 Note on R.H. Reding due 28th Oct. 1859	200.00
Interest on same	
1 note on R.H. Reding due 11th July 1860	188.74
Interest on same	
1 note on R.H. Reding due 21st Sept. 1859	350.00
Interest on same	
1 note on R.H. Reding due 7th July 1860	185.00
Interest on same	
1 note on R.H. Reding due March 1860	9.30
Interest on same	
1 note on R.H. Reding due May 6th 1859	100.00
Interest on same	
1 Note on R.H. Reding due 15 March 1859	59.75
1 note on R.H. Reding due 25th June 1859	20.00
Interest on same	
1 note on L. Lowe due Feb. 9th 1855	60.00
Interest on same	
1 Note on L. Lowe due 24th Nov. 1859	50.00

Interest on same	
(p 199)	
1 note on L. Lowe due 27th Oct. 1853	6.25
Interest on same	
1 note on W.H. Blankenship due 16th March 1853	45.96
June 6th 1853	7.00
Aug. 29 1853	10.00
Nov. 21 1853	5.00
1 note on Elias Harris due 2nd Nov. 1858	13.12
Interest on same	
1 Note on J. Chandown due 4th APril 1858	16.00
Interest on same	
1 note on J.D. Darrow E. Darrow due 1st March 1859	18.00
Feb. 6, 1859	8.00
Interest on same	
1 note on A.L. Fortune due 20th Sept. 1859	16.35
Interest on same	
1 order on B.F. Binkley due 11th May 1860	7.75
Interest on same	
1 note on J.W. Harris due 13 June 1857	9.75
Interest on same	
1 note on J.H. Binkley due 7th March 1860	9.85
Interest on same	
1 note on W? Mumtra and B.F. Binkley due 26 April 1859	27.00
Interest on same	
1 note on J.W. Harris due 15th Jan. 1855	8.00
Interest on same	
1 note on W.H. Bradley & B.W. Bradley due 13 Dec. 1854	330.00
Decr. 27th 1858 Cr. By	350.00
Interest on same	
1 note on James Harris due 20 Oct. 1856	29.50
Interest on same	
1 note on Z. Durham In, due 26 June 1850	85.61
Oct. 15 1857 By Cash	23.40
1 note on C. Cent due 29th Decr. 1859	34.00
1 note on J. Simmons & James Simmons due 1st Feb. 1851	11.00
Interest on same	
1 note of D. Krantz due 12 Dec. 1854	27.00
Interest on same	
1 note on E.L. Darrow due 1st Jany. 1860	14.60
Interest on same	
1 note on Jacob Keeler due 16th Aug. 1851	6.83
Interest on same	
1 note on E.P. Morris due 2 6th Sept. 1848	4.00
Interest on same	
1 note on E.P. Morrisdue 13th Oct. 1848	15.00
Interest on same	
(p 200)	
1 note on Press Binkley due 29th March 1860	12.09
Int erest on same	
1 note on E.P. Moore due 17 July 1857	15.00
Dec. 23 1858 Cr. By	10.00
Interest on same	
1 note on W.W. Williams due 21st Jan. 1849	310.90
Oct. 13th 1857 Cr By	8.58

1 note on David Mosier due 27 Nov. 1858 19.80
Interest on same
1 note on James Walker due 9th April 1857 3.03
Interest on same
1 note on John Simmons due 26th Feb. 1859 8.80
Interest on same
1 note on Nat Farmer due 5 Mar. 1854 11.53
Interest on same
1 note on William Sterry due 4th March 1860 6.00
Interest on same
1 note on D.W. Nye & M.R. Hooper due 18 March 1858 17.35
Interest on same
1 note on Jas. S. Hudgens due 14th Feb. 1860 16.75
Interest on same
1 note on Nathan Morris due 4th March 1860 18.00
Interest on same
1 note on Henry Harris due 31st Jany. 1860 36.03
Interest on same
1 Act. on James Harris due 1st Jan. 1860 2.50
Interest on same
1 note on J.M. & H.H. Binkley due 7th March 1860 13.00
Interest on same
1 note on W. Turner & J.H. Binkleydue 7th March 1860 14.85
1 note on C.C. Bradley due 12th Sept. 1856 5.30
Interest on same
1 note on H. Myers & B.F. Binkley due 4th Aug. 1860 9.00
Interest on same
1 note on James Rose due 9th April 1857 10.71
Interest on same
July 14th Recd.
1 note on Jno L. Adams due 6th June 1856 22.27
Interest on same
(p 201) An Inventory of the personal estate of Anthony Collins decd.

Slaves

Edward, 27 years old
Mary —— 55 " "
Hannah —— 19 years old
Emily —— 17 " "
Mike —— 14 " "
Jenny —— 5 " "
Robert —— 1 " "
Jobe —— 4 " "
Martha —— 33 " "
Kate —— 65 " "
Florence —— 11 " "
Sidney —— 12 " "
William —— 6 " "
Mary —— 3 " "
Thomas —— 6 " "
Betty —— 2 " "

Claims Good
1 Receipt on J.M. Roberts for a note given 27th Aug. 1860 On D. Marr
J.F. Cummings, C.A. Harris, and George S. Deck due the 15th Sept. 1860
for $4200.00
Interest on same

one note on S.M. Roberts due 28th Aug. 1860 for		20.00
Interest on same		
One receipt on T. Harper of Montgomery for claims on J. Fordyth		
due 8th March 1859 for	30.00	30.00
Interest on same		
1 Receipt on T. Harper for claims against Jackson McKennon & Co.		
due April 25th 1860 for		139.06
Interest on same		
1 Receipt of T. Harper for claim on Jackson McKennon & Co. due 21st		
August 1860 for		480.00
Interest on the same		
1 Receipt on D. Mattock for claims on D. Alsbrook due 27th 1859 for		12.75
Interest on same		
1 Act. on A.S. Williams for 1858 & 59 for		28.84

Doubtful claims

1 note on E.W. Mosely due 27th Aug 1859	35.00
Interest on same	
1 Note on Montgomery Williams due 14th Decr. 1857 for	5.00
Interest on same	
1 note on E.R. Craig due 1st January 1860 for	20.00
Interest on same	
1 note on A.H. Douglas due 8th Aug. 1859 for	3.25
Interest on same	
1 note on L. Simpoe due 1st Sept. 1859 for	17.50
Interest on same	

(p 202) One account on James Swift	24.90
Credit April 1859	10.50
Balance Due	18.90
1 account on Thos, Baxter for 1858 & 9	44.00
One account on M. Morgan for	14.10
Credit Nov. 15th 1856 for	5.00
Balance Due	9.10
One account on L. Collins made January 1859	
for Cash loned	125.00

Articles sold him of negroes &C

Edmond	E. Collins	50.00
Martha & 3 children	E. Collins	3.00
Mary	E. Collins	.50
Fill	E. Collins	.25
Hannah & 4 children, lowest bidder	E. Collins	16.00
Florence	E. Collins	5.00
Emily	G.J. Eleazer	42.25
Sidney	N.P. Hagood	11.00
Mike	N.P. Hagood	10.50

Sale property 2nd February 1861

Boxes and Barrels	John Collins	.05
1 Keg nails	N.P. Hagood	.50
1 Wedge and axe	J.L. Wyatt	1.00
1 spinning wheel	W.H. Minor	1.00
2 Do Do	E. Collins	1.05
1 cross cut saw &C	D. Mattock	.60
1 Hand saw	J.B. Hagood	3.05

1 Tongue & groove Plain	W.H. Minor	.50
Augers &C	H.P. Hagood	1.55
Molding plain	W.K. Wyatt	1.05
1 Foot adze	John Collins	1.15
Plain Augers &C	H.P. Hagood	1.00
Chest and contents	John Collins	.25
Box & Cotton	William Ham	2.00
Lounge	E. Carroll	1.55
1 Box & Bell	D. Barton	.60
1 Clock reel	E. Collins	.10
Bucket & Jugs	D. Barton	1.00
1 pair scales	E. Collins	.10
1 candle stand	E. Collins	.15
1 Trunk	E. Collins	.60
1 Dressing Table	E. Collins	.30
(p 203)		
1 Clock	E. Collins	3.00
1 side board	E. Collins	.25
1 Lot Books	Wm. Ham	.70
3 Books	James Wyatt	2.55
1 Lot Books	John Collins	.25
1 Bottle	W.S. Barton	.05
1 Bed Quilt	H. Hagwood	.45
1 " "	H. Hagwood	.30
1 " "	H. Hagood	.40
1 " "	H. Hagood	.40
1 " "	H. Hagood	.40
1 " "	H. Hagood	.25
1 " "	H. Hagood	.25
1 " "	H.P. Hagood	.10
1 " "	H.P. Hagwood	.25
1 " "	H. Hagwood	.55
1 " "	H.P. Hagood	.50
1 " "	H.P. Hagood	.55
1 " "	E. Carroll	.65
1 " "	E. Carroll	.55
1 " "	Robert Sim	.40
1 " "	J.B. Hagood	.30
1 " "	J.B. Hagood	.55
1 " "	H.P. Hagood	.20
1 " "	H.P. Hagood	.25
1 " "	E. Carroll	.15
5 cains	H. Hagood	1.20
Tub & Books	E. Carroll	.35
Bed Stead & Clothing	R. Mills	13.00
1 Bed Stead & Clothing	E. Carroll	15.00
1 Bed Stead & Clothing	Robert Sim	6.00
1 Trunnel Bed	Elijah Trotter	5.45
1 Bed Stead & Clothing	Tho. Hathert	13.50
3 weeding Hoe	J.W. Freeman	.45
1 Grubbing Hoe	W.A. Workman	.10
1 Grubbing Hoe	J.W. Freeman	.25
1 Hay Fork	B.R. Freeman	.10
1 Stone Hammer	D. Barton	1.00
2 Raw Hydes	W.B. Stokes	1.60
1 Spinning Wheel	C. Ellison	2.00
1 Fan Mill	E. Collins	.25

1 Pair Wagon Geer	A. Jackson	2.75
1 Set Plow Geer	W.R. Wyatt	1.00
1 Set Plow Geer	J.W. Freeman	.65
5 Barrel Corn	S.D. Watkins	25.50
(p 204) Amount brot up		
5 Barrels Corn $5.00	S.D. Watkins	25.00
5 Barrels corn --$5.05	D. Murgrove	25.25
5 Barrels corn -- $5.10	E. Carroll	25.50
8 Barrels, 1 Bu. Surplus corn -- 5.10	E. Carroll	41.82
1 Stack Fodder	S.D. Watkins	5.50
1 Stack Fodder	Josephine Collins	5.85
1 Ox Waggin	L. Collins	66.00
5 second choice hogs	S.D. Watkins	25.05
8 Hogs-- $2.20	G.W. Gossett	17.60
1 Gray mule, Gabriel	R.W. Workman	95.00
1 sorrel mule colt	F.M. Green	66.50
1 Gray mule. Peter	Thomas Martin	76.50
1 Sorrel Mare	James Gamble	8.00
1 SorrellM Mare	Thomas Martin	80.00
1 Yellow colt	Thos. Stephens	40.00
1 Lot lumber	J. Blackford	6.25
1 Lot bacon	T.Y. Dixon	21.50
100 Lot Bacon	T.Y. Dixon	21.50
480 " "	T.Y. Dixon	108.00
1 Lot crockery ware	D. Grimes	.30
1 Table	E. Collins	.05
1 Wash Kettle	E. Collins	.50
1 Yoke Oxen	T.Y. Dickson	46.25
1 Yoke Oxen	H. Davis	44.50
1 cow and calf	D. Mills	13.50
1 yellow cow and calf	E. Harris	10.75
1 spotted cow and calf	William Organ	13.00
1 yellow cow and calf	J.T. Swift	25.00
1 Broken Horn cow	W. Grimes	18.00
1 Speckled cow and calf	J.M. Daniel	21.00
1 motley face cow	E. Harris	12.05
1 Black Stud	E. Harris	7.75
1 white face yearling	E. Harris	5.50
1 Spotted Yearling	E. Harris	6.15
1 Brindled Heifer	E. Harris	9.00
1 pair two horse plows	N.P. Hagood	.30
1 Lot old plows	C. Elerson	.75
1 Plow and shovel	C. Elerson	1.05
1 Bull Tongue plow	J.B. Hagood	2.35
1 Harrow & Clevis	Thos. Rogers	2.30
1 Grind Stone	E. Ellerson	2.00
1 Set B.S. Tool	E. Elgerson	33.40
1 Drill & Rod	E. Ellerson	.50
1 Stack Fodder	Z. Groves	8.00
1 Stack Fodder	J.B. Hagood	1.19
(p 205) Amount brot up.		
2 wheat cradles	H. Hagood	.05
2 wheat cradles	D. Jones	.05
3 Rawhydes	W.B. Stokes	4.00
1 Lot chare cole	C. Elerson	5.00

10 First choice sheep	E. Collins	10.00
11 second choice Sheep	E. Collins	11.25
2 sheep	E. Collins	2.75
1 Bell wether	E. Collins	1.00
4 sow and pigs	John Collins	26.25
1 Sow and pigs	T. Harper	4.00
2 Barrels shattered corn	Louida Collins	4.00
5 1/5 barrels short corn	W.H. Minor	8.32

(p 206) Will of Jacob Bell decd.

I, Jacob Bell do make and publish this as my last Will and Testament hereby revoking and making void all other wills by me at any other time made.
1st.
I direct that my funeral expenses and all my just debts be paid as soon after my death as possible out of any monies that I mat die possessed of, or may first come into the hands of my executor.
2nd
I give and bequeath to my son G.W. Bell all my lands except two hundred acres where John H. Harper settled at. Also I give to me son G.W. Bell one negro man named Henry, one negro woman named ---- two negro boys, one named Tom the other named Parker, Also all my horses except one, also one yoke Oxen, one wagon and geer, one ox cart, three shot guns, One case of bottles, all my farming implements, first choice of my bedsteads and furniture, half of my stock of hogs, one silver watch. The cropthat may be on hand to be divided equally between my son G.W. Bell and my daughtersRebecca and CarolineBell.
3rd
I give and bequeath to my two daughters Rebecca & Caroline Bell two hundred acres of land , the place where John H. Harper settled on, to have as a home during their natural lives, then go to my sonG.W. Bell forever, and that my son G.W. Bell have the management of the land during their lives, also I give to them all my cattle except the oxen, and the other half of my sock of hogs.
Fourthly
I give and bequeath to my daughter, Rebecca Bell six hundred dollars of the money I sold the girl June for, if I do not buy her another negpo with the money, also I give to her my second choice of Bedsteads and furniture. I also give to my daughters Rebecca and CarolineBell, one horse.
Fifthly
I give and bequeathto my daughter Caroline Bell one negro boy named Jim, one bed stead and furniture one safe and one trunk,
Lastly, it is my wish and desire that my executor should sell every species of property that I may die possessed of except what has been specially willed away and if I should have any money (p 207) left on hand after paying my debts. I wish it together with the amount of the sale of the above named peoperty equally divided between my son G.W Bell and my two daughters, Caroline & rebecca Bell.
Seventhly
I give and bequeath to my daughter Cynthia Moore fifty dollars, also one bedstead and furniture an after her death to her son Charles Moore.
Eightly--
I give and bequeath to my two grandchildred John and Lucy Evans, fifty dollars each.
Ninthly
It is my wish and desire that my son G.W. Bell pay out of his part of my estate the three bequests made to my daughter Cynthia Moore and John and Lucy Evans.

Lastly,
I nominate and appoint my son G.W. Bell & James J. Wilson my executor to this my last will and Testament.

In Testimony whereof I Jacob Belldo set my hand and seal this day 20th July 1854.

Jacob Bell (Seal)
Signed, Sealed and delivered in presence of
W.W. Williams
J.D. Nicholson

Settlement of A.J. Bright Admr. of G.W. Stack dec.
A.F. Bright Admr. of G.W. Stack. Dr.

To Amount Inventory	$399.33
Contra.	
By cash for Bond &C	2.00
Letters of Administration	.50
Copy of same	.50
Recording Inventory	.25
2 Receipts	2.00
2 Refunding bonds	1.00
Allowance to Admr.	10.00
Settlement &C	.24
	16.49
Amount due Legatees	382.83

(p 208) Settlement of H.V. Hooper Exr.of John J. Hooper
H.V. Hooper Exr. of John J. HooperDr.

To cash left on hand	39.00
Proceeds Crop Tobacco 1859	575.00
Amt cash received from N.V. Bryant	10.00
Amt. Thos. J. Shaw act.	16.95
Amt. John D. Dismukes act.	45.79
Amt. W.E. Felts act.	8.33
Amt. A.L. Fortune	33.50
Amt. A.E. Souel	27.14
Amt. received from W. Weatherford	84.75
	780.46
Contra	
By cash paid coffin	20.00
" Fee to clerk	5.42
" Amt. S.T. Fortune note	236.25
" " pais Souel	22.09
" " paid Raines & brown	1.15
" " paid H.J. Shaw	10.85
By Amt. paid John D. Dismukes	60.90
By Amt. paid Thos. W. Harris	11.24
By Amt. paid W.E. Felts	61.33
By Amt. paid Dr. Sam Arnold	50.00
By Amt. paid Bang Walker & Co.	139.00
By Amt. paid A.L. Fortune	23.25
By Amt. paid W. Weatherford Trustee	487.11
By Amt. paid W. Weatherford	79.91
By Amt. paid A.H. Williamson	5.00
By Amt. paid Cheatham Watson	14.25
By Amt. paid Thos. J? Shaw	85.27

By Amt. paid Boy, Ned	$ 20.00
By Amt. paid Boy, Murphey	9.15
By Amt. paid Taxes 1859	31.45
By Amt. paid bal. N.L. Fortune act.	13.75
By Amt. paid family expenses	50.00
By Clerk for settlement	1.50
	1433.87

Amt. paid by W.V. Hooper more than rec'd 658.41
Insolvent claims in the estate of John J. Hooper.

1 note on Eli Grisham	14.00
1 note on Wm. F. Bennett	50.00
1 note on Mrs. F. Bennett	60.00
1 note on J.E. Felts	70.00
1 note on Thornton & Co.	123.10
	317.10

(p 209) Amount bad claim belonging to the estate of John J. Hooper dec.

brought up	$317.10
1 note on W. Blankenship	11.47
1 Note on E. Ferfeson & Co.	21.85
1 account on Jacob Woodall	9.86
1 account on Wm. Simpson	17.02
1 account on D.A. Wilkins	27.63
(Having been paid)	
Amount of Insolvent claims	404.66

Last Inventory of John W. Shaw adm. of E.G. Murphey, dec.

To cash received from James Mallory	.50
To cash recd. from R.J. Mallory on acct.	0.23
To cash received from A.J. Bright Clerk	20.00
To cash received from S.H. Bracy	.50
To cash received from G.W. Gossett	2.25
To cash received from H. Hunter	1.00
To cash received from J.W. Hunt	.50
To cash received from C.& M. Clarksville	6.00
To cash received from C & M Nashville	42.50
To cash received from County Court Nashville	1.15
To cash received from J.W. Hunt adm. T. King	1.50
To cash received from William W. Williams	1.00
To cash received from R.J. Mallory for poplar trees	84.00
To cash received from Cross & Sons on Execution	10.50
To cash received from E.P. Mosier	1.70
To cash received from W.P. Matthews	.50
To cash received from W. Durham Rent of land	5.00
	184.73

An Inventory and account of sale of the personal Estate of Charles G. Lovell dec. sold Oct. 2 1861.
W.G. Shelton, Administrator.

Names of Purchaser	Articles sold	Amt.
N. Jordan	1 small bull	$ 2.00
N. Jordan	1 Black Bull	2.80

Widow Lovell (C.G.)	2 Heifers	$5.00
Widow Lovell (C. G.)	2 Steers	10.00
Widow Lovell	1 Bay mare & Colt	25.00
Jno. Cullum	1 Bay horse colt	75.50
Widow C.G. Lovell	1 clay bank mare	17.50
Jesse Hooper	1 Bay colt	21.00
Alex Work	1 sorrel colt	50.00
W.T. Hooper	Rent of land	46.00
	Total Amt. Sales	234.80

(p 210) Amount Sale C.G. Lovells estate brot over 234.80
Inventory of notes of C.G. Lovell found in his possession at time of his death.
1 note on J.F. Russell rendered by C.C. Hooper due Feb. 1st 1861 for 600.00
1 note on J? F. Russell indorsed by C.C. Hooper due Feb. 1st 1861 for 200.00
1 note on James Brummett due Feb. 11th 1860 (D) 3.40
1 constable receipt of Wm. Jordan for the collection of a note on D.T. McCavock due Aug. 25. 1859 $500.00
1 Due Bill on Jesse Jordan for ½ of five hundred Dollars on D.T. McCa McCavock held by Jesse Jordan due to C.G. Lovell when collected dated Nov. 14th 1859 (D) 250.00
1 due bill on J. Jordan for ½ of a $500.00 note on J.C. Darden due June 10th 1859 for (D) 250.00
Cr. on the above note 100.00
1 due bill on J.Jordan for ½ of anote given by C.B. Peacher due January 15th 1856 for (D) 500.00
The above three due bills of J. Jordan are due by him when collected, and nor before to the estate of C.G. Lovell.
1 claim on heatham County for 20.00
1 claim on Cheatham County 4.37
1 Constable receipt of W.W. Creel dated Sept. 11th 1860 for the collection of a note on T.Y. Northern due Sept. 1860 (D) 450.00
One note on Jesse Jordan dated Aug. 31st 1860 for 700.00
1 note on J.A. Work dated Oct. 20th 1857 (Doubt) 22.45
Sworn in open court May 6th 1861
W.G. Shelton Admr's

(p 211) Inventory of personal property of J.J. Hooper estate as given by H.V. Hooper, Executor, Mat 4th 1861

1 Negro man	Dred	About	47	years of age
1 " "	Ned	"	28	"
1 " "	Murphey	"	37	"
1 " Woman	Caroline	"	37	"
1 " "	Becky	"	32	"
1 " "	Matilda	"	27	"
1 " Girl	Bedda	"	13	"
1 " Boy	Ruben	"	11	"
1 " "	Tom	"	10	"
1 " "	Don	"	8	"
1 " "	William		5	"
1 Infant John	John		3	"

1 Negro Boy	Lewis	About	5 years
1 " "	Frank	"	4 "
1 Infant	Harriett	"	2 "
1 "		"	2 months

5 mules
1 Horse
1 mare
10 heads cattle
32 head sheep
50 head hogs
1 Four horse wagon
1 two horse wagon
1 water cart
1 Buggy (Worthless)
13 plows
6 sets harness
6 weeding hoes
2 grub hoes
1 cross cut saw
1 hand saw
1/3 interest in wheat fan
12 or 15000 pounds tobacco
8 bedsteads
4 feather beds
2 mattresses
Bedding
2 clocks
1 Book Case
1 cupboard
1 Press
1 Bureau
1 Lounge
2 Dining Tables
3 small Dressing Tables
3 wash stands
2 work stands
1 candle stands
2 Doz. chairs
1 wheel
1 clothes chest
1 Looking Glass
H.V. Hooper Ex.
Sworn to before me May 4th 1861

(p 212) An account of sales made of the personal property of W.D. Edwards dec. at his lateresidence in Cheatham County after having advertised according to law.

Articles sold	Purchasers names	Amt.
2 Spades	L.J. Pardue	.25
1 Lot of plows	G.W. McCarley	1.20
1 Pot 9	M.R. McDaniel	.10
3 wedges, 2 Renches	John T. Hooper	1.10
1 Lot scrap iron	John T. Hooper	7.75
1 Sledge	G.W. McCarley	.25
1 DO	G.W. McFarley	.45

1 crow bar & poker	G.W. McFarley	1.05
1 Lot Lumber	Wm. Hand	1.00
1 Lot cedar	Wm. Hand	4.00
1 Lot clamps &C	John T. Hooper	4.25
1 Lot Lumber	W. McFadden	1.00
1 Lot Cherry Lumber	W.M. McFadden	1.10
1 cross cut saw	G.W. McCarley	5.00
1 Lot short lumber	W.M. McFadden	1.00
1 Jack	John T. Hooper	3.50
1 Lot Lumber	Jas. S. Stewart	5.00
1 " "	W.M. McFadden	2.75
1 Grind Stone	John T. Hooper	3.25
1 Lot waggon spokes	Mariah Edwards	5.00
1 skift	Mariah Edwards	1.75
1 wood boat & cable	Mariah Edwards	66.00
1 Lot Cord Wood	Mariah Edwards	15.00
192 lbs bacon -- 15	Catherine Mayfield	28.00
100 lbs bacon -- $14\frac{1}{2}$	Jonathan Sanders	14.50
200 lbs. bacon -- $14\frac{1}{2}$	H.W. Turner	29.00
200 lbs. Bacon -- 16	H.W. Turner	30.00
42 lbs. Bacon -- 16	H.W. Turner	6.72
1 Heifer	L.J. Perdue	10.50
2 small steers	Mariah Edwards	10.50
1 cow and calf	L.J. Perdue	16.25
1 sow and pigs	Mariah Edwards	6.00
2 sows & 15 pigs	L.J. Perdue	14.00
6 1st choice Hogs	L.J. Perdue	27.00
1 sow and four pigs	L.J. Perdue	4.00
6 2nd choice Hogs	L.J. Perdue	24.00
Remainder 7 $3.75	L.J. Perdue	26.25
1 pair steel yards	J.S. Stewart	.50
2 files	John T. Hooper	1.10
1 foot adz	R.L. Weakley	.25
1 Broad Axe	L. Barton	.50
1 Lot Butts scisors	John T. Hooper	.45
(p 212) Amt. brot up		
1 shot gun	G.W. McCarley	3.00
1 Lot Paints	R.B. Bright	3.25
1 Bedstead & Furniture	Mariah Edwards	6.00
1 clock	Mariah Edwards	1.00
1 Cedar chest	Mariah Edwards	3.00
1 Jug and Jar	J.S. Stewart	1.00
		397.52

The foregoing is a full and perfect account of all the property of the estate of W.D. Edwards, decd. directed by law to be sold which has come to my hands, notes with good security due 12 months after date were taken from the purchasers.
This 20th day of April 1861.

James H. Williams Admr. of W.D. Edwards dec.

Sworn to before me this day, 1861
W.W. Williams, Clerk

The following is a perfect Inventory of the personal effects belonging to the estate of W.D. Edwards, dec. which has come into my hands Independent of the property sold at his sale.

1 note on Jonathan Fambrough for$12.85 due the 27th Jan. 1860 $12.85
1 note on W.P. Hooper & son for 14.81 due 25th Feb. 1860 9.81
With a credit of $5.00 the 1st March 1861 4.50
1 due bill on Lewis Reader, Clerk Steamer, V.K. Stevenson for$15.00 due Nov. 20th 1860 15.00
1 account on Jonathan Hollis 15.00
1 account on Jackson McKinnon & Co. 88.59
1 account on Jonathan Sanders 18.41
1 account on John C. Weakley for 9.00
2 Inventory on page 214.
J.H. Williams Admr.

(p 214) Inventory of the personal property of Mary Harris decd. sold on the 15th June 1861 by John L. Harris Admr.

Articles Sold	Purchaser	Amt.
3 chairs	D. Harris	.25
1 Bed and Clothing	D. Harris	18.00
1 saddle	D. Harris	.25
1 Bed and furniture	D. Harris	18.00
1 Lot sundries	D. Harris	.10
1 Bed Stead	D. Harris	.50
1 Chest	D. Harris	2.50

Notes and accounts

1 note on A.H. Williams & W.W. Williams for one hundred dollars due 17th Jan. 1859. $100.00
Interest.
1 note on Thos. W. Felts due 25th Nov. 1858 for 15.00
Interest on same
1 note on Thos. W. Felts due 20 January 1858 for 2.70
Interest on same.

(2 Inventory)
Account Sale of W.D. Edwards property on the 15th of July 1861 on a credit until the 20th April 1862.

Purchasers name	Articles sold	Amt.
W.H. Stewart	1 yoke Oxen	45.00
T.J. Miles½	1 Bu. wheat.50c	5.00
J.S. Stewart	10 Bu. wheat .40c	4.00
R.L. Weakley	10 Bu. wheat 42c	4.20
Thos, McDaniel	10 Bu. wheat .42c	4.20
J.S. Stewart	10 Bu. wheat .42c	4.20
R.L. Weakley	10 Bu. wheat .38	3.80
Thos. J. Miles	10 Bu. wheat .36	3.60
R.L. Weakley	10 Bu. wheat .36	3.60
R.L. Weakley	10 Bu. wheat .35	3.50
Maria Edwards	10 Bu. wheat .33	3.30
Mariah Edwards	37 Bu. wheat .23½	8.69
		93.09

Lemuel Morris	G.C. Binkley Admr.	
1 Tin Bucket	James Read	.20
1 Hand axe and Hammer	E.L. Darrow	.10
1 Walnut Table	E.L. Darrow	.50
1 Ten safe	J.D. Darrow	6.10
1 Tray and sifter	J.W. Darrow	.30

1 Lot Barrels	N.B. Binkley	.05
1 basket and sundries	J.D. Darrow	.50
1 lot sundries	W.L. Binkley	.50
1 Large Jug	W.L. Binkley	.15
1 Pocket Knife	James Cochran	.30
2 candle sticks	J.D. Darrow	.15
1 Box and three chairs	A.L. Hudgens	.70
7 chairs	J.D. Darrow	.65
1 cupboard	E.L. Darrow	5.00
1 shot gun	J.D. Darrow	3.25
1 clock	N.N. Binkley	2.50
1 small table	J.W. Darrow	.95
1 Bed and clothing	J.D. Darrow	9.50
1 stead & Cord	H.H. Binkley	3.80
1 Bed and clothing	W.L. Binkley	19.05
1 Bed and Stead	J.D. Darrow	1.00
1 Bed and Blanket	J.W. Darrow	1.75
1 Quilt	A.L. Hudgens	.50
2 Blankets	J.W. Darrow	.95
1 Quilt	Mrs. Cochran	.60

(p 215) Lemuel Morris — G.C. Binkley Admr.

Articles sold	Purchaser	Amt.
1 Tin Bucket	James Reed	.20
1 Hand axe and Harness	E.L. Darrow	.10
1 Walnut table	E.L. Darrow	.50
1 Ten Safe	J.D. Darrow	6.10
1 tray and sifts	J.W. Darrow	.30
1 Lot Barrels	N.N. Binkley	.15
1 Bakket & Sundries	J.D. Darrow	.50
1 Lot sundries	W.L. Binkley	.50
1 Large Jug	W.L. Binkley	.15
1 Pocket knife	James Cochran	.30
2 candle sticks	J.D. Darrow	.15
1 Box and three chairs	H.L. Hudgens	.70
7 chairs	J.D. Darrow	.65
1 cupboard	E.L. Darrow	5.00
1 Shot gun	J.D. Darrow	3.25
1 clock	N.N. Binkley	2.50
1 small Table	J.W. Darrow	.95
1 Bed and clothing	J.D. Darrow	9.50
1 Stead and Cord	H.H. Binkley	3.80
1 Bed and clothing	W.L. Binkley	19.05
1 Bed and Stead	J.D. Darrow	1.00
1 Bed and Blanket	J.W. Darrow	1.75
1 Quilt	A.L. Hudgens	.50
2Blankets	J.W. Darrow	.95
1 Quilt	Mrs. Cochran	.60
1 Lot sundries	J.W. Darrow	.10
1 Razor and Strap	E.L. Darrow	.60
1 Lot Pocket Books	William Rose	.05
1 Press	J.H. Binkley	5.00
1 Lot Bacon, 100 lbs. .14c	Nancy Morris	14.00
1 Lot "	N.N. Binkley	11.20
1 Lot bacon	W.L. Binkley	10.07
1 Lot tallow 19qts. .10c	J?D. Darrow	1.90

1 Stand Beef	E.L. Darrow	.50
1 Keg Vinegar	H.H. Binkley	.40
1 Bucket & lard	E.L. Darrow	.60
25 Lbs. Lard	Nancy Morris	2.50
Lard	William Rose	3.20
1 Keg Salt	J.R. Binkley	.45
1 Wash Tub	A.S. Hudgens	.60
1 Lot sundries	E.L. Darrow	.05
1 Lard Trough	J.R. Binkley	.10
1 Pad Lock	James W. Darrow	.10
1 Lot Sundries	E.L. Darrow	.05
1 Axe Handle	H.H. Binkley	.05
(p 216)		
1 Lot lard	H.H. Binkley	.92
1 Lot Kegs	J.D. Darrow	.20
1 Trough	J.R. Binkley	.05
1 Crock	N.M. Binkley	.10
1 Lot Hogshead	N.M. Binkley	.15
1 Milk Pan	J.D. Darrow	.15
1 Wash Pan	J.D. Darrow	.15
1 Dish	J.W. Darrow	.30
1 Bucket	J.D. arrow	.25
1 Cup & Bucket	J.D. Darrow	.15
1 Pewter Basin	J.W. Darrow	.25
1 Pewter Basin	J.W. Darrow	.25
1 Pewter Plate	J.W. Darrow	.05
2 Pans	W.F. Simpson	.10
2 Pitchers	Mrs. Cochren	.10
1 pair cotton cards	m. Follis	.15
6 paltes	W.L. Binkley	.30
6 plates	J.H. Binkley	.10
2 small dishes	A.L. Hudgens	.30
1 Jug Bowl & C	J.R. Binkley	.20
1 Lot cups and saucers	Mrs. Kedler	.30
1 Plate	James Darrow	.15
1 Lot tea spoons	J.H. Binkley	.20
1 " " "	J.H. Binkley	.05
1 Demi John	J.D. Darrow	.15
1 Lot knives	A.L. Hudgens	.30
2 mollasses Bottles	A.L. Hudgens	.20
1 Glass Jar	N.M. Binkley	.15
1 Bag shot	J.W. Darrow	1.05
1 Lot nails &C	E.L. Darrow	.05
1 Lot Bottles	N.M. Binkley	.35
1 Lot Sundries	A.L. Hudgens	.10
1 Pot rack	J.D. Darrow	.20
1 Pot rack	J.D. Darrow	.25
1 Pair Shovel and tongs	J.R. Binkley	.20
Hand Irons	Henry Binkley	.60
1 Lot Sundries	H.H. Binkley	.10
1 Pair Hand Irons	J.R. Binkley	.10
1 Reap Hook	E.L. Darrow	.05
1 Coffee Mill & Lot	N.M. Binkley	.15
1 Bucket	R.H. Newman	.05
1 Pail	J.W. Darrow	.10
1 Water Bucket	A.L. Hudgens	.05
1 Water Bucket	A.L. Hudgens	.20

(p 217)

½ Bushel & B arrel	H.H. Binkley	.05
1 Stand & Saddle	H.H. Binkley	.05
1 Box & Keg	J.D. Darrow	.10
1 Lot plow geers	H.H. Binkley	/30
2 Baskets	J.D. Darrow	.30
1 Saddle	E.L. Darrow	2.55
1 Plow	J.R. Binkley	.30
1 Shovel	J.W. Darrow	.05
1 Shovel plow	A.H. Binkley	1.25
1 Avery Plow	J.D. Darrow	1.00
1 Clothes line	J.D. Darrow	.30
4 hoes	J.W. Darrow	.25
1 Log chain	A.L. Hudgens	1.55
1 Lot Sundries	B.F. Binkley	.25
Corn	W.L. Binkley	6.02
71 Bundles Fodder	J.D. Darrow	1.00
1 Cow and Calf	H. Simmons	10.00
1 Mare	E.S. Simpson	31.50
1 Lot growing corn	J.R. Binkley	10.50
Irish Potatoes	J.H. Binkley	1.05
1 Axe	Levi Binkley	.30
1 Axe & Wedge	H.H. Binkley	.15
1 Axe	H.H. Binkley	1.25
1 Lot Sundries	H. Simmons	.05
2 plains	A.H. Binkley	.50
1 Lot sundries	J.H. Binkley	.10
1 Large Pot	H.H. Binkley	.65
1 pr. pot hooks	H.H. Binkley	.25
1 Frying pan	A.L. Hudgens	.25
1 small pot and hooks	J.R. Binkley	.35
1 skillet & Lids	Mrs. Keelor	.40
1 Pot	J.H. Binkley	.30
1 Oven & Lid	W.L. Binkley	.10
1 skillet & Lid	J.D. Darrow	.65
1 shaving skillet	J.D. Darrow	.30
1 smoothing iron	Mrs. Keejer	.25
1 pair candle molds	A.H. Binkley	.30
1 Coffee pot	H.H. Binkley	.30
Cash left on hand		.20
1 note on J.J. Binkley due on the 10th August 1850 for		157.50
with a credit		27.88

(p 218)

1 note on B.F. Binkley due on 20th day of August 1857 for	200.00
Interest on same	45.00
	245.00
1 note on H.H. Binkley & B.F. Binkley due 20th August 1857 for	200.00
Interest on same	45.00
Total	685.22

A list of property sold of Polly T. Hudgens dec. on the 18th June 1861.

Articles sold	Purchasers name	Amt.
1 bedstead and furniture	A.L. Hudgens	$12.25
1 Bedstead & Furniture	A.L. Hudgens	9.75
1 Chest	W.L. Hudgens	3.50
1 Chest	James Hudgens	2.05

1 Cupboard	Daniel Hudgens	1.05
1 Bowl, Knives & Forks	Daniel Hudgens	.30
1 Pitcher &C	Daniel Hudgens	.45
1 Lot Bottles	W.L. Hudgens	1..10
1 Black Mule	W.W. Hudgens	20.00
5 shoats	Thomas W. Perdue	6.25
1 sow and pigs	W.W. Hudgens	4.45
5 head sheep	W.L. Hudgens	6.25
1 Cow and calf	James Hudgens	38.00
1 Yoke Oxen	A.L. Hudgens	53.00

(p 219)

Settlement of Moses Jones Administrator of H.W. Hannah. dec.

Moses Jones Administrator of H.W. Hannah	Dr
To amount Inventory	$254.85
Amount notes and accts.	27.05
	281.90

Contra.

By 1 note to A. Hannah		$10.00
By 1 proven account to	M.A. Hannah	15.00
By 1 " " "	Jno. A. Clark	12.00
By 1 " " "	M.L. Clark	7.77
By 1 " " "	J.M. Fulghum	5.35
By 1 " " "	S.A. Thompson	1.90
By 1 " " "	W.W. Hutton	.50
By 1 " " "	W.P. Hays	3.65
By Tax in the year 1861		2.30
By Clerks for bond letter Adm.		3.00
By Proven act to Moses Jones		1.90
By 1 proven account Dr. E.S. Exum		2.00
By Allowance to Administrator		20.60
By Tax for year 1862		2.52
By Recording Inventory		.30
By Settlement		.50
By 1 account on H.W. Whitfield (Insolvent)		5.00
By 1 Account on B.F. Hannah Dr.		1.00
		96.29
Amount due heirs Aug. 1st 1861		185.61

(p 220P

A list of the property of John Cochran dec. sold on the ----
by Mrs. E. Cochran Admrx

Purchasers names	Articles sold	Amt.
John Simmons	1 Jointed stove	.50
John Simmons	1 stock Hanel	1.00
J.F. Underwood	1 stock hanels	.50
John Simmons	Cooper knives	3.00
John Simmons	Whetstone	1.60
F.G. Boyt	1 Hand Axe	1.40
W.H. Blankenship	1 Lot sundries	.30
John Forbes	1 Iron wedge	.50
John Simmons	1 set tin hoops	.25
John Simmons	1 hand axe	.75
Jno. Forbes	1 stock	.30
W.H. Blankenship	1 lot chesels	.25
Jno. Adams	1 Razor strop &C	25
R. Smith	Bottle and Moles	.25
W. Bobbitt	1 Jug	.25

E. Smith	1 Water Barrel	.20
Jno Adams	1 axe handle & sack	.20
F.G. Hoyt	1 Plow	1.00
E. Smith	1 Barrel and Basket	.20
E. Smith	1 Flour Barrel	.30
Virginia Bobbit	1 Lard Stand	.40
W.B. Gower	1 small Keg	.10
Elijah Smith	1 small keg	.15
Virginia Bobbit	1 weeding hoe	.55
E. Smith	1 grubbing hoe	.85
W.C. Gower	1 Axe	.25
W.H. Blankenship	1 Set Geer	1.60
		17.40

Notes and accounts

1 note on T.W. Harris due on 13th Oct. 1855	$200.00
Interest on same	70.00
1 note on T.W. Harris due on the 24th Feb. 1856	70.00
1 Credit January 9th 1860	26.00
1 credit Aug 15th 1860	76.25
	60.25
Balance principal on said note	9.75
Interest on same	18.66
	328.41
Amount of Estate	315.81

(p 221) Settlement of E. Cochran of John Cochran decd.
Mrs. Elizabeth Cochran Admrx. of John Cochran

To amount of Inventory	315.81
Contra.	
By Jo Hudson proven acct.	28.25
By John C. Hale proven acct.	7.58
By D.W. McFadden proven acct.	15.00
By Tax 1859	1.00
By W.D. Wall proven acct.	1.75
By amount paid Thos. W. Harris	1.50
Allowance Admx.	20.00
Clerks fee	3.50
Account on J. Cochran	3.00
Amount due acc settlement	234.28

A list of property sold notes and accounts of A.H. Binkley dec. sold on the 16th Aug. 1861 by G.C. Binkley.

1 Shovel plow	James Demumbreun	.55
1 Half Shovell	E.J. Binkley	.35
1 Cary plow	G.C. Binkley	.30
Plain AC	James Demumbreun	.50
1 Cutting Box	Henry Binkley	.50
1 pair geer	John Shivers	2.40
1 Gun	Henry Simmons	4.35
1 Shot gun	Henry Binkley	10.50
1 mans saddle	James Demumbreun	10.00
4 shoats	B.F. Binkley	10.00
4 shoats	James Demumbreun	8.00
1 sow & eight pigs	B.H. Newman	10.25
1 serrel mule	Thos. O'Brien	151.00

Accounts

One account on G.C. Binkley	1.50
One account on Joseph Binkley	2.00
One account on Isaac Nabors	2.00
One account on Jesse Chivers	5.00
One account for his part proceeds of horse and feeds	5.84
	255.24

(p 222) Amount slae of property belonging to the estate of R. Sanders Dec sold by A.W. Sanders on the ---- day of ------

Purchasers named	Articles sold	Amt.
Susan Durham	1 Pot and hooks	.10
W.C. Sanders	1 Oven	.10
Martha Edwards	1 Tea Kettle	.35
B.J. Barnes	1 Skillet &C	.30
W.C. Sanders	1 Pot & Hooks	.70
Susan Durham	1 Skillet	.30
Susan Durham	2 shovels	.35
Susan Durham	1 Pot rack	.85
Jno. Sanders	Kettle	2.00
Susan Durham	Grubbing and Weeding hoe	.35
E.G. Hudgens	1 Axe	10
Jno. Sanders	1 Set geer	.80
Jno. Sanders	1 plow & single tree	1.50
Jonathan Sanders	1 mans saddle	1.25
Susan Durham	2 Lard stands	.10
David Sanders	1 Straw cutter	1.35
David Sanders	1 lot glass tumblers	10
David Sanders	1 candle stick	.15
Melby Sanders	1 Dining table	.15
Melby Sanders	1 Coffee Mill	.20
John Z. Hudgens	1 Coffee Mill & Shears	.05
Daniel Hudgens	1 sugar bowl & crock	.25
Melby Sanders	1 Piggin &C	.10
Jonathan Sanders	5 chairs	3.00
Jno. Sanders	1 Bible & Hymn Book	2.00
A.J. Teasley	1 Chest	.50
H. Maxey	1 Bureau	12.25
Jno. Z. Hudgens	1 Clock	1.75
Jno. Sanders	1 Chest	2.50
Sam Hudgens	1 Cupboard	8.00
John Sanders	1 pitcher	.20
Jonathan Sanders	1 pair fire dogs	1.00
Susan Durham	1 bed and furniture	14.00
Melby Sanders	1 bed and furniture	12.00
David Sanders	1 pair scissors	.15
David Sanders	1 quilt	3.25
Sam Durham	1 counterpane	2.25
Sam Durham	1 Turf Counterpane	1.55
Daniel Hudgens	1 quilt	1.00
H. Maxey	1 quilt	.80
Jonathan Sanders	1 Quilt	1.50
Jno. Sanders	1 Quilt	1.00
(p 223)		
John Sanders	1 quilt	1.00
Sally Farrer	1 Blanket	1.00
Jno. Sanders	9 bushels wheat @ 55	4.95

Sam Durham	5 bushels wheat @ 1.00	$5.00
Jonathan Sanders	9 bushels wheat @ .55	4.95
Jno. S. Hudgens	279 shares oats 1¾	4.88
Daniel Hudgens	686 shares oats @ 1.62	11.11
Jno. Sanders	2 Barrels corn @ 3.00	6.00
Jno. Sanders	1 Cart	2.00
James Perry	1 water bucket	.40
Jno. Sanders	1 Ring and Steeple	.25
Jno. Sanders	1 Sorrel Horse	15.00
Jno. Sanders	1 wheat stand	.25
Jno. Sanders	1 meal sack	.20
Henry Maxey	1 saddle	.25
David Sanders	1 set knives and forks	.40
Susan Durham	2 Pans	.25
W.C. Sanders	1 Pitcher	.35
Meltry Sanders	1 bowl and contents	.45
David Sanders	4 plates	.05
Henry Maxey	2 dishes	.50
Meltry Sanders	1 set teaspoons	.40
Melbey Sanders	1 set cups and saucers	.40
Milley Sanders	1 Table with draws	.25
Martha Edwards	1 Jar	.50
Susan Durham	1 churn	.90
Melbey Sanders	1 wash tub	.40
Susan Durham	1 Tray & Sifter	1.00
James Perry	6 chairs	1.65
Melbey Sanders	1 wheel reel	2.40
J.L. Edwards	1 Iron wedge	.40
A.J. Teasley	1 side saddle	10.00

(p 224) Will of John J. Chamblis
I, Jno. J Chambliss do make and publish this my last will and Testament herely making void all other wills made by me at any time.

Ist. I direct that my funeral expenses and all my debts be paid as soon after my death as possible out of any monies that I may die possessed of or may first come into the hands of my executor.

2nd. I give and bequeath to my beloved wife Betheney B. Chambliss during her natural life or widowhood, my land with all the appurtenances after her marriage or death to be equally divided between my children, Fredonia Chambliss, Sophronia Chambliss, Pleasant M. Chambliss, Harriet E. Chambliss and John H. Chambliss.

3rd. I give and bequeath to my wife a sufficient number of horses and cattle to cary on the farm and also a sufficient quantity of other stock for the use of the family.

4th. I desire in case of sicknesswhere medical aid is required that each one after they are twenty one years of age pay their own medical bills out of their distributive share.

5th I desire that all surplus be sold when time promise renumeration prices.

Lastly, I herely nominate and appoint my friend James Frazier my executof, in witness whereof I do this my last will set my hand and seal. This June 20th day 1861.

J.J. Chambliss.

Signed sealed and published in our presence and we have subscribed our names in the presence of the testator, This 20th day of June 1861.

Attest. David B. Barton
Lemuel Barton

(p 225) An account of the sale of the property of G. Hudgens, dec. sold by B.G. Hudgens, one of the e xecutors, of said dec. and on the 24th Sept 1861

Articles sold	Purchasers Names	Amt.
Two trays, 1 Pot	B.W. Bradley	.25
1 Kettle	B.W. Bradley	1.25
1 Tea Water	B.W. Bradley	.05
1 shot gun	B.W. Bradley	5.00
1 Frow	B.W. Bradley	.25
1 claw Hammer	B.W. Bradley	.25
1 Iron wedge	B.W. Bradley	.35
1 Bridle	B.W. Bradley	.20
1 Oven	B.W. Bradley	.80
1 set cart Tyin	B.W. Bradley	1.55
1 Pot	B.S. Williams	2.05
1 saw scythe &C	W. Bradley	.25
1 Pot & 2 trays	W. Bradley	.15
1 Jug	B.L. Williams	.50
1 Bedstead &C	J.W. Owen	13.00
1 Bedstead	B.L. Williams	4.00
1 Bed	T.H. Hudgens	12.00
1 Bed and Stead	W. Bradley	2.30
1 Trunk	B.L. Williams	.10
1 Counterpaine	RodaSanders	2.05
2Counterpaines	Roda Sanders	[illegible].95
1 Bed Quilt	R. Sanders	1.00
2 Sheets	R. Sanders	1.30
2Sheets	R. Sanders	2.55
1 Counterpaine	R. Sanders	.50
2 Pillow slips	R. Sanders	.40
3 pillow slips	R. Sanders	.40
1 Bed Quilt	R. Sanders	.25
2 Bed Quilts	R. Sanders	.95
1 Lot bed clothes	R. Sanders	1.35
1 Bed Stead	R. Sanders	.55
1 Cupboard	W.W. Hudgens	12.50
1 Lot geese @ 5 cts. each	B.W. Bradley	
6 bTurkeys	R. Sanders	1.90

Hire negroes

Sarah	B.L. Williams	6.50
Martha	W.W. Read	1.50
Nice and four children until 25th Dec. 1861.	B.W. Bradley to have $40.00 for keeping	
Seal and Amos till 25th Dec. '61	B.W. Bradley to have $20.00 for keeping	

(p 226) Inventory of the personal property belonging to the estate of Hiram Langford sold by Josh Humphreys, sold on the 16th day of August 1861.

Purchasers names	Articles sold	Amt.
J.J. Thorn	1 Bee Gum	$1.50
J.J. Thorn	1 Bee Gum	1.35
Jno. Duke	1 Bee Gum	1.00
Henry Felts	1 Bee Gum	.50

Henry Felts	1 Bee Gum	.60
A.J. Thorn	1 Bee Gum	.90
Thomas Shores	1 Bee Gum	.35
Thomas Justice	1 Bee Gum	.40
A.J. Thorn	1 Bee Gum	.50
Thomas Justice	1 Bee Gum	.90
R.L. King	1 Bee Gum	.90
Obidah Knox	1 Bee Gum	1.75
George Garason	1 Bee Gum	1.00
R.J. King	1 Bee Gum	1.00
John Aakins	1 Bee Gum	1.25
R.J. King	1 Bee Gum	1.00
John Pambrough	1 Bee Gum	2.00
Martha Langford	Contens of garden	1.00
A. Swift	1 cross out saw	2.65
Henry Felts	1 Grind stone	2.60
I.P. Blankenship	5 first choice hogs	29.50
I. P. Blankenship	5 second choice hogs	21.00
I.P. Blankenship	5 third choice hogs	21.00
I.P. Blankenship	5 fourth " "	21.00
Wlias Johnson	5 fifth choice of hogs	11.25
A.J. Perdue	5 sixth " "	7.00
I. P. Blankenship	5 seventh choice hogs	5.00
"	5 eighth choice hogs	5.00
"	5 ninth choice hogs	5.00
"	5 out of pen	6.00
R.D. Mosely	1 Bay mule	40.50
Panister Wright	1 sorrel male	42.50
Jno. S. Majors	1 Bay mare	85.00
William Padden	1 Bay horse	3.00
H.W. Turner	1 yoke oxen	54.25
R.J. Mabry	1 Heifer	21.50
E.L. Williams	1 spotted bull	10.00
E.L. Williams	1 white bull	6.25
William McFadden	1 cow and calf	25.00
Jno. Hogan	1 Fan Mill	20.00
J.B. Blankenship	1 Ox Cart	2.00
J.B. Blankenship	1 cart	2.50
(p 227)		
Gid Nicholson	1 field corn	100.00
Gid Nicholson	1 Turnip patch	5.25
G.R. Harris	1 Oat stack	6.00
Henry Blanton	1 Oat stack	5.50
G.R. Harris	1 Oat stack	4.50
David Carnes	1 Oat stack	4.50
G.R. Harris	1 Oat stack	4.50
David Justice	1 Oat stack	4.50
G.R. Harris	1 Oat stack	4.50
Martha Langford	1 Field corn	15.00
Martha Langford	1 Lot fodder	2.00
James Gill	1 Pistol	1.30
J.P. Blankenship	1 Barrel Vinegar	1.45
J.P. Blankenship	1 Lot Barrels	.10
Ebin Gupton	1 stack oats	2.25
Ebin Gupton	1 Lot in crib	1.50

Alsey Jones	1 Lot soap	.65
Alsey Jones	18 head geese	3.06
M.G. Turner	1 Lot	4.00
Joshua Stroud	2 stacks wheat	5.20
A. Jones	1 Lot Bacon	12.00
David Carnes	3 Hogs	3.00
John S. Major	7 chickens	.70

2nd account of sale made of the personal state of Martha A. Harris dec. on the 10th of November 1860.

Names	Articles	Amt.
E. Harris	163 barrels of corn	$554.20
E. Harris	1 Pen shucks	2.20
E. Harris	1 Lot millet hay	4.60
E. Harris	1 Lot shucks	4.00
Ben Howell	5 Barrels corn	17.00
Thos. Sesler	52 Barrels corn	205.40
Thos. Sesler	1 Pen shucks	7.10
		794.50

(p 228) 2nd sale of the propertyof Mary T. Hudgens made by B.F. Walker on the 30th day of August 1861.

Purchasers names	Articles sold	Amt.
Daniel Hudgens	19 Bbls & 4 Bu. @$1.65	32.67
James Hudgens	1 Lot shucks	.75
John Forbes	1 Mare	15.50

2nd Account of Sale of property Sold by G.C. Binkley. Administrator of A.H. Binkley dec. Sold on the 7th day of Decr. 1861.

Purchasers names	Articles sold	Amt.
H. Williams	1 Lot corn	7.50
E.L. Darrow	5 Barrels corn	15.00
E.L. Darrow	3 Bushels Corn	1.80
Adam Binkley	5 Barrels corn	15.00
J.P.B. Henderson	5 barrels corn	14.00
C.D. Lawrence	500 Bundles Oats	3.75
Jno. Shivers	500 Bundles Oats	7.50
C.D. Lawrence	565 Bundles oats	9.88
Jno. Shivers	500 Bundles Oats	8.25
C.D. Lawrence	500 Bbls refused corn	7.75
		95.43

(p 229) An account of the sale of the property by E.C. Allem Trustee for J.A. Work. sold at private Sale except mule and Boat Gunnel.

Purchasers names	Articles Sold	Amt.
E.J. Wadkins	10 barrels corn @ 3.25	$32.50
15 barrels fed to stock		
Benjamin Greer	1 Yellow mare	7.50
Dr. Williams	3 head of cattle	42.00
R.P. Work	1 Bay Mare	20.00
R.P. Work	1 Yearling	5.00
G.W. Allen	1 Mule	60.00
G.W. Allen	1 town lot	40.00
James Lenox	1 Set boat gunnel	7.00
		214.00

Contra.

By cash paid to A.L. Demoss drawing deed	$10.00
By cash paid Bond and recording Deed	2.25
By cash paid Howling corn	2.50
By Commissioner 5/100 per cent	10.70
Net amount of proceeds	188.55

Will of William A/Fortune Dec.

I, W.A. Fortune have this day appointed J.W. Hunt my agent to act for me in my absence as my lawful attorney to collect and receipt in my name and to pay my debts that I owe, also leave all my papers Books &C also my horse, bridle Blanket & saddle in case of any accident I empower him to sell the articles and Should I Never return. I will and desire that whatever remains after paying my debts, shall be equally divided together with what remains in the hands of my guardian, between my three sisters, Jane, Elizabeth and Ellen in regard to the portion that will go to my youngest sister Ellen. I desire that it remain in the hands of J.W. Hunt until she is twenty one years or marries and she dies it to be equally divided between Jane and Elizabeth Should J.W. Hunt die he shall appoint one in his place .

This 11th day of May 1861.

P.S. In case of the death of the said J.W. Hunt the county court appoint someone to carry out the provisions of the above articles.

William A. Fortune
Witnesses
Geo. W. Hunt
W.W. Williams

(p 230) An account of the sale of the personal property belonging to the estate of James B. Moore sold by J.J. Bradley on the 14th Sept. 1861

Articles sold	Purchasers name	Amt.
3 weeding hoes	James Moore	.05
1 spade	James Moore	.05
1 Bull Tongue plow	Robert Lane	.40
2 plows & Ox Yoke	James Moore	.10
1 Lot Hames &C	Robert Lane	.35
1 Pr traces	Robert Lane	.45
1 2 horse wagon	James Walker	8.25
1 Cross cUt saw	Sterling walker	5.50
1 Bed	Elizabeth Moore	3.00
1 Bed	Mary Moore	3.00
1 spade	Mrs Moore	.35
1 Wedge	H. Williams	.65
1 wheel	Mrs. Moore	.25
1 Pot	Mrs. Moore	1.00
4 chairs	Ben Moore	.50
2 chairs	Mrs. Moore	.25
1 Bed Stead	Eliz. Moore	.10
1 Feather Bed	Julia A/Moore	6.00
1 Bed stead	Mrs. Moore	.10
1 Bed Stead	Mrs. Moore	.10
1 Bed Stead	Mary Moore	1.60
1 Pot	Mary Moore	.35
1 Grind Stone	Ben Moore	.45
1 Grind Stone	James Moore	.05

1 Hand Saw	Daniel Hudgens	.40
1 Seive	Ben Moore	.10
1 Clock	Mrs. Moore	.25
1 Clock	James Moore	3.25
L1 Table	Mrs. Moore	.10
1 Chest	Mrs. Moore	.25
1 Chest	Julia Moore	.10
1 Side Board	S. Walker	19.50
1 pair fire Irons &C	Mrs. Moore	.15
1 smoothing Iron	William Durham	.25
10 Bushels wheat @76	Ben Moore	7.60
10 bushels wheat @ 75	S. Walker	7.50
10 bushels wheat @ 75	Sterling Walker	7.50
10 Bushels wheat @ 73	S. Walker	7.31
1 Clock Reel	Mrs. Moore	.10
7 shoats	Robert Lane	35.50
1 mule	James P. Davis	25.50
6 pigs	Robert Lane	9.00
(p 231)		
1 Horse	Mrs. Moore	48.00
1 Horse	Lit Perry	50.00
1 Mare	Mrs. Moore	5.00
1 Stack Oats	S. Walker	4.25
1 " "	S. Walker	4.25
1 " "	S. Walker	4.10
1 " "	James Moore	3.00
1 Fan Mills	James Moore	.50
1 Cow	W.H. Stewart	20.00
1 Axe & Grub Hoe	James Moore	.45
1 Pair Geer	John Head	1.00
6 sheep	Mrs. Moore	5.00
10 Barrels of corn	William Gower	12.70
10 Barrels corn	William Darden	12.60
10 Barrels Dorn	William Darden	12.50
10 Barrels Corn	William Darden	12.50
$11\frac{1}{2}$ Barrels corn	William Darden	1.37
1 Lot shucks	William Darden	7.75
2 Barrels	Ben Moore	.70
3 Trout lines	Jesse Shearon	1.50
547 lbs. tobacco $4\frac{3}{4}$ cts. $25.98 8 BBls.4 Bu corn 1760		43.58
Money left on hand		15.00
1 Note on James H. Moore due 3 May 1861		24.85
Interest on same		
1 Account on Henry Smith		.70
1 Note on Jno. Z. Hudgens due 25th Dec. 1860		5.00
Interest on same		
1 account on Thomas Perry		.50
1 Account on William S. Bradley		4.50
Cash paid by Jordan Special Commissioner to sell the land of J.B. Moore		16.00
To interest		6.43

An account of the property sold by JamesFrazier belonging to the Estate of Jno. J. Chambliss dec.

Cash left on hand		8.95
1 note on W.J. Stewart due 28th April 1861 for		13.00
3 head young cattle to John Majors		33.00
1 Milk Cow	Bradberry	20.00
60 lbs. bacon @15	B.F. King	9.00
166 lbs. bacon	John S. Majors	24.90
2965 pounds pork @ 10	L.J. Perdue	296.50
		475.35

(p 232) Settlement of E. S. Gleaves administrator of the Estate of Joseph W[I]llis Dec.

To amount of property sold	40.50
To amt. of notes sold	1073.47
	1138.97

Contra.

By S.T. Willis	370.00
Tax Receipt for 1859	4.35
" " " 1860	2.04
E.B. Harris Corporation Tax	.30
Tax Receipt for 1861	1.08
Thos. Hunt proven acct.	9.00
R.H. Reding	12.00
Thos. J. Shaw Rec.	19.91
L.E. Gleaves ac.	8.00
Ewing Cooper, Receipt	5.00
J.A. Hudson proven acct.	20.00
F.A. Allen " "	19.47
Harris Williams	1.19
W.C. Burk & Co.	8.24
Bater Randle Willisford	29.75
County Coms. note town lot	235.00
James Hudgins proven acct.	1.50
Hnery Harris " "	2.00
W. Moore " "	12.00
L.E. Lowe " "	93.12
Allowance to Admr.	33.00
Bond	2.00
Letters Admr.	.50
Copy of same	.50
Order lay off years provisions	.25
Record & report	.25
Order confirming report	.25
Recording Inventory	.35
making settlemmnt & recording same	1.62
Bond	.50
Order of appointment	.25
	895.72
Amount due on settlement Jany. 1862	218.25

(p 233) Acct. of sale of the property of Annie Scott. Dec. sold by W.H. Scott. July 25th 1865.

T.J. Biggers	1 Large Kettle	$5.50
A. Scott	1 Pot	5.00
T.J. Riggins	1 oven and lid	1.00
G.T. Hooper	1 skillet & oven	.50
J.S. Hale	1 pot and kook	2.00

J.S. Hale	Tea Kettle & Oven	.50
J.S. Hale	2 Stone Jars	1.05
A. Scott	1 Pewter basin	.80
J.S. Hale	1 Strained Piggin	.80
J.S. Hale	1 Sifter	.25
J.S. Hale	3 Coffee Pots	.65
J.S. Hale	1 churn and cake form	1.60
J.S. Hale	1 Table	8.60
Miss Narcissa Scott	1 set tea cups & saucers	2.00
J.S. Hale	1 set plates	2.00
R.T. Scott	1 Dish	.50
W. Cruch	Pitcher & Book	1.25
J. Sears	Jar Molasses	1.40
W.H. Scott	1 sett silver spoons	5.00
Miss Narcissa	3 glasses & dish	1.25
W.H. Scott	1 Tea Pot & bowl	.30
Philip Williams	3 pitchers	2.00
Wm. Setters	2 plates and butter dish	.50
W.J. Clark	1 preserve dish	.50
J.S. Hale	2 Pans	1.00
T.J. Riggins	Beeswax	.75
Dock Bell	1 sausage horn	.45
T.J. Riggins	1 Coffee Mill	2.00
W.H. Scott	1 Cupboard	7.00
" " "	1 Clock	3.50
R.T. Scott	1 Bible	1.00
J. Sears	1 Jar	.50
R.T. Scott	1 Desk	7.50
T.J. Riggin	1 Sugar chest	3.00
W. Bratten	1 Bed and Bolster	26.00
J.S. Hale	1 Bed Stead & Mat	6.00
J.J. Larken	1 Fly Brush	1.00
J.S. Hale	1 Blanket	4.00
J.S. Hale	1 Coverlet	10.25
T. Dunn	1 Coverlet	5.50
W.H. Scott	1 Blanket	3.00
Jack Hutton	1 Lounge and mattress	7.00
T.J. Riggins	1 Bed	27.00
James Wynn	1 Bed boaster & pillows	41.00
(234)		
Miss Narcissa Scott	1 bed quilt	6.00
W.J. Clarke	1 Bed quilt	4.00
T.J. Riggins	1 Counterpane	7.50
W.H. Scott	1 Counterpane	10.50
R.T. Scott	1 Quilt	5.00
James Wynn	2sheets	5.50
J.S. Hale	2 sheets	4.00
Jno. Hutton	2 Table Cloths	6.00
Wm. Setten	1 Quilt	5.00
Mrs. Caruthers	3 sheets	7.25
James Wynn	1 quilt	6.00
A. Scott	1 Counterpane	9.50
Mrs. Setten	1 Blanket	4.25
W.J. Clark	1 Rocking chair	4.00
W.J. Clark	1 candle stand	1.00
W.J. Clark	1 Hackle	.50

W.J. Clark	1 Basket	.25
T.J. Riggin	4 chairs	2.40
T.J. Riggin	5 chairs	3.25
W.H. Scott	1 Looking glass	.25
A. Scott	1 Bed mattress	.90
W.H. Scott	1 " "	1.00
W.J. Osborne	1 Loom	20.75
G.J. Hooper	1 wheel	3.50
G.J. Hooper	1 wheel	1.75
W.H. Scott	1 Sley	.90
W.H. Scott	3 Sley	1.25
M. Bell	1 red cow	22.00
W.H. Scott	1 Heifer	18.00
W.H. Scott	1 Lard Stand	2.50
W.H. Scott	2 Hogshead	1.00
W.J. Clark	2Sheets	6.00
W.J. Osborne	1 wheat fan	3.50
W.H. Scott	1 Cow Bell	1.00
Cash on hand		30.00
Total Amount		444.25

This is a true and perfect Inventory of all the goods and chattels rightd and credits of the said Annie Scott Deceased which have come to my hands possession Knowledge or the hands of any other person for me to the best of my knowledge & belief this the 7th day of August 1865.

Sworn to in open court 7th day of Aug. 1865,

W. Jordan Clk.

Will of James Jones

In the name of God Amen. I, James Jones of the County of Cheatham State of Tennessee being of sound mind and memory but under much bodily affliction and knowing that is appointed for all to die but the hour of desolution unknown, and desiring to make such disposition of thw wordly effects as it has been my fortune to be possessed of as well be satisfactory to my own mind and feelings and hoping the same will be satisfactory to all concerned do ordain make and execute the following as my last will and testament to wit,

Item 1st It is my last will and desire that all my just debts be paid out of any means I may die possessed of.

Item 2nd. I give and bequeath to my beloved wife Martha Jones for and during her natural life or widowhood all my property and effects of every descriptions to be by her used for her own comfort and the interest of our children and at her death I want an equal division made of my effects among my children following to wit. Mary Ann Hunt. Elizth Majors. Martha Gupton Robert Jones, James C. Jones, Nancy Miles, Harriet Gupton, Judah Majors, and Sarah Jones.

Should my wife marry after my death she will receive a childs part.

Lastly, I nominate and appoint my son James C. Jones my Executor.

Given under my hand this 4th day of September in the year of our Lord 1863.

James his x mark Jones (seal)

Signed and acknowledged in presence of
W.D. Weakley
D.G. Teasley

Will of Elizabeth Hunter
I, Elizabeth Hunter of the County of Cheatham and State of Tennessee being of sound mind and memory do make and publish this as my last will and testament hereby revoking and making void all former wills by me at any time made.

1st. I desire that my Executor as soon after my death as practicable pay my funeral expenses and all my just debts out of any monies I may be possessed of or may first come into his hands.

2nd. I give and bequeath to my sister Rachel Hunter one negro girl named Katy and one rocking chair.

3rd. I give and bequeath to my sister Catherine McCarley one negro girl named Betty.

4th I give and bequeath to Mary T. Hunter daughter of Jno. A. Hunter one hundred dollars for the purpose of educating her.

5th I give and bequeath to my nephew G.W. McCarley my Bed and furniture if he never returns the bed and furniture to go to my sister Katherine

6th I have yet and undivided interest in my uncle David's estate when collected it is my will and desire that the whole amount be equally divided between my three sisters Rachel, Peggy and Katherine, share and share alike.

I nominate and appoint my nephew Allen Hunter my Executor to this my last will and testament. In testimony whereof I have hereunto set my hand and seal this 1st day of February 1864.

Elizabeth x Hunter (her mark)

Signed sealed and delivered in our presence and in the presence of the Testator & in each others presence the 1st Feb. 1864

Willie W. Williams
D.G. Teasley

(p 236) I, Thomson Biggers of the County of Cheatham and State of Tennessee being of sound and disposing mind and memory do make and publish this my last will and testament hereby revoking all other wills by me at any time heretofore.

1st. And principally I commit my soul into the hands of Almighty God trusting alone in the merits of his son the Lord Jesus Christ for Eternal Salvation and my body to the earth in humble hope of a ressurection to eternal life and which I wish buried with as little expense and show as comports with simple decency.

2nd My will is that the expenses of my sickness & funeral be first paid.

3rdly All just debts by me owing at the time of my debt.

4th Having given my daughter Catherine a Bed, I also give and bequeath to each of my children Robert, William and Jane a Bed to be received at their marriage or at the death of their mother.

4th I give and bequeath to my dear wife Eliza W. Biggers all my personal property of whatever kind of which may die possessed during her life or widowhood with power to sell or dispose of any surplus stock of any kind as she may elect.

5th I give and bequeath to my dear wife Eliza W. the tract of land on which now live with every thing appertaining thereto to be held by her during her life or widowhood & after her death it is my will that the said tract of land consisting of one hundred and fifty acres, be equally divided among my four children, Catherine, Robert, William and Jane if surviving or their lawful heirs or if they so elect I wish it to be sold and the proceeds equally divided as above.

6th. Lastly I do hereby constitute and appoint my two sons Robert B. Biggers and William H. Biggers to be Executors of this my last will and testament.

In Testimony whereof I have hereunto set my hand and seal this 20th day of May A.D. 1865

Thomson Biggers (seal)

Signed sealed and published in our presence and we have subscribed our names hereto in the presence of the testator.

This 20th day of May A.D. 1865

Attest. Sterling Brewer
W.C. Hunter
Wm. Durham

Will of Samuel King

Dear Willie, I want you to take possession of all my/notes/accounts and Books and collect them or as many of them as you can. Some will pay and others will try to avoid it. But make as many as you can do it. There is anote for $100.00 on Thomas W. King also another for $80.00 also one for $100.00 which has some credits on it that I want you to settle with him. (p 237) he has sent me some medicine which is not credited on it. I expect the balance on it will be as much or more than the amount of the medicines, If not settle it on one of the others and as soon as thereis any law compel him to pay them. Do not give him a day to play about them, for he has treated me very unkind about them, which I want him to know and that I think very hard of him for the manner he has acted towards me.

You will find an account against Ben Moore. It is in a judgement in B. Barnes office. I want you to show him no favors when you have any law to act on. His brother Lype Littleton Perry serve likewise.

You will find an account against Clay Starnes in favor of B.L. Hudgens for $8 which you will try and get him to pay Ben. Give it to me for what he owed me. You will find various accounts which collect if you can. I was particular in the above as you might understand the nature of them. My satch I want Aramintas little Cornelius to have if you think be best to sell it and buy him one when he gets grown, do so.

When you have collected them I want you to pay Bright, Jas. Lenox Jr. B. Barnes, Henry Shaw, any other debts I owe none that I intend to pay. There is an old Claim of Cheathams which ought not to pay and would have set aside long since if there had been any law in the land as Gen. Cheatham/& John S. Cheatham told me that for the medical services rendered them once when they were expected to die that they would give them to me which they were well able to do and I spent 4 weeks, night and day attending them in which time I slept but very little. You will find an account against Sam S. Williams which is several hundred dollarsnow that it is lost to me, he had some claims against me which I want the account to pay.That will be all that I will ever get.

You will find an account against Willie Sanders for Books. I left the books with him to sell for me which he promised to do after which he quit Ashland. I saw him a few days before he left he told me he was going away and asked what he should do with the Books. I told him to give them to Mr. Asa Carney and ask him to take of them for me which he promised to do, as Mr. Carney was going to occupy the same house he left and Carney went into the house. Mr. A. Edwards as Carney told me saw cause to put him out of the house Carney left and went into Brights House, the said Sanders without saying anything to Carney about the Books all the time on the promises, I think it nothing but right that Sanders pay me for the Books. He has my note for some 20 or 30 dollars which the account he must pay and he pay me the balance. There is a little account some 60 cents I think that I owe Jim Gray for Shoeing my mare which pay when you have collected and paid the above claims if there is any left, I want you to give Nancy, your little daughter $5.00 to buy her a ring and Breast pin (p 238) I give her this as a mimento not for value as I also know you would not have anything I might give you also I want you to give Delilah Hudgens to buy her a ring & Breast Pin. My mare I said I give to Araminta Herron 2 or 3 years ago to pay her for taking care of me some 13 Or 14 years and I Leave her to her sole use and benifit, her husband having no claim to her in any manner, nor if she to be sold for any of his debts or contracts and for the surety thereof I leave her to you in trust for the above purposes.

After all the above has been affected and there should be anything left, I want you to pay yourself for your trouble and then if anything remains give it to Araminta Herron. My saddle, bridley Books and chest you will sell, in testimony whereof I have hereunto set my hand and seal this 12th day of Sept. 1864 .

Sam King (seal)

A list of the property sold at the sale of T.W. Scott Dec.
By John S. Hale Administrator July 25th 1865.

G.J. Hooper	2 Plows	
G.J. Hooper	3 Plows	
G.J. Hooper	2Double Trees	
W.H. Scott	1 whip saw.	
J.C. Harris	3 Hoes	
W.H. Scott	2 Hoes	
A. Scott	1 Pick & axe	
J.B. Parkison	1 Spade	
J.C. Harris	1 Pair Breecing	
G.W. Hannah	2 Blind Bridles	
J.C. Harris	1 Pair chains	
J.C. Harris	1 Pair chains	
Moses Jones	1 " "	
J.C. Harris	1 Pair lines	
T.J. Riggin	1 Set plow geer	
E.G. Sears	1 " " "	
E.G. Sears	1 Grind Stone	
E.G. Sears	1 Lot chains	
E.G. Sears	1 lead harness	
A. Scott	1 Halter chain	
W. Lewis	1 pair sheep shears	
W.J. Clark	1 hand saw &C	
W.J. Clark	1 Lot Augurs	
W.J. Clark	Adz & Hammer	
W.H. Scott	1 scythe Blade	
(p 239)		
J.C. Harris	1 Lot tools	$1.00
J.C. Harris	1 Lot Irons	2.00
T.J. Riggin	2 chairs	2.55
J.C. Harris	1 Lot sundries	2.00
W.J. Clark	1 scythe & Cradle	2.70
W.J. Clark	1 mowing blade	1.80
G.W. Hannah	1 Large pot	4.55
W.J. Clark	1 Lot ware	3.25
W.J. Clark	Pots &C	3.10
T.W. Osborne	1 Kettle	1.10
Dave Thompson	1 Lot shoe tools	3.25
M.A Catlin	Braic & Bit	5.00
Mrs. Setton	1 Reel	2.00
J.C. Harris	1 candle stand & wheel	3.75

J.B. Parkinson	1 Spinning Wheel	80.00
T.J. Adkinson	1 Bed Bolster and pillows	32.00
W.H. Scott	1 Bed Stead & Bed	7.50
Phillip Williams	1 clock	3.00
G.W. Hannah	1 Press	16.00
W.J. Clark	6 chairs	13.00
A. Scott	2Bottles & Spittoons	2.00
G.J. Hooper	1 Small table	7.85
R.T. Scott	1 Silver Watch	17.00
Mrs. Setten	1 Bed Bolster & Pillows	33.00
G.W. Hannah	1 Bed stead	13.50
W.H. Scott	1 Lot Deather	6.75
Judge Palmer	1 Piece Deer skin	1.25
J.C. Harris	1 Basket & Contents	2.60
G.W. Hannah	1 Lot earthenware	2.30
Dock Bell	1 Set knives and forks	4.00
W.J. Clark	2 Dishes	2.75
Phillip Williams	Earthenware	1.00
Phillip Williams	1 Wash Basin	.85
G.J. Hooper	Cards & Scales	1.60
W.H. Scott	1 Lot vials	1.00
T.J. Riggins	2 cupping glasses	.50
A. Scott	1 Jug	4.00
W.J. Clark	1 Jar	1.00
W.J. Clark	1 Butter stand & Carpet sack	1.75
S.H. Dunn	10 Bushels wheat @ 1.35	13.50
S.H. Dunn	100 lbs. Bacon @ .25¾	23.75
T. Owens	75 lbs Bacon	19.31
J.M. Dunn	50 lbs Soap @ 4¾	2.37½
W.J. Clark	1 Lard Stand	2.80
Moses Jones	1 Barrel Salt	9.42
W.J. Clark	1 Lot Wool	5.25
(p 240)		
W.H. Lawrence	2 Hogs	24.50
John Hutton	1 sow	15.00
" "	1 sow	17.00
W.J. Clark	11 head sheep @ 3.00	33.00
W.W. Deal		
J.C. Porch	Mule	153.00
G.W. Hannah	1 Mule	130.00
W.H. Scott	1 Mule	95.00
C.M. Nichols	146 Bush Corn @ $1.20	160.60
J.C. Harris	1 - 2 horse wagon	76.00
	Total Amount	1230.45

This is a true and perfect Inventory of all the goods and chattels, rights and credits of the said Thos. W. Scott Dec. so far as I have gone or has come to my hands to the best of my knowledge and belief.
This 7th day of August 1865.

John S. Hale, Admr.

Sworn to in Open court 7th day of August 1865.

Warren Jordan, Clerk

The following is a true list of the property belonging to the estate of W.G. Shelton Deceased, sold on the 5th day of October 1864.

John King	Bellows, two hammers & anvil	$10.00
G.W. Murphey	10 lbs wool @ 90 cents	9.00
W. Oliver	10 lbs. wool @ 90 cents	9.00
T. Cessler	10 lbs wool @ 85 cents	8.50
H. Douglas	10 lbs. wool @ 85 cents	8.50
Jesse Jordan	1 saddle	20.00
John Gallaher	1 mans saddle	15.00
Thomas G. James	1 buggy and harness	200.00
A.J. Simmons	1 mare	100.00
Thomas G. James	1 Horse Mule	50.00
Thomas Crouch	1 mare mule	66.00
Thomas Cessler	1 Jack	50.00
Thomas James	1 white ox	35.00
J.P. Bell	1 Red ox	35.00
J.P. Bell	1 white faced ox	40.00
N. Jordan	1 Frost and brindle steer	25.00
N. Jordan	1 white steer	10.50
N. Jordan	1 Red heifer	8.00
Thomas G. James	One cow and calf white	20.00
N. Jordan	1 cow and calf Black	

(241)

Thomas G. James	1 Red cow and calf	28.00
David Hooper	1 Heifer	18.25
E. Cox	1 st. lot of hogs 10.	52.50
W.N. Dozier	2nd " "	50.00
John Gallaher	3rd " " 10	30.00
Thomas Cesler	4th " " @ 10	21.00
Andrew Hogue	5th " " 10	17.00
James Thompson	6th " " 10	28.00
A.J. Crockett	2nd lot of sheep	31.00
David Hooper	3rd lot sheep	30.00
Jesse Jordan	4th lot of sheep	26.00
Thomas Crouch	5th lot of sheep 10	24.00
Andrew Hogue	6th lot of sheep	22.50
James Thompson	7th " "	13.30
Thomas J. Crouch	1 spinning wheel	2.75
Thomas J. Crouch	1 Kettle	10.00
Oct. 2nd 1865		1148.80

Sworn to and suscribed Before me Oct. 2nd 1865.
Warren Jordan. Clerk

The following is a list of property on hand belonging to the estate of W.G. Shelton Decd.

4 Bed steads Bed & Clothing	80.00
1 Lounge Bed and clothing	20.00
1 Burrough	5.00
1 Parlor Looging glass	6.00
4 folding tables	20.00
2 small tables	3.00
1 Book case	5.00
1 Press	6.00
1 Wardrobe	10.00
1 Small looking glass	1.00

1 Large Looking Glass	3.00
1 Clock	10.00
2 Safes & Tables furniture	15.00
11 chairs	5.00
2 wash stands	3.00
1 Spinning wheel	1.50
1 Cook stove & Furniture	12.00
½ pair Balances	3.00
1 Barrel Salt	8.00
40 lbs wool	25.00
50 lbs soap	2.50
3 Lard stands	3.00
2 plow gears	8.00
One ox cart	20.00
One Larnip	1.50
One Keg white lead	1.50
One can linseed oil	1.75
One crow bar	1.50
4 sides leather at tan yard	12.00
1 yoke of cattle	50;00
# milch cows & Calves	60.00
5 other cattle	20.00
One Mule	125.00
31 head of hogs	150.00
1 Shovel	2.00
1 spade	2.00
1 grindstone	1.50

List of notes on hand

One note on G. Green	230.00
due March 5th 1861 with a credit Jan. 3rd 1862 for 100.00	
One on Wm. Demunbra for	40.00
due Dec. 10th 1859 with a credit Dec. 10th 1858 for 2.00	
(p 242) One note on John H. Cullum due April 12th 1862	125.00
One note on A.B. Gibbs due April 29th 1857 Cr. Sept 10th 1861,$50.00	146.03
One on A.J. Bright for $200 due Feb. 26, 1859, with a credit April 4th 1859 for	135.00
One on A.J. Bright due Jan. 9 1861 for	40.00
One on H. Dowlen due Oct. 1, 1860 for	26.25
One on B.H. Gibbs due Jan. 8th 1862 for	287.30
One on R.B. Gibbs due Jan. 8th 1862 for	258.17
One note on R.B. & R.H. Gibbs due Jan. 8th 1862 for	115.17
One on Henry Stewart due Oct. 1st 1860 for	33.00
One on R.B. Gibbs due April 1st 1861 for	5.00
One on J.H. Cullum due Dec. 25th 1860 for	33.06
One on John S. Majors due Aug. 12th 1860 for	117.00
One on J.J. Lenox due January 10th 1863 for	200.00
One on J.B. Demunbra due Dec. 10th 1859 for	40.85
with a credit of 30.72 the 17th day of Feb. 1861	
One on A.G. Demunbra, due Jan. 1st 1860 for	45.00
with a credit of 11.00 on the 7th January 1860	
One on Wm. M. Hooper due Aug. 16th 1860 for	93.74
One on Wm. M. Hooper due Sept. 20th 1860 for	25.00

One on John H. Allen due May 27th 1860 for	50.00
One on G.W. McQuary due Dec. 4th 1860 for	10.00
One on T.J. Crouch and T.N. Hooper due Dec. 23rd 1860 for	1000.00
One on R.B. Gibs due April 1st 1858 for	95.00
One on S.T. Hooper and T.N. Hooper due March 2nd 1860 for	21.00
with a credit May 29th 1860 foe 15.00	15.00
One on G.W. McQuary due Feb. 27th 1861 for	30.70
One on T.W. Rupst (Rupke) due Jan. 15th 1862 for	15.00
One on D.M. Lovell due Dec. 9th 1861 for	8.00
One on B.H. Gibbs due Jan. 4th 1859 for	100.00
with $20.35 cr. Aug. 3d 1858 and cr. By $56 Jan. 8th 1861	
One on A.H. Williams due Dec. 18th 1859 for	568.00
with a credit of $300.00 on the 18th Jan. 1859 for	31.75
One on Wm. Demunbra and A.H. Williams due March 3d 1860	65.15
One on Jesse Jordan (Paid)	$1375.00

October 2nd 1865
G.W. McQuary
W.W. Fulgham
Admrs.

(p 243)
A list of peoperty sold at the sale of J.W. Darrow deceased
By George C. Binkley administrator August 19th 1865.

James Binkley	2 plows	.50
Nathan Morris	1 Bull tongue plow	.50
J.W. Felts	1 " " "	.50
J.W. Felts	2 Shovel plows	.20
John Webb	1 grubbing hoe & wedge	.55
J.H. Binkley	Coopers tools	6.60
N.D. Farmer	one hand axe	.50
Jno. Webb	One pair harness	1.60
George Felts	One bellows & saddle	.60
J.W. Felts	One wagon wheel & C	2.00
J.W. Felts	One saddle	2.00
John Webb	One shovel	.10
B.H. Newman	One chopping axe	.60
W.A. Henderson	One Bed stead	1.25
James Cochran	One pot and hooks	.50
James M. Binkley	" " "	2.25
James Cochran	" " "	.75
W.E. Felts	One tub	.25
Hiram Cochran	One skillet & LId	.40
Uames Mosier	One pot	1.75
James Mosier	One skillet & Lid	.45
Aaron Williams	One Oven	.25
Aaron Williams	One small skillet	.55
Aaron Williams	One tea kettle	.65
James Mosier	One spinning wheel	.90
Hiram Cochran	One fish net	.50
E.H. Simpson	One piggin & Onions	.60
Nathan Morris	Old Irons	.25
James Cochran	One Loom	.30
E.H. Simpson	One tub and onions	.70
N.D. Farmer	One ox yOke	.10
David Cullum	One cask vinegar	.80
William Clark	One cask vinegar	.25

B.H. Newman	One bell and auger	.30
B.F. Binkley	One auger and chain	.40
James Mosier	One set chairs	3.50
Nathan Morris	One set chairs	.50
John A. Hudson	3 hogs 1st choice	9.75
John A. Hudson	4 hogs 2nd choice	6.30
James Harris	One lot chains	.20
Hiram Cochran	One cow and calf	17.00
James Mosier	One cow and calf	21.00
(p 244)		
A.J. Fentress	One black cow and calf	35.00
Levi Binkley	One heifer	13.00
Levi Binkley	One heifer	15.00
N.D. Farmer	One calf	12.35
Thomas Farmer	One mule	25.00
James Cochran	1 mare	68.00
B.F. Binkley	One colt	26.25
James Winters	one sow and pigs	5.75
Hiram Cochran	1 sow and six pigs	8.25
E.H. Simpson	One black sow	6.50
James Harris	Two hogs	14.50
A.N. Binkley	one sow and2pigs	5.10
Wm. Dowling	5 1st choice sheep	12.25
Wm. Dowling	5 1st choice sheep	10.50
Wm. Dowling	4 1st choice sheep	8.00
David S. Binkley	One ,, 1 horse wagon	22.00
James Mosier	cotton & POtatoes	5.00
James Cochran	Garden and vegetables	5.30
James Mosier	Chest and contents	6.75
James Cochran	One bed and clothing	23.00
Aaron Williams	One bed	20.25
Hiram Cochran	One clock	3.40
John A. Hudson	One pr sheep shears	1.40
Nero Harris	One pr cotton cards	1.30
H.J. Binkley	One pr cotton cards	.55
W.E. Felts	One lot bottles	.10
E.J. Clark	One set knives and forks	2.50
W.E. Felts	One sugar bowl	.10
Jno. Bess	1 Pitcher & Sugar dish	.25
James Mosier	1 set cups and saucers	1.10
James Rose	One lot cups &C	.70
H.J. Binkley	One sett plates	2.10
James Mosier	One pepper box &C	.30
John Bess	2 glasses & qt cup	.40
H.J. Binkley	One white pitcher	.75
James Cochran	4 plates &C	.35
Aaron Williams	One coffee mill, dishes	1.90
S.A. Richardson	One coffee pot	.25
Dock Hooper	One basin	,.50
John Bess	One gal. jug	.10
James Demumbra	One cupboard	5.00
J.H. Binkley	One small table	1.25
James Mosier	One folding table	3.00
Hiram Cochran	1 lot bed clothing	2.00
Aaron Williams	1 lot bed clothing	3.10
Hiram Cochran	One rifle gun	10.25

(p 246)

Silvester Dowlen	1 shot gun	3.25
John A. Hudson	1 shot gun	3.50
James Harris	One sack wool	6.30
James Cochran	One lot wool	6.30
Hiram Cochran	One lot cotton	4.70
James Mosier	One lot cotton	1.15
Jakes Demunbra	Shoels & Steelyards	1.05
William Rose	Andirons	.50
James Cochran	2 jars	.30
N.N. Binkley	1 jar	.25
Ed Sulliman	1 jars	.35
Joseph Darrow	" "	.50
James Mosier	One breas tray & Sifter	1.85
S.A. Richardson	One dish & Basin	.75
Leonard Binkley	1 water bucket	.25
G.C. Binkley	1 stone churn	.25
Hiram Cochran	One basket	.70
James Cochran	One razor strap	1.55
James Harris	One cedar bucket	.60
James Cochran	2 smmoth irons	.50
J.L.Felts	Saddle bags	.65
John Bess	one lard stand	.15
James Cochran	One box onion sets	.50
Dock Hooper	One lot salt	.43
N.D. Farmer	One water bucket	.50
James Mosier	One lot corn	3.75
William Gower	One Bed stead	.40
S.A. Richardson	One lot lard	2.25
James Cochran	One lot soap	5.50
Hiram Cochran	One side bacon	6.09
James Cochran	2 sides bacon	13.32
James Mosier	2 sides bacon	9.62
Alex Rose	One lard trough	.30
James Cochran	2 bushels meal	2.50
John A. Hudson	18 chickens @ 48c	8.64
W.D. Darrow	1 lot younf chicks	3.75
S.A. Richardson	1 lot ducks	1.00
S.A. Richardson	1 lot Books	.50
S.A. Robinson	Oats 125 Bundles	1.33
Jmaes Cochran	Lot Fodder	.80
Cash on hand at time of sale		50.00
Total amt of first sale		

(246) Account of sale of property of J.W. Darrow decd. sold October 28, 1865 by G.C. Binkley Admr.

Hiram Cochran	One sley	.75
E.J. Clark	3 barrels corn @ 3.00	9.00
James Cochran	9 barrels corn	27.00
J.H. Binkley	3 barrels corn @ 2.50	7.50
J.H. Binkley	One lot remainder	2.60
E.J. Clark	One frow	.75
James Cochran	One grub hoe	.10

H.J. Binkley	Lot refuse corn	13.20
G.C. Binkley	$\frac{1}{2}$ barrel corn	1.50
James Cochran	Amt. account	12.40
W.A. Henderson	Note due Dec. 26th 1864	206.80
L.R. Darrow	Note due Dec. 26 1858, cr. Aug 24th 1860	22.65
R.C.F. Cagle	Note die Aug. 17, 1857 $ 2.15	30.00

The foregoing contains a true and perfect inventory of all the goods chattel rights and credits of J.W. Darrow Dec. that have come to my knowledge or possession, This Nov. 6th 1865

George C. Binkley Admr.

Inventory and account of the property of B.F. Hannah Dec. By Moses Jones administrator on the day of -----1865

H.L. Clark	One steel trap	1.00
Mrs. L. Bledsoe	1 vise, ame, scythe & Cradle	1.15
" " "	4 hoes	.50
" " "	1 two horse plows	.50
" " "	2 one horse plows	1.10
" " "	1 bull tongue plows	1.00
" " "	1 bull tongue plows	.25
" " "	2 plows	3.20
George A. Russell	1 coulter	.10
William Deal	One steel cock	.20
James Hannah	One cutting box	1.00
Mrs. L. Bledsoe	$2\frac{1}{2}$ bush salt 1.20	3.00
G.B. Hannah	One flax wheel	.25
Mrs. L. Bledsoe	1 cross cut saw	2.60
Mrs. L. Bledsoe	1 pair plow gear	1.00
James Hannah	1 " " "	1.00
James Hannah	1 Pair harness	.25
William Kellum	1 two horse wagon	70.00
John H.C. Kellum	1 shot gun	14.50
(p 247)		
B.F. Hannah	1 bed stead , bed and furniture	40.50
Mrs, L. Bledsoe	1 " " " "	40.00
James Hannah	1 bed single, no furniture	22.00
---------------	1 counterpane	1.50
Mrs. L. Bledsoe	One counterpane	.50
C.H. Hoskin	One counterpane	4.00
G.B. Hannah	One coverlet	7.75
G.B. Hannah	One coverlet	9.00
G.B. Hannah	one coverlet	5.00
Mrs. L. Bledsoe	One quilt	.60
Stephen Hale	One quilt	1.25
G.B. Hannah	One quilt	1.50
G.A. RUssell	1 clock frame	.20
Mrs. L. Bledsoe	1 Large chest	1.20
G.B. Hannah	1 Dining table	1.30
Mrs. L. Bledsoe	1 Bureau	8.00
Mrs. L. Bledsoe	1 sugar chest	3.00
Mrs. L. Bledsoe	pair fire Irons	1.25
Mrs. L. Bledsoe	1 Pair tongs & Shovels	.30
James Hannah	1 chest	.25
G.B. Hannah	1 Paor Shears	2.00
G.B. Hannah	1 pr compasses	.25
James Hannah	2 augers	1.25

James Hannah	1 drawing knife	1.05
G.B. Hannah	2 fore planes	.80
G.B. Hannah	6 groove plains	.50
Jas. Hannah	Oil stone & Square	1.75
Jas. Hannah	1 lot shoe tools	2.00
Moses Jones	1 box sundries	.10
W.N. Thompson	1 bag flaxseed	.10
James Hannah	One Book	1.25
James P. Clark	One Book	.50
W.H. Kellum	One Book	.25
John Sutton	One Book	.15
Mrs. James Hannah	1 Bible	.10
J.P Clark	One Book	.50
G.A. Russell	One Book	.50
Frank Atkinson	1 lot coon skins	.30
Mr. L. Bledsoe	1 low bed stead	.70
Geo. W. Hannah	1 bed stead	1.45
Mrs. L. Bledsoe	1 large pot	2.60
James Hannah	1 small pot	1.00
Mrs. L. Bledsoe	1 Oven	.60
Jas. Hannah	1 skillet	.30
Jas, Hannah	1 ½ bu. Measure	.35
G.B. Hannah	1 spinning machine	25.00
(p 248)		
Mrs. L. Bledsoe	5 chairs	2.00
Mrs. L. Bledsoe	1 Brass kettle	2.60
Mrs. L. Bledsoe	1 check Reel	.25
Mrs. L. Bledsoe	1 Loom and gear	1.00
Joseph Hannah	1 small cow	9.25
Mrs. L. Bledsoe	1 cow and calf	36.00
Jas. Hannah	4 head of sheep	10.00
Mrs. L. Bledsoe	5 head Small hogs	8.00
Joseph Hannah	One shoat	3.75
Mrs. L. Bledsoe	One large sow	13.00
G.B. Hannah	One roan Filly	85.00
N. Dozier	One Bay mare	22.00
Mrs. L. Bledsoe	One sorrel mare	31.00
Mrs L. Bledsoe	One cupboard	.50
Mrs. L. Bledsoe	One table	1.00
Mrs. L Bledsoe	One bread tray	.25
Mrs. L. Bledsoe	One bowl and pitcher	.80
C.H. Hoskins	Mollasses jar & cruet	1.00
A. Fletcher	One plow	1.15
A. Fletcher	One set blacksmith tools	15.30
G.A. Russell	One broken kettle	.20
J.P. Clark & Warren Jordan	One iron tooth harrow & s hot pouch	1.75
One note on Houston Clark(disputed) due Jan. 4, 1843 for		40.00
One note on W.J. Carter Jan. 1st 1847 to be accounted for at end of year		100.00
One note on W.J. Broadey (doubtful) due Jan 1, 1862 hire of slaves		120.00
One note on Pellus & Lawrence due 25th Dec. 1848 (worthless)		170.00
G.B. Hannah	Account	280.00
Jas. Hannah	Account year 1865	78.00
Jas. P. Clark	Account year 1864 & 5	32.00
Moses Jones	Account year 1865	7.50
J.M. Bagwell	Board for G.A. Bagwell	60.00

The above contains a true and perfect inventory of all the goods and chattel rights and credits of B.F. Hannah Decd. which has come to the hands, knowledge or possession of Moses Jones Administrator this Nov. 6th 1865.

Inventory of the goods and chattels notes and money belongin g to the estate of William Knight Dec.

One note on Ally Smith due Jan. 1st 1863 for 35.00
One note on Ally Smith due Jan. 1st 1864 30.00
To money in the hands of Winfield Knight/Guard.$1170.83
David W. Knight
Sworn to in open court Nov. 6th 1865
Warren Jordan, Clerk

(p 249)
Inventory and account of sale of the property of Harris Williams Dec. sold July 29th 1865.
By Sterling Walker Admr.

G.W. Maxey	2 Coopers adz	1.25
A.J. Teasley	1 Iron Wedge	.35
Wyatt Shearon	1 chopping axe	.60
A.R. Byron	1 Auger	.40
John H. Hooper	2 lbs soda	.10
A.J. Teasley	2 Plane bits	.60
J.W. Shearon	2 papers Pepper	.10
A.J. Teasley	3 bottles ink	.10
W.H. Morris	3 bottle Ink	.10
J.A. Harper	3 bottles Ink	.10
W.D. Shearon	2 bottles ink	.10
James Walker	1 bottle glue	.20
J.D. Vankook	3 paper pepper	.10
G.W. Maxey	3 paper pepper	.10
J.W. Shearon	3 " "	.12
Hard Hudgins	3 " "	.15
James Waker	2 " "	.10
Wm. Hudgins	2 " "	.10
H. Hudgins	2 " "	.15
A.J. Teasley	1 " "	.05
Wm. Hudgens	1 Lot buckles	.10
Wm Hudgens	1 lot buckles	.10
Wm. Hudgens	1 Lot buckles	.10
Wm. Hudgens	1 lot buckles	.10
Wm. Hudgens	1 lot cabbage seed	.10
Warren Hudgens	1 glass jar	.80
James Walker	2 Bottles	.50
William Hudgins	1/2 quire paper	.15
Z.F. Shearon	1/2 Quire paper	.10
W.H. Morris	1/2 Quire paper	.13
Warren Hudgins	1/2 quire paper	.15
Dick Byron	1/2 quire paper	.13
Warren Hudgins	1/2 quire paper	.13
W.H. Morris	1/2 quire paper	.13
W.H. Morris	1/2 quire paper	.13
A.J. Teasley	1/2 quire paper	.14

A.J. Teasley	½ quire paper	.14
J.W. Shearon	½ quire paper	.15
W.H. Morris	½ quire paper	.15
C.A. Harper	½ quire paper	.15
W.H. Morris	½ quire paper	.20
Leander Walker	½ quire paper	.16
C.F. Williams	½ quire paper	.20
(p 250)		
G.W. Harris	1 lot paper	.35
William Hudgins	Pocket Book	.30
G.W. Harris	1 Razor	.80
Warren Hudgins	1 Pocket Book	.15
J.W. Shearon	1 Razor	.1.50
Rosa Walker	1 Razor Strap	.85
Mary Walker	1 pr shoes	2.00
Warrem Hudgins	1 pr shoes	2.05
Bettie Walker	pr shoes	2.30
Nancy Hudgins	1 pair shoes	2.25
Hard Hudgins	pair shoes	2.05
J.W. Shearon	1 Table	2.10
G.E. Harris	1 Bed Blanket	1.00
G.E. Harris	1 bed blanket	1.65
James Walker	1 bed & 2 Pillows	7.50
W.D. Shearon	1 cutting knife	2.05
H.B. Hutchinson	1 wheel barrow	

Officers receipts

1 Note on Aaron Cagle due Jan. 1st 1859 cr. $5.00 Nov. 5/59	21.15
1 note on B.H. Newman due Jan. 1st 1860	25.92
1 note on A. Lowe due Jan 1st 1860	136.09
1 note on A. Lowe due June 26th 1860	25.17
1 note on Wm. Simmons due April 4, 1860	6.00
1 note on Henry Harris due Jan. 1st 1860	
1 note on Wm. Rediker due March 10, 1860	25.50
1 account on Robert Knox due Jan. 1st 1859	9.85
Cash on hand Tennessee money	33.00
Cash on hand Georgia Money	4.00
Cash on hand Greenback	19.05
On Due Bill Will R. Felts due April 25th 1861½	4.80
One due bill on M.R. Hooper Due Nov. 21st 1860	3.50
One acct A.E. Sewell due Nov. 21st 1862	12.50
One acct. Frank Binkley due Oct. 25, 1863	.87

Constable Receipts

1 Due Bill J.G. White due Sept 3, 1860 for	12.50
1 note on W.C. Clark & E.W. Carney due Dec. 25, 1860	5.26
1 note on A.J. Ramer & Jas. Knight Due Dec. 25, 1860	16.70
1 note on Gideon Lowe Due Jan 12th 1860	12.50
1 note on J.M. REad & W.W. FeltsDue Feb. 27th 1860	20.00
1 note on S. Watson due April 10, 1862	300.00
1 note on C.D. Lawrence due Jan. 25, 1862	53.61
1 note on W.F. Gower due May 1, 1862	1.90
1 note on Samuel Watson due May 1862	13.75
1 note on W.E.C. Gower due May 1862	15.08
1 note on J.A. Hudson due June 2, 1862	1.55
(p 251)	
1 note on J.D. Dismukes due Nov. 6th 1862	30.54

One note on S. Walker due Oct. 22nd 1862	72.95
One note on A.W. Hooper Due Oct. 22nd 1861	17.75
One note on J.T. Harris due 1862	3.65
One note on James/Harris due 1862	3.10
One note on David Wilkins due 1862	.25

Sworn to and suscribed before me the 15th day of September 1865

Sterling Walker Admr.

Attest Warren Jordan Clerk

Additional Inventory of the notes and acts of Harris Williams Dec.

One note on G.W. Felts due Jan. 1st 1860	7.18
One note on G. Gallaher due March 27th 1860	47.50
One note on H.J. Binkley due May 23rd 1861	3.66
One note on Hiram Cochran due Jan. 1st 1860	18.08
One note on Elias Harris due Jan. 21st 1861	7.17
One note on Nathan Morris due Jan. 1st 1861 (cr. $10.00)	23.18
One note on Neri Harris due Jan 1st 1860	2.98
One note on H.J. Gower due Jan 1st 1861	8.10
One note on T.M. Parish due May 10th 1861	13.23
One note on Will R. Felts due Jan. 1st 1861	21.57
One note on W.A. Nichols Due April 13th 1861	13.10
One note on W.L. Binkley due May 23rd 1861	7.50
One note on Levi Simmons due Jan. 1st 1861	13.18
One note on S.P. Knox due May 8th 1861	4.93
One note on Hiram Felts cr. $16.00 Oct. 21/61 Jan 1st 1861	26.56
One note James Cochran due (cr. $1.58) March 8, 1859	6.07
One note on A.L. Fortune APril 7th 1860	10.00
One note on J.J. Nichols Jan. 1st 1861	3.00
One note on Henry Harris Jan 1st 1861	38.89
One note on John Bennett Jan 1st 1861	22.68
One note on M.P. Frey May 11th 1861	23.08
One note on W.E.C. Gower Jan 1st 1861	10.28
One note on J.F. Underwood Mch. 19, 1860 cr. Aug 31, 1860 $ 13.00	16.85
One note on Elias Harris Jan. 1st 1860 cr. Feb. 1861 $4.00	6.54
One note on Elias Johnson due Nov. 9th 1857	2.71
One note on H. Dowlen due Sept. 13th 1860	1.70
One note on T. O'Brien due Jan. 1st 1860.	25.15
One note on T. O'Brien due Dec. 3rd 1860$18.09	
One note on W.A. Nichols due Nov. 20th 1859	5.16
One note on James Perry due April 5th 1862	9.65
One note on Thos. Keeler due May 11th 1859	4.03
One note on J.C. Newland due April 15th 1861	4.50
One note on Wm. R. Herron Felts due Dec. 25th 1862	3.75
One note on Elias Harris due June 1st 1861	2.25

(p 252)

One acct. on Thos. O'Brien due July 6th 1861	.73
One acct. on J.F. Underwood due Nov. 22. 1860	2.45
One ac. on Tempz Shivers due Jan. 2d 1858	2.30
One ac on Jesse Shävers due Nov. 28, 1860	5.45
One note on Joel Krantz Due Nov. 28 1861	2.75
One ac. on Wm. Fortune due May 10th 1859	2.05
One ac. on James Moore Due Dec. 18 1860	1.88
One ac. on Edward Wren Due Nov. 12 1858	2.73
One ac. on B.W. Bradley Due Nov. 20 1860	5.28
One ac. on J.F. Underwood Due 22nd 1860	2.45
One ac. on B.F. Binkley Due April 23, 1862	6.45
One ac. One ac. on A.Rose, due Aug. 14, 1860	9.88
One ac. on Thomas Perry due Jan. 10 1861	1.95

One ac. on A.L. Fortune Due Aug. 2, 1862	24.34
One note on A.L. Fortune Due Oct. 25, 1860 cr. note on M.R. Hooper $3.50	6.00
One note on A.L. Fortune due Aug 14, 1861	4.25
One act. on Jo Darrow Due April 13, 1861	2.83
One ac. on W lliam Dowlin Due Aug. 20, 1861	28.83
One ac. on Sam'l King due Dec. 8, 1861	18.40
One ac. on W.W. Williams due Dec. 8, 1860	3.40
One act. on H. Dowlen due Dec. 9 1860	52.15
One ac. on G.W. Teasley due Dec. 22, 1860	2.75
One ac on J.H. Harper due Nov. 10, 1860	18.04
One ac. on Wm. R. Felts due Mch. 25, 1861	6.97
One ac. on B.F. Binkley due April 23, 1862	6.45
One ac. on H.W. Hooper due 1861	3.63
One ac. on B.B. Hudgens due June 19th 1863	3.60
One ac. on Wm. Sterry due Aug. 18th 1862	4.60
One ac. on A. Rose due Aug. 14th 1862	7.95
One ac. on C.A. Hudgens due June 12th 1862	11.75
One ac. on Edward Sullivan due Dec. 20th 1860	9.45
One ac. on Gad E. Harris due Aug 19th 1862	8.90
One ac. on Elias Harris due Oct. 1861	10.83
One ac. on A.L. Fortune, Bal on acct 1858 & 1859	32.70
One ac. on W. Agent due Jan. 13th 1858	3.20
One ac. on W.W. Bennett due July 26, 1859	3.00
One ac. on Thomas Hunt due Aug. 1st 1859	39.91
One ac. on L.L. Hünt due Aug. 5, 1859	27.24
One ac. on G.W. Binkley due July 2, 1859	13.65
One ac. on Jas. Hudgens due Aug. 2, 1859	23.88
One ac. on F.M. Underwood Aug 10, 1859	14.95
One ac. on C.A. Hudgens due June 5th 1859	17.52
One act. on H.J. Gower due Aug. 6, 1859	31.09
One ac. on Leander Felts Due May 16th 1859	12.25
One ac. on George Arrington 1860	13.03
One Ac. on Em Hudgens due Aug 9, 1860	2.86
(p 253)	
Robert A. Smith Dec. 17th 1860	4.30
George Cantrell Nov. 26, 1860	1.65
J.M. Read May 12th 1860	3.45
Joseph Darrow Nov. 1st 1860	1.10
W.P. McCormick July 6th 1860	3.80
Leonard Binkley, April 25th 1860	1.95
Tempy Shivers, Jan. 2nd 1858	2.20
Mary Cullum, Sept. 3, 1859	2.23
J.N. Briant, Oct. 23d 1859	2.23
David Mosier 1859	22.78
Joseph Mosier 1859	31.56
Nancy Felts, July 28, 1860	5.25
James Barnes, April 30th 1860	2.75
James Rose, Aug. 8th 1861	1.40
Miss Cullum, Dec. 29th 1859	12.72
James Rose, April 8th 1860	1.48
Tempy Holmes, April 8th 1860	4.30
W lliam Farmer April 8th 1860	2.00
Polly McCormic " " "	4.25
M.V. Binkley " " 1862	3.25

Elizabeth Binkley, April Aug. 8th, 1860	1.95
Miss Sarah Hooper, Oct. 31st, 1360	2.95
LLL. Galligan, March 1st 1860	5.62
J.D. Dismukes, March 1st 1858,	54.29
J.D. Dismukes " " 1859	57.28
J.D. Dismukes " " 1860	56.76
J.D. Dismukes " " Sundries	51.62
Daniel Glenn " " May 17th 1861	2.41
Hiram V. Hooper, March 19th 1861	11.12
William L. Hudgens 1862	9.50
D.W. Nye 1859	9.05
David Cochran 1862	19.50
L.A. Sears 1862	45.09
M.R. Hooper 1859	34.51
A. Lowe 1862	10.87

Inventory of the property of Marvel Harris Dec. By Sterling Walker. Administrator Sept. 1st 1865

Marvel Harris portion of Land amtg to $76.20

The above contains a true and perfect Inventory of all the goods and chattel rights and credits of Marvel Harris Dec. that have come to my hands. Knowledge of possession this Sept. 1st 1861

Sterling Walker Admr.

(p 254) An Inventory of the personal Estate of D.E. Robt. & Lemuel Barton Decd.

Cash on hand United States Currency	119.00
Cash on hand Banks of Tennessee old issue	438.00
Cash on hand New Issue	116.00
Cash on hand Gold and Silver	2.30
T.H. Baxter note due Jan 1st 1860	188.00
Lewis Lowe " " July 1st 1859	22.00
David Sanders " June 18th 1857	27.00
John C. Weakley " April 14th 1842	35.43
Thomas Barton due Jan. 1st 1841	28.00
Ira Clark due Oct. 26th 1845	10.20
Lem Adkins due Dec. 25	15.50
James Walker due Jan. 16th 1858	35.00
Constable Read receipt note on John Lacy for	197.00
dated Oct. 17th 1855 due in 20 days with a credit Apr. 26, 1856	11.25
and one other credit Feb. 18th 1857	100.00
G.A. Edwards ac. ½ Barrel sugar 7½	
L J. Perdue, Oct. 2nd 1860	3.75
Robert Weakley June 16th 1865	40.00

6 head mules, 4 head horses
2 yoke oxen, 11 head cattle
50 head hogs, 70 head sheep
8 goats, 1 four horse wagon
2 carts, 2 log chains
1 Thresher, 1 Reaper
1 pair patent balances, 1 wheat fan
1 lot farming tools, 1 set blacksmith tools
1 lot carpenter tools. 1 cross cut saw
1 Lot tobacco, 150 or 200 Bushel wheat

1 lot of Bee stands, 1 lot of barrel heading
1 mans saddle, cutting knife and scythe
1 large kettle. 1 lot cider stands & flax
5 Beds & furniture. 2 Bureaus & 1 cupboard
1 lot Cupboard Ware

The above is a true and perfect inventory of all the goods and chattel rights and credits of the said Darwin E. Robert and Lemuel Barton, deceased that have come to our hands possession or knowledge of the hands of any other person for us to the best of our knowledge & belief.
William Frazier)
Wash Wall) Admr.
Sworn to and suscribed Oct. 30th 1865 before me
Warren Jordan, Clerk

(p 255) Inventory of the personal estate of John Walker Dec. byHenry Hunter Executor.Isaac Eatherly due April 2nd 1860 $200.00
with a credit of$15.18 June 10, 1861 also cr. Feb. 2nd 1864 of $48.80
Henry Hunter due Feb. 20th 1862 186.00
with a credit of $10 July 12th 1862 also cr. Oct. 10th 1863 for $170.00
G.W. Harris & Nancy Harris due Dec. 25th 1859 60.00
with a credit of $8.00 Nov. 23rd 1861 also a credit of $10 no date a credit of 31.05 Feb. 25th 1862.
J.D. Teasley one note due Nov. 1st 1860 for 5.00
Uriah Murff & R.J. Mallory due Dec. 24th 1859 for 50.00
with a credit of $25.00 March 26th 1862.
Joshua Walker Due March 26th 1862 25.00
" " due January 1st 1865 20.00
Josh Walker, H.A. Pool & T.J. Battsdue Sept. 17th 1865 (paid in repairs) 10.00
Mourning L. Stewart due Jan. 1st 1863 24.00
J.T. Batts & T.W. Williams due Jan. 1st 1864 43.15
S.P. Knox due Jan. 1st 1864 35.00
Eliza Prichett & Gid Nicholson due Sept. 17th 1865 21.00
John Perdue & David Council due Sept. 17th 1865 71.50
T.W. Williams & David Council Due Sept. 17th 1865 110.75
Cash Collected 60.00
James Nicholson & E.L. Williams 699.90
J.H. Webber & James Hunter 236.00

The above is a true and perfect inventory of all the goods and chattels, rights and credits of the said John Walker dec. that has come to my hands, possession or knowledge. or the hands offany other persons for me.
This Sept. 28th 1865
Henry Hunter, Exr.

Sworn to and suscribed before me November 6th 1865.
Warren Jordan, Clerk.

An account of the rent of the lands of T.W. Harris Dec. for the year 1865 By Sterling Walker Exr.

J.W. Binkley	Rent	$23.25
G.E. Harris	13 acres at $2.00 per acre	26.00
" " "	7 acres @ 1.00 for wheat	7.00
William Binkley	4 acres @ 1.00 oats	4.00
J.R. Binkley	8 acres for wheat	8.00

Sterling Walker	23 acres for corn @ 2.00	$46.00
Sterling Walker	7 acres @ 1.00 for corn	7.00
A.L. Fortune	13 " 2.00	26.00
G.E. Harris	House Garden & Etc.	

Inventory and account of sale of the personal estate of A. Walker Dec. Sept. 4th 1865

William Binkley	6 head of sheep @ 3.00	$18.00
William Hudgens	1 Hog	5.00
James M. Walker amt. due on settlement		2.00
Sterling Walker	100 lbs bacon @ 12¾	12.75
Alexander Lowe	415 lbs. bacon @ 10	41.50
Alexander Lowe	181 lbs. bacon	14.48
Jas. W. Walker	To Salt	3.00
Jas. W. Walker	wheat, oats, potatoes & staves	8.50
Sterling Walker	To one mule	125.00
Jas. W. Walker	1 Shoat	3.00
B.F. Binkley	To Bacon	24.70
C.W. Starnes note due Dec 24th 1861		12.00
W.W. Hudgens	Due Jan. 1st 1866	45.00
J.W. Shearon	Due Jan. 1st 1866	1.40
G.W. Maxey	Due Jan. 1st, 1866	3.00
A.H. Walker(not good)	Due Ja. 1st 1866	12.00
B.F. Pace	Due Jan 1st 1865	11.00
Daniel W. Nye	54½ barrels of corn @ 3.00	163.00
		505.33

The above contains a true and perfect inventory of all the goods chattel rights and credits of A. Walker Dec. that have come to my hands knowledge or possession
Sept. 4th 1865
Jas. W. Walker, Admr.

Inventory of the personal estate of James C. Jones, Dec.. Due Sept. 1st 1860.

Joseph Gupton	Note Due Sept, 1st 1860 or. Sept 17th 61, $30 -	76.65
Thomas Gupton	Due June 5th 1864	45.00
Robert Jones	Due Jan. 1st 1865	129.00
James C. Jones	Jan. 16th 1861 or. June 26th ' 62, $10	16.00
James C. Jones	Sept. 5th 1864	13.00
J.W. Hunt	Sept. 26th 1864	213.75
James C. Jones	Jan. 1st 1865	27.00
Jacob C. Jones	Dec. 2nd 1861	55.00
Jaes C. Jones	Mch. 21st 1863	33.60
Cash on hand		124.00
Joshua Jones (doubtful) May 1st 1862		5.00
		738.50

The above is a perfect inventory of all the notes and chattel rights and credits of the sd. James C. Jones Dec. which have come to my hands, possession or knowledge Nov. 4th 1865
James C. Jones, Exr.

(p 257)
Account of the sale of the personal estate of David Jones, Dec. sold by T.J. Read Administrator on the ---- day of ---- 1865.

G.W. Daniel	1 no. 8 Plow	.90

G.W. Daniel	1 Lot plows	.35
G.W. Daniel	1 Pair cart wheels	4.50
Howell Hagewood	3 sheep	5.25
Howell Hagewood	3 sheep	3.75
Howell Hagewood	3 sheep	4.25
Howell Hagewood	1 sheep	1.40
Howell Hagewood	Spinning wheel	1.00
E.J. Jones	3 sheep	2.00
E.J. Jones	1 spinning wheel	1.00
E.J. Jones	1 Bed	5.00
G.W. Gossett	1 cow and calf	25.00
John P. Elazer	1 cow and calf	15.00
William Hand	1 Ox	15.00
G.M. Forsythe	1 cow	20.00
E. Carroll	1 yearling	4.95
E. Carroll	1 pair cards	.95
S.W. Patterson	1 pair cards	.25
Amos Tally	1 yoke oxen	40.00
J.A.M. Nesbitt (note)	---------- G	120.00
McClelland & Maberry	- -------- D	122.33
John Step (as admr. of) --D		7.12
W.L. Lang ------------ D		17.51
Isaac Groves ----------- D		27.80
M. Morgan Hagewood & Jones D		13.80
Wash Maberry " " D		52.96
J.M. Morgan, Hagewood & JOnes D		17.60
John Farmby date 1829 Bad		4.50

The above contains a true and perfect inventory of all the goods chattel right and credits belonging to the estate of David Jones, dec. which have come to my hands possession or knowledge this November 6th 1865

T.J. Rye, Administrator

(p 258) Inventory of the property of W.W. Read Dec.

One note, Plaster & Weakley due March 22nd 1859 with a credit of 125 April 28th 1866	250.00
J.M. Read Due Dec. 25th 1859	50.00
W.W. Walker Due Sept. 15th 1856	150.00
B.F. Read April 19th 1860	25.00
J.D. Nicholson Aug. 6th 1860	14.00
James Read Oct. 4th 1859	155.84

The above contains a true and perfect inventory of all the goods and chattels rights and credits of W.W. Read Dec. that have come to my hands, possession or knowledge This Oct. 1865

Rawls Maxey, Admr.

Inventory of the personal effects of Jno. W. Maxey Dec.

Henry Maxeys note $20 due 31st Jan. 1859, or.13th April 1859	11.25
Jan. 3rd 1862	5.00
Henry Maxey note January 1st 1860	74.25
Cr. Jan. 2nd 1861	25.00
Jan. 3rd 1860	40.00
Jan. 5th 1861	2.50

J.J. Shearon	March 5th 1860	20.00
J.J. Shearon	January 1st 1861	43.50
J.J. Shearon	May 1st 1860	110.00

The above contains a true and perfect inventory of all the goods and chattel rights and credits of J.W. Maxey Deceased that have come into my hands possession or knowledge.

This October 1865

Rawls Maxey Admr.

(p 259) Inventory and account of sale of the personal estate of W.W. Williams Dec. sold Aug. 30th 1865. By A.J. Bright Admr.

Mrs. Mary Ann Williams	1 Bed and furniture	$10.00
" " " "	1 bed and furniture	12.00
" " " "	1 Table	2.00
" " " "	1 Lounge	3.00
" " " "	1 Chest	4.00
" " " "	1 Book Case	4.00
" " " "	1 small table	1.00
Thomas Williams	1 watch	12.00
Mrs. Williams	1 pair saddle bags	2.00
Mrs Williams	1 spinning wheel	.05
Mrs Williams	1 spinning wheel	.25
Mrs. Williams	4 Shoats	5.50
Mrs. Williams	5 sheep	7.00
Thomas Bell	5 sheep	11.25
Thomas Harris	1 cow and calf	19.00
Mrs. Williams	2 hogs	2.00
Mrs. Williams	3 Hoes	.55
Mrs. Williams	1 Plow and Gear	1.75
Jo Williams	1 cow	20.00
Jo Williams	1 yearling	6.00
George W. Harris	1 Heifer	8.25
W.H. Stuart	1 Star	9.00

Cash on hand Tennessee Money		90.00
Cash on hand	Kentucky Money	25.00
Cash on Gold and Silver		44.75
Note on David Sanders due Sept. 11th 1863		1.75
Note on John Sanders Feb. 8th 1860		3.00
Note on B.J. Barnes	April 7th 1861	31.00
Note on G.R. Harris	Aug 13th 1860	20.00
Note on W.J. Gray	Nov. 1st 1864	56.00
Note on R. Simmons	July 15th 1861	9.19
Note on J.B. Moore	Feb. 27th 1861	5.00
Note on J.T. Sexenn	Nov. 5 1861	2.00
Note on A.B. Gibbs payable to Sanders Jan. 2nd 1860		10.00
Note on W.P. Bryan	Sept. 21st 1861	2.00

The above contains a true and perfect Inventory of all the goods and chattel rights and credits of WW. Williams Deceased that have come into my hands possession or knowledge.

This day Aug31st 1865

A.J. Bright Admr.

(p 260) An Inventory of the personal property of W.C.Pinson, Dec. sold by W.J. Nicholson Admr. on the 21st February 1862.

J.H. Adkins	3 old axes	.30
R.L. King	1 Shovel	.35
J.H. Adkins	1 Old axe &C	.10
J.H. Adkins	Old Trumpery	.15
Joshua Humphres	2 weeding hoes	.10
J.H. Adkins	1 single tree	.40
Eben Gupton	2 Barrels	.25
Sam'l Ennis	1 stone hammer	.30
Eben Gupton	1 stone hammer	.25
Mrs. Pinson	1 Shovel	.30
Mrs. Pinson	1 shovel	.56
Mrs. Pinson	1 harrow	4.00
Albert Clifton	2 Augers	.10
Gid Nicholson	2 Augers	.50
George Burton	2 chisels	.20
G.W. Harris	1 Drawing knife	.80
Robert McCormic	2 Rasps	.25
Wm. Nicholson	Bar Iron	.35
Dempsey Nicholson	1 pair steelyards	.10
J.H. Adkins	1 Lot trumpery	.10
Sam'l Ennis	1 Frow	.40
Dempsey Hunter	3 Harrow Teeth	.25
Mrs. Parsons	1 saw	.20
Wm. Nicholson	3 Planes	.55
Wm. Steels	1 plane	.25
Wm. Nicholson	1 plane	.25
Dempsey Nicholson	1 chopping axe	.75
Thomas Stewart	1 cross cut saw	2.00
Mrs. Pinson	1 Dinner pot	1.00
Mrs. Pinson	1 Oven	1.00
Mrs. Pinson	1 Skillet	1.00
Will Jeff Nicholson	1 Pot	.50
G.W. Harris	1 Skillet	.75
G.W. Harris	1 Oven	.80
W. Nicholson	1 Pot	1.00
Mrs. Pinson	2 pair hooks	.25
Mrs. Pinson	1 Spinning wheel	2.00
Dempsey Nicholson	1 Bee Gum	1.25
Mrs. Majors	1 Bread Tray	.15
Mrs. Pinson	1 Bread Tray	.15
Wm. Nicholson	1 Bucket & Barrel	.55
Jno. S. Majors	1 Barrel Vinegar	4.00
John Blankenship	1 Barrel cider	10.00
(p 261)		
D. Barton	1 cow hide	1.50
Will J. Nicholson	1 Sheep Skin	.35
Will J. Nicholson	1 Sheep skin	.35
Will J. Nicholson	1 sheep skin	.25
Samuel Ennis	1 cow hide	1.50
Henderson Pinson	1 Set shoe tools	2.00
J.H. Adkins	1 cradle & Clock	.25
Wm. Nicholson	1 Table	1.25
Henry Blanton	1 Mans saddle	7.50
Allen Hunter	Barrel and flax seed	.75

Nancy Pinson	1 Bed and Stead	10.00
J.H. Adkins	1 Jar Pickles	.45
J.H. Adkins	Coffee Pot &C	.10
O.O. Knott	1 Iron and spoons	.40
J.H. Adkins	1 Poplar Table	.30
O.O. Knott	1 Lot books	.30
H. Pinsom	1 Small table	2.00
Mrs. Pinson	1 Reel	.50
J.H. Adkins	1920 bundles oats	19.20
Wm. Jones	800 bundles oats	12.00
Mrs. Pinson	1 Gray Mare	20.00
John W^h^ite	1 Filly	68.00
Wm. Durham	1 Sorrel Colt	42.00
Wm. Durham	1 Heifer	5.00
Mrs. Pinson	1 Heifer	5.00
Hawkins Frazier	1 Red cow & calf	20.00
John Nicholson	1 muly heifer	17.00
David Council	5 head sheep	17.50
H.C. Pace	1 sheep skin	1.05
Mrs. Pinson	R nt of farm	75.00
Joshua Stroud	Rent of land	27.00
Eben Gupton	Rent of land	31.35
John Nicholson	Rent of land	23.50
W.J. Nicholson	1 sow and pigs	8.20
H.C. Pace	5 shoates	15.25
H. Pinson	5 shotes	12.75
Robert McCormic	5 shotes	10.00
Henderson Pinson	6 shotes	26.00
W. Page	4 outside	7.50
H.C.Pace	1 sandy sow	5.25
H. Pinson	1 spottish sow	7.25
H. Pinson	1 Diamond Plow	1.00
H. Pinson	1 Cary plow	.50
J.S. Majors	1 Lot pickles	1.75
Cash Received		33.00
Note, John S . Majors	1 note	37.21
T.L. Justice	1 note	8.42
(p 262)		
D. Blanton and others	One note for	100.00
Wm. Fambrough & Majors	one notefor	18.00
R.J. Mallory	One note for	15.00
H.B. Blanton (Doubtful)	One note for	25.00
Mrs. Pinson	1 Flax Wheel	.50
Mrs. Pinson	1 trundle bed	3.00
Darwin Barton	1 set chairs	1.50
W.C. Hunter	1 Basket Onions	.60
Mrs. Pinson	2 smooth Irons	.50
Mrs. Pinson	1 cupboard	1.50
Mrs. Pinson	1 Spser	.05
Mrs. Pinson	Candle Molds	.25
Henry Blanton	Trot lines & net	1.50
Eben Gupton	1 lot trumpery	.30
Eben Gupton	2 plow points	.10
Mrs. Pinson	1 womans saddle	2.50
Mrs. Pinson	1 Log chain	2. 25
Henderson Pinson	1 still and tubs	40.00
Gid Nicholson	1 plow	1.50
Mrs. Pinson	1 plow	1.50

Mrs. Pinson	1 plow	.50
W. Nicholson	1 Carey Plow	.25
David Council	1 Dorris plow	1.90
Will Jeff Nicholson	1 Avery Plow	3.75
G.W. Harris	1 Bull tongue Plow	1.05
W. Nicholson	1 old plow	.15
Eben Gupton	1 old plow	.50
W. Nicholson	1 pair Hames	.10
Joshua Humphries	2 Blind bridles	.55
Gid Nicholson	Back Band & Traces	1.55
J.A. Simpson	2 Bridles &C	.50
Joshua Humphreys	1 double tree	1.50
J.S. Harris	1 Pair Harness	.65
R.L. King	2 curry combs	.40
J.S. Harris	1 scythe and cradle	2.00
John White	1 wheat fan	15.25
William Nicholson	1 Lot flax	1.00

The above contains a true and perfect Inventory of all the goods chattel rights and credits of W.C. Pinson Dec. that have come into my hands knowledge or possession April 1862.

Wm. J. Nicholson, Admr.

(p 263) Second Invemtory of W.J. Nicholson admr. of the estate of W.C. Pinson Dec. sold on the 25th December 1862

W.J. Nicholson	1 sow and pigs	8.25
H.C. Pace	5 shotes	13.25
H. Pinson	5 shotes	12.75
Robert McCormic	5 shotes	10.00
H. Pinson	6 shotes	26.00
Wm. Pace	4 outside	7.50
H.C. Pace	1 sandy sow	5.25
H. Pinson	1 spotted sow	7.25
H. Pinson	Diamond plow	1.00
H. Pinson	1 Carey Plow	.50
John S. Major	1 Lot pickles	1.75
John S. Major	2527 pound bacon @ 20c	505.40
R.J. Mallory	515 " " 15c	77.25
Cash Received	May 6th	9.00
One officers receipt	9 barrels corn @	9.00

1 Receipt on J. Murphey vs. N. Sanders payable to A. Gupton due Oct. 10, 1859 with a credit $5.00 June 2nd 1860 one for 2.50 April 10th 1860 2.50
with a credit June for $2.50 April 10, 1859 3.50

An account od sale of property of Catherine Pinson Dec. By Wm. J. Nicholson Admr. of W.C. Pinson Dec. Nov. 12th 1865.

W.J. Nicholson	Weeding hoes	.25
O.O. Knox	1 single tree	1.25
D.H. Nicholson	1 Avery Plow	2.50
Wm. Page	1 Turning plow	1.00
O.O. Knox	1 Avery	3.50
A.J. Perdue	1 Double tree	1.05
John Nicholson	1 Axe	1.60
H.C. Pace	1 Harrow	7.10

W.J. Nicholson Jr.	1 Kettle	8.50
R. King	1 Shovel	2.05
F. Perdue	1 Paor Hooks	1.00
W. Plaster	Pair Forge Irons	1.00
W.J. Nicholson	2 Fire Pokers	.30
W.J. Nicholsog	1 Spillet	1.25
J.J. Buckner	2 Harrow teeth	.30
S. Stewart	1 frying pan	.50
H. R. Pool	1 Shovel and Ladle	.30
J.J. Buckner	1 Tea Kettle	2.00
Nancy Pinson	2 Flat irons	2.75
Buck Denney	1 dinner pot	1.25
Nancy Pinson	1 Large pot	2.45
Carrol Hunter	1 Spice Mortar	2.20
(p 264)		
Buck Denney	1 Bell	.55
Mary Major	1 Coffee Mill	.50
J.J. Buckner	Lap Rings	.50
J.J. Buckner	1 Water Bucket	1.05
J.J. Buckner	1 Water bucket	.55
Buck Denney	1 Tin Bucket	.75
J.J. Buckner	1 Pail	.30
J.J. Buckner	1 Can & Strainer	.50
J.J. Buckner	1 Churn	1.30
Buck Denney	1 Basket	.45
Buck Denney	1 Basket	.15
Nancy Pinson	1 Basket	.20
W.J. Nicholson	1 wash board	.30
Buck Denney	1 Bread Tray	.55
W.J. Nicholson	1 Lard Stand	4.00
Wash Smith	1 Lard stand and lard	7.00
J.T. Albright	1 Piggin	.10
J.J. Buckner	1 spinn ng wheel	5.35
J. Mosely	1 cook stove	17.50
A.W. Frazier	1 meal stand	.25
O.O. Knox	1 Water can	2.00
John Gupton	1 Barrel &C	.10
W.J. Nicholson	1 sausage mill	4.25
J.J. Buckner	1 Table	3.00
G.W. Gossitt	1 Flax wheel	2.35
W.J. Nigholson	1 Kage	.10
Nancy K ox	1 Bill	2.50
J.J. Bubkner	1 Claw hammer	.50
W.J. Nicholson	1 Hatchet	2.00
J.J. Buckner	1 work basket	.15
John Adkins	Basket & Flax	1.70
Wm. Tims	1 Spinning Wheel	3.80
A.J. Perdue	1 Lot Feathers	3.50
Robert McCormic	1 side saddle	1.30
J.J. Buckner	1 Bridle	1.40
J.J. Buckner	8 plates	2.90
Nancy Pinson	2 china plates	1.25
Nancy Pinson	Plates, cream jug &C	3.25
M. Williams	1 Sett plates	2.90
J.J. Buckner	Cups, saucers Dish &C	3.55
John Albright	1 sugar bowl	.50

J.J. Buckner	2Dishes &C	1.70
D.H. Nicholson	1 Pitcher	.65
J.J. Buckner	1 Pitcher	1.00
Miss Fielder	Molasses stands, knives and forks	2.70
J.J. Buckner	1 Jar	.35
(p 265)		
J.J. Buckner	1 Table	1.00
O.O. Knox	½ Bushel	.15
F. Evans	1 Barrel Salt	10.55
Wm. Page	1 Lard Stand	1.50
Frank Perdue	1 Barrel soap	1.75
John Albright	1 side bacon	2.50
Rufus King	1 Barrel Vinegar	4.15
Wm. Nicholson	1 Barrel, grindstone &C	2.35
Joseph Gupton	1 Razor & Strap	1.60
F. Evans	2 Traces	.80
J.J. Buckner	3 glasses	1.15
Jno. Adkins	1 Lot Bottles	.50
John Nicholson	1 Salr set	.20
T.L. Justic	3 Bottles	.40
W.J. Nicholson	1 Bark &C	.30
Nancy Knox	1 Grater &C	.10
W.J. Nicholson	Trumpery	.05
Wm. Reynolds	Bees Wax	.25
J.J. Buckner	1 Press	12.50
W.J. Nicholson	1 Lot books	.80
T.L. Justice	1 Lot books	.55
Nancy Pinson	1 Bureau	12.00
Alsey Jones	1 Gun	3.50
Allen King	1 pair cards	1.50
J.J. Buckner	2 pair cards	2.75
Wm. Lewis	2 pair cards	.70
Alsey Jones	1 Basket	.35
Mary Robertson	1 Bed shelf and clothes	44.50
T.L Justice	1 Bed Quilt	2.25
J.J. Buckner	Bed clothes 46.50	46.50
Nancy Pinson	1 lot bed clothes	35.00
Sac Stewart	1 Bed quilt	1.65
Nancy Knox	1 Bed quilt	2.25
Robert Mosely	2 mules	283.50
Calvin Adkins	1 Mule	52.50
R.D. Mose;y	1 Mule	100.00
A.J. Perdue	1 chair	2.80
E. Gupton	1 Lot gear	2.60
Wm. Page	1 scythe and cradle	3.25
Joseph Gupton	1 S otted cow	16.00
B.F. King	1 cow and calf	28.75
Wm. Blanton	1 cow and calf	25.00
James King	1 white heifer	8.00
B. Davis	1 red yaarling	5.00
B.F. King	1 cow and calf	30.00
John S. Majors	1 Large hog	17.50
(p 266)		
H. McCormic	6 hogs	17.25
W.J. Nicholson	1 Basket	.40
Frank Perdue	Chickens and geese	7.99
John Pace	1 Large shovel	1.10

W.W. Fizer	1 Set chairs	5.00
Alsey Jones	1 Set chiars	3.00
Josh Humphries	1 Hatchet	.55
George Garrison	1 Grub hoe	.35
R. King	25 Bbls corn	75.00
Willie Stewart	2 Iron Wedges	1.00
Sac Stewart	4 sheep	13.00
John Fambrough	8 sheep	24.25
James Fielder	Rent land	20.00
John Mosely	Home place	50.00
J.B. Taylor	$50 to be taken off	2.50
Robert McCormic	1 Leather apron	.55
Wm. Blanton	1 seald stand	.75
G. Nicholson	1 sow and shotes	11.00
Wm. Blanton	5 hogs	19.00
G. Nicholson	6 hogs	18.00
Robert McCormic	1 shot bag	.30
M. Major	1 Barrel Flax	4.25
James H. Major	1 pr pot hooks	.35
Robert McCormic	1 Flask	.75
W.K. Hollis	1 Lot Books	.75
D.H. Nicholson	1 Bucket	.75
Jo Gupton	2 pr shears	.40
Dock Pace	1 cizrun	1.50
Willie Stewart	1 "	1.30
Bud Coleman	1 sifter	1.00
John Nicholson	Gear & Hand saw	.45
C.W. Gossitt	Mall	.25
G. Nicholson	Fire Irons	3.50
Jo Gupton	Knife Box	.05
W.J. Nicholson	Pot rack &C	1.10
John Nicholson	1 Lot wool	1.50
W. Blanton	2 Barrels	.55
Rent of land 1862		75.00
Expenses Repair of House, taking care of negroes &C		70.00

The above contains a true and perfect Inventory of all the goods & chattels rights and credits of Catherine Pinson Dec. that have come to my hands possession or knowledge.

W.J. Nicholson, Admr.
of W.C. Pinson Dec.
(p 267)
A list of the preishable property belonging to William Clifton Decd. Sept. the 26th 1865.

Thomas Bell	1 lot oak scantlin	.50
Wm. Plaster	Sheeting by hundred $1,85 cents	6.06
Wm. Plaster	500 feet weatherboarding $1.65 pr. h.	8.25
L.J. Hooper	500 ft. weather boarding $1.53 pr h.	7.75
W. Plaster Remainder	" " 526 ft. @ 1.80 pr. h.	9.46
Thomas Bell	130 ft. scantling @ $1.85 per h.	2.40
L.T. Hooper	500 ft. fencing @ $1.65	8.25
L.T. Hooper	Remainder 236 ft. @ 1.60 per	3.77
G.W. Harris	4 axes & Bell	.25
C.C. Knox	1 wedge & yoke	.80
T. Gupton	1 Fow p	.90
W.H. Pace	1 cow and calf	15.00

T: Bell	1 cow		10.00
T. Bell	1 Heifer	p	7.00
T. Bell	1 steer	p	7.00
T. Bell	1 grey mare		40.00
G.W. Gossett	1 old saddle	p	3.50
Ann Clifton	1 fine saddle	p	14.00
Ann Clifton	1 chest		3.00
T. Bell	1 small table		5.00
G.W. Harris	1 razor & Strap		.50
T. Bell	½ doz chairs by the piece 1.15		6.90
Widpw	1 small table		1.00
Widow	1 sugar chest		2.00
R.H. Johnson	3 pair cards	p	1.65
W.H. Pace	2 balls shoe thread		.45
A.Hunter	Alls and locks	p	.30
W.H. Morris	shoe makers tools	p	2.85
Andy Cane (Cain)	1 small bed stid		1.00
Parris Teasley	1 spinning wheel		.70
Widow	1 spinning wheel		1.00
Widow	1 Reel		1.00
N. Johnson	1 noggin p		.30
L.Perdue	1 pairsbiliards	p	2.00
L. Perdue	1 crock p		.40
G.W. Harris	1 crock		.25
Widow	1 crock		.75
G. Williams	1 churn		1.00
T. Bell	1 churn		1.55
W.H. Plasters	1 churn		1.30
G.A. Shearon	1 lard barrel		.10
Widow	1 lard barrel		.50
T. Bell	1 lard barrel	p	.25
T. Bell	1 can		.10
(p 268)			
J.C. Smith	1 water barrel		1.15
T. Bell	1 water barrel		1.10
Widow	1 pair fire irons		1.50
Widow	1 pot		.50
Widow	2 pr fire irons		.25
Widow	1 big kettle		2.75
T. Bell	1 Book case		3.25
Ann Clifton	1 Big chest p		2.00
T. Bell	1 Bed quilt		1.35
E.H. Clifton	1 counter pane	p	1.00
Widow	1 Counter pane		.50
Widow	1 counter pane		.50
T. Bell	1 clock		3.50
T. Bell	1 bed and stead		41.00
T. Bell	1 bed and stead		22.00
Ann Clifton	1 looking glass		.50
Widow	1 Safe		2.00
"	2 tin buckets		.30
"	2 " "		.50
"	1 brd tray		.15
"	1 dish pan		.10
"	1 table		.05
"	1 chest p		.25

W. Weakley	1 Bee hive p	3.25
W. Smith	1 lot bee gum	.25
M.M. Chambliss	1 mowing blade p	.70
T. Bell	1 grubing hoe	.25
T. Bell	1 weeding hoe	.10
T. Bell	1 weeding hoe	1.30
Widow	1 Spade	.60
T. Bell	1 Tung plow	.25
T. Bell	1 digger & Harness p	.10
T. Bell	2 plows and harness	;30
M.M. Chambliss	1 pr. chians & plows p	.25
T. Bell	1 Lot of flax	.25
T. Bell	1 Flax brake	.25
T. Bell	1 pair of gear	1.10
Widow	1 grind stone	1.75
T. Bell	1 Jack plain	1.00
T. Bell	1 Fore plain	1.00
T. Beal	1 smoothinf plain p	.80
M.M. Chambliss	1 Iron square p	.25
T. Bell	2 chisels	.60
T. Bell	2 augers	.80
T. Bell	1 pair of gears	1.10
E.K. Clifton	1 grind stone	1.75
W. Plaster	1 Jack plain	1.00
W. Plaster	1 Fore plain	1.00
H. Sanders	1 smoothing plain p	.80
T. Bell	1 Iron square p	.25
T. Bell	2 chisels p	.60
C. Smith	2 Augers	.80
W. Plaster	2 augers	.75
D.G.Beasley	1 hand axe	.10
(p 269)		
W.D. Weakley	1 broad axe	1.10
W. Plaster	1 Oil stone	.25
G.W. Harris	1 hand saw	.30
J.W. Hunt	1 lot of nails	.25
T. Bell	1 lot nails and hamer	.60
G.W. Harris	4½ bushels wheat @ 55 cts	2.47
G.W. Harris	6½ bu. old wheat at 80c	5.20
Widow	2 boxes & Stands	.90
W.D. Weakley	1 wheat fan	5.60
T. Bell	1 half bushel	.60
J.W. Hunt	1 scolding stand	.50
T. Bell	1 work bench	2.00
J. Bebbett	6 first choice hogs	37.00
D.W. GUpton	6 second choice hogs	30.00
D.W. Weakley	1 sow and shoats	13.00
J. Smith	Salt by the bushel 65 cts.	2.35
Widow	1 Land stand	1.00
Widow	[illegible]	2 sheep
T. Bell	2 sheep $3.25 each	6.50
W. H. Stuart	11 gallons brandy	22.00
T. Bell	Rent of land west of the lane	20.00

Sale of Remainder of property of WM . Clifton Decd. on the 25th day of Nov. 1865.

I.N. Clifton

Widow	10 Bu seet potatoes	5.00
W.D. Weakley	5 " " " @ 1.00	5.00
S.H. Cliftod	5 " " " @ 70 cents	3.50
W.D. Weakley	1 lot sweet potatoes planting	1.00
W.D. Weakley	12 bbl. corn @ $2.00	24.00
W.H. Plaster	16 bbl. 2 bu corn @ $2.55	41.80
I.N. Clifton	6 bbl short corn @ $1.25	7.50
Calvin James	1 lot shucks @ $3.10	3.10
W.D. Weakley	500 bundles oats @ 1¼ cts.	6.25
W.D. Weakley	300 Fodder 1.30 pr bundle	3.90
W.D. Weakley	250 " @ 1.25 pr hund.	3.12
Elvin Jones	210 Fodder @ 1.10 per hund.	2.30
W.D. Weakley	250 damaged fodder 40 cents per hund	1.00
Widow	21 lbs pict cotton 20 cts.	4.20
W.E. Clifton	21 lbs. cotton at 30 cts	6.30
Edwards & Cross	285 lbs. leaf tobacco at 15cts.	42.75
Edwards & Cross	175 lbs lugs @ #3.00 per hundred	5.25

(p 270)
A list of funds belonging to the estate of Wm. Clifton Decd.

Confederate Money on hand	$122.00
State Bank of Tennessee, Old Issue	19.00
Silver on hand	1,35
One note on Plaster & Weakley	44.50
One note on L.J. Perdue pr. & Int	86.00
One note on R.H. Weakley	29.00
One note on J.W. Gupton	6.97
One note on John Fambrough	3.04
One apo on S. Bobbitt	2.68
One apc on B. Felts	24.00
One apo on S.A. Clifton	10.00
One apo on Sarah Smith	3.44
One apo. on Sarah Smith	1.70

Inventory of the goods and chattels of P.W. Randolph that has come into my hands as administrator.

1 Saddle and bridle	7.00
1 Buggy and harness	52.00
1 Feather bed	19.00
1 silver Watch	22.50
1 silver watch	3.00
Notes and accounts about	100.00

One half of which I Consider doubtful
John D. Tucker, Admr of P.W. Randolph

Inventory and account of sale of the estate of B.L. Williams Decd.

James Watts	1 mattock	.30
Frank Ellis	3 hoes 2 grub and weed	.65
G.W. Hunt	2 weeding hoes	1.10
W.J. Hunt	1 Bull tongue plow	.50
W.J. Hunt	2 cottars	.60

G.W. Hunt	2 old plows	.05
E.J. Binkley	2 weeding hoes	.25
J.E. Turner	1 grubbing hoe	.50
G.F. Ellis	1 Froe	.50
W.J. Hunt	1 grub Hoe	.05
A.H. Williams	1 Axe	.50
A.H. Williams	1 Iron Wedge	.50
(p 271)		
G.W. Hunt	1 Iron Wedge	.70
A.H. Williams	1 Axe	1.00
R. Head	1 Plow &C	.15
T.H. Felts	1 Livingston Plow	6.25
Williamson	1 Livingston Plow No. 8	5.00
W.J. Hunt	1 Rake	.20
W.J. Hunt	1 swingle tree	.30
C.A. Hudgens	" "	.35
W.J. Hunt	1 clivis	.30
James Watts	1 clivis	.30
M.P. Frey	1 Lot trumpery	.12½
G.W. Williams	1 Bell	.25
L. Thomas	1 Bell &C	.10
Wm. Edgent (Edgin)	1 draw knife	.45
J.W. Williams	1 half bushel	.30
W.J. Hunt	1 Pot rack	.35
G.W. Hunt	1 Lot trumpery	.30
G.F. Ellis	1 chisel &C	.25
Wm. Dowlen	1 set gear	1.35
C.A. Hudgens	1 set gear	1.00
W.J. Hunt	1 set gear	2.55
M.V. Dowlen	p pair steelyards	.25
C.A. Hudgens	1 plow No. 12	2.75
W.E. Felts	1 par Crads	.25
M.V. Dowlen	1 pr cards	.25
W.J. Hunt	1 pr cards	.10
Nancy Felts	1 Tin Bucket	.35
Nancy Felts	1 Tin bucket	.25
G.W. Hunt	1 Tin bucket	.25
M.V. Dowlen	1 Tin bucket	.25
J.W. Wilson	1 water bucket	1.00
C.A. Hudgens	1 water bucket	.25
M.V.Dowlen	1 d can	1.60
G.W. Hunt	1 cedar bucket	.10
Meri Harris	1 churn	.50
N.W. Felts	1 coffee mill	.25
Nancy Felts	1 straner &C	.40
J.W. Wilsom	1 spinning wheel	2.00
W.E. Felts	1 spinning wheel	1.00
M.V. Dowlen	1 Reel	.10
N?V? Dowlen	1 cook stove	5.00
N.V. Dowlen	1 chamber	.50
N.V. Dowlen	2 smoothing irons	.40
Sack. M. Stewart	1 stew pot	.60
J.W. Owen	1 Oven	1.05
M.P. Fry (Frey)	1 Oven	1.00
	$47.12	

(p 272)

(p 272)

J.W. Owen	1 Oven	.45
A. Latimore	1 Skillet	1.10
M.P. Frey	1 Lot Trum -	.40
A. Latimore	1 stew pot	1.70
G.F. Ellis	1 large Pot	2.25
L.L. Williams	1 pot rack &C	1.10
Wm. Dowlen	1 Skillet	.30
G.F. Ellis	2 Tubs	.50
G.F. Ellis	1 water can	.25
M.V. Dowlen	1 Kettle	.50
M.V. Dowlen	1 Table	.10
N. Felts	1 Tray	.50
N. Felts	2 pans	.10
L.L. Williams	1 Tray	.20
A.H. Williams	1 Sifter	.55
W.E. Felts	1 Swift	.10
J.J. Brdley Jr. (Bradley)	1 dining table	5.00
M.V. Dowlen	1 dining table	1.00
W.R. Ramer	1 chest	3.75
W.J. Hunt	1 Lot vials &C	.20
S.M. Stewart	1 dressing table	2.75
M.V. Dowlen	1 Bureaux	7.00
M.V. Dowlen	1 Looking glass	.50
W.E. Felts	1 sugar Boll	.30
J.J. Brdley (Bradley)	1 pitcher	.70
M. Binkley	2 Pitchers	.90
L.L. Williams	2 plaits &C	.40
Jack Ramer	1 Grater	.15
S.M. Stewart	1 Sett knives and forks	.35
J.W. Wilson	1 molasses stand	.45
J.J. Bradley	1 Lot bottles	.20
Jack Ramer	1 Glass Jar	.55
Lewis Thomas	1 stone jar	.30
J.W. Wilson	1 Clock	5.50
W.E. Felts	1 candle stand	2.00
M.V. Dowlen	1 Bed stead	1.00
M. Binkley	1 Bead	22.00
G.W. Hunt	1 "	22.00
M.V. Dowlen	1 Sett of chairs	3.60
W.E. Felts	1 set of chairs	3.90
M.V. Dowlen	1 set of chairs	1.00
A.G. Felts	1 Testament	.55
John Dolen (Dowlen)	1 looking glass	.90
Jo Grant	1 History of the world	3.30
M.V. Dowlen	1 cupboard	70.00
	$167.25	

(p 273)

Tom Bracey	1 set shoe tools	1.80
Rob Head	1 sett shoe & Lasts	1.70
M.V. Dowlen	136 lbs. picked cotton @ 35	12.60
H. Dowlen	116 lbs. seed cotton @ $10\frac{1}{2}$	1.68
G.W. Hunt	1 Bed stead &C	5.20
George Felts	1 Lot books	.60
Wm. Dowlen	1 Flax Wheel	2.00
W.J. Hunt	1 Trundle bead stead	.60
S.M. Stewart	1 Bed stead	.50

S.M. Stewart	1 bed stead	.25
S.M. Stewart	1 safe	.25
A.H. Williams	1 Flax Brake	.25
Jo Krantz	16½ Gallons vinegar @ 16	2.64
G.W Hunt	1 Hhd. & Mortar	.25
M.P. Frey	12½ lbs.soap .04	.50
H. Dowlen	2 Hhds. 1.20	2.40
Green W. Hunt	1 Lot broom corn	.45
M.V. Dowlen	1 Bay mare	.61
M.V. Dowlen	1 Fire screen	.20
W.E. Felts	1 Muly yearling	5.25
G.W. Hunt	1 Red yearling	6.25
A.N. Hooper	1 red cow	13.00
M.V. Dowlen	1 cow and calf	20.60
W.N. Rose	1 cow ando calf	12.75
B.H. Bradley	1 muly cow	12.50
Robt. Williams	1 Bay mare	37.05
A.H. Williams	1 mule colt	60.00
A.H. Williams	1 bay colt	25.00
A.H. Williams	1 yoke oxen	55.00
W. Gent	1 cury comb	.30
W. Gent	1 saddle	3.00
Sylvester Dowlen	1 sow & piggs	6.75
Jo. E. Agent (Edgin)	1 side saddle	.25
T. Bracy	1 Bench & Tools	.65
A.H. Williams	4 1st choice Sheep 4.00	16.00
A.H. Williams	4 2nd choice " 4.00	16.00
A.H. Williams	3 3rd choice " 3.50	10.50
G.F. Ellis	1 Knif	.50
Marilla Dowlen	1 churn	1.00
A.H. Williams	100 lbs. bacon 16	16.00
A.H. Williams	100 lbs bacon 16	16.00
A.H. Williams	100 lbs, bacon 16	16.00
A.H. Williams	100 lbs. bacon 16¼	16.25
A.H. Williams	100 lbs bacon 16¼	16.25
A.H. Williams	182½ lbs bacon 16½	30.03
A.H. Williams	100 lbs lard 17¼	17.25
	524.91	

(p 275)

Green Hunt	1 Lot sundries	.10
Wm. Harris	1 Grub Hoe	1.30
A.L. Fortune	1 Lot hoes	.25
W. Hawkins	1 Clivis	.25
Green Hunt	2 hoes	.20
W. Hawkins	1 Lot sundries	.10
Wm. Hunt	1 Lot sundries	.15
John Walker	1 Iron wedge	.25
Green Hunt	1 Iron Wedge	.60
T.N. Walker	1 Iron Wedge	1.10
John Williams	1 Iron Wedge	1.00
Wm. Hunt	1 Saddle	2.00
Wm. Harris	1 Grind stone	4.25
Green Hunt	1 whet stone &C	.50
R.R. Felts	1 scythe & Cradle	.50
Green Hunt	1 Auger 2 inch	1.00
A.H. Williams	1 inch	.45

M.V. Dowlen	1 Auger ½ inch	.25
Wm. Harris	1 "	.25
Green Hunt	1 Yoke &C	.25
Green Hunt	1 Hand saw	2.00
Green Hunt	1 Plane & Chisel	.15
Wm Harris	1 Lot olers	.25
Wm. Hunt	1 Lot sundries	.30
W.W. Felts	1 Scythe & Blade	1.60
Green Hunt	1 Drawing knife	.80
R. Murphey	1 Drawing knife	.85
Frank Williams	1 Apple Pealer	.10
M.V. Dowlen	1 Feed trough	.10
D. Fort	1 Trowel	.30
Green Hunt	1 Shovel Plough	.25
Lewis Williams	1 Hand saw	.50
Green Hunt	1 Pitch Fork	.25
Wm. Hunt	1 cross cut saw	5.00
Green Hunt	2 lock chains	1.00
Green Hunt	1 work bench	.50
Wm. Harris	1 - 2 horse plow	1.00
R.R. Felts	1 Pr stretcher	.50
W. Hawking	1 Log chain	.50
Wm. Hunt	1 Lot plough	.25
M.V. Dowlen	1 swingle tree	.05
John Bradley	1 Peock Plough	.50
Wm. Hunt	1 Lot lumber	.10
Green Hunt	1 coalterplow	.60
Wm. Hunt	2 Avery Ploughs	.50
(p 276)		
Green Hunt	1 Bull tong plow	.25
Green Hunt	1 Lot sundries	.50
Green Hunt	; Avery Plough	1.00
A.H. Williams	1 cart & Bed	6.00
Green Hunt	1 waggon bed	1.00
A.H. Williams	1 Harrow	5.00
Green Hunt	2 Bee Gums	3.00
Green Hunt	5 Bu wheat @ 1.60)	
Green Hunt	5 bu wheat @ 1.55) not sold	
D.A. Wilkins	3 Bu rye @ 40	1.20
Green Hunt	1 scalding tub	.35
Green Hunt	1 wheat fan	15.00
Thos. Harris	1 wheat fan	.50
John Bradley Jr.	1 clivis	.05
Frank Williams	1 straw cutter	5.00
Wm. Turrentine	3 hogs	34.00
Green Hunt	3 Hogs	23.00
Green Hunt	6 pigs	6.00
Richard Reding	1 sorrel mare	5.00
John Bradley	1 muly cow	15.50
Mrs. E.C. Hunt	1 Heifer	5.00
Mrs. E.C. Hunt	1 Head sheep	7.00
Green Hunt	1/3 straw stack	1.00
Wm. Hunt	1 waggon	9.50
Green Hunt	1 Lot tobacco	5.00
Mrs. E.C. Hunt	1 Axe	.05
Mrs. E.C. Hunt	2 lard stands	.25
Green Hunt	7 Bu. Salt	5.75

Mrs. E.C. Hunt	1 Lot sundries	.25
Rob Williams	1 Pot	1.00
A.B. Carlin	1 Pot	3.25
Wm. Hunt	1 Bake Pot	.45
A.B. Carlin	1 Bake pot	.50
Wm. Hunt	1 Freying pan	.10
Wm. Hunt	1 skillet	.10
Thom. Ventries	2 bread bakers	.25
John Chamblis	1 pot rack	.25
Mrs. E.C. Hunt	1 pot rack	.05
Green Hunt	1 large pot	2.50
Mrs. E.C. Hunt	3 pots	.10
Mrs. E.C. Hunt	1 old stove	.65
Wm. Hunt	1 side saddle	1.50
Mrs. M.J. Hunt	1 Flax Wheel	.50
Mrs. E.C. Hunt	1 spinning wheel	.10
W.W. Felts	1 water keg	.05
(p 277)		
Mrs. E.C. Hunt	1 Cedar pole	.50
A.H. Williams	4 forceps	2.00
A.H. Williams	1 Stone jar	2.00
Wm. Hunt	1 copper Bbbler	2.75
John William	1 churn	.25
C.M. Walker	1 pr. sheep shears	.50
Green Hunt	1 Hatchet	.50
J.E. Turner	1 Straner	.10
Wm. Ramer	1 Tray	.50
Wm. Ramer	2 smoothing irons	.20
A.B. Corlew	1 Basket	1.10
Green Hunt	1 pr steelyards	.50
D. Fort	1 pr. steelyards	2.75
M.V. Dowlen	2 Howels	.25
Wm. Hunt	1 Lot sundries	.10
W.W. Felts	1 T[R]undle bed stead	.35
Robert Williams	1 Table	.05
Mrs. E.C. Hunt	1 Tin Bucket	.05
Mrs. E.C. Hunt	1 Tin Bucket	.05
Mrs. E.C. Hunt	1 Brass kettle	.10
Mrs. E.C. Hunt	1 Jar	.05
Mrs. E.C. Hunt	1 Jar	.10
Mrs. E.C. Hunt	1 cedar piggin	.05
Mrs E.C. Hunt	1 Table	.10
Mrs. E.C. Hunt	1 Demajohn	.50
Mrs. E.C. Hunt	1 Lot bottles &C	.10
Mrs E.C. Hunt	2 cake tallow	.10
Mrs. E.C. Hunt	2 jugs	.10
Mrs. E.C. Hunt	1 Jar	.05
Mrs. E.C. Hunt	1 Table & Contents	2.00
Mrs. E.C. Hunt	1 Table & Contents	.25
Mrs. E.C. Hunt	1 Table & Contents	.10
A.B. Corlew	2 dishes	.10
Wm. Ramer	1 Pitcher	.30
Mrs. M.J. Hunt	1 Dish	.25
Mrs. E.C. Hunt	1 candle stand	.25
Wm. Hunt	1 writing Disk	2.50
Mrs. E.C. Hunt	1 cupboard & contents	1.00

Mrs. E.C. Hunt	1 Clock	1.00
Mrs. E.C. Hunt	2 Brass candlesticks	.05
Mrs. E.C. Hunt	1 Bed stead	.10
Mrs. E.C. Hunt	1 Trundle Bed stead &C	2.00
Mrs. E.C. Hunt	1 Lot bed clothing	1.00
Mrs. E.C. Hunt	1 lot Bed clothing	1.00
Mrs. E.C. Hunt	1 Feather Bed	1.00
Thomas Ventress	6 chairs	5.75
(p 278)		
Green Hunt	6 chairs	5.00
Mrs. E.C. Hunt	1 Trunk & Chest	.10
Mrs. E.C. Hunt	4 chairs	.10
Wm. Hunt	2 Books	1.00
Green Hunt	3 Books	.50
Green Hunt	1 Book	.50
Wm. Hunt	2 books	.50
Wm. Hunt	1 book	.60
Green Hunt	2 Books	.25
Green Hunt	3 books	.50
Wm. Hunt	1 Book	.25
Green Hunt	1 Book	.25
Green Hunt	2 Book	.25
Green Hunt	1 Book	.25
Green Hunt	1 Book	.25
Green Hunt	3 Books	.50
Green Hunt	1 Book case	8.25
Green Hunt	Bureaux	5.00
Green Hunt	1 Brace & Bitts	2.50
Robt. Williams	1 Bed stead	.10
Mrs. E.C. Hunt	1 Bed stead and contents	1.00
Mrs. E.C. Hunt	2 meal sacks	1.00
Mrs. E.C. Hunt	5 bbl.	.25
Robt. Williams	1 Table	.10
Green Hunt	1 pr. saddle bags	.25
Green Hunt	white lead	.10
Green Hunt	1 pr and irons	.10
Mrs. E.C. Hunt	1 pr and irons & shovel	.25
W. Hawkings	1 Beef hide	1.00

The following is a full and perfect account of the sales of the property of the sales of the estate of J.W. Hunt Decd. directed by Law to be sold notes with good secutity Due four months and ten days after date ware taken from to the purchasers, this the 3rd day of Jan. 1866

Geo. W. Hunt, Administrator.

An Inventory of the personal estate of J.W. Hunt, Decd. Amount witness fees, Bell and Moore	12.02
Cash in Greenbacks	9.00
Cash in Bank of Tennessee	7.00
Cash in bank of Tenn Sept. 1st 1861	5.00
Cash in bank Shelbyville Tenn.	1.00
Cash in Augusta Insurance & Banking Co. Georgia	1.00
(p 279)	
One note on the Estate of B.L. Williams due 14th March 1861	22.90
One note on the Estate of B.L. Williams made payable toR.C. Williams, Due the 1st of May 1845	5.00
One account on the estate of B.L. Williams Due for	10.00

One account on the estate ofB.L. Williams taken upof W.E. Felts, Due 1st Jan. 1846 for $5.55
One account on A.H. Williams for the year 1854, 56, 57, 58, and 59 without interest being counted for 482.77
(For which there Rebuting Claims)
One note om W.W. Felts Isham W. Felts made payable to J.J. Binkley Due 27th Feb. 1849 for 8.25
One note on W.W. Felts and R.D. Felts made payable to B.F. Binkley Due 25th December 1848 for 8.50
One account on W.W. Felts for the year 1846, 47,48,49,50 and 52 without interest counted for which there are Rebuting claims 56.18
One due bill on Wilie Williams without date 1.80
One note on James Watts due 27th August 1862 (Doubtful) p 24.47
One note on W.R. Ramer due 24th May 1852 for 1.26
One note on Edward Sullivan due 26th Dec. 1860 1.95
One account on D.W. Nye due Jan. 1st 1863
For which there rebuting claims 43.75
One account on Dr. A. Lowe 1st Jan. 1864
Some credits to be allowed
Balance if any Insolvent 64.45
One account on A.J. Gower, Due Jan. 1st 1863 Doubtful 5.10
The foregoing contains a full true and perfect inventory of the estate of Jas. W. Hunt Decd. so far as the same has come into my possession or knowledge this the 30 day of December 1865

Geo. W. Hunt
Administrator of J.W. Hunt. Dec.

(p 280)
A list of the perishable property of John Perdue Decd.
Sale by John W. Perdue Administrator on the 25th Sept. 1865.

1 Mule	R.W. Williams	24.00
1 Coller	R.W. Williams	.90
1 corn sheler	Johnatham Fambrough	15.
1 Salt Bettle	" "	3.25
1 Ox Cart	Thomas Bell Senr.	7.25
2 Plows	Thomas Bell Senr.	.25
1 Pork Hog	W.A. Etherly (Eatherly	16.00
5 1st choice hogs	W.A. Eatherly	29.00
1 sow 1st choice	W.A. Eatherly	8.00
1 sow 2nd choice	Thomas Shores	8.00
12inch auger	Thomas Shores	1.00
1 plow	Thomas Shores	.50
2 axes and hoe	Thomas Shores	.50
1 Lard Barrel	Thomas Shores	.50
1 3rd choice sow	Joseph J. Williams	8.25
1 4th choice sow	Joseph J. Williams	8.00
1 5th choice sow	Joseph J. Williams	6.25
5 2nd choice shoats		18.25
1 Hay Fork	Joseph J. Williams	1.00
1 Hay Fork	Joseph J. Williams	1.25
1 Frow	Joseph J. Williams	.75
5 3rd choice shotes	A.J. Perdue	13.25
10 shotes per head	A.J. Perdue	29.00
1 Grind stone	A.J. Perdue	3.25
1 shovel plow	A.J. Perdue	.50
1 Hand saw	A.J. Perdue	.65

1 Cross Cut saw	A.J. Perdue	1.00
1 Trunk	A.J. Perdue	1.00
1 Chest	A.J. Perdue	1.25
1 Turning Plow	J.C. Perdue	1.50
1 Cutting Knife	J.C. Perdue	1.20
1 Shovel	J.L. Perdue	2.00
1 Hay fork	J.L. Perdue	1.10
1 DoubleTree	J.L. Perdue	.75
2 turning plows	J.L. Perdue	.50
1 B. Hook	J.L. Perdue	1.30
1 Hf. Bu. Measure	J.L. Perdue	.40
1 sealed tmb.	J.L. Perdue	.50
1 Tin	J.L. Perdue	.25
1 Lot plank	W.H. Stewart	11.50
1 shop gun	W.H. Stewart	.50
1 yoke of oxen	James Vestoe	40.00
(p 281)		
1 Heifer	James Vestoe	15.25
1 Pick	David Counsel	.50
1 fan Mill	David Counsel	19.50
1 rope	Uriah Murff	1.30
1 Basket	Uriah Murff	.70
1 shovel	Thos. Bell	1.60
1 single tree	Thos. Bell	.50
1 lot of gear	Thos. Bell	.85
1 Pole ax	Thos. Bell	.50
1 Lot of sundries	Thos. Bell	.10
1 Colter	Thos. Bell	.15
1 Colter	Thos. Bell	.15
1 Iron Bar	Thos. Bell	1.25
1 pr steelyards	Thos. Bell	.30
1 Lot sundries	Thos. Bell	.30
1 Lot old plows	Thos. Bell	.25
1 Pick & sundreis	Thos. Bell	.60
1 Pork hog	Mrs. A. Perdue	8.00
1 Lard Barrel	Mrs. A. Perdue	.75
½ Lard Barrel	Mrs. A. Perdue	.25
1 Lot barrels	Mrs. A. Perdue	1.00
1 Lot buckets½	Mrs. A. Perdue	1.00
1 chest	Mrs. A. Perdue	1.00
1 Table	Mrs. A. Perdue	.10
1 clock	Mrs. A. Perdue	5.00
1 small table	Mrs. A. Perdue	.50
1 Trunnel bed	Mrs. A. Perdue	2.00
1 Trunk	Mrs. A. Perdue	.10
1 Lanton	Mrs. A. Perdue	.50
1 Pr. dog irons	Mrs. A? Perdue	.25
1 Plow	Alexr Pool	.50
3 Hoops	Wash Smith	.15
1 smoothing iron	Wash Smith	.15
1 pr. steel yards	H.R. Felts	.60
1 Dish	W.B. Hooper	1.00
1 Grind stone	W.B. Hooper	1.00
1 pouch and belt	W.B. Hooper	1.00
1 plow	Claborne Sanders	.60
1 Basket	Claborne Sanders	.25

1 Desk	D.C. Perdue	.25
2 Pitch Forks	R.T. Gupton	.50

(p 282) Report of John W. Perdue Decd.
Sept. 15 1865

Money on hand Bank of Tennessee	11.00
Claims on hand thought to be goos	
1 account on W.D. Edwards for	21.30
1 Officers receipts on A.W. Stewart & Bro. for $400 with four credits	
Balance	255.00
1 Note on Isaac Eatherly for	15.00
with of $2.00 Balance	13.00
1 note on THomas Biggers	8.00
Payable to Duke and Gupton	
1 note on W.B. Hooper	8.00
1 note on W.B. Hooper	4.56
In favor of Ralls Maxey and Wilson Wall	
1 note on J.J. Williams	3.83
1 note on H.J. Carner (Carney)	20.75
with a credit of $10.00 Balance	10.75
1 note on Henry Maxey	80.00
with a credit of $50.00 Ballance	30.00
1 Officers receipt on R.H. Weakley	15.82
1 acct. on L.J. Perdue	27.70
1 note on L.J. Perdue	40.00
1 note on L.J. Perdue	60.75
1 note on L.J. Perdue	20.00
Doubtful Claims	
1 note on W.C. Duke	7.00
1 officers receipt on R.H. Weakley	17.87
1 note on J.H. Cain	13.10
1 note on A.J. Perdue	14.00
1 note on G.W. McCarley	11.00
1 note on Johnathan Sanders	8.75
1 note on " "	16.89
with credit of .92/100 $1.92	14.95
1 note on Jonathan Sanders for 12 barrels corn.	
Worthless claims on hand	
1 note on H. Murry	298.38
1 note on Z. Owen	3.20
1 note on R.C. Jones	5.65
(p 283)	
1 noteon T. Adkins	21.12
1 note on H. Hollis	6.75
1 note on John Stewart	10.18
1 note on J. Jonns (Johns)	9.78
1 note on Jas. H. Gupton	200.00
1 note on A. Vick	31.34
1 note on John Fambrough	5.90
1 note on John Fambrough	1.75
1 note on John Walker	1.75
1 note on John Walker Jr.	4.22

J.W. Perdue Adm. for John Perdue Decd.
A list of notes and accts come into my hands belonging to the estate

of John Perdue Decd.

Cash on hand Bank of Tennessee	11.00
1 note on hand on L.J. Perdue for	40.00
1 note on hand on L.J. P erdue for	60.75
1 note on hand on L.J. Perdue	
1 note on hand on T.D. Hunter for	12.70
1 note on H.J. Carney for	20.75
with a credit of $10.00 Ballance	10.75
1 note on James H. Cain for	13.10
1 note on Henry Maxey for	80.00
with a credit of $50.00 Ballance	30.00
Judgement against R.H. Weakley	17.87
1 Judgement against R.H. Weakley and G.W. Gossett for	15.82
1 note on John Stewart for insolvent	10.13
1 note on Hiram Mowery (Mallory)	298.34
1 note on JohnWalker Jr. for	4.22
1 note on Thompson Bigger made payable to Duke & Gupton for	8.00
1 note on Jonerthan Sanders	16.87½
cr. by $1.82 cents Balancedue	15.5½
1 note on Jonerthan Sanders for	
12 Barrels merchantable corn	
1 note on W.B. Hooper & Moses Reed made payable to Rawls Maxey and Wilson Wall for	4.56
1 note on Jas. H. Gupton insolvent for	200.00
1 note on R.J. Jones for	10.65
1 note cr. by R.J. Jones $5.00	5.65
1 note on Z. Owens payable to J.S. Car for	3.20
1 note on Samuel Adkins insolvent for	21.72
1 note on W.B. Hooper for	8.00
1 note on W.E. Duke doubtful for	7.00
(p 284)	
1 note on J.J. Williams for	3.83
1 Receipt on R.D. Mosely Constable for a note of hand on A.W. Stewart & Bro. for	400.00
With four credits, one for $45, & one for $20.00 and one for $30 and one for $50 Ballance	255.00
1 note on Isaac Eatherly for $15.00, cr by $2.00 Balance	13.00
1 acct. on W.D. Edwards for	22.25
1 note on John James insolvent for	9.75
1 note on A.J. Vick for	31.34
Cr. by $3.87 ½ cts. Ballance insolvent	27.47½
1 note 1 note on A.J. Perdue for $14.00	14.00
1 note on G.W. McCarely for	11.00
1 note on John Fambrough insolvent for	1.75
1 note on John Fambrough insolvent for	5.90
1 noteon H. Hollis made payable to James Morgan insolvent for	6.75

The most of the above notes are doubtful and never can be collected.

Sept. 23rd 1865
An Inventory and acct of sale of the personal property of Mrs Maria EDwards Decd. sold at his late residence for cash on the day specified above

Purchasers Names	Articles Bought	Amount
Jno. Fambrough	1 grubing hoe	1.00
Thos. BellJr.	1 Grubing hoe	.80
Thos. Bell Sr.	1 Plough	1.05
David Council	1 Log chain	1.60

Hiram Sanders	1 Iron wedge	.85
Thos. Bell Jr.	1 single tree and clives	.25
Boney Pool	1 pair harness	.60
L.J. Mayfield	1 pair hammer	.50
L.J. Mayfield	1 lot chisels	.50
T.H. Eatherly	1 lot tools	.55
L.J. Mayfield	2 augers & square	.55
Thos. Bell Jr.	1 Brace & Bit	1.00
T.H. Eatherly	1 Lot Gouges & Chisels	.25
M.M. Chambliss	1 hand saw & drawing knife	1.05
Jas. S. Stewart	2 small saws	1.05
Jas. S Stewart	Plow planes & BIts	.75
T.H. Eatherly	1 jack 4 planes & oil stove	2.75
A. Hunter	4 Rabbit planes	.25
(p 285)		
Thos. Ball Jr.	1 Jack & 4 planes	1.75
Thos. Bell	1 smoothing plane	1.10
T.A. Eatherly	1 Tool chest	.80
T.A. Eatherly	2 pots & 1 pr hooks	.65
Thos. I. Miles	1 skillet & tea kettle	1.75
T.A. Eatherly	2 jars, 1 pot	.25
Thos. Bell Jr	1 Poker and shovel	1.05
Wm. D. Weakley	1 skillet & Pot	2.00
Mrs. Samuel McDaniel	Skillet Lids &C	1.10
T.J. Miles	1 Jar	1.00
M.M. Chambliss	1 Spring Balance	.55
L.J. Mayfield	Sugar Bowl Glasses &C	.55
Thos. Bell Senr.	9 plates & 1 dish	1.00
Thos. Bell	1 set kives & Forks	.90
Mrs. Samuel McDaniel	1 pitcher	1.00
T.A. Eatherly	2 Glass Bowls & pitcher	.25
Thos. Bell	1 dish & spoons &C	.30
Thos. B. Perdue	1 Table	1.00
Wm. D. Weakley	1 coffee mill	.20
Thos. B. Perdue	1 Safe	5.50
Thos. Bell Senr.	1 Coffee Box	.10
Mrs. Sam'l McDaniel	1 spinning wheel	$5.10
Thos. Bell Sr.	1 Book Case	1.25
Mrs. Samuel McDaniel	1 small table	.50
Thos. Bell Jr.	1 water bucket	.50
J.H. Williams	1 water bucket	.25
J.H. Williams	1 Jar	1.00
Thos. Bell Jr.	1 clock	2.00
T.W. Williams	1 Cedar chest	7.50
Thos. Bell Jr.	1 willow basket	.25
H.D. Edwards	1 Bureau	10.75
H.B. Edwards	1 Bed stead & Furniture	35.00
Laura Edwards	1 Bed stead & furniture	21.75
Thos. Bell Jr.	1 Set and irons	2.80
H.D. Edwards	1 Bed stead and furniture	11.75
Richard Fambrough	1 Rat trap	.25
Thos. Bell Jr.	8 chains	2.00
Thos. Bell Senr.	1 Keg salt	.75
A.J. Gupton	5 Hogs	25.00
Thos. Bell Jr.	1 cow	14.50
Thos. Bell Jr.	1 yaerling	4.00
Jno. Fambrough	2 Hogs	3.50
Thos. Bell Jr.	1 Kettle	.80

J.H. Williams	1 scythe & Cradle	2.50
Thos. B. Perdue	1 small Bed Stead	.25
Wm. D. Weakley	1 Ox Cart	6.75
H.D. Edwards	700 Bundles oats at 2cts	14.00
(p 286)		
I.N. Clifton	$13\frac{3}{4}$ Bu wheat @ 120	16.50
Wm. Gunter	10 bu. wheat $1.05	10.50
T.H. Eatherly	1 Work Bench	.30
Thos. Bell Ser.	1 Mistaker Bar	1.50
W.D. Weakley	1 Ox Ring	.25
Samuel McDaniel	1 Tray & Wash board	.20
T.H. Eatherly	1 chopping axe	.25
		242.75

Sept. 23rd 1865

This day the farm belonging to said estate was put up and rented to the highest bidder for the year 1866, notes taken for the same due the 25th of Decr. 1866, as follows

Renters names	Place rented	Amount
Henry D. Edwards	Homeplace on the River Mrs. Weakleys	248.00
John Fambrough	Place on the road near Mrs. Weakleys	21.00
		269.00

Nov. 18, 1865

This day sold at public Sale the Rent corn belonging to said estate on a credit of six months, notes taken in accordance thereto.

Purchasers names	Amount bought	
T.H. Eatherly	$5\frac{1}{2}$ barrels merchd Corn $2.40	$13.20
T.H. Eatherly	$1\frac{1}{2}$ bbl. Short Corn @ 1.35	2.03
		$15.23

The above is a true and perfect Inventory of all the goods and chattel rights of the said Maria Edwards Decd. which have come into my hands possession or knowledge or the hands of any other person for me to the best of my knowledge and belief.
This 20th day of November 1865.

James H. Williams, Admr.

An account of sale made of the personal property of the estate of E.S. Exum D ed. at his late residence Chesnut Grove, Cheatham County, March 19th 1866.

Naes	Articles	
J?N? Dunn	1 Gum Speclum	5.00
J. Hooper	1 " "	2.00
Dr. Dixon	1 case & Instruments	6.45
W.H. Scott	1 Spring Lance	1.75
J.C. Porch	1 Self syrnge	.50
J.N. Dunn	1 " "	.95
J. Hooper	1 Spring Lance	.40
		7.05
(p 287)		
Wm. H. Scott	1 scales & Weight	
J. Hooper	1 steth Scope	1.00
Dr. Dixon	1 " "	.25
J. Hooper	1 graduated measure	.25
J.N. Dunn	1 box callomel	.45
Wm. H. Scott	1 Glass Sying	1.00

Dr. Dixon	contents of drawer	1.25
Wm. H. Scott	1 mortar & pestle	2.25
S.H. Dunn	1 cuping glass	.50
Wm. H. Scott	1 Peter Syinge	.50
Dr. Dixon	1 pr. saddle Bags	5.50
J. Hooper	W.S.D. Book	5.00
J. Hooper	M.D. Book	1.50
A. Smith	Rothalogg Book	.20
S.H. Dunn	" "	.85
J.A. Dunn	2 B Book	.50
A. Smith	1 " "	.30
S.H. Dunn	1 Book	.25
J.A. Dunn	1 Book	.40
Dr. Dixon	Armstrong Practise	.40
S.H. Dunn	3 Books	.40
S.H. Dunn	1 Bot Nitre	.60
J.C. Porch	1 Bot. Linseed Oil	.40
M. Jones	Cincoonia	.40
Dr. Dixon	1 Bot. Salts	.25
Jo Hooper	1 Lena	.40
Jo Hooper	1 Bot. Cantharides	.30
S.H. Dunn	1 Gal. Sugar Lead	.55
J. Hooper	1 croton oil	.75
J?N. Dunn	1 Bot Oil Viteral	.25
J. Hooper	1 Bot. Amonia	.35
J.N. Dunn	1 Gumbush	.25
Dr. Dixon	1 Oil Annis	.65
Dr. Dixon	1 squills	.50
J. Hooper Cloves	1 cloves	.35
S.H. Dunn	Tinct. cabacia	.10
J. Hooper	grnd lotion	.30
J.J. Ussery	contents of shelf No. 1	.25
J.J. Ussery	" " " No. 2	.40
S.H. Dunn	" " " No. 3	1.20
J.N. Dunn	" " " No. 4 & 5	1.60
J.J. Ussery	" " " No. 6	.40
T.W. Osborne	1 Ox Cart	7.00
J.S. Osborne	1 cow and calf	30.75
J.B. Hooper	1 Bureau	10.00
(p 288)		
H.T. Stringfellow	1 gun barrel	1.25
T.W. Osborn	1 Hand axe	.60
H.F. Stringfellow	1 pair saddle bags	2.50
Wm. Sears	1 Silver watch	16.00
Wm. H. Scott	1 Grind Stone	3.75
S.H. Dunn	Coping glass	.75
Dr. Dixon	1 Bed and stead	30.00
		54.85

The above is a full and perfect account of the sales of the property or the estate of E.S. Exum Decd. notes with good security Due twelve months after date ware taken from the perchasers this March 19th 1866.

W.J. Osborne, Admr.

Inventory of the Solvent claims Belonging to the Estate of E.S. Exum Dec.

Thompson Osborne	1 act. 1865	10.12
Wm. Greer	1 act. 1865	4.00
Wm. Lee	1 act.	25.00

Moses Jones	1 act 1865	10.50
John Johnson	1 act. 1865	7.00
T.J. Riggin	1 act. 1865	27.50
J.H. Fulghum	1 act 1865	7.00
R.J. Stringfellow	1 act 1865	23.50
J.P. Pegram	1 act 1865	21.50
J.B. Parkerson	1 act	21.75
Mrs. L. Bledsoe	1 act	3.00
Mrs. Francis Pack	1 act.	13.00
S.W. Adkisson	1 act 1865	17.75
Felix Curfman	cr. by ten dollars $10.00	18.00
Warren Jordan	1 act. due on settlement	5.00
Mastin Ussery	1 note March 29th 1865	16.00
J.M. Brown	1 note Feb. 7 1865	12.25
H.T. Stringfellow	1 note June 2th 1860	15,50
Jas. Harris	1 note Sept. 8th 1865	45.00
W.F. Ussery	1 note April 1st 1864	73.00
T.W. Osborne	1 note Feb 1865	17.25
T.W. Osborne	1 note 1864-1865	17.25

The above is a true and perfect of all the notes and accounts of the said E.S. Exum Dec. which have come to my hands, possession or knowledge or the hands of any other persons for me to the best of my knowledge and belief that are solvent claims.

This April 2nd 1866
W.J. Osborne, Administrator

(p 289)

An Inventory of the accounts on Dr. Exum Decd. that are doubtful claims.

Ledfords Act. 1865		7.25
Chreech One Act. 1865		23.00
Henry Sayles, One act.		21.00
J.P. Bell	one act 1865	8.50
W.Y. Brown	One act 1865	14.00
Mont Bell	One act 1864	30.50
Josh Dillingham	One act. 1865	5.00
Albert Morris	One act 1865	6.00
David Thompson	One acct. 1865	10.00
Andrew Thompson	One act. 1865	13.00
M. Moore	" " "	5.00
James Harding	" " 1863 & 64	13.50
Ezra Holstead	" " 1865	10.00
Thomas Fulghum	" " "	15.00
A. Smith	" " "	13.00
James Nolls	" " "	1.50
Stephens Hale	" " "	14.50
S.Y. Brown	" " "	9.50
James Owens	" " "	7.50
Ambrose Sitton	" " "	13.50
Mont Pack	" " "	4.00
Ben Crumpler	" " "	15.00
James Darity	" " "	39.00
E.H. Brown	" " "	5.00
J. Newsom	" " "	3.00
B. Hawkins	" " "	8.25
S.A. Blocker	" " "	5.50
Mrs. E.D. Bell	One note July the 8th 1865	29.00

Peter Andrews	One act due 1865	4.50
Feb Benningfield	One act due 1865	3.00
John Hill	" " " "	14.00
S.F. Bell	" " " "	10.00
James Wyatt	" " " " 1863	16.00
A.W. Turner	" " " " "	10.00
T.J. Crouch	" " " " "	8.00
James Noll	" " " "	15.00
R. Crumpler	" " " "	11.00
Wm. Oakly	" " " 1862	14.00
Frank Russell	" " " "	12.50
Wm. Brown	" " " "	3.00
A. Page	" " " "	6.00
J. Russell	" " " "	4.00
John Puckett	" " " "	2.00

(p 290)

C.C. Lotwell	" " " 1861	13.00
W.G. Shelton P.L. Pack Heirs	One act 1861 "	25.00
B.P. Lovell	One act 1861	13.00
Wm. Philip	" " "	5.00
George Weams (Weems)	Note due Sept. 28th 1860	12.00
E.H. Brown	" " Apr. 4th 1860	51.50
S.A. Woods	" " May 20th 1864	10.00
S.A. Thompson	Note due June 1st	11.85½
S.N. Smith	Note due Nov. 7th 1862	8.00
Mrs. E. Hartley	1 act due 1864	15.50
R.Feribee	Note due Oct. 17th 1861	7.00
PaterAndrews	Note due 1862	7.50
G.A. Repell	note due Feb. 8th 1865	32.40
John R. Anderson	Note due Dec. 4th 1861	5.00
Wm. Smith Note due Jan. 30th 1862		42.00
James Taylor	Note due Jan. 18th 1861	14.00
B. Sawyer	" " Oct 8th 1862	5.00
Ben Howel	One act due 1862	51.00
R.W. Barcliff	One act due Jan. 8th 1858	8.55
St. Scotts	One act. due 1856	29.50
Wm. Carather	" " " 1863 &4	18.00
B.A. Jackson	" " " 1855 & 56	19.25
S.M. Cathy	" " " 1866	6.00
Green Jackson	" " " 1862	22.50
H. Jackson	" " " 1861	9.90
A.C. Stockard	" " " 1856	11.25
E.N. Phipps	" " " 1856	20.00
Joe Kellum	" " " 1863	34.00

The foregoing is a full and perfect account of the accounts and notes that are on E.S. Exum Book for practise that are doubtful claims this April 2nd 1866

William J. Osbornes, Adm.

(p 291)

A list of the property sold at the sale of H.H. Binkley Aug.14th 1865.

William Edgin	1 Avery Plow	2.00
G.C. Binkley	2Hoes	.50
G.C. Binkley	Shovel & Grubbing hoe	.30
J.W. Felts	1 Briar Hook	.50
A.N. Binkley	1 5th chain	.50

N.N. Binkley	1 pair waggon Gear	1.60
E.J. Binkley	Plow Gear &C	.50
E.J. Binkley	Trace Brithing &C	.75
J.W. Felts	1 cutting box and knife	2.00
H.J. Binkley	One lot of oats	2.50
Montgomery Binkley	1 Heifer	21.00
E.H. Simpson	1 cow and cFell	17.50
E.H. Simpson	One bull calf	4.25
William Winters	1 Two horse wagon	50.00
George Felts	1 single tree	.30
J.R. Binkley	7 geese at 30	2.10
H.W. Binkley	One roan mare	150.00
Thomas Morris	1 curry comb	.10
George Felts	Garden of vegetables	16.00
E.J. Clark	1 sett chairs	5.50
Widow Felts	1 set chairs	1.50
N.N. Binkley	1 spinning wheel	4.00
E.J. Binkley	1 spinning wheel	1.00
E.J. Binkley	1 Water bucket	.80
Widow Felts	1 Pail	.40
J?R? Binkley	1 wash pan	.25
N.N. Binkley	1 Loom & Gear	2.50
Jacob Binkley	1 Bureau	20.00
J.M. Binkley	1 Clock	2.00
J.R. Binkley	1 lot woolen yarn	5.10
Wm. Rose	s pair cards	1.00
Widow Felts	Basket & Cotton	.60
E.J. Clark	1 Bed	23.00
A.N. Binkley	1 Bed & Stead & Cord	3.60
Dock Dnes	5 lbs wool	5.00
J.R. Binkley	4 lbs. wool	4.00
Mont Binkley	3½ lbs. Black wool	2.62
J.R. Binkley	4 lbs cotton @ 40	1.60
William Ramer	4½ lbs cotton 50	2.25
William Winters	2 bll Feathers	3.75
A.J. Binkley	1 Irom Wedge	.35
William Ramer	1 Bedstead	.50
N.N. Binkley	Bedstead &C	.50
(p 292)		
J.R. Binkley	1 carpet	1.00
N.N. Binkley	1 Old quilt	.50
J.R. Binkley	1 lot red pepper	.10
H.J. Binkley	1 Bed and stead	30.50
J.R. Binkley	1 Pitcher	.75
B.B. Binkley	1 Pitcher	.25
George Felts	1 Jar	.50
J.R. Binkley	Knives and forks	.50
Mont Binkley	5 plates	1.30
Wm. Rose	1 dish and plate	.60
Montgomery Binkley	4 suacers & 5 cups	1.00
Wm. Winters	½ dozen Glasses	1.25
Mont Binkley	1 sugar bowl	1.80
J.M. Binkley	molasses can	.50
J.W. Felts	1 cup	.25
Widow Felts	1 Jug and bottles	.60
William Clark	2 coffee Pots	.20
J.M. Binkley	1 coffee mill	.55

John Bess	1 smoothing Iron	.80
G.W. Binkley Jr.	1 smoothing Iron	.40
N.N. Binkley	1 cupboard	5.80
H.J. Binkley	1 Table	1.70
Angeline Ford	1 Tea Kettle	.60
B.B. Binkley	1 Tea kettle and skillet	.65
Widow Felts	Pot and lid	.80
Widow Felts	1 oven and hooks	.40
W.F. Simpson	~~1 oven and hooks~~	.40
W.F. SIMPSON	1 Oven and lids	1.25
G.C. Binkley	Candle Mould	1.00
E.J. Clark	Fire Irons	1.50
Wm. Edgin	1 Fire Iron	.50
Montgomery Bell	1 Fire shovel	.50
J.R. Binkley	1 churn and jar	1.80
E.J. Clark	1 folding table	2.00
S.A. Richardson	1 white counterpane	3.35
Allen Newlands	1 white counterpane	4.05
Allen Newlands	Fringe for counterpane	.65
Montgomery Binkley	1 Bureau Toilet	1.60
Montgomery Binkley	1 Table toilet	1.05
Montgomery Binkley	½ doz. towels	2.00
E.J. Clark	1 looking glass	2.00
N.N. Binkley	1 pr Pinure & Float	.20
E.J. Binkley	Sheep shears	.65
Mont Binkl y	1 lot sheep	14.50
Mont Binkley	1 Bucket Lard	1.90
William Rose	19 lbs. Bacon @ 22½	4.27½
J.M. Binkley	8 lbs @ 23	1.84
(293)		
Nancy Farmer	2 Jowls	.35
William Rose	1 Lard trough	.25
W lliam Ramer	1 Lot Soap	1.40
Widow Felts	1 lot soap	1.50
Nancy Knight	1 lot soap	3.60
David Krantz	3 empty kegs	.65
William Rose	1 salt barrel with salt	.45
E.J. Clark	1 Tray and sifter	1.00
T.W. Morris	1 meal barrel and sack	.25
J.R. Binkley	1 chair	.20
H.W Binkley	1 saddle and surricingle	5.00
John Bess	1 strainer	.25
N.N. Binkley	1 chest	.85
J.H. Binkley	1 lot chickens	3.40
N.N. Binkley	1 square	.45
Chunk Felts	1 lot old iron	.75
Jacob Binkley	1 Sheep Bell	.40
J.H. Binkley	1 wash kettle and tub	1.10
John Bess	1 old saddle	.25
N.N. Binkley	1 Table cloth	1.00
N.N. Binkley	1 yard linsey	.25
H.J. Binkley	14 lbs. bacon 22¼	3.15
Jas. R. Binkley	1 Jar	.25
N.N. Binkley	1 Table cloth	.10

Account of 2nd sale November 25th 1865.

C.F. Binkley	1 potato patch	3.00
H.J. Binkley	5 barrels corn ¢ $2.80	14.00
H.W. Binkley	5 " " @ 3.00	15.00
H.J. Binkley	3 barrels corn @ 2.90	8.70
G.R. Felts	1 Lor refuse	6.05
A. Washington	1 lot shucks	1.50
E.J. Binkley	1 plow point No. 13	.30
N.N. Binkley	1 Satchel	.35
C.F. Binkley	1 knife and fire shovel	
N.N. Binkley		
Nancy Felts	7 Bushel corn @ 60	4.20

A list of the notes and accounts on hand

One note on J.R. Binkley Due Dec. 1861	100.00
One Note on N.N. Binkley Due Dec. 1861	100;00
" " " " " " " "	100.00
" " " " " " " "	100.00
One note on B.F. Binkley Estate Due Dec 1861 cr. $35	100.00
Receipt on W.W. Williams Clk. vs. E^State of R.D. Felts	
Due Jan. 1st 1861	55.00
One ac J.R. Binkley Due January 1864	25.00
(p 294)	
ONe note on C.F. Binkley Due Dec. 1865	45.00
One note on J.R. Binkley due Dec. 1865	10.50
One note on H.J. Binkley Due Dec. 1865	5.90
One Note on N.N. Binkley Due Dec 1865	19.50
One note on H.W. Binkley Due Dec 1865	5.00
One acct on G.W. Binkley Due Dec 1865	3.60
Cash on hand	43.50
One account James Rose Due Dec. 1865	43.50
One ~~One~~ note on J.M. Read doubtful Due Feb. 1863 cr. 65 cts	18.00
One note Jno. R. Binkley Due 1863 cr. $6.10	26.80
One account John Bess Due Nov. 1863 cr. .75cts	10.70
One note Jno. R. Binkley Due Dec. 1864	7.50
One judgement against James HarperDue Nov. 7th 1859	20.00

Inventory <u>an</u> account of Sale of the property of B.F. Binkley Dec. October 30th 1865.

A.F. Binkley	Two old plows	.10
A.F. Binkley	1 Peacock Plow	.75
A.F. Binkley	2 Hoes &C	.10
A.N. Binkley	1 pick and grubbing hoe	.35
A.N. Binkley	1 lot old iron	.25
Elijah Harris	1 single tree & Bull tongue	.55
Geo. C. Binkley	1 Two horse plow	1.00
James Harris	Stretcher & Clevis	.80
Wm. Binkley	Mollasses Keg	.75
W.E. Felts	1 X cut saw	.15
James Harris	1 X cut saw	6.50
A.F. Binkley	1 cutting knife	.25
B.B. Binkley,	1 Pot	2.00
Hulda Felts	1 Dinner pot	
Hulda Felts	1 Bucket	.10
Hulda Felts	1 Bake Oven	.40
William Nichols	Old scrap Iron	1.00
A.F. Binkley	1 Sett Plow gear	.20
Wm. Nichols	1 log chain	2.05

A.N. Binkley	1 pr steel yards	1.00
W.E. Felts	Harness, Axe & etc.	.20
Hulda Felts	1 Lot old axes	.10
W.E. Felts	1 hay fork	1.30
Church Felts	2Hatchets	.25
A. Rose	1 Hand saw	1.10
D. Krantz	1 Hand saw and hammer	.15
W.E. Felts	Shoe tolls & Wedge	.60
(p 295)		
HuldaFelts	1 Box Sundries	.10
Wes Felts	Part set Coppers tools	1.35
B.B. Binkley	" " " "	1.00
G.C. Binkley	Palne &C	.50
John Binkley	1 Old Clock	.25
J.M. Binkley	1 candle stand	.40
J.R. Binkley	1 Sett chairs	2.00
William Clark	1 rocking chair	1.00
James Harris	1 " "	1.25
Latita Carpenter	4 painted chairs	1.50
A.F. Binkley	1 Looking Glass	.55
James Harris	1 Small table	2.05
J.R. Binkley	1 Large desk	5.00
James Harris	4 sleys	2.10
J.M. Binkley	Picture President	.50
A.F. Binkley	Man of World	.60
A.F. Binkley	History of the World	1.70
L. Carpenter	1 Dictionary	.80
Virginia Binkley	Life of Christ	.65
B.B. Binkley	Travel of World	1.25
Mrs. Rose	Lives of President	.50
W.E. Felts	Armageddon	1.30
R.S. Demunbra	2 Religious Books	.50
A.F. Binkley	Revolutions of Europe	.30
George Felts	Life of Clay and Jackson	.20
D. Krantz	Life of Clay and Sparks	.15
D. Krantz	2 Small Books	.30
G. Felts	Boatman Pilot	.25
W. Ramer	Report Patent Office	.30
R.S. Demunbra	Report Patent Office	.25
N.N. Binkley	Report Patent Office	.20
L. Carpemter	Bookcase & Contents	.55
A.F. Binkley	1 Clock	3.00
Virginia Binkley	1 Bureau	3.00
Virginis Binkley	4 Pictures in Frame	.75
L. Carpenter	Flower Pot & Tray	.10
B. Binkley	1 Trunk	.50
L. Carpenter	1 Spinning wheel	1.00
Virginia Binkley	1 Folding table	.50
L. Carpenter	1 Safe and ware	5.25
E. Harris	Straw bed	4.05
N.N. Binkley	1 Sett -----	.80
B.B. Binkley	1 Bedstead	14.00
A.N. Binkley	1 Old Table	.50
A.F. Binkley	1 Feather Bed	7.00
(p 296)		
Wash Felts	1 Thermoter	1.10

L. Carpenter	1 Chest	.25
B.B. Binkley	1 Bed Quilt	1.10
B.B. Binkley	1 Bed Quilt	.25
James Harris	1 Bed Quilt	.25
B. Binkley	1 Comfort	.50
W. Nichols	1 Lard Can	1.00
G. Felts	1 Frying pan	.40
W.E. Felts	2 Fruit cans	.25
L. Carpenter	One Churn	.25
Mrs. Rose	1 Coffee Mill	.10
C.F. Binkley	Waffle Iron and Table	1.25
J.M. Binkley	1 Lot Bottles	.35
A.F. Binkley	1 Lot Bottles	;35
L. Carpenter	1 Loom	.50
Mrs. Rose	1 Cupboard	1.00
B.B. Brinkley	1 Muley cow	35.50
L Carpenter	1 Horned cow	20.00
James Harris	1 sow & pigs in Range	5.00
H.J. Binkley	2 Sheep	3.00
B.B. Binkley	1 Lot oats	29.60
James Harris	1 Jug and oil	.50
L. Carpenter	Fire Irons	.25
B.B. Binkley	Smoothing Irons	.50
Virginia Binkley	Bed Stead and Bed	16.00
L. Carpenter	Bed Stead and Bed	32.40
L. Carpenter	Old Chairs & kettle	.60
L. Carpenter	Shovel	.10
Received cash cost from N.N. Binkley		1.40
Paid A. Rose	Auctioneer	2.00
W.A. Henderson Clerk		1.00
Net Amount		233.20

December 1st 1865

John A. Hudson, Admr.

Notes and Accounts

One note J.R. Binkley Due 16th Aug. 1862	
Cr. $13.35	
One note on A.L. Hudgens	
Due Aug. 1861 cr. 7.00	14.00
One note on J.H. Binkley Due 7 May 1861 or. 5.75	6.00
One note B.H. Newman Due 24th Dec. 1861 cr. 34.10	75.00
One note T.W. Osborne due 15 Aug. 1857	
One note T.A. Anderson due 20 Nov. 1863 cr. 75.00	125.00
One note J.D. Darrow due 1st March 1861	20.19
One note J.W Felts Due 18th May 1856	15.00
One note James T. Davis Due5 March 1862 or. 28.00	35.00
One note J.R. Binkley due1st Nov. 1868	15.00

(p 296)

One note on John R. Binkley payable to A.F. Binkley due Dec. 25th 1864	7.50
One note on Burton Neighbors (Nabors) due July 1st 1860 cr. by 5.00	52.90
One note Charles D. Lawrence due Aug 24th 1861	50.00
C.J.C. Shivers,Receipt for note on E;L; Darrow $60 payable toG.W. Harris due Dec. 25, 1868	
W.W. Read Receipt note on W.E.C. Gower and J.L. Durham due Dec 24th 1861	75.00

J.H. Binkley	Receipt note due 17th Nov. 1859 on D. Krantz	18.30
J.H. Binkley	Judgement on E.W. Carney & A.J. Mayo assigned	
by A. Lowe		27.00
One note due Sept. 26th 1860 on W.W. Bennett cr. of $13.40		45.00
One note on W.L. Brinkley payable to T.J. Felts Due 25th Dec. 1862		200.00
Rec'd Levi Binkley dated 14th February 1863		35.34
Fifa B.F. Binkley) vs) Leoncidas Hunt)	July 27th 1861	21.50
Fifa B.F. Binkley) vs) Webb & Morris)	June 5th 1861	9.45

John A. Hudson, Admr.

Inventory and Account of sale of the property of Jesse D. Nicholson Deceased By G.W. Maxey, Administrator.

Greenville Nicholson	2 Augers	.60
J.A. Nicholson	2 Cary Plows	.10
J.A. Nicholson	1 Bull Tongue	.25
Amy Nicholson	2 Weeding Hoes	.10
J.A. Nicholson	1 Lot shoe tools	1.20
W.D. Wall	1 Pair lasts	110
J.A. Nicholson	3 pr lasts	.10
J.W. Walker	2 pair lasts	.30
J.A. Nicholson	4 pr lasts	.60
G.B. Nicholson	1 Ox Cart	11.00
E.K. Clifton	1 Lot Plank & Santling	2.15
J.W. Walker	1 Lot weather boards	16.55
J.A. Nicholson	1 Sorrel Horse	50.00
Amy Nicholson	1 Yoke Oxen and Sundry other articles	11.95

Accounts on Solvent men	
One on L. Fox	1.85
William Graham	1.55
G.W. Harris	800.00
W.W. Read	15.23
Nancy Harris	5.40
Thomas Walker	18.50
Martha Pace	3.00
B.J. Barnes	4.65
Mrs. Majors &. G. . Nicholson	51.20
James Rudolph	11.05
J.W. Walker	7.80
E.K. Clifton	5.88
J.J. Bradley	.60
A.J. Teasley	5.30
W.H. Morris	4.20
Allen Hunter	50.00
Doubtful Claims	
Wash Stewart	3.88
W.W. Williams	1.85
Edward Clifton	2.00
Julia Clifton	.75

G.W. Maxey Admr.

Sworn to Feb. 3 1866. Warren Jordan. Clk.

(p 298) Inventory and account of Sale of the property of Rachel Bobo Decd. By Sampson Rosson, Administrator.

A.W. Fizer	Rent of Farm	45.00
W.W. Connell	1 Plow and single tree	1.00
Hartwell Reeks	1 Plow & Singletree	1.00
A.W. Fizer	1 Drawing Knife	.15
H.C. Pace	1 Tongue Plow	.25
D.W. Stack	1 Mattock	.50
H.C. Pace	1 weeding hoe	.25
J.B. Walton	2 axes	;50
R.R. Gill	1 Axe	1.00
W.R. Rosson	1 Log chain	.35
J.T. Darden	1 Sett. gear	1.50
John Duke	1 chain rope	.10
A.W. Fiser (Fizer)	1 Grind stone	.30
A.W. Fiser	1 Tin Bucket	.95
W.R. Rosson	1 Tin Bucket	1.00
J.E. Morrow	1 " "	.65
J.E. Morrow	1 sett plates	2.55
John Shearon	1 Dish	.90
John Shearon	2 Dish	.35
A.W. Fiser(Fizer)	1 sett broken plates	1.20
R.R. Gill	1 set cups and saucers	2.00
J.E. Morris	1 coffee pot	.50
J.E. Morris	Sett glass tumblers	1.05
A.W. Fiser	1 salt pepper & vinegar	.35
A.W. Fiser	1 Pitcher	.20
T.L. Gray	1 coffee pot	.25
D.W. Stack	1 sett knives and forks	.05
D.W. Stack	1 set spoons	.80
A.W. Fiser	1 churn	1.15
A.W. Fiser	1 sad iron	.55
F.P. Pennington	1 sad iron	.10
W.R. Rosson	2 pair cards	.50
A.W. Fiser	1 Pitcher	.35
W.R. Rosson	1 chamber	.40
Zopher Smith	1 Reel	4.25
D.W. Stack	1 Pr steel yards	.25
A.J. Hamlett	1 Box Trumpery	.50
A.W. Fiser	1 stone jar	.50
W.R. Rosson	1 pot and hooks	2.00
H.C. Pace	1 Pot rack	.75
J.D. Tucker	1 Pot rack	.75
A.W. Fiser	1 Stand pickles	.75
(p 299)		
A.W. Fiser	1 Pair Hooks	.45
* A.W. Fiser	1 Lot bottles & Oil	.10
A.W. Fiser	1 Shaving skillet	.10
A.W. Fiser	1 Oven and lid	.50
H.C. Pace	1 Skillet and grid iron	.30
Jacob Stack	1 Lot Trumpery	.15
A.W. Fiser	1 Lard Stand	.55
W.G. Pickering	2 Boxes Peas	.35
Jo Alley	1 Wash tub	.25
R.R. Gill	1 Stone jar	.40
*Young Gardner	1 lot bottles & oil	.10

W.G. Pickering	1 Coffee Mill	.05
W.G. Pickering	1 Shovel and poker	.05
John Duke	1 Coffee Mill	.10
W.R. Rosson	1 Dining Table	.90
A.W. Fiser	1 Pair sad irons	.10
T.L. Gray	1 Hand saw	.10
A.W. Fiser	1 Safe	.15
Solomon Crotzer	1 lot Water Buckets	.25
A.W. Fizer	1 Water Pail	1.00
J.R. Drake	1 Water barrel & Cart	7.50
Young Gardner	1 Water Barrel	2.50
A.W. Fizer	2½ Bu salt 2.40	6.00
D.W. Stack	1 Tray & Sifter	.05
W.R. Rosson	1 Barrel & Contents	.25
J.R. Drake	1 Barrel Vinegar	8.25
W.R. Rosson	97½ lbs Bacon 20	19.50
W.R. Rosson	1 Lot soap	2.10
W.R. Rosson	1 Lard Trough	.20
J.T. Stack	1 Bushel Meal	1.50
W.W. Connel	1 Bu. Oats	.70
W.R. Rosson	1 Spinning Machine	.10
A.W. Fiser	6 chairs 65	3.90
Young Gardner	4 damaged chairs	.30
W.R. Rosson	1 Box carpet Rags	.50
Solomos Crotzer	1 Feather bed &C	25.50
H.C. Pace	1 Bedstead & Cord	7.00
E.M. Nolen	1 Comfort	1.50
W.R. Rosson	1 Candlestand	2.00
W.R. Rosson	1 Feather Bed & Bes Staed	21.00
Wesley Harrison	10¾ lbs feathers	9.15
A.W. Fiser	1 Lot Rags	.25
Zopher Smith	1 Bed balnket	2.75
Zopher Smith	1 Bed balnket	3.00
(p 300)		
W.R. Rosson	1 chest	3.00
W.R. Rosson	1 Stone jar	.25
A.W. Fiser	1 Dining Table	3.00
W.R. Rosson	1 Hammer	.20
J.D. Tucker	1 Jug	.30
W.W. Connel	1 Jug	.30
Austin Elliott (C.M.)	1 Bed stead	1.00
W.R. Rosson	18 Geese	3.60
Young Gardner	16 chickens 25	4.00
A.W. Fiser	10 Hens 40	4.00
W.R. Rosson	12 chickens 40	4.80
W.R. Rosson	side saddle	6.00
W.G. Pickering	1 Yoke oxen	75.00
W.R. Rosson	1 milk cow	20.00
A.J. Hamlett	1 milk cow	15.00
A.W. Fiser	1 yearling	9.25
A.W. Fiser	1 Yearling	13.00
A.W. Fiser	1 sow & Pigs	10.50
H.C. Pace	5 choice hogs	33.75
W.R. Rosson	1 Sow	2.00
T.L. Gray	6 shotes 2.75	16,50
W.G. Pickering	432 bundles oats	11.88

W.R. Rosson	1 Two year colt	57.00
A.W. Fiser	1000 Bu oats	27.50
A.W. Fiser	265 bundles fodder	5.96
W.R. Rosson	6 barrels & 2 Bu corn	15.27
W.R. Rosson	1 lot corn in field	40.00
J.R. Drake	1 Lot corn in field	30.00
A.W. Fiser	One Brown mare	65.00
A.W. Fiser	1 Lot cabbage	1.10
A.W. Fiser	1 lot cabbage	-------
Asa Barfield	One old clock	1.00
A.W. Fiser	$7\frac{3}{4}$ lbs nails	1.62
A.W. Fiser	1 Turnip patch	.50
W.T. Gossett	1 Turnip Patch	.50
W.T. Gossett	1 sweet potato patch	3.00
A.W. Fiser	1 sweet potato patch	.50
A.W. Fiser	1 stone jar	.50
W.R. Rosson	1 Avery plow	2.00
J.R. Drake	1 Lot cabbage	3.75
J.F. Stack	1 Wood Frame	.25
A.W. Fiser	4 Boxes	.75
W.R. Rosson	1 Box	.15
W.R. Rosson	1 ax	.15
A.W. Fiser	2 Meal Bags	1.00
(p 301)		
A.W. Fiser	One sugar scoop	.25
W.R. Rosson	One Basket	.25
A.W. Fiser	One meal bag	.10
A.W. Fiser	220 Bundles oats	5.50
A.W. Fiser	$12\frac{1}{2}$ lbs bacon	2.50
A.W. Fiser	One Iron wedge	1.00
J.S. Rosson	Cash Borrowed	25.00
T.L. Gray	On settlement	1.50
Mrs. S. Weakley	On settlement	1.00
Sampson Rosson	Cash on hand	22.50
J.E. Turner	Auction fee	5.00
W.T. Gossett	Clerk & Drawing acct.	6.00
The money on hand	G.B.	42.00
Silver $10.30 Amm. Bank 1.00		53.30
W.R. Rosson	Cotton yarn	8.00
Total amt. of sale cash, accts, notes &C		725.31

I, Sampson Rosson, Administrator of Rachel Bobo Decd. Do hereby certify that the foregoing contain a true and perfect inventory of all the property that has come into my hands as administrator of said estate.

Sampson Rosson.

Inventory of the effects of Joseph Kellums Dec. Nov. 1st 1865.

One note on Nancy Greer due the 24th Dec. 1860 for	198.90
One note on John T. Beck Due 25th Dec. 1862 for	50.00
One acct. on Caleb Capps for 1863	72.87
One acct on James E. Newsom Dec. 1st 1861	109.50
One acct. against Houston Cooper for 1861	18.53
One acct against John T. Beck for 1863	50.00
Wm. H. Kellum To cash in Tenn. Money at his fathers death	125.00
To spen in hand same time	20.00
To articles sold before his date od sale and rents for 1864 & 1865	340.00

To amount of sale of all perishable property sold by him 841.50

I, Mosses Jones Administrator of Joseph Kellums Dec. do hereby certify that the above is a true and perfect inventory of all the effects of the estate of said deceased which have come into my hands as administrator of said Estate Witness my hand and seal this the first day of Nov. 1865.

Moses Jones Ad,r.

Certified in my presence
Warren Joedan Clk.

(p 302) Inventory and account of sale of the property of H. Reeks Deceased September 20th 1865.

John Reeks	1 Shoe Bench &C	.50
John Tucker	Ax, Teakettle &C	.50
Mrs. Reekes	1 Hand saw	.25
Mrs. Reekes	1 Drawing knife	.25
John Tucker	Hoes & Pots	.55
Sam'l Reeks	1 Jug	.10
J.D. Drake	1 Biscuit Baker	.35
Martha Pennington	1 Lot barrels	.30
Joseph Gray	2 Barrels	.25
Mrs. Reekes	1 Lard Stand	.25
Mrs. Reekes	1 wheel and cards	.25
Sam(l Reekes	2 chairs &C	.15
J.D. Drake	Dish & Knives	.10
John Tucker	2 Decanters	.15
D. Fort	1 Lot bottles	.10
Mrs. Reekes	1 Coffee Pot	.05
Mrs. Reekes	2 Candle sticks	.10
Mrs. Reekes	1 chest	.25
Mrs. Reekes	1 clock	.50
Mrs. Reekes	1 sugar chest	.25
Samuel Reekes	1 wardrobe	.10
Mrs. Reekes	2 slays	.10
Mrs. Reekes	2 Table cloths	.40
John Tucker	One Jar	.10
Mrs. Reekes	Table and Books	.25
Mrs. Reeks	3 Shoats	.75
Mrs. Reekes	One plow	.40
A. Adkins	One plow	1.00
John Reekes	1 cart	1.25
John Reekes	1 Red Bull	5.25
Mrs. Reekes	One Black Bull	3.50

I, James Reekes Administrator of H. Reekesdecd. do hereby certify that the foregiong is a true and perfect inventory of all the g ods, chattels, rights and credits of the deceased that have come into my hands knowledge or possession. Sept. 20th 1865.

J.J. Reekes, Adm.

(303) Inventory of notes and accounts belonging to the Estate of David E. Barton, Decd. December 25, 1866.

One note on G.E. Elazer due May 1st 1862	55.68
One note on J.T. Fielder due June 21st 1860	2.25
One note on J.M. Read due Dec. 17, 1859	10.80
One note on M. Bell due April 24, 1861	18.00
One note on T.M. Williamsdue Dec. 25th 1860	7.00

One acct. on F.S. Evans	5.00
One acct on G.A. Nicholson	10.00
One Acct on W.J. Nicholson	6.00
One acct on J.B. Taylor	5.00
One acct. on Joseph Wheeler	6.00
One acct. on James Wilson	5.00
One acct. on Josh Humphreys	10.00
One acct. on Hogan Anderson	6.00
One acct. on Quince Jarrell	5.00
One acct. on Thomas Adkins	10.00
One acct. om Anthony Swift	5.00
One acct. on Garland Jarrell	5.00
One acct. on Pace & Wall	12.00
One acct on Thomas Stewart	6.00
One acct. on Willie Bagwell	15.00
One acct. on King & Gill	5.00
One acct. on William Albright	7.50
One acct. on Mrs. Pool	5.00
One acct. on John White	5.00
One acct on Albright & Evans	7.50
One acct on George Reynolds	5.00
One acct on Wesley Nicholson	5.00
One acct. on John Rhinehart	15.00

The foregiong Contains a true statemant of the effects of David E Barton, Dec. that have come to my hands possession or knowledge this January 1st 1866.

W.D. Wall, Admr.

Inventory of the effects of S.M. Roberts Dec. Sale Oct. 4th 1865.

One note of Thomas Rogers		34.70
One note	J.M. Trotter	46.00
One Note	S.C. Harris	46.00
Catherine Roberts		25.00
L.S. Collins		28.10
Sim Roberts		11.40
P. Eleazar		11.00
J.B. Hagewood		17.00
Thomas Batson		17.30
W.B. Batson		13.50
Peter Neblett		21.00
R. Edmond		160.00
B.A. Neblett		5.00

The foregiong is a true statement of the notes that have come into my possession as admr. of S.M. Roberts dec. Feb. 5th 1866.

Smith Batosn.

(p 304) Inventory an account of sale of the property of Elizabeth Walker Decd. Sold by Jesse D. Nicholson admr. Feb. 12th 1862.

M.G. Turner	1 cooking stove	25.00
B.J. Barnes	1 Brass Kettle	3.00
John D. Tucker	1 wash pan & dipper	.35
G.W. Harris	1 Iron Wedgw & gate hinge	.60
James Mallory	1 chopping axe	1.55
A. Walker	1 Lot old iron	.35
G. Nicholson	1 Bell & Iron tooth	.15
Martha Woodson	1 churn	.20
E?H. Nicholosn	1 wash tub	.75

Mr. Majors	1 Large pot	1.00
J.J. Wilson	1 large kettle	2.55
M.B. Stewart	1 pr cotton cards	3.50
James Mallory	1 spinning wheel	4.60
Henry Hunter	1 cooking stove	5.05
John D. Tucker	1 skillet and lids	.75
Mrs. Majors	1 Oven	.80
L.J: Hunter	1 Tin Bucket	.85
D.A. Hunter	1 Tin buc ket	.90
Allen Hunter	1 Tin Bucket	.40
L.J. Hunter	1 Bucket & Strainer	.40
L.J. Hunter	1 Bread Tray	.50
G.W. Harris	1 Bread Tray	.30
John Perdue	1 mortar	.15
L.J. Hunter	1 cedar bucket & sifter	.60
G.W. Harris	3 old barrels	.25
Joshua Humphreys	1 Bbl onions	.55
W.J. Gossit(Gossett)	½ Barrel vinegar	2.55
Thomas Bell	1 stove	2.35
J.S. Harris	1 Spinning machine	.25
M.V. Walker	10 Bushels Wheat 1.30	13.00
Lorenzo Fox	5 Bu. Wheat @ 1.25	6.25
G.W. Harris	5 Bu wheat @ 1.25	6.25
D.H. Nicholson	2½ Bu. wheat @ 1.00	2.50
A. Walker	1 Ox Cart	7.25
Henry Hunter	1 Avery Plow	5.05
Jo Shearron	1 Dorris Plow	.75
J.W. Perdue	1 Diamond plow	1.05
G.B. Nicholson	1 Bull Tongue Plow	1.05
D.H. Nicholson	2 Back bands	.25
George Bell	1 Grubbing hoe	.75
J.D. Nicholson	1 Grubbing hoe	.50
Allen Hunter	3 weeding hoes	.35
(p 305)		
J.S. Dismukes	1 Shovel	.70
G.W. Gossett	1 Pair stretchers	1.00
R.H. Knox	1 Log chain	1.05
Dempsey Hunter	1 cutting knife	2.70
Mrs. Majors	1 wagon and harness	21.00
R.J. Mallory	1 Lot Oats	4.50
W.J. Gossett	1 Lot oats	4.00
Henry Felts	1 Lot oats	2.56
G.B. Nicholson	4 Guns	.80
G.B. Nicholson	1 Lot shucks	1.00
M.V.B. Walker	1 Stack Fodder, 200½ lbs @ 20¢	2.00
Greenville Nicholson	5 Barrels corn, @ 2.00	10.00
L.J. Hunter	16 barrels Corn @ 2.00	32.00
A.L. Vanhook	5 barrels corn , @ 2.05	10.25
L.J. Huuter	15 barrels corn	30.75
Rufus King	2barrels corn	4.10
M.M. Chambliss	1 Ox Yoke	.20
G.W. Harris	1 cow and calf	20.00
M.V.B. Walker	1 cow and calf	22.50
M.V.B. Walker	5 shotes 1st choice	19.00
G.B. Nicholson	5 shotes 2nd choice	17.50
G.B. Nicholson	3 shotes 3rd choice	9.50

G.B. Nicholson	Bal per head	1.00
M.V.B. Walker	1 black sow and pigs	10.75
James Bobbit	1 white sow	6.10
H.C. Pace	2 white sows	5.50
H.C. Pace	1 spotted sow	5.05
M.V.B. Walker	1 stack fodder	2.00
H.J. Shaw	1 Mule	130.00
Mourning Stewart	1 Buggy and harness	50.00
A.J. Perdue	1 mans saddle	7.25
G.W. Gossett	1 womans saddle	m3.25
Mrs. Majors	1 Mule	125.00
Henry Hunter	1 Bag cotton	1.00
Robert King	1 Gray Mare	45.00
M.V.B. Walker	1 Colt	28.00
James Mallory	6 sheep	20.00
J.J. Williams	5 sheep	18.00
Rufus King	4 sheep	6.25
M.V.B. Walker	206½ lbs bacon @ .20c	41.30
G.B. Nicholson	294 lbs bacon	55.86
M.G. Turner	673 lbs. bacon @ 19	107.68
Rufus King	90 lbs. bacon @ 16	14.40
M.G. Turner	64½ lbs. lard @ 16	10.24
John Turner	1 clock	7.00
Henry Hunter	1 Pitcher & Wash bowl	1.00
(p 306)		
James Walker	1 Jar	.50
Mourning Stewart	1 large dish	1.90
Mourning Stewart	1 Tea pot	.70
Dempsey Hunter	1 Sett plates	1.90
G.W. Harris	1 Dish &c	1.35
Dempsey Hunter	1 lot plates	1.50
G.W. Harris	2 pitchers	1.55
Dempsey Hunter	1 Sausage stuffer	.50
Allen Hunter	1 sett knives and forks	4.00
W.C. Hunter	1 sett knives and forks	1.10
M.V.B. Walker	1 Candle stick	.75
Mourning Stewart	1 pitcher & Bowl	1.50
Allen Hunter	1 sett glasses	2.00
W.C. Hunter	1 set cups & Suacers	2.70
Mahala Walker	molasses & Bowl	.50
James Bradley	Preserve stand	.75
W.H. Morris	1 basket & Contents	.85
W.H. Morris	Jar & Jug	.75
Allen Hunter	2 Table cloths	2.05
Green Nicholson	1 Table cloth	1.05
G.W. Harris	2 Table cloths	3.15
Mourning Stewart	1 Reel	.25
Allen Hunter	Old nails	.10
J.W. Perdue	Basket Wool	.95
James Walker	2 Bu sweet potatoes	.90
Green Nicholson	Irish Potatoes	.75
Jo Alley	Window Curtains	1.50
G.W. Harris	1 Cupboard	4.00
G.B. Nicholson	1 Clock	.05
W.C. Hunter	3 Books	.10
H.R. Felts	1 Slate & Books	.45
W.C. Hunter	1 Lot books	.35
S. Knox	1 Lot books	.10

W.H. Morris	1 stack Oats	12.46
R.H. Knox	6 turkeys @ 50	3.00
Allen Hunter	1 lot peafowls	5.25
Martha Woodson	On e churn	.05
G.W. Harris	1 lot butter	.70
William Durham	1 basket eggs	.65
Allen Hunter	1 dish pan	.85
James Hunter	1 Fluter	1.30
L. Pace	1 Waiter	.50
M.V.B. Walker	1 looking glass	2.20
William Durham	1 fiddle	.35
J.S. Harris	1 hymn book & C	.75
(p 307)		
D.H. Nicholson	1 Bunch feathers	.15
J.S. Harris	1 fly broom & whip	.35
Thompson Biggers	1 Lot feathers	.35
Wm. Durham	1 han	.10
Allen Hunter	1 han	.10
R.H. Knox	1 pr sheep shears	.45
Mourning Stewart	1 chamber	1.05
Henry Hunter	1 chamber	.05
Rufus King	1 bag dried fruit	2.00
Allen Hunter	1 bag dried fruit	25
Dempsey Hunter	1 folding table	8.05
G.B. Nicholson	1 pr fire dogs	.35
Jesse Sheeron	1 pr fire dogs	.40
James Walker	1 shovel and tongs	1.25
Thomas Walker	1 flat iron	.70
A. Walker	1 sugar jar	.85
W.W. Read	1 lot coffee	1.85
W.H. Pace	1 flask	.20
Mourning Stewart	1 table cloth	1.00
H.R. Felts	5 head geese @ 16	.80
A.J. Perdue	12 head geese@ 17	2.62
R.H. Knox	4 head geese @ 13	.52
Josh Humphreys	1 slate	.15
G.W. Harris	1 pr fire dogs	.55
Allen Hunter	1 scythe blade	.40
Allen Hunter	1 lot tobacco	18.00
Mourning Stewart	2 bu sweet potatoes @ 45	.90
Cash on hand		2.00
Total amount sale, notes & C		$1272.70

Last Will and Testament of E.S. Exum.
In the name of God Amen.
I, Elijah S. Exum of the County of Cheatham and State of Tennessee, being of sound mind but bodily infirmity do make this my last Will and Testament "that is to say" that I have twice married and my son Wm. C. Exum, the issue of my first wife inherited all her Estate, Therefore I give to my present wife Elizabeth F. Exum and my two children Sallie Bettie Exum and Elijah Robert all my effects which I have in possession the sale of which is to be determined by W.H. Scott, W.L. Osborn and my wife witness.
Wherefore I have hereunto suscribed my name and affixed my seal the twenty fourth day of January 1866.

E.S. Exum, (seal)

Attest.
R.H. Thomas
W.H. Scott.

(p 308) Inventory and acct of sale of the effects of T.W. Scott Decd. By John S. Hale Administrator, February 17th 1866.

R.H. Thomas 1	103 lbs cotton at 3	3.09
R.H. Thomps	1 Bull Tongue Plow	1.00
R.T. Scott	1 wagon sheet	2.00
R.T. Scott	1 scythe sheet	1.00
R.H. Thomas	1 water bucket	.40
R.H. Thomas	1 claw hammer	.50
R.H. Thomas	42 Barrels corn @ 2.20	92.40
R.H. Thomas	1 half bushel	.50
Amount of cash on hand		21.00
Amount of notes on hand		20.00
Amount of accounts on hand		24.73

State of Tennessee)
Cheatham County)

I, J.S. Hale do hereby certify under oath that the above inventory is correct and true to the best of my knowledge and belief.
April 2nd 1866
J.S. Hale

Inventory of the effects of Samuel A. Thornton Dec.

I, James M. Thompson Admr. of Sam'l L. Thompson Dec. do hereby certify that the following is a true and perfect Inventory of all the goods of the said Samuel A. Thompson Dec. which have come into my hands or knowledge viz: One sett blacksmith tools, one waggon and some and gear. One cotton Gin, a lot of farming tools, one scythe & cradle, one lot of Corn, One bed Bedstead & furniture, One table, One clock, one watch, one cutting box, one wagon Bed, One lot of Books , one pr. Balances.

One note on John A. Pullen due Sept. 29th 1861 for	90.00
One note on Jo Hannah due March 15th 1863 for	10.00
One note on Jo Kellum due 26th Feb. 1860 with a credit of $100 Int.	$13.50
One note on G.A. Russell for due Oct. 30th 1862.	35.00
One on G.B. Hannah due Feb. 21st 1864 for	20.00
One acct. on A.J. Noll for	86.30
One on Sam White (colored) for (doubtful)	15.00
One on W.N. Thompson for	12.23
One Thos. W. Fulghum for	9.10
One on Jno. A. Clark for	3.75
One on B.F. Hannah Dec. for	31.05
One on John Y. Dortch (doubtful) for	27.97
One on Jo Kellum for	11.00
One on Wm. Sears for	1.00
One on J.M. Bagwell for	38.93½
One on S.D. Thompson for	14.15
One on James Mays for	2.00
One on W.D. Henry for	3.15
One on Ezra Halstead for	15.02

James M. Thompson Admr.

(p 309)
Inventory and account of sale of the property of Nancy G. Murphy Decd.

William Durham	1 stove	16.75
J.J. Bradley	1 kettle	4.75
W.C. Hunter	1 coffee mill	.70
J. Hunter	1 washing machine	.10

G.W. Farmer	1 skillet and lid	1.75
D.A Hunter	1 Keg soap	.75
G.W. Farmer	1 Tea kettle	.55
S.H. Bracey	1 seive	.50
D.A. Hunter	1 pr hooks &C	.35
B.H. Bradley	1 bread tray	.40
J.J. Bradley	1 pr large hooks	.30
D.A. Hunter	1 Barrel soap	1.00
J.J. Wilson	1 Keg	.65
B. H. Bradley	1 pot	.65
G.F. Ellis	1 pot and tub	1.25
B.H. Bradley	2 pails	.45
J.J. Wilson	1 pr candle sticks	.45
James Hunter	1 Bucket	.15
William Durham	1 Box Glass	1.25
H.W. Turner	1 lot tallow	2.10
B.H. Bradley	1 churn	.75
Jo Alley	1 Shovel	.10
Wm. Durham	1 Barrel vinegar	2.50
R. Murphey	1 Barrel mollasees	8.00
G.F. Ellis	1 weeding hoe	.90
M.W. Winters	1 weeding hoe	.90
J.J. Bradley	1 spade & 2 hoes	1.90
B.F. Pace	3 old axes	.40
William Harris	1 Irom wedge	.50
J.J. Wilsom	2 old Barrels & vinegar	.25
Wm. Brian	1 Box and oven	1.00
William Durham	1 lot salt	12.20
H.C. Pace	1 plow	4.50
D. Felts	1 plow	4.50
James Hunter	1 plow and double tree	6.15
Wm. Harris	1 pair plow gear	4.00
E.J. Allen	1 plow and shucks	2.40
W.J. Gossett	500 bundles fodder	4.75
G.W. Hawkins	500 " "	4.75
James Walker	634 bundles fodder	6.00
B.W. Bradley	1500 " oats	16.75
D. Felts	500 " "	6.00
B.W. Bradley	660 " "	7.26
Wm. Rediker	1 lot hogs	18.00
(p 310)		
William Durham	4 shoats	14.20
H.V. Murphey	4 shaots	10.40
Martha Woodson	7 pigs	5.80
R. Pennington	4 sheep	21.00
T.W. Perdue	9 sheep	36.00
J. Stack	5 barrels corn	7.50
H. Turner	10 barrels corn	20.00
D.J. Fort	5 barrels corn	10.25
G.W. Hawkins	5 barrels corn	10.25
W.J. Gossett	5 barrels corn	10.50
R. Murphey	27 barrels corn	57.97½
Wm. Durham	5 barrels corn	10.00
W.B. Link	7½ barrels corn	15.75
M.G. Turmer	1 lot otbacco	17.25
H. Turner	1 brown colt	75.00

D.J. Fort	1 bay mare	149.00
R. Connell	1 yoke oxen	72.60
H.C. Pace	1 black heifer	16.00
S. Durham	1 white cow	25.25
B.W. Bradley	1 ox cart	19.00
J. Teasley	1 log chain	3.00
Wm. Durham	1 bedstead & Caster	10.00
B.F. Pace	6 tumbler	.55
H. Turner	3 Bottles	.25
S.H. Bracy	1 sett plates	1.10
B.H. Bradley	1 set paltes	1.15
M.W. Winters	2 plates	.20
Wm. Durham	1 sugar bowl	.25
J. Tucker	1 bottle Ink	.25
D.J. Hunter	2 Dishes	1.00
W. Hawkins	1 dish	.75
Wm. Durham	1 dish	1.05
W.B. Link	1 dish	.50
S.H. Bracey	1 set cups and saucers	1.15
Wm. Durham	2 cups & Cream pot	.40
J. Hunter	1 set knives and forks	.45
Wm. Durham	1 Lot bottles	1.00
W.J. Darden	1 whet stone	.30
W. Durham	1 sett knives and forks	3.00
R. Murphey	2 books	1.00
W. Brian	3 books	1.10
H.C. Pace	4 books	1.30
Wm. Durham	1 Table	.10
P. Harris	1 powder horn &C	1.55
B.W. Bradley	1 safe	11.50
(p 311)		
William Durham	1 table& Tin bucket	8.20
Z.W. Winters	1 bureau	3.00
J. Stack	1 sett andirons	.25
C.S. Gupton	2 sett chairs	8.30
B.H. Bradley	1 sett andirons	.45
J.E. BRAdley	1 water bucket	.55
James Hunter	1 water can	.50
J. Huggins	1 wheel barrow	.15
J. Tucker	1 Red cow	22.00
B.W. Bradley	1 cutting knife	2.60
Robert Knox	1 lot hens	2.38
George Murff	1 lot Gun	.50
W. Durham	1 lot brick	.60
J.J. Bradley	1 Hearth cloth	.25
Cash on hand	Silver $10.53 Paper $33.00	43.53
1 note on hand	T.W. Hunt due June 4th 1862	37.50
1 note on	M.V.B. Walker due March 17th 1860	247.00
	G.W. Murphey & H.W. Turner	
1 note	Talton Watson due Aug. 29th 1860	15.00
1 note	Elizabeth Walker due Aug 28th 1860	20.00
1 note	William Durham due June 18th 1862	64.00
1 note on G.W. Murphey	due Feb. 12th 1861	47.60
1 note	R.L. Williams due Oct. 11th 1860	61.53
1 note	J.W. Shaw due May 14th 1861	47.32
1 note	J.W. Shaw due Feb. 16th 1861	20.00
1 note	J.W. Shaw due Sept 21st 1861	35.00

1 note	J.W. Shaw & R.L. Williams due July 26th 1860	230.30
1 note	J.W. Shaw due Sept. 19th 1859	51.00
Shaw & Bros. due April 17th 1861		10.00
	Accounts	
One acct.	A.H. Williams 1859	84.75
C.A. Hudgens Receipt due Feb. 22nd 1860		135.00
E.L. Williams Receipt due Feb. 3rd 1862		52.63
1 note	W.T. Logan, B.M. Smith A. Williams L.L Williams due Feb. 22nd 1860	269.75

The foregoing is a true and perfect Inventory of all the goods and chattel rights and credits of said Nancy G. Murphy Dec. which have come to my hands possession ot knowledge or the hands of any other person for me to the best of my knowledge.
C.C. Williams
Test
W.W. Williams Clk.

(p 312) Inventory and account of Sale of the property of Samuel King Dec.

E.T. Herron	1 Trunk	.50
E.T. Herron	1 chest	1.50
E.T. Herron	1 bridle and saddle	5.55
A.W. Hooper	1 pr saddle bags	3.95
A.W. Hooper	1 pr medical bags	1.50
C.F. Williams	1 mortat & Pestle	.50
E.G. Hudgens	2 Razors	1.09
E.T. Herron	1 razor strap	.10
A.W. Hooper	Spectacles	.20
James Walker	1 Hone	.50
C.F. Williams	1 Surveyor & Case	.25
W.C. Charlton	2 Lanuts	.50
A.W. Hooper	1 Pocket case	1.50
E.T. Herron	1 Syringe	.25
C.F. Williams	1 Tooth Key	1.00
J.H. Harper	Forceps	.25
E.T. Herron	2 Books	.15
C.F. Williams	3 Books	.47
W.C.Charlton	4 books	3.60
C.F. Williams	Sundry books	4.70
C.F. Williams	" "	10.05
W.C. Charlton	" "	4.85
E.T. Herron	1 watch	14.00
J.W. Walker	1 Watch	10.00
One note on Thomas King		100.00
One note on Thos. King		80.00
One note on Thomas King		100.00
With credits		100100
One acct. on Jesse Shearon		4.00
One acct. on Plummer Feasley Amt. not remembered.		
One acct Clay Starnes (doubtful)		8.00
Total		353.96
Int. on Tom King note		22.00
		380.96

State of Tennessee
Cheatham

Cheatham County)
This day personally appeared A.F. Carney before Warren Jordan, Clerk of the County Court for and made oath in due form of law to the correctness of the withinInventory, December 18th 1865
A.F. Carney
Warren Jordan, Clk.

(p 313) Inventory and account of sale of the property of Elizabeth Bobo, Dec. April 1866, By E.M. Nolin(Nolen) Admr.

Mrs. Nolen	1 small pot	.25
John Elliott	1 griddle	.50
Mrs. Nolen	1 pot and pot rack	.85
John Elliott	1 Oven and lid	.25
Logan Gray	1 Oven and lid	1.85
A. Adkins	1 shovel &C	.25
Jo Gray	2 Tubs and kegs	.65
G. Isenstien	1 Spinning wheel	.50
D.W. Stack	3 barrels & contents	.70
Logan Gray	1 Barouch & Irons	3.30
T.H. Cage	1 Barrel	.65
W. Rogers	3 Hides	.40
Mrs. Nolen	1 lot tin ware	.30
D.W. Stack	1 pan &C	.50
Jo Gray	1 pr scales	.70
Mrs. S. McGee	1 pr cards	.30
A. Adkins	1 cow and dipper	1.30
Mrs. Nolen	1 coffee mill &C	1.40
Green Elliott	1 churn	.50
Logan Gray	1 Demijohn	1.25
W.J. Grant	1 Demijohn	1.00
Jo Nolin(Nolen)	1 Hammer	.10
Mrs. Nolin	1 Reel &C	.60
Mrs. Nolin	1 Preserve dish	.30
Mrs. Nolin	1 sett cups and saucers	.60
T.A. Fizer	1 lot bottles	.50
G. Elliott	1 Lantern	.25
Charlotte Vanleer	1 crock	.40
Mary Drake	1 Jar	.40
W.B. Gardner	1 wash pan	.55
Mrs. S. McGee	1 sugar and contents	1.55
Logan Gray	1 Table	.75
Logan Gray	1 Table	1.50
A.A. Fizer	1 Bureau	4.05
W.B. Allsbrook	1 Looking glass	2.90
A.A.F izer	Bolster slip	1.35
G.W. Farmer	1 lot pillowslips	.70
G.W. Farmer	1 lot pillowslips	.70
G.W. Farmer		
A.A. Fizer	Table Cloths &C	2.00
G.W. Farmer	Table Cloths &C	2.00
Mrs. S. McGee	one pr sheets and towels	1.25
A.A. Fizer	one lot towels	.15
W.G. Pickering	One comfort	1.50
A.A. Fizer	One comfort	3.25
(p 314)		
G.W. Farmer	1 comfort &C	1.55

W.J. Gossitt	2 counterpanes		2.00
W.B. Allsbrook	1 Press		2.25
Mrs. Nolen	1 clock		2.55
Mrs. McGee	1 candle stand		1.95
W.T. Gossitt	1 stone Jar		1.40
Mrs. Nolen	1 Jar lard		9.30
D.W. Stack	1 clothes brush &C		.25
Charlotte Drake	2 Flat Irons		1.00
L.J. Bagwell	1 Tea kettle		.50
W.J. Gossitt	1 Brass Kettle		2.00
P.T. Williams	1 shovel and tongs		1.05
W.J. Gossitt	1 pt Andirons		.50
Mrs. McGee	1 Pr. Andirons		.10
A.A. Fizer	1 sett plates		.30
Mrs. S. McGee	1 set plates		.45
A.A. Fizer	1 set plates		.95
Mrs. S. McGee	1 dish		.65
Mrs. Nolen	2 dishes		.65
W.B. Alsbrook	1 sett knives and forks		2.05
W.B. Gardner	3 spoons		.50
Mrs. Nolen	1 sett teaspoons		1.35
G. E lliott	1 caster		.25
Mrs. Nolen	1 sett cellars & C		.20
John Nolen	1 sugar Bowl		.25
Mary Drake	1 bowl and dishes		.40
Mrs. McGee	2 Pitchers		.55
D.C. Smith	1 cream pitcher		.25
Charlotte Vanleer	5 glass Tumblers		.65
Mrs. Nolen	1 dish and teapot		1.00
D.W. Stack	1 molasses stand		.70
Mrs. Nolen	1 Tea pot		.50
Mrs. S. McGee	2 bowls		.35
W.G. Pickering	1 cupboard		3.25
Logan Grey	1 bed stead		3.10
W.B. Allsbrook	4 chairs		.75
W.B. Allsbrook	4 chairs		.55
R.H. Moody	4 chairs		.25
W.G. Pickering	1 chamber		.10
Jo Gray	1 Feather bed and Matress		26.50
Mrs. Nolin	1 Feather bed		14.00
W.B. Allsbrook	1 feather bed		18.00
W.B. Allsbrook	1 thread bed		8.17
W.G. Pickering	1 Lounge		8.17
W.G. Pickering	1 Lounge Mattress &C	5.90	[illegible]
(p 315)			
W.G. Pickering	1 wash stand		1.25
Mrs. S. McGee	1 Bureau		5.50
W.G. Grant	1 Lot books		.25
A.A. Fizer	4 pr window curtains		.30
Mrs. Nolen	33 lbs cotton @ .15		4.95
W.J. Gossett	Buggy harness		1.00
Mrs. Nolin	1 flax wheel		.05
W.G. Pickering	1 lot wool		3.00
Cricy Walton	1 chest		1.10
Logan Gray	5 barrels corn@ 3.05		15.25
D.W.Stack	5 barrels corn @ 3.90		19.50
D.W. Stack	5 barrels corn @ 4.00		20.00

J.E. Cage	5 barrels corn @ 4.00	20.00
W.J. Gossitt	5 barrels corn @ 4.15	20.75
J.E. Cage	Remainder	15.85
John E. Lynch	1 white cow	22.25
G. Isenstien	1 speckled heifer	35.00
John Elliott	1 white cow and heifer	36.00
W.B. Gardner	1 white heifer	10.25
T.H. Cage	1 Oat stack	18.35
G. Isenstien	8 sheep	14.00
John Nolen	5 hogs 1st choice	25.50
John Nolen	5 hogs 1st choice	20.50
G. Isenstein	1 sow and shoats	15.00
John Elliott	1 lot tobacco @ 6.00 per hd	
Logan Gray	1 piece iron	.25
P.T. Williamsmm	1 plow point	.25
Mrs. Nolen	1 lot soap	.80
Mrs. Nolen	11 chickens	1.25

The foregiong contains a true and perfect Inventory of all the goods chattels rights and credits of Elizabeth Bobo Dec. that have come into my hands possession or knowledge this May 7th 1866

E.M. Nolen Admr.

Account of sales of the personal property belonging to the Estate of J.T. Bradley Dec. April 21st 1866.

E.G. Hudgens	1 Bay Mule	120.00
B.F. Smith	1 Black Mule	142.50
S.H. Hudgens	1 Carryall	50.00

This is to certify that the above is a true copy of the amount of sales. Sworn to and sucribed before me.

B.L. Hudgens Admr.
G.W. McQuary Clk.

May 7th 1866

(p 316) Alist of theproperty sold at the Sale of James Binkley Dec. April 20th 1866.

E.J. Binkley	1 Lot sundries	1.00
Burton Neighbors	3 Froes	.60
G.S. Lock	1 lot iron tolls	1.50
Jack Crocket	3 Plows &C	3.00
David Binkley	2 plows	.25
Jack Crockett	1 plow & Snead	2.00
David Binkley	3 plows &C	.55
Burton Neighbors	1 cross cut saw	7.00
Pat Mannison	1 sledge hammer	1.00
Moses Ragan	2 match planes	.60
Jack Crockett	2 other planes	.60
David Binkley	Sundry Articles	4.20
Jack Crockett	1/5 Fan mill	2.00
W.C. Charlton	2 Kegs	1.55
M.H. Boyd	1 keg	.60
David Binkley	5 old barrels	.50
Pat Mannison	1 Cant hook	.25
H.J. Binkley	1 Fan Mill	1.00
David Binkley	1300 Lathes	2.25

George Binkley	1 corn sheller	2.00
David Binkley	1 Large Kettle	12.00
John Locke	1 old red cow	25.10
Leonard Binkley	1 black cow & calf	22.50
Leonard Binkley	1 white cow	41.50
John Locke	1 speckled cow	18.00
Widow Binkley	1 small yearling	3.00
Burton Neighbors	1 small yearrling	4.00
Burton Neighbors	1 Large sow	16.25
J.W. Felts	4 shaots 1st choice	17.50
Jack Crockett	1 Lot lumber	1.75
David Binkley	1 Lot lumber	1.75
Jack Crockett	1 Lot lumber	11.75
George Binkley	1 Log chain	1.40
H.B. Carney	Rent, house in Ashland	10.00
T.T. Thompson	1 Lot fence posts	1.02
Jack Crockett	1 lot scantling	8.40
Jack Crockett	1 lot joists	1.55
H.B. Carney	1 lot lumber	16.50
T.T. Thompson	1 lot oak lumber	3.60
H.B. Carney	1 lot loose lumber	4.25
T.T. Thompson	Work bench & Lumber	1.25
Pat Mannison	1 pile oak lumber	1.05
(317)		
Jack Crockett	1 lot Posts	.45
David Binkley	saw mill machinery and lease	110.00

The above is a true and perfect Inventory of the goods and chattels, rights and credits of the said James Binkley Dec. which have come into my hands or possession or knowledge or the hands or possession o f any other person for us to the best of our knowledge and ability.
This May 25th 1866
Adam Binkley Jr. Admr.

Inventory and account of Sale of the personal effects of T.W. Teasley Dec. M March 24th 1866.

1 Trowel	No names	.50
1 Hammer		3.00
1 Saddle		21.00
1 Horse		110.00
1 Slate		.35
1 Rifle		17.00
One note		248.93
One note		1.90
One note		15.75
One note		3.50
One note		9.41

The above is a true and perfect Inventory of the goods and chattels rights and credits of the said T.W. Teasley which have come into my hands, possession or knowledge or the hands of or knowledge or possession of any other person for me to the best of my knowledge and belief this April 1866.
T.F. Teasley, Admr.

G.W. Basford Inventory of the psoperty sold by G.W. Basford Admr. of Elizabeth Miles Decd.

1 lot of chairs	E.D. Basford	3.00

1 Spinning wheel	E.D. Basford	1.50
1 Pr Andirons	E.D. Basford	.30
1 Spice Mortar	E.D. Basford	.25
1 Tea kettle	E.D. Basford	.25
2 Skillets and lid	E.D. Basford	.25
1 Pot &C	E.D. Basford	1.00
1 Pot	E.D. Basford	1.50
1 Table	E.D. Basford	.50
1 Shovel &C	E.D. Basford	1.00
(p318)		
2 pr pothooks	E.D. Basford	1.00
1 Chest	E.D. Basford	2.50
1 Trunk	E.D. Basford	4.00
1 Desk &C	E.D. Basford	.75
1 Featherbed	B.J. Stack	14.00
1 Bed Sted	B.J. Stack	1.50

Personally appeared before me G.W. Basford and made oathin due form of law that the above is a true and perfect Inventory and account of sale of the effects belonging to the estate of Elizabeth Miles Dec. this July 2nd 1866

G.W. McQuary, Clk.

Joel F. Mays, Inventory and account of the personal effects of W.J. Berry Dec. that have come into my hands possession or knowledge.

To cash $2355.71

The above is a true and perfect Inventory of all the goods and chattels rights and credits of the said W.J. Berry Dec. which have come into my hands possession or knowledge or the hands of any other person for me to the best of my knowledge and belief.

Joel F. Mays

Sworn to before me date as above
G.W. McQuary Clk.

Settlement of H.W. Sanders Administratorof the Estate of Rebecca Sanders Dec.

To Amt. property sold	160.34
To notes on John Sanders	98.20
	258.54
To notes on W.W. Sanders	7.75
	266.29
Cash on hand	9.25
Leather	2.60
	278.14

Contra

By fees	W. William Clerk	3.20
Baid	E.G. Hudgens for selling property	2.00
Account of J.W. Paid for burial expenses		7.30
H.P. Shaw	Proven acct.	12.87
A.J. Teasley	Proven acct.	6.00
B.J. Barnes	Fees as clerk at sale	2.00
Clerk for settlement & Recording same		2.50
(p 319)		
Administrators allowance		20.00
		55.87
Balance due to Legatees		222.27

A list of the property of the estate of Leonard Frazier Dec.

1 Carryall & Harness	J.W. Dhearon	20.00
1 Plow and trumpery	W.J. Nicholson	.50
1 Tung plow and saw	G.W. Harris	.75
1 Axe and chain	Widow	.10
1 Bay mare	Widow	1.00
1 Lot books	Henry Frazier	.25
1 Lot books	Henry Frazier	.10
1 lot books	Henry Frazier	.10
1 Book	G.W. Harris	1.25
1 Dress Table	Widow	.25
1 Clock	Widow	.10
1 Watch	Widow	.50
1 Chest	Widow	.50
1 Flax wheel	"	.25
1 Spin Wheel	"	.05
2 Augers	Henry Frazier	.25
3 Augurs	Henry Frazier	.05
3 Chisels	Henry Frazier	.75
1 pair Grooves	J.T. Hooper	1.00
3 planes	Henry Frazier	.10
1 screw	"	.15
1 Tool chest & Contents	"	.10
2 plows	"	.05
2 plows	"	.30
3 do	"	.25
1 two horse plow	"	3.00
1 Lot gear	"	.50
1 scythe	"	.50
1 cow and calf, augers & barrels		21.50
1 Yearling	Widow	1.00
1 Yearling	"	.50
1 sow and 5 pigs	"	1.00
1 sow and 4 pigs	"	1.00
1 Shoat	"	.10
1 Bryar Hook	Henry Dozier	.10
1 Frow	Henry Dozier	.10
		57.00

(p 320)
State of Tennessee)
Cheatham County)
Personally appeared before me G.W. McQuary Clerk of the County Court of said County G.W. McQuary Clerk of the County Cout of said County and make oath in due form of law that the above is a true and perfect Inventory of the personal effects belong to the estate of Leonard Frazier Decd.

G.W. Maxey Adm.

Sworn to before me 6th Augt. 1866
G.W. McQuary Clk.

Inventory & account of sale of the personal property belonging to the estate of E. & Nute Harris Decd.

1 Gray Mule	C.J.C. Shivers		166.00
L bay mare mule	E.C. Harris		152.00
1 Gray horse mule	W.J. Lyles		160.00
1 mouse colored Horse mule	Thos. Pack	75.00	75.00
1 Bay horse mule	Catherine Harris		122.00

1 Gray Horse	Minerva Harris	124.00
1 Red cow and calf	Minerva Harris	51.00
1 White cow and calf	Mansfield Watkins	47.00
1 Red cow and calf	Minerva Harris	31.00
1 White yearling	Catherine Harris	11.00
1 Red steer & Yearling	E.C. Harris	8.00
1 Brindle Heifer	Minerva Harris	11.00
1 white speckled steer	Thos. B. Oakley	15.00
1 Red Heifer	Minerva Harris	22.00
1 crumply horned heifer	Catherine Harris	18.00
7 head sheep	Virgil Patterson	21.00
1st choice sow	Minerva Harris	14.00
2nd choice sow	Catherine Harris	12.00
3rd choice sow	E.C. Harris	13.00
5 1st choice sheep	Minerva Harris	22.25
4 - 2nd choice sheep	Catherine Harris	16.20
7 head sheep	Jno. Jones	21.35
1st lot corn 10 bbls	Minerva Harris	27.00
2nd choice Corn	E.C. Harris	25.00
3rd choice "	Catherine Harris	25.00
4th choice "	Wm. Sears	30.00
5th choice Corn	Wm. Sears	30.00
6th choice "	Wm. Sears	30.00
7th choice Corn	MinervaHarris	14.00
8th choice Corn	Catherine Harris	14.00
Remainder	Minerva Harris	-----
1 four horse wagon	E.C. Harris	62.00
(p 321)		
1 Two horse wagon	MinervaHarris	80.00
All the fodder per bundle @ 2½	Minerva Harris	7.50
1 lot shoats	Minerva Harris	21.50
2nd choice shoats	Catherine Harris	20.50
3rd choice Shoats	Minerva Harris	19.00
2 Cast plows	G.W. Jackson	5.00
3 old plows	W.P. Mayberry	.25
1 wheat fan & hogshead	E.C. Harris	.35
1 Avery Plowno 8	Minerva Harris	2.00
1 Diamond Plow	James Brummet	4.00
1 Diamond plow	Wm. Howell	4.00
1 Grubbing hoe	Minerva Harris	.50
1 grubbing hoe	Samks Harris	.50
1 weeding hoe	J.B. Williams	1.00
1 lot gear	Minerva Harris	1.50
Backband & chairs	Minerva Harris	2.20
1 Trace chain	Minerva Harris	.75
1 set harness	Minerva Harris	11.00
1 Iron wedge	Minerva Harris	.55
1 Lot old harness	Francis Russell	.50
1 Log Chain	Minerva Harris	3.60
1 Pot	Minerva Harris	.50
1 Skillet and lid	Jim Sears	1.40
1 Oven and lid	Henry Stringfellow	1.10
1 Oven and lid	Minerva Harris	.75
1 Hand Saw	Minerva Harris	.75
1 Drawing knife	Thos. Sears	1.90

1 Inch Auger	Wm. Howell	.40
2 chisels & sheep shears	Wm. Howell	.35
1 Briar Hook	Berry Jordan	1.25
1 Mowing blade and pitch fork	James M. Brown	.60
1 Grind stone	Minerva Harris	1.15
1 Wash Kettle	Minerva Harris	2.70
1 Waddrobe	Minerva Harris	5.00
1 Trunnel Bed	Minerva Harris	10.00
1 Large dining room bed	Minerva Harris	15.00
1 Candle stand	Minerva Harris	.15
1 Looking glass	Minerva Harris	.40
1 Bed and Furniture	Catherine Harris	18.00
L lounge and furniture	Samps Harris	10.00
1 small table	Minerva Harris	3.00
1 Bed and furniture	Minerva Harris	24.00
2nd bed	Minerva Harris	27.00
1 Table	Catherine Harris	.20
1 clock	Catherine Harris	.50
1 chest	Minerva Harris	1.00
(p 322)		
1 double barrel gun	Minerva Harris	21.00
1 Bureau	Catherine Harris	9.00
1 Large looking glass	Catherine Harris	1.00
1 Book case	Minerva Harris	2.00
1 set chairs	Minerva Harris	1.00
1 set chairs	Minerva Harris	2.00
1 Loom	Minerva Harris	6.00
1 Spinning wheel	Minerva Harris	4.00
1 Real	Minerva Harris	.50
1 Folding leaf table	Minerva Harris	7.00
1 Cupboard	Catherine Harris	10.00
1 Cooking stove	Minerva Harris	9.00
1 Large table	Minerva Harris	2.25
1 stone churn	MinervaHarris	1.00
1 Tin Bucket	MinervaHarris	1.00
1 Half Bushel	Minerva Harris	.25
1 square table	Minerva Harris	.10
1 Pail	MinervaHarris	.30
1 Can	Catherine Harris	1.00
1 Rifle gun	W.P.Mayberry	7.00
1 Carall	Minerva Harris	35.00
4200 lbs. pork @ 12c	Minerva & Catherine Harris	500.00

State of Tennessee)
Cheatham County)

Personally appeared before me G.W. McQuary Clerk of the County Court of said Joseph Harris and made oath in the form of law that the above is a true and perfect Inventory and account of sale of the personal effects belonging to the estate of E. and Nute Harris.

Joseph Harris

Sworn and suscribed to before me May 7th 1866

G.W. McQuary Clerk

Cash & Notes on land belong to the estate of E. and Nute Harris Dec.

One note on James Slight for rent of land	40.00

One note on M.A. & W.C. Harris for	92.90
One note on James Speight for rent of land	40.00
One note on Minerva and C.W. Harris for rent of house and land	60.00
Cash Union and Planters Bank	25.00
J.B. Williams Dr for Rent House and land	35.00
Cash on hand	289.32

State of Tennessee
Cheatham County
Personall appeared before me G.W. McQuary Clerk of the County Court, Joseph Harris and made oath in due form of law the above is a true account of all the monies & notes belonging to the estate of E. and Nute Harris sworn to and sucribed before ma me 7th day of May 1866.
Joseph Harris, Admr.
G.W. McQuary, Clerk

(p 323) A list of the property sold on the 7th of June 1866, belonging to the Estate of Allen Thompson Dec.

Names of persons	Property Sold	Amount
Jack Hullen	1 oven lid and skillet	.50
Jack Hullan	1 baking oven & pot	1.00
Spencer White	1 pot and oven & skillet	1.25
S.D. Thompson	1 Brass kettle & Pot	4.00
H. Cooper	2 water buckets	.50
H. Cooper	1 Pot and Waffle Irons	.50
Jack Hutton	1 pale cup and stainer	1.75
H. Cooper	1 Pail & Wagon sheet	2.40
H. Cooper	1 wash pot	2.00
Jack Hutton	2 Boles	.25
H. Cooper	1 coffee pot & lot tin ware	2.00
H. Cooper	2 Piggins	.50
Miss Julia Thompson	1 Table and jar	.75
Wm. Thompson	1 stove and Utensils	10.00
H. Cooper	1 Barrel and cotton	1.50
H. Cooper	1 lot of barrels	.25
S.D. Thompson	1 Lot sundries	.50
H. Cooper	1 Carpet	2.25
H. Cooper	1 Bag cotton basket &C	.50
Jack Hutton	1 Reel	.50
W.N. Thompson	1 Flax Wheel	1.00
Jack Hutton	1 spinning wheel	1.75
Spencer White	1 spinning wheel	6.00
J.M. Dunn	1 bed stead & Cord	.50
Neal Thompson	2 peaces leather	2.50
W.N. THompson	1 peice leather	.50
Frank Smith	1 pr of haims	1.00
J. Travis	1 calf skin and umbrella	.60
Lewis Thompson	1 bag cotton & Basket	1.75
John Porch	1 sheet of wool	15.50
B.F. Smith	1 steel trap and leather	.10
M. Gartner (Gardner)	1 steel trap and leather	.70
Stephens Hale	2 Brooms	.60
George Cooper	1 Bedstead	2.25
M. Garton	2 bunch peafowl feathers	.25
S.D. Thompson	1 Bunch feathers	.35
B.F. Smith	1 lamp and coffee mill	.25
Wm. Henry	1 smoothing iron	1.20

Jack Hutton	1 smoothing iron	1.25
Geroge Cooper	1 cradle	1.00
Wm. Taylor	1 jug, honey and bowl	1.50
Bill Thompson	1 jug molasses	.50
(p 324)		
W.N. Thompson	4 jars and lot of sundries	2.15
Jack Hutton	2 Oilcloths	.50
W.P. Mays	2 Oilcloths	1.15
S.D. Thompson	2 window blinds	.25
Anderson Greer	1 pr cotton cards	.80
Lucy Woodward	2 pr cotton cards	.50
J. Travis	1 box sundries	.50
W.N. Thompson	1 Basket	.55
Jack Hutton	2 baskets	1.00
Mary Greer	2 candle sticks	.70
Wm. Hammel	1 par scales	.50
W.P. Mays	1 set plates	1.05
Lucy Woodward	8 plates	.50
Spencer White	2 dishes and 2 plates	.50
Lucy Woodward	2 dishes	.40
J. Travis	1 large dish	.30
Sam'l Dunn	1 dish, pitcher & Bowl	.25
Wm. Henry	1 sugar dish	.55
Spencer White	1 Pitcher	.85
J.M. Dunn	1 pitcher	.90
E.H. Brown	1 pitcher	.75
Bill Thompson	1 teapot	.25
Jack Hutton	2 teapots	.50
Wm. N. Thompson	1 sugar bowl	.35
S.H. Dunn	1 Bowl	.15
Joseph Greer	1 set chiney cups and saucers	1.55
Bill Thompson	1 set china cups and saucers	.80
Wm. Taylor	2 saucers, 1 glass, 1 bowl	.25
W.C. Hutton	2 glass preserve dishes	.50
Steven Hale	1 castor & Cruet	.50
Jack Hutton	1 molasses stand	.85
W.N. Thompson	1 sugar bowl	.75
Moses Jones	1 set salt cellars	.25
George Cooper	5 glass tumblers	.90
Wm. N. Thompson	1 set table spoons	1.00
Lucy Woodward	6 spoons &C	.40
Lucy Woodward	6 spoons &C	1.40
Wm. Taylor	1 set knives and forks	.30
E.H. Brown	1 cake tallow @ 1.80 per lb	1.80
J.M. Dunn	1 lot beeswax & tallow	.40
Sarah Thompson	2 framed pictures	1.10
Lucy Woodward	1 looking glass	1.40
W.N. Thompson	1 Bible Testament & lot of books	3.95
S.D. Thompson	4 socks	1.60
Jack Hutton	2 chambers	1.00
Anderson Greer	1 bed blanket	1.65
(p 325)		
Wm. Thompson	1 Bed blanket	.50
J. Travis	1 bed blanket	1.30
Moses Jones	1 coverlid	3.00
Lucy Woodward	1 bolster case & Pillowslip	1.55

Mary Greer	2 Sheets	1.80
Bill Thompson	3 sheets	2.25
Mary Greer	2 sheets	2.50
Zacker Rayne Esq.	1 counterpane	6.50
Zacker Rayne Esq.	1 counterpane	4.25
Zacker Rayne Esq.	1 counterpane, fringed	4.25
W.P. Mays	1 counterpane	5.75
Zack Payne	1 counterpane	5.75
J. Travis	1 counterpane common	2.00
Lucy Woodward	1 counterpane. flowered	4.00
Anderson Greer	1 coverlid	4.75
W.N. Thompson	2 coverlid	24.50
W.N. Thompson	3 coverlid Gettia	11.25
Lucy Woodward	2 coverlid old	1.60
Frank Smith	1 Comfort	1.25
W.N. Thompson	1 bed bolster & Sheet	15.50
W.N. Thompson	1 bed bolster 2 pie sheets	17.00
Lucy Woodward	1 Bolster 1 sheet	15.00
George Cooper	1 bed bolster & Sheet	19.00
S.D. Thompson	1 Moss Mattress	8.50
J.N. Dunn	1 Bed Quilt	1.25
John F. Greer	Straw bed	1.50
Joseph Greer	1 Bedstead	3.00
Lucy Woodward	1 low headed bed and quilt	5.00
Miss J. Thompson	1 Bureau	15.00
Joseph Greer	1 Desk and bookcase	11.75
S.D. Thompson	1 Cupboard	2.50
Sam'l K. Dunn	1 clock and sugar chest	4.55
Neal Thompson	1 Bedstead	1.00
J. Travis	1 chest	.75
Thomas Deel (Deal)	1 Table	10.00
A. Aken	1 safe	3.25
Jack Hutton	1 Table	7.05
J. Travis	1½ round table	.25
S.K. Dunn	1 small table	.50
W.C. Stuard (Stewart)	1 set chairs	5.00
John S. Hale	7 chairs 25 cents each	1.75
J.M. Bagwell	1 lot bacon	15.00
Jerry Thompson	7 middles bacon 24c per lb	34.92
Zack Payne	7 hams, 23c per lb.	28.06
Zack Payne	1 keg lard 12½ cts per lb	24.50
B.F. Smith	1 lot tallow	.55
(p 326)		
Frank Smith	1 half barrel molasses	11.25
Allen Thompson	1 lot soap	15.00
Thomas Biggers	1 Beef hide	.75
W.P. Mays	1 bbl vinegar	4.00
Jack Hutton	1 loom and 2 slays	9.00
J.N. Dunn	2 slays	1.50
Jack Hutton	2 pr loom harness	2.00
S.D. Thompson	1 spinning machine	30.00
Wm. Carter	2 meal sacks	2.00
Frank Smith	1 meal sack	.80
Len Shelton	1 meal sack	.30
G.A. Russell	1 cow and calf	19.50
Jack Hutton	1 cow and calf	37.00

Neal Thompson	2 cows and 2 calfs	69.00
Lewis Thompson	1 cow and calf	20.00
Spencer White	1 spotted cow & Calf	37.00
Zack Payne	1 black heifer 7 spotted heifer	19.50
Jack Hutton	1 red steer	9.75
S.B. Hale	1 pided steer	------
Spence White	6 - 1st choice hogs per head	40.00
Anderson Greer	1 black and blue sow	22.00
Wm. Thompson	4 sows and pigs	17.00
Ivy Thompson	7 - 1st choice shoats $2.50 per	17.50
Bob T onpson	7 shaots 2.30 per head	16.10
Zack Payne	4 first choice sheep 3.00 per head	12.00
Zack Payne	4 second choice 2.75	11.00
Moses Jones	1 Ram	1.00
David Thompson	10 barrels corn @ 3,25 per bbl.	32.50
David Thompson	10 bbl. corn @ 3,.25	32.50
Wm. Thompsom	1 4- horse wagon	35.00
R.W. Pegram	1 sorrel mare & mule colt	161.00
Jack Hutton	1 mule	110.00
Wm. Thompson	1 buggy	16.00
S.D. Thompson	1 side saddle	15.00
Wm. Hamble	1 bed stead	5.00
Wm. Deal	1 basket of bottles	.10
B. Smith	1 pan drwaer knife & shears	.20
J. Travis	1 pr. steelyards	.25
Spencer White	2 Iron wedges @ 45 cents each	.90
George Cooper	1 gridiron	.10
Spencer White	1 pot rack, 3 tin buckets	1.00
Wm. Carter	1 pot rack	.60
S.D. Thompson	1 bell & sheep shears	.10
John Kellum	2 Tin buckets & Dipper	.50
S.D. Thompson	1 water -----	.25
Wm. Nawl	1 stone jar	.50
(p 327)		
A.J. Noll	1 stone jar	.60
Spencer White	1 tray, seive &C	.50
Charley Cross	1 churn	1.50
Wm. Taylor	1 basket hand iron shovels &C	1.00
S.D. Thompson	2 single horse plows each 1.50	3.00
Jack Hutton	1 single horse plow	2.00
*Charley Cross	1 bull tongue plow	.60
G.W. Hannah	1 grind stone	1.10
Wm. Hamble	1 chopping axe	.15
Wm. Deal	1 chopping axe	1.00
Jack Hutton	2 Hoes	.60
Spencer White	4 hoes assorted	.60
Wm. Carter	2 Hoes	.55
G.W. Hannah	2 mowing hoes	1.50
J. Travis	1 mowing blade	.60
Jack Hutton	1 scythe& cradle	3.00
Jack Hutton	1 set waggon harness	6.75
Wm. Thompson	1 set waggon harness	1.25
Lewis Mays	1 pr plow harness	1.00
Spencer White	1 pr plow harness	1.00
John Kellum	1 Kettle	6.50
Zack Payne	1 red heifer	10.00
* Allen, Thompson,	2 horse plow	4.50

Charley Cross	5 bu. wheat 2.35 per bu	11.75
Wm. Harvell	Remainder @ 2.20 per bu	16.00
Zack Payne	1 lot cabbage	3.00
Wm. Taylor	1 lot cabbage & onions	1.50
Wm. Hamble	1950 bundles oats @ 2.30	46.00
Wm. Hutton	5 hogs $5.50 per head	27.50
J.M. Dunn	4 hogs @ 3.90	16.60
Wm. Thompson	2 hogshead	.85
S.D. Thompson	1 hamper basket	.35
Wm. Hamble	1 Basket	.15
Bob Thompson	1 mule - dick	57.00
Jo Hendricks	1 mule Suse	210.00
Jo Hendricks	1 mule Fred	200.00
Wm. Thompson	1 pickle stand	.35
Spencer White	1 Truck wagon	1.00
		607.55
Ampt. on 6th page		39.30
Ampt. on 5th page		826.20
Ampt. on 4th page		316.24
Ampt. on 3rd page		64.20
Ampt. on 2nd page	25.20	25.20
Ampt. on 1st page		55.80
To cask on hand at death		60.50
1 acpt. on A.T. Brown (doubtful)		35.00
		2024.99

(p 328)
State of Tennessee)
Cheatham County)

Personally appeared before me W.N. Thompson Administrator of the estate of Allen Thompson Decd. and made oath in due form of law that the wihth is a true and perfect inventory of the estate of Allen Thompson Decd.

W.N. Thompson Admr.

Sworn to and suscribed before me Aug. 24th 1866

G.W. McQuary , Clerk.

A list of the personal property of Dr. B.L. Hudgens, Dec. sold by G.W. Maxey Admr. on the 24th of August 1866.

Names	Property sold	Amt.
Sandy Crantz (Krantz)	1 violene	7.75
A.J. Teasley	1 trunk	6.50
T.H. Hudgens	1 tin bucket	.60
Len Teasley	1 pr martin gales	.55
Dr. Hooper	1 medical book	.50
Dr. Williams	" "	.50
Dr. Hooper	" "	.75
W.H. Stuart	" "	.75
W.H. Stuart	" "	1.25
W.H. Stuart	" "	1.75
W?H. Stuart	" "	1.20
W.H. Stuart	" "	1.25
W.H. Stuart	" "	2.25
W.H. Stuart	" "	.50
Dr. Hooper	" "	2.00
W.H. Stuart	" "	.25

W.H. Stuart	1 Medical book	.75
Dr. Hooper	1 medical book	1.00
W.H. Stuart	1 medical book	2.50
Dr. Hooper	1 pair scales	.25
Dr. Williams	1 speculen	.10
Dr. Hooper	1 coffelers	.50
Dr. Hooper	2 ceoping glasses	.25
* Dr. Hooper	1 lot vesals	.50
Dr. Hooper	contents	.25
Dr. Hooper	1 mortat and pessel	.50
Dr. Hooper	1 serring	.10
G.W. Harris	1 nipple glass	1.15
A.J. Teasley	1 pr tooth pullers	.50
W.H. Stuart	1 pr tooth pullers	.55
J.W. Walker	1 pr tooth pullers	.30
(p 329)		
Dr. Hooper	1 pr tooth pullers	.50
J.W. Shearon	1 bottle	/45
Dr. Hooper	2 Antimoney wine	.25
Dr. Hooper	3 " tanner	.30
Dr, Hooper	tincture cathardise	.10
T.J. Harris	1 bottle have surrep	.20
** Dr. Hooper	1 bottle guacum	.05
Dr. Williams	Lemon acid	.10
W.H. Morris	1 bottle pulverized comoney	.40
Dr. Williams	cathetin	.25
Dr. Hooper	Ipacoo	
Dr. Hooper	3 Bot Forovence	.30
Dr. Hooper	Potash & Oil Sassafras	.25
Dr. Williams	1 Bot Pepereen	.20
T.H. Hudgens	1 Bottle	.50
Dr. Hooper	1 Glass	.40
Dr. Hooper	1 Speculum	1.20
G.W. Harris	1 meg grater	.15
G.W. Harris	1 Jar	.15
Dr. Hooper	wine of ergate	.10
Dr. Hooper	Wine of ergate	.10
T.J. Harris	1 Bottle	.30
T.J. Harris	1 Bottle Rhubarb	.30
Dr. Hooper	1 Jar senna	.10
T.J. Harris	1 jar allows	.05
Jo Crantz (Krantz)	Wine Lobelia	
G.W. Harris	2 Bottles	.10
J.A. Nicholson	2 bottles	.10
Jo Crantz	Bottles &C	.15
T.J. Hudgens	1 medical case	12.50
Dr. Hooper	1 Overcoat	7.00
G.W. Harris	1 stable horse	68.00
* Dr. Hooper	1 Fill knife	.25
Morris, W.H.	Borox	.35

Notes Solvent

1 note on E.G. Hudgens, due July 14th 1860	750.00
1 Note on Wm. Hudgens, Due Aug. 3rd 1861	12.50
1 Note on Matthew Hunt due Aug 2nd for	3.00
1 Note on J.R. Binkley due 2nd ---1861	7.50
** Dr. Hooper — 1 lot violes	.10

Accounts Solvent

C.A. Hudgens due Jan. 1st 1863	1.50
Wm. Sterry due Jan. 1st 1862	7.00
Jesse Shearondue Jan. 1st 1862	8.00
Alexander Walker due Jan. 1st 1861	8.00
B.F. Smith due Jan. 1st 1862	6.00
Edmond Sullivan due Jan 1st 1862	5.50

(p 330) Accounts doubtful

Samuel Durham due Jan 1st 1862	5.00
B.B. Hudgens due Jan 1st 1862	5.75
Thomas Walker due Jan 1st 1862	.75
One order on E.G. Hudgens from Plummer Teasley solvent for due Jan . 1st 1867	8.00
Money on hand	19.20
T.E. Hudgens ac.	3.50

I , G.W. Maxey admr of B.L. Hudgens do solemnly swore that the foregoing is a true and perfect Inventory of all the goods and chattel rights and credits that have come to my hands possession or knowledge.

Witness my hand and seal Sept. 3rd 1866

G.W. Maxey Admr.

Sworn to before me,
G.W. McQuary Clk.

Inventory and account of note cash &C that have come into my hands of S.W. Adkison as administrator of B.L. Pack Dec.

One note on Mrs. Francis Russell for	140.00
One note on John Simpkins for	102.00
One account on receipt from Brummett	92.00
Elizabeth Packs note	59.15
Amount rec. from Mcquary & Fulghum	328.15

The foregiong contains a true and perfect Inventory of all the notes accounts, and effects of B.L. Pack Dec. that have come into my hands as administrator of said estate this Sept. 12th 1866.

S.W. Adkisson Admr.

Carried to page 340.

Settlement of W.H. Lovell, administrator of C.G. Lovell Decd. who was executor of B.L. Pack Dec. C.G. Lovell to the estate of B.L. Pack dec. Amount received from the estate 2778.06

Contra Interest		62.90
Money paid by C.G. Logell ,P.A. Miller proven acct.		20.00
May 10th 1859	J.N. Brown receipt	25.50
June 4	L.D. Pack	15.05
June 5 for Dud		1.40
June 6	Receipt Thomas M. Dunn	17.00
Oct. 9	Receipt Thomas M. Dunn	520.20
B.L. Pack	Note	8.00
J.A. Shearon	Proven acct.	1.75
(p 331)	Tax receipt 1859	8.67
J.F. Davis	proven acct.	9.00
G.W. McQuary	Receipt 1860	6.75
J.M. Larkin	proven acct.	10.00
J.T. Collier	Proven acct.	2.25
April 7th years support to widow		377.75
John Jones		2.75
May 20th 1860 Clothing for children		20.00

Leech & Dickson	proven acct.	25.70
Note on C.G. Lovell against estate		384.00
G.W. Perdue	Proven acct.	10.75
E.S. Exum	proven acct.	31.80
E.S. Exum	Note	20.20
J.H. Fulghum	proven acct.	57.98
J.H. Fulghum	note	26.59
Paid to B.D. Packs estate		172.85
		1769.94
Amount paid by W.G. S helton		321.99
		2091.93
Money due from Shelton estate		352.39
Mrs. Russell note		140.00
Simpkins note		102.00
Br ummett &C		95.50
Elizabeth Packs		59.15
		2840.97
An allowance to C.G. Lovell Executor of B.L. Pack Dec. is made of		75.00
Clerk for s ettlement (paid) Lovell		2.00

Settlement of C.C. Williams Exr. of Nancy G. Murphey Dec.

To amount of sale of pr operty		846.66
Cash on hand		43.53
Amount of notes and accounts		1428.10
Interest received		115.68

Contra

By E.L. Williams	Receipt Feb. 25th 1862	491.00
By E.L. Williams	May 5th 1863	196.00
By E.L. Williams	Feb. 29th 1864	110.00
By E.L. Williams	Feb. 1st 1862	561.02
By E.L. Williams	Aug 21st 1862	92.14
By E.L. Williams	March 10th 1864	43.05
By E.L. Williams	Jan. 9th 1863	101.98
By E.L. Williams	Feb. 27th 1866	332.00
H.C. Murphey	Recd Feb. 12th 1866	52.37
B.M. Alley	Rec'd. Feb. 12th 1866	52.37
(p 332)		
George Ellis recd.	Feb. 12th 1866	52.37
G.A. Nicholson	Recd. Feb. 12th 1866	52.37
T.W. Hunter $\frac{1}{4}$	Insolvent	37.50
G.W. Murphey	Insolvent	47.00
Talton Watson	Insolvent	15.00
R.J. Mallory	Proven acct.	25.00
W. Hawkins	for coffin	18.00
Shaw & Bro.	proven acct.	8.88
E.L. Williams	proven acct.	3.50
Paid Court Cost (Rec. A.J. Bright)		10.00
Allowance to Exr.		120.00
Balance for settlement		2.00
		2423.55

Amount of sale Notes &C	2433.97
Amount of credits	2423.55
Amount due on settlement	10.42

State of Tennessee)
Cheatham Cou nty) THOMAS PERDUE'S WILL

I, Thomas Perdue having been afflicted in body but of sound mind and perfect memory do make and Publish this my last will and Testament hereby revoking all others made by me at any time.
I, first desire that my Soul should return to the Great God who gave it and my body to be decently buried.

Then I direct and desire that all my just debts be paid and funeral Expenses be paid.

Then, I Give and bequeath to my beloved wife Mary M. Perdue all my monies notes and accounts, all my stock household and kitchen furniture and all my land. Everything belonging to my Estate Real and personal of every description during her natural life free for the use or dispose of in any way she may desire while living and to make any disposition of all she has at her death that she may desire.
I, also hereby appoint my beloved wife Mary M. Perdue Sole Executor of this my last Will and Testament in witness whereof I have hereunto Suscribed my name and affixed my seal this 18th day of November A.D. 1861.

Thomas Perdue X his mark.

Witness, James M. Dunn
William Deal

(p 333) B.H. Gibbs Will

I, Benjamin H. Gibbs of the County of Cheatham and State of Tennessee do make and Publish this my last Will and Testament hereby revoking and making void all former wills by me at any time made.
Item 1st. I direct that my Executor as soon after my death as possible pay all my just debts and funeral expenses out of my money I may die seized and posessed or may first come into his hands.
Item 2nd. I give and bequeath to my beloved wife Sarah B. Gibbs during her natural life or widowhood all my property both real and personal and mixed to govern Control and manage the same just as I would just as I would was I living provided my wife should marry she shall return ~~the services of Will~~ during her life and a equal share of the balance of my property with all my children but the same should she marry not to be liable for any of her future husbands contracts and upon the death of my wife I direct that the boy will and her share of my property return to my estate and be equally divided among all my children Share and Share alike. I hereby empower my wife Sarah B. Gibbs by the advice of JamesLenox Sr. and Benjamin C. Robertson to sell my part of the tract of land purchased from James Lenox or the home tract if she wished to do so or any surplus property that may be on hand during her widowhood.

In case the advice of James Lenox and B.C. Robertson could not be had from any cuase I wish the County Court to appoint two suitable persons to advise my wife.
Myself and R.B. Gibbs are in copartnership in wood buisness I wish him to carry out the same. If we have negroes hired at my death I want him to work them their time out and to sell the wood that may be on hand as though I was living. I dont wish the said R.B. Gibbs to account to court for my part of the procedds of the Sale of the said Wood but pay it to my wife and he is to have the services of my boy Will to help him sell the wood when my wife can spare him.. When she cannot Spare him I aothorize the said R.B. Gibbs to hire someone to help him to be paid out of my share Sale.
Item 3rd.
I also empower my wife to purchase Land on the same conditions she is aothorized to sell.
Item 4th
I aothorize and empower my brother R.B. Gibbs at the close of our partnership to sell all the partnership property and pay my part of theproceeds to

my wife.
Item 5th .
I also authorize my wife to sell all my interest in the lands of Hardy D. Miles Dec. Estate also wish my wife to have the proceeds of all my property for the purpose of educating & supporting my children until they become of age.
6th.
I nominate and appoint my wife Sarah B. Gibbs my sole Executor to this my last Will and Testament and that she be permitted to qualify as such executor without giving Security.
June 28th 1862.
B.H. Gibbs.
Signed Sealed and delivered in our presnets and in the presents of the Testator and that we witnessed the same at his request this 28th day of June 1860.
W.W. Williams
Alexander Boyt
G.W. Miles

It agreed by the undersigned that the dividing line between us of our tract of land we purchased from James Lenox shall commence at the stump of a fallen down beech on the South Bankoh of Cumberland River, a little below the said R.B. Gibbs corn cribs and rund so as to make a fore and after tree of a large white oak near the center of the bottom marked R.& B. Greene. Given under our hands and seals.
June 28th 1862
B.H. Gibbs
R.B. Gibbs
Attest.
W.W. Williams
Alexander Boyt.

Inventory and account of sale of the personal property of Mrs. Judith Sanders Decd.

Names of Purchasers	Property Sold	Amt.
Mrs. David Sanders	1 side saddle	4.00
Mrs. E. Edwards	2 chairs	.25
*Mrs. E. Edwards	1 spinning wheel	1.00
Mrs. E. Edwards	1 set sad irons	.20
Rhody Sanders	1 looking glass	.30
G.W. Harris	1 Folding table	5.00
Mrs. Rhoda Sanders	1 Loom	.15
Mrs. Rhody Sanders	1 cupboard	5.00
Wash Edwards	1 clock	5.95
Mrs. Wash Edwards	1 Bureau	10.00
Thos. Harris	1 Bed and clothing	9.00
Thos. Harris	1 Bad Stand	1.35
Wm. Eatherly	1 bed and contents	17.35
(p 335) Mrs. Edwards	2 do do	.25
Wm. Eatherly	1 Bedstead	.60
Benjamin Walker	1 bed quilt	1.50
Benjamin Walker	1 bed quilt	.75
Benjamin Walker	1 Bed quilt	1.80
Lucy Sanders	1 Blanket	1.50
G.W. Harris	1 Bed quilt	.80
G.W. Harris	1 Slay	.75
John Fry	1 cow and calf	30.00
		102.10

One note on Jas. W. Hunt due 1 day after date and dated Augt. 1, 1857 for $43.00

Cash on hand 24.00

169.10

State of Tennessee)
Cheathan County)

I do hereby certify that the within inventory and account of sales of the personal effects of Mrs. Judith Sanders is true to the best of my belief this 6th day of August 1866.

Williams S. Sanders, Judith Sanders
Exr.

1 Tract of land 106 acres sold for six dollars per acre	$636.00
1 Tract of land of 173¾ acres sold for four dollars per acre	699.00
	1335.00

State of Tennessee)
Cheatham County)

Personally appeared before me Henry Hunter Exr. of JohnnWalker Dec. and made oath in due form of law that the above is a true and perfect Inventory of all the real estate belonging to the estate of John Walker Dec.

Henry Hunter Exr.

Sworn to and suscribed before me this 3rd day of Oct. 1866

G.W McQuary, Clk.

(p 336) An Inventory of the personal property of the estate of Isaac Frazier Dec. sold on the 26th day of July 1866 at his late residence in Cheatham County after having advertised according to law.

Names	Articles	Amt.
J.M. Smith	1 No 8 Avery Plow	1.25
Henry Hunter	1 No 8 Avery Plow	2.60
Doub (colored)	1 No 13 Avery Plow	4.00
Doub "	" " " "	4.00
Wes Barton (colored)	1 lot old plows	1.70
John Mosely	1 log chain axe & plow	2.00
Doub (colored)	2 old and 2 hoes	1.00
Burgess Harris	1 Raw hide	.55
W.H. Stuart	1 good hoe	.80
Doub (colored)	1 good hoe	.85
Doub "	1 grub hoe	.60
William Williams	Briar hook and mow blade	.65
Doub Frazier (colored)	1 doubletree	.35
Henry Hunter	1 set plow gear	1.50
Doub(colored)	1 set plow & gear	1.50
Zac Shearon	Sive hoe & hames	.10
Doub(colored)	1 stand and trumpery	1.80
Ben Alley	3 chisels 1 auger	.50
Doub (colored)	1 draw knife	1.00
J.W. Perdue	1, 2- inch auger	.90
Will Williams	1 iron square	.50
Henry Hunter	1 role axe	1.60
Doub (colored)	1 colter	.10
Doub (colored)	1 hand saw	3.50
L.J. Perdue	6 1st choice hogs	60.00
George Harris	6 2nd choice hogs	55.00
John Hooper	7 3rd choice hogs	39.00
Joh Hooper	7, 4 Choice Hogs	32.00
Will Williams	1 Blue sow, 8 pigs	14.00
Will Williams	1 spotted sow & 8 pigs	11.50
George Harris	1 big hog	15.00
Wes Barton colored	1 sow and four pigs	8.25

Thos Bell	1 sow and five shoats	20.25
Don Price	1 red cow and calf	30.00
Roof Jackson	1 pided cow and calf	34.50
L.J. Perdue	1 dry cow	22.25
John Hooper	1 Bay Mule	154.00
Burgess Harris	1 brown mule	129.00
Pleas Chambliss	1 two horse wagon	83.50
Pleas Chambliss	1 set two horse harness	10;00
Don Fox	10 bu. wheat 1.40½	14.00
Thos. Bell	10 bu. wheat	14.00
(p 337)		
Thos. Bell	10 bu wheat @ 1.40½	14.00
Don Fox	5 bu. wheat	7.00
Henry Hunter	10bu. wheat	14.00
Thos. Bell	5 bu. wheat	7.00
G.W. Gossett	1 wheat Box	2.25
Robert Stewart	1 Fan Mill	11.00
John Shearon	1 scythe & Cradle & half bu.	.50
Coop Gupton	1 Sorghum mill	15.25
Will Shearon	3 barrel corn @ 3.50	10.50
Will Williams	10 bbl corn @ 3.00	30.00
Will Williams	10 bbl. corn @ 3.00	30.00
Will Williams	7 bbl. corn ;@ 3.35	23.45
Wes Barton(colored)	shelled corn rubbage	3.00
Henry Hunter	1 Ox Cart	5.00
Thos. Bell	1 Pr traces & single tree	.50
R.J. Watts	100 lbs bacon @ 23cts.	23.00
R.H. Weakley	111 lbs bacon @ 22½	24.97
D. Gupton	100 lbs bacon @ 22	22.00
D. Gupton	100 lbs. bacon @ 22	22.00
D. Gupton	Remainder @ 22	24.20
W.H. Stuart	1 barrel salt	6.00
W.H. Stuart	1 Barrel salt	5.00
Doub Frazier (colored)	2 land Triangles	.60
G.W Gossett	1 keg of tar	.40
Doub (colored)	2 empty barrels	.10
Doub (colored)	1 meet axe	.05
Howell Frazier	1 large kettle	5.00
Doub (colored)	1 small kettle	1.25
Doub (colored)	1 dinner pot	1.25
Doub (colored)	1 Tea Kettle	.55
G.A. Nicholson	1 large oven &C	1.50
Mrs. Doub (colored)	1 cook stove &C	
Thomas Miles	6 plates	.60
Mrs. L. Frazier	2 plates	.10
.G.W. Gossett	1 Pea dish	1.00
Mrs. W.J. Nicholson	1 tea pot sugar bowl	.70
Mrs. W.J. Nicholosn	1 cream mug	.10
Ben Davis	1 Pitcher	.70
Thos. Shores	1 bowl and jug	.25
James Walker	2 preserve dishes	.40
Henry Hunter	6 glass tumblers	1.25
Mrs. John Cain	2 glass tumblers	.10
Thos. Shores	1 candle stick	.25
James Bobbitt	1 preserve stand	.40
Jno. Nicholson	1 crock and bottles	.40
Mrs. Doub (col)	1 cook stove	1.50

Robert Batson(colored)	1 Tin bucket and jar	1.50
(p 338)		
Thos. Shores	2 dishes and tea pot	.25
W.H. Stuart	500 bundles oats @ $1\frac{1}{4}$	6.25
Thos. Council	500 " "	6.25
W.H. Stuart	500 " "	5.00
Thos. Bell	500 " " @ $1\frac{1}{4}$	6.25
Thos. Bell	500 " "	6.25
W.H. Stewart	400 " "	5.00
D.C. Perdue	Bed stead &C	25.00
D.C. Perdue	1 bed atead &C	30.00
Widow Carrigan	1 Lounge &C	10.00
Don Price	1 cupboard	10.00
Zac Shearon	1 Lot chains	3.00
Coop Gupton	1 folding table	9.00
Don Price	1 coffee mill	.25
Henry Frazier	1 Saber	.25
Wohn Duke	1 candle stand	.30
W.H. Stuart	1 sausage mill	3.05
James Walker	1 lot trumpery	.40
Zac Shearon	1 side saddle	13.50
Henry Frazier	1 Bead stead	3.00
John Duke	1 chest	2.50
Robert Stewart	1 Bureau	7.25
A.S. Blankenship	1 Trunk	.50
Mrs. W.J. Nicholson	1 small chest	3.75
D.C. Perdue	1 look glass &c	3.00
Robert Batson(colored)	1 Bureau	10.80
A.W Stewart	1 clock	1.00
John Kelly	1 shot gun	12.00
F.M. Jennett	1 slate	.25
L.P. Stewart	1 book	1.50
Ferney Evans	2books	1.25
F. King	1 book	.60
H. Pinson	1 book	1.00
F. King	1 lot books	.10
F. King	1 spinning wheel	7.00
D.C. Perdue	1 counterpin & quilt	4.00
W.H. Stuart	1 counterpin	4.25
Mrs. W.J. Nicholson	2 counterpins &socks	.50
D n Price	1 counterpin white	3.50
Doub (colored)	1 clock real	1.00
Thos. Bell	2 stove hammers	1.80
Pleas Chambliss	1 lot nails @ 11 c	2.20
C.D. Gupton	the vegatables in garden	16.00
(p 339)		
Thos. Bell	All apple fruit	5.00
W.J. Nicholson	The growing tobacco	27.00
Doub (colored)	All the sweet potatoes	1.00
G.A. Nicholson	1 Irish potato patch	2.75
Doub (colored)	13 gees @ 13cents	2.25
W.J. Nicholson	40 acres Paster	1.00

Property resold on 27

L. Fox	1 mans saddle	3.00
W.H. Stuart	1 childs crib	.15
L. Fox	1 pr steel yards	.25
Mrs. Frazier	1 smooth irons	.10

W.H. Stuart	1 pr & irons	.25
Burgess Harris	1 grind stone	.25
L. Fox	1 Iron hoop	.25
Thos. Bell	1 Bay Mare	55.20
Thos. Bell	1 Brown Mule	132.00
Burgess Harris	1 Riding Bible	.50
Burgess Harris	1 Mule	.10
Howell Frazier	1 Ring and steeple	1.00
		$1564.37
D.C. Perdue	1 note due Jan. 30 1861	3.37½
Doub(colored)	1 act. for pork	113.00
Doub (colored)	1 acct. for corn	21.00
Thos. Bell	for rent of land for 1867	126.00

Cooper Gupton
Corn sold at Isaac Fraziers Dec. for rent of land 1868 — 200.00
Good corn $1.03 Rubbage
H. Frazier $2.05 Bbl. good corn Thos. Jones — 137.25

The above is afull and perfect account of the sales and rent of land and all the property of Isaac Frazier Dec. this 27th day of Aug. 1866

G.W Harris Admr.

Sworn to before me this 30th Oct. 1866

G.W McQuary Clk..

AAn Inventory of all the personal property of Pheraby Allen Dec. sold Oct. 11, 1866.

4 head of hogs sold for	21.00
Two cows and calves	52.00
1 grindstone	2.10
1 bed pillows & bolster for	14.35
1 Bed pillows and bolsters	9.50
1 Bedstead	.70
1 Clock	12.50
Five bedqilts	4.90
2 chests	4.25
1 Table	.25
1 cupboard	3.10
(p 340)	
1 Looking glass sold for	1.05
1 coffee Mill	.25
1 Hammerr	.30
1 Pitcher	1.50
1 Smoothing iron	1.05
1 Safe	3.85
1 Stew Kettle	1.20
1 Skillet	.25
1 Tea Kettle	1.25
1 Pitcher Hooks & pot rack	.50
1 churn	1.50
1 Fat stand	.85
5 chairs	1.00
1 lot sundries	.25
1 axe & piggin	.35
1 Table	.30
1 Kettle	3.25
1 Shot gun	.50
1 Keg	.50
1 Auger	.25
	144.60

WILLIAM HUDGEN'S WILL

I, William Hudgens /of Cheatham County, and State of Tennessee being of sound mind and memory but remembering that all men must die, do see proper to make and publish the follwoing as my last will and testament hereby revoking and making void all other wills by me at any other time made. First it is my Will and desire that my Executor after my death first pay my burial expenses and all my just debts out of any money that may be on hand at my death or may first come into my hands.

2nd.

I will to my beloved wife Ann P/Hudgens during her natural life or widowhood the House, gardens, orchard and so much of my lands as may be necessary for support, one horse, one yoke of oxex and cart and log chains, one milch cow and calf, one sow and pigs and six shoats and such household and kitchen furniture as may be necessary for her to keep house with, also some plough & gear (p 341) and my negro man Jesse, all to be under control of my Executor, one chopping axe, one grubbing hoe, one weeding hoe, all her own choice, and at her death to be disposed of as hereinafter named.

3rd.. I will to my granddaughter Lucy Ann Conley, one sixth of all my estate including lands and other effects that may be in the hands of my Executor at the death of my wife.

4th I will to my son Elijah Hudgens the same as I have to my grand daughter Lucy A. Conley and should he die without children he can will it to any of h his brothers or sisters but in default of children and will then to be equally divided between his brothers and sisters and their represenatives.

5th. I will to my son C.A. Hudgens the same amount that I have my grand daughter and son above named.

6th. It is my wish to pay my son T.E. Hudgens for his care of me extra from the above named heirs and I will to him to be laid off by my Executor after my death five acres of land in such form as my son T.E. Hudgens may wish so as to include his house and gardens and that he have the use of the oxen and cart which I have willed to my wife at any time he may want them when not in her use. And that he have free of any rent any of the land not used by my wife during her life.

7th.

I will to my daughter Martha A.R. Sterry the same that I Hvae to my granddaughter L.A. Conley, Elijah and C.A. Hudgens but to be under her own control and not liable of the debts, contracts or control of her present or any future husband and at her death to go to the children of her body.

8th.

As with my son T.E. Hudgens I wish to my daughter Elizabeth I Hudgens something extra for her care of me. I will to her besides what I have willed to my grand daughter L.A. Conley and E & C.A. Hudgens one bedstead, bed and furniture of her own selection, one wardrobe and saddle and bridle, and it is my will that she live at home at or with her mother during her mothers life, unless she marry, and should she die without child or children she may will what I will to her any of her brothers or sisters but in default of any child or children or will, then it is to be divided Equally between her brothers or sisters or their represenatives.

I appoint my friend R.H. Alley, my Executor to carry out and execute the provisions of this my last Will and that after my death he have laid off hands besides what is named in the will section of this my will one years provisions for my wife and that he sell all the perishable property not willed away by me on such time and terms as he may think best and rent such of my lands as are not used by my wife and son T.E. Hudgens as he may think best and hire out my negro man Sam during my wife's lifetime giving either of my sons, preference to hire him and to divide annually his hire and any rent that may arise from the land equally amongst my children and at the death of my wife Ann P. Hudgens to sell my lands and negroes and such other perishable willed (p 342) to my wife as may be on hand at such time and on such terms as he may think best but should he think best not sell, to rent and hire out until he may think proper to sell and divide the proceeds amongst my children as directed in the foregoing Will. Signed and sealed in our presents and witnessed by his requests.

November 5th 1863

WilliamsHudgens (seal)

ATTEST

F.A.Miles

Mathew Hunt

An Inventory of the personal Estate of W.B. Evans Decd. that come into the hands of W.H. Stuart Admr. sold 14th Sept. 1866

1 note on J.S. Majors due Dec. 15th 1859	$118.42
* 1 note on J.W. Gupton due 30th May 1860	1230
1 note on R.S. Evans due 11th Feb. 1861	10.10
with credit $1.20 given 7th Jan. 1861	
1 note on J. Gupton Due 1st Feb. 1859	15.00
1 note on J.B. Williams due 25th Apr. 1859	10.00
1 order on J.H. Mayo for	3.00
made by Griff Lankford Aug. 26. 1860 with a credit for	2.55
1 Acct. Harris Williams due 1859	5.00
1 acct. Elias Johnston due 1859	5.00
1 acct. N.W.Sanders due 1859	3.50
1 acct. Abner Gupton due 1859	10.00
1 note J.W. Gupton Jan. 4th 1861	2.75

State of Tennessee)

Cheatham County)

Personally apppared before me G.W. McQuary Clerk of the County Court of said County Wm. H. Stuart and made oath in due form of law that the above contains a true and perfect inventory of the personal estate of W.B. Evans Dec.

Wm. H. Stuart

Sworn to and suscribed before me Dec. 8th 1866

G.W. McQuary Clk.
Cheatham County Court

(p 343) An Inventory of the Personal Estate of F.S. Evans Dec. Sold by Wm.H. Stuart Admr on the 14th of September 1866,

1 sorrel horse	Robert Weakley	90.00
1 Bridle	James W. Stuart	1.00
1 saddle and blankét	Jas. B. Stuart	12.00
1 old horse	Curtis Bush	22.50
1 Bridle	Curtis Bush	.05
5 1st choice hogs	George Perdue	38.50
3 2nd choice hogs		18.00
6 3rd choice hogs		21.00
1 lot old Corn	Curtis Bush	5.25
4 pigs in pen	George Perdue	8.00
500 bundles oats	J.W. Shearon	6.25
300 bundles oats	J.W. SHearon	5.25
1 lot quininebottles	Fanny Evans	.60
1 lot Quinine bottles	Thos. Bell	.50
1 lot jars	G.W. Maxey	.10

1 box vials	Dr. Smith	.10
1 pr saddle bags	Johnathan Simpkins	1.00
1 bottle Alkahall	Dr. Hooper	1.00
1 Bottle Magnetia	J.B. Walton	.40
1 lot bottles &C	H.P. Pool	.25
1 Jar Borax	Dr. Hooper	.50
1 Bowl &C	Dr. Smith	.50
1 Bowl	G.W. Warren	.70
1 medicine on bottom shelf	Dr. Smith	1.00
1 neset on bottom shelf	Dr. Smith	.25
1 neset " " "	Dr. Smith	.50
1 neset " " "	Dr. Smith	.70
1 " " " "	" "	1.00
1 " " " "	" "	1.00
1 " " " "	Dr. Hooper	1.30
1 medicine case	Dr. Smith	19.75
1 Bureau with glass	Thomas Bell	25.00
1 Pan & Coffee pot	Elizabeth Watt	.20
1 Pitcher	Elizabeth Watt	.65
1 molases stand	Thomas Shores	.50
5 tumblers	Moody Page	.50
3 Saucers & 5 cups	Curtis Bush	.10
1 Bowl	Curtis Bush	.05
1 set knives & forks	G.W. Maxey	1.00
2 sets of spoons	Curtis Bush	.80
(p344)		
1 Desk	Henry Maxey	.15
1 set plates	Delpha Bush	.40
1 Desk	Elizabeth Watt	.35
1 folding tablw	Burgess Harris	5.50
1 Water stand	Harriett Wall	.60
1 Knight mug	Thomas Bell	.50
1 Feather bed	Elizabeth Watt	23.50
1 Lot cotton	B.J. Barnes	2.75
1 Dema john	David Evans	2.25
1 Little Table	Faney Evans	3.00
1 Bureau	Burgess Harris	25.00
1 Trunk	David Evans	2.75
1 Sugar Chest	David Evans	5.25
2 razors & Straps	T.D. Stuart	1.75
1 Bed quilt	Elizabeth Watt	5.75
1 counter pin	B.W. Binkley	11.00
1 counterpin	B.W. Binkley	8.00
1 Bed Quilt	B.W. Binkley	2.25
1 Bed Quilt	Faney Evans	.75
1 Bed Quilt	Faney Evans	.75
1 bolster slip	B.W. Braley	.10
2 Bolster slips	B.W. Braley	.80
2 bolster slips	B.W. Braley	.35
1 Towel	Elizabeth Watt	.10
1 survey Book	F.A. Harris	.50
1 medical book	B.W. Bradley	.75
2 medical book	Dr. Williams	.80
James Bobbitt	1 cow and calf	16.00

2 medical books	J.B. Walton	1.00
2 medical books	J.B. Walton	1.00
1 medical book	J.B. Walton	1.60
1 medical book	Jo Justice	.50
2 medical books	Dr. Williams	.50
2 medical books	J.B. Walton	1.00
2 medical books	J.B. Walton	1.80
2medical books	J.B. Walton	4.50
2 medical books	Jo Justice	2.00
1 lot surgical Instrument	Dr. Perdue	11.50
1 lot teeth Instrument	Dr. Williams	5.00
1 walking cane	Faney Evans	1.60
1 Bottle Harts horn	J.W. Stuart	.75
1 lamp	Moody Page	1.00
1 Water &C	Jöhnerthan Simpkins	1.00
1 sugar bowl	R. Coleman	.20
Lantern	Dr. Hooper	.30
(p 345)		
1 Bot & Oil can	Faney Evans	.25
1 Oil can	Moody Page	.50
1 Black Brush	J.W. Shearon	.10
1 Decanter	Faney Evans	.60
1 morter &C	Dr. Williams	1.25
1 lot medicine	Dr. Hooper	.25
1 steth scope	Dr. Hooper	.25
1 lot medacine	Dr. Hooper	1.00
1 lot medicine	Dr. S ith	1.00
1 lot Medicine	Dr. Smith	1.25
1 " "	Dr. Smith	.10
1 " "	Dr. Smith	.10
2Jares &C	Dr. Hooper	.25
1 Lot medacine	Dr. Smith	.10
1 Lot medicine	Dr. Smith	.10
1 " "	Dr. Hooper	.30
1 " "	Dr. Smith	.25
1 " "	Faney Evans	.20
1 Medacine Glass	Dr. Williams	.10
1 lot medacine	Dr. Smith	.10
1 Scope	Dr. Williams	.20
1 lot medacine	Dr. Hooper	1.50
1 lot medicine	Dr. Smith	.10
1 lot medacine-	Faney Evans	.15
1 lot medicine	Dr. Hooper	.25
1 lot bottles	Billy Shearon	.10
1 whiskey cock	Thomas Bell	.25
1 Book Case	T.C. Stuart	8.50
1 pr fire dogs	W. Wall	1.25
5 chairs	James Bobbitt	3.75
1 Avery Plow	George Perdue	1.35
1 Hoe	Billie Shearon	.10
1 Grub Hoe	Hiram Sanders	.35
1 Axe	W. Wall	.15
1 McRunels plow	Gid Harris	3.50
1 par plow gear	John Farmey(Farmer)	2.00
1 tub	Curtis Bush	1.25
1 big pot	Curtis Bush	1.25
1 lot of instruments	J.B. Walton	3.00

1 little pot	Polly Stuart	.50
1 skillet	D.G. Teasley	.25
1 Tea kettle	Curtis Bush	.20
1 skillet	Curtis Bush	.50
4 barrels and basket	W.H. Plaster	.65
1 coffee mill	Virge A. Stuart	.65
1 Tin Bucket	Thomas Bell	.70
1 churn	B.F. Walker	1.00
(p 346)		
1 milk piggin	B.F. Walker	.70
1 flat Iron	Burgess Harris	.45
1 wash board	Jo Shearon	.35
1 Lot bacon	Jesse Simmons	30.10
1 lot bacon	Curtis Bush	10.36
1 lot bacon	David Evans	4.00
1 lot bacon	James W. Stewart	4.00
1 Barrélsalt	David Evans	3.30
1 Barrel 1 rd	David Evans	5.57
1 barrel meal	Curtis Bush	.10
1 lot onions	G.W. Harris	.30
1 Cable	L.J. Perdue	.30
1 Spinning wheel	Delpha Bush	4.00
1 pr cotton cards	Delpha Bush	.40
15 chickens	Curtis Bush	3.00
1 cotton patch	Curtis Bush	1.00
1 sweet potato patch	Curtis Bush	5.60
1 Bookcase	David Evans	3.00
1 Watch	David Evans	10.25
1 patch of corn	Curtis Bush	11.00
1 Lot journals	Dr. Hooper	.10
1 Bucket	Burgess Harris	.05
1 dipper	Curtis Bush	.10
1 Lock	V.A. Stuart	.10
5 barrels, 2 bu. corn	W.H. Stuart	12.17
50½ Bu. corn	Z. Shearon	23.44
50½ Bu. corn	Sterling Shearon	23.44
11 Bu. corn	Curtis Bush	4.65

A listtof notes and come into my hands as Admr. of the estate of Dr. F.S. Evans Dec.

Solvent

1 note on S. Bobbitt due		
1 acct. on same for $3.00 due Jan. 1st	1867	3.00
1 acct. on Jon Simpkins due 1st Jan.	1863	10.00
1 acct. on Wash Smith " " "	1867	.50
1 acct on S. Shearon " " "	1867	8.25
1 act. on Mrs. M. Stewart due 1st Jan	1867	1.00
1 acct. on Jesse Shearon " "	1865	1.00
1 acct on Jesse Shearon	1866	12.00
1 acct. H. Sanders	1866	3.15
1 W.H. Stuart	1867	1.00
1 acct. on Jo Shearon " " "	1867	16.50
1 acct. on W.H. Stuart	1865	12.00
1 acct on Jas. S. Stewart	1867	47.00
1 acct. on Mrs. S. Sanders	1866	2.00
(p 347)		
1 acct. on Jesse Shearon due Jan 1st	1863	1.00
1 acct. on Mrs. E. Shearon $100.00 due	1864	17.00

Due $4.00 Due 1866	22.00
1 acct. on Thos. Spores due Jan. 1867	4.00
1 acct on Sims Smith due Jan. 1867	.50
1 acct. Mrs. Mary Smith " 1864	1.50
1 acct. R. Stewart " 1867	4.00
1 acct. Mrs. Sally Smith # 1867	7.00
1 acct Ben Stewart " 1867	4.00
1 acct. Robert Jones " 1867	15.00
1 acct A. Hunter " 1866	4.00
1 acct. Wm. Harris 1864	3.00
1 acct. B.J. Barnes 1867	5.00
1 acct Jim Bobbitt 1867	3.00
1 Mrs Nancy Barton 1865	1.00
1 acct. on Miss Scott Clifton 1866	4.00
1 acct. Miss Ann Clifton 1865	2.00
1 acct. E.K. Clifton 1865	5.00
1 acct. D.E. & Lem Barton 1st Jan. 1865	30.00
Due Jn. 1866 56.60	85.50
Amt. forwarded 290.90	
1 acct. on Miss S. Bearden Due Jan. 1867	10.00
1 acct. Mrs. Sarah Bobbitt 1866	10.00
1 act on Thos. Harris 1867	14.00
1 act G.W. Harris $4.00 due Jan. 1865 25.00 due Ja. 1867 cr. by 1.50	
Jan. 1867 35.00	35.00
1 act. on Delila Hudgens Due Jan 1st 1867	5.00
1 act. Miss Sarah Harrison due Jan 1st 1865	7.00
1 act. John Hand $6.00 due Jan. 1863 $1.50 due Jan. 1865 $2.00	
due Jan. 1866 and $31.00 due Jan 1866 in all	41.00
1 act on Mrs. Mary Hunter due Jan. 1866	14.00
1 act Jo Krantz due Jan. 1866	8.00
1 act Thos. Justice due Jan. 1867	1.50
1 act due Jan 1867 Tom Maxey	.50
1 act H.W. Miles due Jan. 1867	13.00
1 acct. W. Howard Miles due Jan 1867	1.50
1 acct. H. Mxaey for	14.00
1 acct. Sarah Magers due Jan. 1865	1.00
1 acct. Mrs Amanda Majors due Jan. 1866	12.00
1 acct. T.J. Miles due Jan 1863	3.00
and Jan. 1866 $10.00	13.00
1 act George Maxey due Jan. 1867	1.00
1 acct S. Morris due Ja. 1866	3.00
1 acct. Jim Mosely due Jan. 1862	1.00
1 acct Thos. Miles due Jan. 1864	1.50
1 acct Jno. Gupton due Jan. 1867	34.00
1 acct. Wm. Graham due Jan. 1867	12.00
1 acct Cooper Gupton due Jan. 1867	1.50
1 acct. due Jan 1866	15.00
(p 348)	
One acct on Calvin Gupton due Jan 1865	26.00
One acct on Jno Fambrough Due Jan. 1867	13.00
One acct. on Howel Frazier due Jan 1867	4.00
One acct. T. Fowler due Jan. 1867	29.00
One act. H. Felts due Jan. 1866	1.00
One acct. Isaac Frazier due Jan 1866	87.00
Forwarded $738.90	
One acct. Wash Owen due Jan. 1866	5.00
One Acct B. Pool due Jan. 1866	1.50

One Act. W.H. Pace due Jan 1867	5.00
One act Wash Wall, " " "	5.75
One Act. B.F. Walker " " " 1865	9.00
1866	100.00
1867	11.75
And in all	21.75
One acct on Jo J. Williams 1864	2.00
One acct. W.H. Plaster Jan. 1867 $2.50	15.50
	17.50
One Act on Jas Walker due Jan. 1866	14.00
and Jan 1867	5.50
In all	19.50
One acct on JohnnTeasley due Jan. 1867	8.00
One act. on W.D. Wall due Jan. 1866	10.50
and Jan. 1867	1.00
	11.00
One act. on Jno. Edwards due Jan. 1864	5.00
One Act. on W. Eatherly due Jan. 165	3.00
and Jan. 1866	2.00
In all	5.00
One act. on James Read due Jan. 1866	1.50
One Act. on Lucinda Teasley Jan. 1866	5.00
One act. H.D. Edwards Jan. 1867	3.00
One Act. on Thos. Edwards Jan. 1867	57.00
One act. on Mrs. E. Read 1867	4.00
One act Green Nicholson 1866	2.00
One act Greem Nicholson Sr. Jan 1867	2.50
One act H. Nicholson Jan 1865	8.00
and Jan. 1866	4.00
In All	12.00
1 note on G.H. Shearon 26th Feb. 1866	12.00
1 note on H.W. Miles due May 8, 1866	17.20
1 note on Thos. C. Jones for	37.50
Due 16th Feb. 1866 with a cr. of	20.00
the 7th July 1866	
1 note on Alsey Jones Due 7th May 1866	18.00
1 note on W.W. Hudgens Due 3rd April 1866	17.00
1 note on Thos. Justice for	30.00
due 7th March 1866 with a cr. of	10.00
the 9th of May 1866	20.00
1 note on Delila Hudgens Due Jan. 2nd 1866	40.00
1 note on S. Bobbitt Due Feb. 14, 1866	3.00
One note on D.E. Barton for	87.00
Due Feb. 24th 1864 with a cr. of	50.00
July 1st 1864	37.00
Carried Forward $1,115.60	$1115.60
One act on Mrs. Martha Williams Due Jan. 1863	12.00
One act. on Jno. B. Taylor Due Jan. 1864	34.00
One act. Guss Sheraon Due Jan. 1867	2.00
Tennessee Money found on hand	12.00
Carried Fo rward	$1175.60

(p 349) A list of the doubtful claims

One note on John Batts Due 1st Jan. 1864	30.00
One note on Augustus Bearden due 28th Dec. 1865	12.35
One note on James Bearden due 28th Dec. 1866	12.00

One note on Jno. B. Cain Due Jan. 1864	28.00
One note on A. Cain due 8th Feb. 1864	31.00
One note on Shepherd due 17th Jan. 1866	15.00
One note on Newton Due 4th Nov. 1865	5.00
One note on Abner Hunter Due 8th Feb. 1864	42.00
One note on B.B. Hudgens Due 10th Mch. 1866	24.50
One note Isaac Hollis for $18.00	18.00
Due 12th Jan. 1861 with a credit of	7.00
Due 16th Jan. 1861	11.00
One note on W.H.H. Gent Due 25th Jan 1866	15.05
One note on R.T. Gupton guardain of James Gupton Due Jan. 25, 1865	12.05
1 note on Jesse D. Nicholson due 28th Apr. 1866	30.00
1 Note on Wm. G. Marrah due April 28th 1866	31.50
1 note on Isaac Hollis for	35.76
1 Note on Jo Pool due 1st Jan 1863	3.00
1 note on James Fielder due 1st Jan 1864	.50
1 Note on P.H. Frazier due 1st Jan 1864	2.50
1 note on Nis Fambrough due 1st Jan 1864	4.50
1 note on Richard Fambrough due 1st Jan 1866	4.00
1 noteon M. Fambrough due Jan 1864	3.00
1 note on James H. Majors due Jan 1864	2.00
1 noteon Nick Gupton due Jan 1864	2.00
1 note on A?Galloway due Jan 1864	5.00
Carried forward $355.16	
1 act. on Polly Swift due Jan. 1863	2.00
1 act on Jo Powell due Jan. 1864	12.00
1 act on A. Eatherly due Jan. 1867	5.00
1 act on M. Felts due Jan. 1866	9.00
1 acct. on T.H. Eatherly due Jan. 1867	35.00
1 note on Geo. Eleazir Due Jan. 1867	2.00
1 note on Isaac Eatherly Due Jan. 1865	2.00
1 note on Plummer Teasley Due Jan. 1865	15.00
1 note on D. McCarley Due Jan. 1863	18.00
with a cr. of $2.75, $10.00 the 1st Jan. 1864	25.35
1 note on T.M. Williams Due Jan. 1863	12.00
1 account on same Due Jan. 1863	11.50
1 acct. on Jno. Smith $ 3.50 due Jan. 1861 and $4.00 due Jan. 167	7.50
1 acct. on N. Sanders due Jan. 1867	14.00
1 acct. Samuel McDaniel due Jan. 1863 for $30.00 and Jan. 165 $3.00 and Jan. /67 $4.00	43.00
1 account on R.H. Weakley due Jan. 1863 $14.00 Jan/64 $12.00	26.00
1 acct. on Jno Sanders Jr. Due Jan 1867	2.00
(p 350)	
L acct. on Wm. Whitehead Due Jan. 1862	12.50
and Jan. 1867	5.00
1 acct. on Henning Williams due Jan. 1866	3.00
1 acct. on Rebecca Williams due Jan. 1864	15.00
1 accountn R. Williams due Jan. 1867	2.00
1 acct. Wash Williams due Jan. 1864	25.00
1 acct. Wm/ Page due Jan. 1865	6.00
1 acct. Robert Perdue due Jan. 1863 $19.00 and Jan. 1866 $22.00 and Jan. 1867 $2.00 In all	43.00
1 account on Susan Walker due Jan. /65	12.00
1 acct. L.Perdue due /66 30.00 and Jan. /67 $15.00 In all	35.00
1 account on J. Pool due Jan. 1864	3.00
Amt. Forward	738.41

1 acct on Jno H„mphrey Due Jan. 1865	10.00
1 acct. on Wm. H. Miles due Jan. 1863 and $5.00 due Jan. 1867	23.00
1 acct. on Martha Langford due Jan. 1864	18.00
1 acct. on Tennie Langford due Jan. 1864	31.00
1 acct. on W.H.H. Gent due Jan. 1864	6.00
1 acct. on Delila Miles due Jan. 1866	8.00
1 acct. on Polly Miles due Jan. 1867	2.00
1 acct. on S.P. Knox due Jan. 1866	17.00
1 acct. on Mrs. Johnson due Jan. 1865 #13 and Jan. 1866 $5.00	20.00
1 acct. on Abner Hunter due Jan. 1865 $20.00 and Jan. 1866 $10.00	30.00
1 acct on Jno. Hunter due Jan. 1864	1.00
1 acct. on W.K. Hollis due Jan. 1863$2.00 and 1865 $16.00 In all	18.00
1 acct on J. Hall Due Jan. 1866	5.00
1 acct. on Jonathan Hollis due Jan. 1861 $8.00 Jan. 1868 $25.00	33.00
1 acct. on E. Humphries due Jan. 1864	5.00
1 acct. on B.F. King due Jan. 1853	.15
1 acct. on Thos. Logan due Jan. 1865	4.00
1 acct. B.B. Hudgens due Jan. 1867	24.00
1 acct. Sam Durham due Jan. 1866 $18.00 also Jan.,1867 $18.50	36.50
1 acct. on James Cain due Jan. 1867	4.00
1 acct. Wm. Cothran Due Jan. 1865	3.00
1 acct. Wm. Druney Due Jan. 1866	2.00
1 acct. on John Blair due Jan. 1867	12.00
1 acct. Andrew Cain due Jan. 1865	13.00
1 acct. Polly Batts Due Jan. 1865	4.00
1 acct. Rebecca Coleman Due Jan. 1862	5.00
1 acct. Jno. Cain Jr. Due Jan. 1864 $10.00 and Jan /66 $14.00	24.00
1 acct. on Jane Batts Due Jan. 1865	13.00
1 acct. Jane Coleman Due Jan. 1863	1.00
1 acct. J.T. Batts Due Jan 1861	3.00
1 acct. on W. Blanton due Jan. 1866	.15
(p 351) Amount Forward	$1113.71
1 acct on B.F. Read Due Ja. /67	27.00
1 acct on Jno Pool Due Jan. 1863	2.00
1 acct. on W.J. Nicholson due Jan. /66 $17.00 and Jan. /67 $8.00	25.00
1 acct. on W. Smith due Jan. 1863	5.00
1 acct. on A. Perdue due Jan. /65	27.00
1 acct. Jno Nicholson due Jan. /63 $10 and Jan. /65 $10 making	20.00
1 acct. on Miss Lou Pace Due Jan 1865	18.00
1 acct. on W. Roberson due Jan. /66 $15 and Jan. /67 $7, making	22.00
1 acct. on Geo. Rasberry due Jan. 1865	3.00
1 acct. on Elizabeth Cain due Jan. /64	11.50
1 acct. on Wyatt Shearon due Jan. /67	40.00
1 acct. on M. Stewart Due Jan. /66 $30.00 and Jan. /67 $6	36.00
1 acct. on M. Nicholson due Jan. .62	6.00
1 acct. on Jno. Sanders due Jan. .67	7.50
1 acct. Peep Stuart due Jan. /67	6.00
1 acct. on Claborne Sanders due Jan. /64 $16, also Jan. /65 $10 also Jan /66 $2.00 In all	28.00
1 acct. on Jonothan Sanders Due Jan. /67	4.00
1 acct. Henry Pace due Jan. /63 /65	4.00
1 acct. Tom Walker due Jan .65	24.00
1 acct. W.D. Shearon due Jan. /67	34.00
1 acct. Wash Stuart due Jan. /63	3.00
1 acct. Billy Sib Stuart due Jan. /65	7.00
1 acct. Jno. Shelby due Jan. /65	4.00
1 acct. H. Pool due Jan. /64	10.00
1 acct. John P. Walker due Jan. /64	5.00

1 acct. David Sanders due Jan. .65	11.00
also Jan. /66 $11.08. In all	22.08
1 acct. E.G. Hudgens due Jan. 1865	24.00
1 acct. E.G. Hudgens due Jan. .66	25.00
Amount forward	$1551.79
1 acct on Gid Nicholson due Jan. 1867	25.00
1 acct. on Josephins Bradley due Jan. 1867	2.00
1 note on D.L. Stuart 29th Sept. /66	12.75

A list of colored claims

1 claim Enice due Jan /67	4.00
1 acct. on Carre; Walker due Jan. /67	32.00
1 acct. on Hannah Teasley due Jan. .67	14.00
1 acct. on Tuck Stewart due Jan. /67	4.00
1 acct. David Hunter due Jan. /66	3.00
1 acct. John Walker due Jan. /66	4.50
1 acct. on Big Hannah Teasley due Jan. /66	2.00
1 acct. on Polly Shearon due Jan. /67	.50
1 acct. on Mose Hudgens due Jan. /67	1.00
1 acct. on Green Hell due Jan. .67	5.50
1 acct. Dick Edwards due Jan. /67	11.00
Card Forward	$1697.87

State of Tennessee)
Cheatham County)

Personally appeared before me G.W. McQuary Clerk of the County Court of said County Wm. H. Stuart and made oath in due form of law that the above contains a true and perfect Inventory of the personal estate of F.S. Evans Dec.

Wm. H. Stuart, Adm.
Sworn to and suscribed before me 8th of Dec. 1866
G.W. McQuary, Clk.

Inventory and account of sale of the persinal effects of James Frazier Dec. sold by G.W. Gossett admr. August 28th 1866.

1 lot ploughs	John T. Mosely	.50
1 looking glass	James Frazier	.25
1 Dressing table	James Frazier	1.00
1 Bed stead	Rick Williams	.75
1 clock	Jane Frazier	2.00
1 Fan Mill	Jane Frazier	10.00
50 lbs bacon @ 18c	A.Bearden	9.00
50 lbs bacon @ 15c	Mrs. Cain	7.50
50 lbs bacon "	G.W. Harris	7.50
50 lbs bacon @ 17c	G.W. Harris	8.50
1 Sow	James Frazier	2.00
1 sow	James Frazier	2.00
1 Sow	James Frazier	3.00
5 hogs	Thomas Council	30.00
5 shoats	Rick Williams	12.00
6 shoats	Burgess Harris	12.00
1 sow and oigs	Rick Williams	5.00
1 sow and pigs	J.W. Smith	5.00
1 sow and pigs	J.W. Smith	3.00
5 sheep	Jane Frazier	5.00
5 sheep	Thos. Bell	7.50
Money on hand Green backs		221.00
Confederate		421.00

A list of Notes and Accounts .

1 note & interest on	J.S. Majors	1623.12
1 note and interest	B.F. Pace	94.59
1 note & interest	D.A. Hunter	35.10
1 note & interest J.D. Nicholson		19.91
(p 353)	Doubtful claims	
1 note and interest on	R.J. Mallory	108.02
1 note and interest	Sam Durham	6.80
1 note and interest on	R.H. Weakley	12.25
1 note and interest on	G.R. Harris	9.50
1 note and interest	R.T. Gupton	30.70
Tennessee Money Southern		155.00

I, G.W. Gossett, Admr. of James Frazier Dec. do solemnly swear that the foregoing is a true and perfect Inventory of the effects that have come into my hands as administrator of Jas. Frazier Dec. this Nov. 20th 1866.
G.W. Gossett Admr.

Account of Sale of the erishable property of Wm. Hudgens Dec. sold by me Jan. 2nd 1864.

W. Owens	2 old hoes	.25
T.E. Hudgens	1 Briar Hook	.50
A.E. Suell	1 plough	2.50
W. Sterry	1 pr hames and traces	.30
W. Sterry	1 bull tongue plow	.50
W. Sterry	1 single tree and hames	.05
Jas. Walker	1 pt hubs	.75
T.E. Hudgens	1 set cutting knives	1.00
E.J. Hudgens	1 sorrel mare	25.00
T.E. Hddgens	1 sorrel horse	117.00
J.J. Wilson	1 pr oxen	28.00
J.J. Bradley	1 Bull	6.10
Elijah Hudgens	1 black cow	16.50
Wm. Sterry	1 blue heifer	3.00
G.W. Hunt	2 cow hydes	3.00
D.A. Hooper	1 clock	.25
		203.70
Cash on hand		90.00
Note on J. Sexton when paid		7.00
Amount recd. on sale of tobacco		204.23

R.H. Alley Exr.

(p 354) Inventory of the personal Estate of J.H. Mxaey Decd. Oct. 22nd 1866.

1 note anddue 1st Jan. 1860 J.W. Stack		2.50
1 note due 15th Dec. 1860	John Basford	43.50
1 receipt Due 25th Dec. 1861	J.W. Shaw	100.00
		146.00

State of Tennessee)
Cheatham County)

Personally appeared before me G.W. McQuary Clerk of the County Court of said County. Henry Maxey Admr. of the estate of J.H. Maxey Dec. and made oath in the form of law that the above is a true and perfect Inventory of the personal estate of J.H. Maxey Decd.
Henry Maxey Admr.
Sworn to before me 3rd day of Dec. 1867.
G.W McQuary, Clk.

A list of the Property sold at E. Bobo's Dec. 6th day of Dec. 1866

1 skillet and lid	Mary Drake	1.15
1 pot	Mary Drake	.40
1 pot racks and hooks	E.E. Cage	.60
1 spinning wheel	Louisa Drake	2.00
1 Tray and sifter	Mary Drake	.30
1 Table	E.E. Cage	.20
1 plow no. 8	Wm. McGwhee	2.00
1 plow	E. Fizer	.10
3 Bulltongs	J. Gray	.50
2 weeding hoes	J. Tucker	.10
3 hoes	Jo Rosson	.25
1 cart	A.D. Cage	5.00
1 log chain	W.G. Pickering	2.00
1 yoke of oxen	J. Reeks	69.00
1 brown mare	Peter Williams	100.00
1 brown colt	A. Fizer	60.00
1 lot tobacco per hhd.	C. Langford	6.75
1 plow and gear	Jo Gray	.10
1 lot oats 500 Bu.	Jo Gray	2.75
1 lot oats 500 bu.	T.H. Cagle	2,25
1 lot oats	E. Rawson(Rosson)	2.00
1 lot corn 5 bbl. 10 bu.	J. Gray	3.05
1 lot corn 5 bbl.	J. Gray	3.25
1 lot corn	S.W. Smith	3.30
1 lot corn	J.C. Woodson	3.25
1 lot corn balance	P. William	3.00
1 lot irons		
(p 355)		
One scything cradle	G. Drake	1.50
1 Half Bu.		.05
6 cutting knives	P.T. Williams	1.00

State of Tennessee)
Cheatham County)

Personally appeared before me G.W. McQuary, Clerk of the County Court of said County. E.W. Nolen and made oath in due form of law that the above contains a true and perfect inventory of the personal estate of Elizabeth Bobo Dec.

E.M. Nolen, Admr.
Sworn to before me and suscribed February 4th 1867.
G.W. McQuary, Clk.

Settlement of Sterling Walker Executor of T.W. Harris, Dec. of the estate of James Hudgins Dec. $10645.50

To amount of Inventory, notes cash on hand and amount of sales.

To amount paid Daniel Hudgens, One receipt		184.00
One receipt paid Daniel Hudgens		80.00
One receipt "	Daniel Hudgens	500.00
One receipt "	Daniel Hudgens	66.95
One receipt "	" "	50.00
One receipt "	" "	100.00
One receipt "	" "	10a.00
One receipt "	" "	467.00
One receipt "	" "	50.00
Note paid to	B.W. Bradley note &C	5.30
Sterling Walker Admr. Bell notes &C		4.76

W.H. Stuart Receipt as Stayor of Jesse Durham	58.50
Notegiven at T.W. Harris Sale	36.47
Note to Harris Williams & Interest	82.87
Note to Harris Williams & Interest	11.56
Note given at sale	52.45
Acct paid H.E. Hyde	1.30
T.W. Harris ac	9.62
B.W. Bradley	22.52
	$1929.57

Amount due from Estate	$ 2129.10
Amt. received	1929.57
Bal due	199.53

(p 356) WILLIAM L. HUDGENS

	Dr.
Receipt for	70.00
Receipt for	50.00
Receipt for	58.03
Receipt for	150.00
Receipt for	10.00
Amount paid James Mallory	112.00
Hiram Cochran note & Interest	25.00
Hiram Cochran note & interest	10.16
Receipt for	100.00
Order to Thomas Hudgens	7.20
Receipt for	955.75
Wm. W. Williams order	11.95
A.J. Brights Receipt for	12.55
Harris Williamw note & nterest	33.25
Harris Williams note & Interest	57.65
John Z. Hudgens note	14.70
James S. Hudgens	18.78
Order to W.H. Stuart	38.30
John D. Dismukes note	19.95
A.E. Sowell	42.40
	$1868.63

Amount due W.L. Hudgins	$2129.10
Amount paid	1868 .63
Balance due	260.47

James Hudgins	Dr.	
To note given at Sale		36.95
To note given at sale		256.00
Receipt for		650.00
Receipt for		125.00
Receipt for		50.00
Receipt for		180.00
Cash paid A.J. Brights Clerk		$1509.00
		$1306.95

Amount due James Hudgens	2129.10
Amount paid	1306.95
Balance due	822.15

(p 357) POLLY T. HUDGENS

To cash paid A.J. Bright	9.00
One note for	948.00

Note given at sale	181.00
Note given at sale	186.58
Note given at sale	126.05
Total Amt paid Polly T. Hudgens	$1450.63
Amt. due Polly T. Hudgens	2129.00
Amount paid	1450.00
Balance Due	678.47

WILL OF THOMAS BELL SR. Dec.

In the name of God Amen. I, Thomas Bell Sr. Dec of the County of Cheatham State of Tennessee being of sound mind and memory but under much bodily affliction and knowing it is appointed for all to die, but the hour of dessolution unknown and desiring to make such disposition of the worldly effects as it has been my fortune to be possessed of as will be satisfactory to my own mind and feelings and hoping the same will be satisfactory to my children and their successors. do ordain, make and execute the following as my last will and Testament, To wit.

Item 1st.

1 give and bequeath to my beloved wife Sarah Bell onetract of land, To wit. Beginning at an Ash tree, near the mouth of my lane in the big road leading from L.J. Perdues to Hoopers Shop running from said ash tree due north to the branch, thence up said branch with my line to the beginning so as to include my residence -----. To have and to hold the same during her natural life, at her death said land is to be sold and the proceeds thereof is to be equally divided between my children.

Item 2nd

1 give and bequeath to my beloved wife one horse of medium value, also one saddle and bridle, one cow and calf, one bedstead and furniture, one set knives and forks, one set of plates amd other tableware in proportion and all necessary cooking utensils, also I wish myexecutor to set apart and furnish my said wife with one years provisions to consist of all usual and suitable articles. Such as she is accustomed to, also one Sow and pigs. It is also my will and desire that my said wife is not to bid for any of theproperty at my sale.

Item 3rd

L give and bequeath to my daughter, Martha Smith the eighty acres of land on which she now lives, also onehundred dollars in money so as to make the above mentioned tract of land equal to one hundred acres to have and to hold her and her lawful heirs.

(p 358)

Item 4th

I give and bequeath to my daughter Rebecca Hooper one hundred acres of land on which she now lives to have and to hold her and her lawful heirs.

Item 5th

I give and bequeath to my daughter Mary Hunter one hundred acres of land, said land beginning at L.J. Perdues line and runing so as to include one hundred acres including the residence in which she now lives, to have and to hold her and her lawful heirs.

Item 6th

I give and bequeath to my daughter Sintha Gupton one hundred acres of land on which she now lives to have and to hold her and her lawful heirs.

Item 7th L give and bequeath to my son Thomas Bell one hundred acres of land on which he now lives to have and to hold, him and his heirs.

Item 8th

It is my will and desire that none of my improvements on the several tracts of land that I have given and bequeathed to my children shall be valued in case the ;lands have to be valued.

Item 9th

It is my WILL and desire the ballance of my lands togeather with all my perishable property except what was before mentioned for my wife is to be sold at my death and the proceeds to be equally divided between my children. Item 10th It is further my will and desire that my son Thos. Bell execute and carry out this my Will. Given under my hand this the 17th day of April in the year of out Lord One thousand eight hundred and sixty eight.
Signed ansd acknowledged in the presents of L.J. Perdue, T.W. Perdue
Thomas Bell(x his mark)

WILL OF BENJAMIN ELLIOTT
I, Benjamin Elliott of the County of Cheatham State of Tennessee do make and publish this my last Will and Testament hereby revoking all former wills by me at any time made.
Ist.
I direct that my funeral and burial expenses and all just debts be paid as soon after my death as practicable out of any monies that may come into the hands of my Executor.
2nd.
I give to my daughter Melissa Elliott, grand daughter Elizabeth Hamlett six hundred acres of land it being the tract I now live on. it was granted to John Nichols by the State of North Carolina to be held firmly by said Melissa Elliott and Elizabeth Hamlett forever.
3rd.
All my perishable property. Horses mules and stock of all descriptions, farming utensils Household and kitchen furniture. I will and bequeath to my daughter Melissa Elliott and grand daughter Elizabeth Hamlett to be held firmly by them.
(359)
4th.
I give to my grandchildren; Sally Dame, William Elliott, Robert Elliott, Susan Harris and David Elliott children of my son Thomas Elliott Dec. the tract of land that said Thomas Elliott lived on at his death. Beginning on a double white oak the beginning corner of a grant granted to James Lanier to have and to hold forever after it is equally divided between said children but the diviwion not to take place until the youngest child is twenty one year of age.
5th
I give and bequeath to my son David Elliott Ten dollars in cash.
6th.
All my other property that I May possess that is not willed off by the foregoing articles it is my will that it may be sold, that five hundred dollars of the proceeds be given to my daughter Susan Pennington, the balance to go to my daughter, Melissa Elliott and grand daughter Elizabeth Hamlett jointly to be theirs.
7th.
I do nominate and appoint my friends Alva D. Cage and James E. Cage Executors to this my last Will and Testament.
Benjamin Elliott(x his mark)
Test
J.B. Reeks
Wm. Manneraring.
WILL OF MAZY, TUCKER DEC.
In view of my approaching death I hereby give, Will and bequeath at my death every and all of interest in and to the tract of land on which I now live, lying in Cheatham County, Tennessee Dist. No. 4 togeather with all my personal and real property and effects or any interest I may have in any property or effects both personal and real to my beloved Sisters Mary N. Tucker, Sarah Tucker and Jane Tucker to have and to hold the same and dispose of as

they may think proper/ In testimony whereof I hereunto set my hand this Dec. the 29th 1861.

Mazy Tucker.

Attest
John D. Tucker
A.D. Cage

Inventory and acct. of sale of the personal effects of H.A. White Dec. sold by Z. Payne Admr. on the 31st day of January 1867

3000 ft. of lumber	J.F. Conklin	44.73
1 dump cart	Thomas M. Dunn	16.00
1 Two horse wagon	J.F. Conklin	82.00
3 oxens	J.F. Conklin	90.00
2 log chains	J.F. Conklin	4.00
1 engine and shaving machine	J.F. Conklin	250.00
		486.73

I, Zackriah Payne do hereby certify that the following is a true and perfect inventory of all the effects both real and personal which have come to my hands as Admr. of H.A. White Dec. (p 360) to wit.
one half interest in a steam engine and shaving machine, one two horse wagon and harness, one dump cart, three oxens, two log chains, 3000 ft of mixed lumber, one acct. against J.F. Conklin $126, Good and further I say not.

This 30 day of Jan. 1867
Z. Payne Admr.

Sworn to and suscribed to, before me April 1st 1867
G.W. McQuary, Clk.

A list of the effects belonging to the estate of Benjamin Elliott Dec. now in our hands, April 1st 1867, notes supposed to be good.

1 note on J.S. Williams ans F.P. Pennington due Jan. 3rd 1866	$157.00
1 note on E.M. Nolen due Dec. 25, 1860 for	25.00
1 note on H. Reeks Dec and George Head with John Farmer assigned due Aug. 26th 1865 for	13.65
1 note on John A. Farmer due 8th Dec. 1864 for	67.92
1 note on Wm. H. Farmer and W.W. Winters with John A Farmer assigned due Feb. 19, 1858 for	60.70
1 note on M.E. Pennington and F.P. Pennington due Jan. 2nd 1860	75.00

Notes supposed to be doubtful.

1 note on D.W. Stack & W.T. Dye due Dec. 25th 1863	40.00
1 note on D.W. Stack due Dec. 25, 1863 for	18.00
with a cr. for Oct. 25, 1864 of $2.00	
1 note on W.B. Link, J.D. Tucker & F.P. Pennington due Feb. 14,1862	100.00
1 due bill on Logan Grey due June 11th 1863 for	9.77
1 note on Edward Tucker due Jan. 28, 1862 for	5.00
1 note on Edward Tucker due 13th -- 1859 for	51.00
1 note on W.J. Gray & Joseph Ayley due April 8th 1858 for	100.00
1 note on Sampson Rawson(Rosson) and J.S. Rawson due May 7, 1859	300.00
1 note on T.H. Cage due March 30, 1858 for	25.00
with a credit July the 18th 1859 for	20.00

A list of accounts, receipts and orders that may be collected or may not be.

One receipt for Weatherford and Watson for L.D. Watson dated Feb. 1862 given for 50 flour barrels no price stated but supposed to be $1 per bbl. $50.00

One receipt on Weatherford & Watson for 67 flour barrels at 1.00 per bbl. dated Dec. 18, 1861 for 67.00

One receipt on G.A. Woodson for $128.70 given for acrop of tobacco dated June 25th 1856 128.70 128.70

One receipt on G.W. McQuary County Court Clerk for a note against Hartwell Reeks for twenty dollars due June 15th 1858 filed for proratlx distribution March 4th 1867 20.00

(p 361)

WE certify that the foregoing is a true list of the effects that have come into our hands belonging to the estate of Benjamin Elliott Dec. all of which is respectfully submitted.

William A. Shaw)
James E. Cage) Exrs.

Sworn to before me April 1st 1867
G.W. McQuary Clerk.

Account of Sale made C.J. Gupton admr. of Mrs. M.H. Gupton Dec. Nov. the 17th A.D. 1866.

Stove, sideboard, cupboard	Mrs. C.J. Gupton	2 0.00
1 bed Walnut stad	Mrs. C.J. Gupton	10.00
1 small bed	A.J. Harrison	5.00
1 Bed Stead	Wilie Woodall	200
1 small stead	John Duke	.25
1 Book case	Dr. A.J. Gupton	10.00
1 bed in perlor	Mrs. C.J. Gupton	8.00
1 bed in dining room	Mrs. C.J. Gupton	8.00
1 locking glass	Mrs. C.J. Gupton	1.25
1 bed and stead	Mrs. C.J. Gupton	12.00
1 Bureau	Mrs. C.J. Gupton	8.00
1 small table	Dr. A.J. Gupton	3.00
1 bed stead upstairs	John Duke	.25
1 bed and furniture	H. Felts	1.00
1 lot pictures	John H. Adkind	1.00
1 lot hames &C	John H. Adkins	1.00
1 Trunk	John Duke	.50
1 lot sachels &C	John H. Adkins	.25
1 large jar &C	JOHN Adkins	1.10
1 lot saws &C	Moses Woodall	.50
1 lot jugs &C	Thos. Adkins	.35
1 box Irons &C	H. Felts	.70
1 Lot Baskets &C	John Duke	3.00
1 womans saddle	Thos. Adkins	3.00
1 slate &C	Jo Shiwa Majors	.10
1 small case & Books	John Adkins	1.00
1 set harness & Sleighs	Mrs. C.J. Gupton	.75
1 Gigg	John Mosely	.25
1 cultivator	G.J. Nicholson	1.25
1 cultivator	G. Mallory	1.00
1 set cart wheels	Moses Woodall	3.50
1 waggon		10.00
1 lot raw hides	Nat Sanders	4.00
1 male, Pat by name	A.J. Harrison	131.00
1 male, Beck.	D. Adkins	102.00
1 male Tobe		124.00
(p 362)		
1 RED COW	Mrs. C.J. Gupton	12.00
1 black Heifer	J.D. Hooper	12.00
1 white heifer	A.J. Harrison	13.00
1 calf	Robert Weakley	5.00
1 bed stead	Willie Woodall	1.00

1 lamp	H. Felts	.20
1 lot chairs	Mrs. C.J. Gupton	2.00
1 small table	C.G. Perdue	.50
1 apple mill	Mr. C.J. Gupton	3.00
1 spotted cow, 3 pigs	Moses Woodall	6.20
1 black sow and pigs	Mrs C.J. Gupton	7.00
Mill rent for 1866 & 1867	Mrs. C.J. Gupton	50.00
Mill rent " " "	A.J. Harrison	50.00
1 Buggy	Moses Woodall	15.00

The foregoing is a true and perfect Inventory of all the goods and chattels rights and credits that have come into my hands possession or know ledge as admr. of M.H. Gupton Dec. this Jan. 8th 1867

C.J. Gupton, Admr.

NANCY H. SHEARON WILL.
State of Tennessee)
Cheatham County)

Know all men by these presents that I Nancy Shearon being of sound and disposing and memory and considering the unvertainity of this mortal life do make and declare this my last W ll and Testament in manner and form following. I give and bequeath and desire to my Dear Husband Wyatt Shearon all of the amount coming to me from my Father Thomas Miles E tate both real and personal wherever found or whatever it may be to have and to hold to him the said Wyatt Shearon to his sole and separate use for during his natural life I hereby constitute and appoint my brother William H. Miles executor of this my last will and testament.
Witness my hand and seal this the 26th day of May 1866

Nancy H. Shearon(x her mark)

Signed sealed and delivered and published by Nancy H. Shearon as her last will and testament in the presence of us the suscribing Witnesses who suscribed our names hereto in the presence of the said Testator and in the presence of each other, this May the 26th 1866

F.S. Evans
E.S. Read

(p 363) Inventory of the Estate of R.T. GUPTON DECD.

List of Notes

1 note on A. Carris due 2nd of March 1860 for	$ 35.00
1 note on E. Long due 8th Dec. 1846 for	40.00
1 note on J.T. Batts and G.W. McCarley due 25th Dec. --------	2.50
1 note on Logan Gray due Christmas 1851 for	4.15
1 note on R.T. Mallory due 29th March 1864 for	9.21
1 note on Abner Hunter due 30th Nov. 1858 for	10.00
1 note on John C. Haledue 21st Oct. 1859	17.00
1 note on Joshia Watson (Walton) due 10th Dec. 1840	40.00
1 note on James & Wm. Knox due 2nd April 1842 for	4.00
1 noteon L. Tarpley due 1st Jan. 1852 for	75.00
Credited 4th Oct. 1852 by Bal. $41.00	34.00

List of Constables receipts

Receipt of Thomas M. Duff dated 1st July 1858
To R.T. Gupton for one note on W.D. Moss due 1st Jan. 1857 for $130.00
Also on same const. & note ansd same man for $100.00 due 25th Dec. 1859
100.00
Receipt of A.D. Cochran dated 4th Nov. 1855 for one noteon
Thomas Woodson due July 4th 1835 for 26.00

List of Accounts and Amounts.

1 acc. on L.J. Perdue for sundry articles 1865 for 20.00
1 acc. on R.H. Mallory for 1864 for Sundry articles for 22.50
List of property lot lumber.

State of Tennessee)
Cheatham County)

Personally appeared before me G.W. McQuary Clerk of the County Court of said County J.J. Lenox admr. of R.T. Gupton dec. and made oath in due form of law that the above contains a true and perfect Inventory of the personal estate that has come into my hands as administrator of R.T. Gupton dec. up to this date May 1st 1867

J.J. Lenox admr.

Sworn to before me May 1st 1867

G.W. McQuary Clk.

(p 364) An inventory of the personal property of NANCY HARRIS decd. sold on the 13th day of March 1867.

Avery Plow no 8	Z.F. Shearon	$5.25
Shovell plow	Thomas Bell	.25
Log chain	Thomas Bell	2.24
1 Tea Kettle	Z.F. Shearon	.25
1 lot trumpery	J.D. Tucker	.10
1 Oven	Burges Harris	.25
1 squair table	Burgess Harris	.25
1 cook stove	Z.F. Shearon	3.00
1 alarge kettle	Burges Harris	3.25
1 scythe and cradle	J.D. Tucker	.80
1 Pail	J.D. Tucker	.10
3 1st choice Shoats	W.H. Stuart	10.00
3 2nd choice shoats	J.D. Tucker	7.00
4 3rd choice shaots	Thos. Bell	8.00
1 sow and seven pigs	W.H. Stuart	8.00
1 sow and six pigs	Z.F. Shearon	7.90
1 stackoats @ 1½ p bundle	Joseph Shearon	8.40
1 stack oats @ 146 per hd.	Joseph Shearon	6.30
1 red cow and calf	William Harris	18.00
1 white cow J.D. Tucker		18.50
1 black yearling	W.H. Stuart	10.00
1 bead stead	William Harris	2.00
1 folding table	Z.F. Shearon	6.00
1 lot tableware	Sarah Harris	1.00
1 dish	Thomas Bell	1.25
1 sugar bole	Thomas Bell	.60
6 plates	Z.F. Shearon	.40
cups and saucers	Ben Wilson	.25
1 lot of tableware	Z.F. Shearon	1.00
1 lot ware	Thomas Bell	.50
Cruets &C	Z.F. Shearon	.40
1 pitcher	J.D. Tucker	.70
1 set silver spoons	Z.F. Shearon	4.25
1 set knives and forks	J.D. Tucker	1.50
5 set knives and forks	Wash Smith	.65
1 coffee mill	Thos. Bell	1.15
1 jar and salt stand	Thos. Bell	.10
1 Beaureau	Burgess Harris	13.00
1 looking glass	Wash Smith	1.60
1 sugar chest	Thos. Bell	4.00

1 chest½	Sarah Harris	6.00
6 chairs	D.C. Perdue	3.00
6 chairs	Burgess Harris	2.75
(p 365)		
%) 50 lbs. bacon @ 12 7/8	J.D. Tucker	6.43
1 lot salt	Thos. Bell	2.00
1 small pot	J.D. Tucker	.25
1 basket	Burges Harris	.25
20 lbs lard @ 10c	Burges Harris	2.00
1 coffee pot	J.D. Tucker	.25
1 ten bucket	Z.F. Shearon	.25
1 dish pan	Z.F. Shearon	.40
1 straner	Z.F. Shearon	.25
1 Jair	J.D. Tucker	.45
1 clock	David Vanhook	3.00
1 cupboard	Thos. Bell	1.00
1 loom and gear	Sarah Harris	.50
1 wheel and cards	Sarah Harris	1.50
1 Reel	J.D. Tucker	.30
1 chest	Thos. Bell	.25
1 bead stead	Burgess Harris	.25
1 bed stead	Thos. Harris	.25
1 Trunnel bead stead	John Harris	.10
1 water bucket	Thos. Bell	.25
1 bread tray	Burgess Harris	.15
1 sifter	Burgess Harris	.10
1 lard stand	Burgess Harris	2.00
1 Fire S h ovell	Thos. Bell	.25
1 par fire tongs	Thos. Harris	.50
1 pr traces & Hemes	Burgess Harris	
4 sheep by the head 1.30	Burges Harris	5.20
Irish potatoes	Thos. Bell	
1 shovell	G.H. Shearon	.25
1 weed hoe	G.H. Shearon	.25
1 cutting knife	Burgess Harris	.50
Rent of the land	John D. Tucker	81.00

I, G.W. Harris do hereby certify this is a true and correct inventory of all the effects that come into my hands of Nancy Harris Dec. this 6th day of May 1867
G.W. Harris, Admr.
Sworn to before me May 6th 1867
G.W. McQuary Clk.

(p 366) An I n ventory of the perishable property of T h os. Bell Dec. Sold on the 15th March 1867.

Articles	Names	Amt.
1 basket trumpery	W.B. Hooper	.15
1 Basket trumpery	J.D. Tucker	.10
Hames	L.J. Perdue	.30
1 lot iron	J.D. Tucker	.45
Gait hinges	J.W. Gupton	1.10
1 auger and draw knife	J.W. Smith	.60
1 pr. steel yards	J.D. Tucker	.75
1 pr. steel yards, large	M.M. Chqbliss	2.25
2 Demmey Johns	John Shivers	.30
1 half bushel	J.W. Gupton	.35
1 basket and keg	J.W. Gupton	.35

2 iron wedges	George M. Perdue	1.30
1 keg and contents	J.D. Tucker	.25
1 lot onions	G.W. Maxey	.95
1 jug vinegar	J.W. Gupton	.45
1 box trumpery	T.W. Gupton	.30
1 box trumpery & nails	J.W. Smith	.60
Wool roals by the lb 65cts	T.W. Gupton 3½ lbs	2.27
1 lot barrels	J.D. Tucker	.10
1 lot cotton by the lb.	Sally Bell 05c	
1 lot old axes & frou	L.J. Perdue	.50
1 x saw	Sam Ennis	6.50
1 Reel	Ben Alley	3.50
1 scythe and cradle	Jack Stack	1.00
1 scythe & Cradle	J.W. Gupton	2.50
1 spin wheel	G.W. Harris	.25
1 spin wheel	J.W. Gupton	1.00
1 skillet and lid	J.D. Tucker	.70
Ouben	A.H. Nicholson	.70
1 small pot	Jack Stack	.25
1 skillet	Geo Bell (col)	.40
1 Ouben	Rut Wilson (col)	.40
1 pot	J.W. Gupton	.25
Hooks and tongs	Jack Stack	.60
1 weeding hoe	Widow	1.00
1 lot chains	J.D. Tucker	.35
Plows &C	W.J. Stewart	.80
1 set gear	Widow	3.00
1 set gear	Widow	2.70
1 swingle tree	Sam Jones	.75
Old plows	Sam Jones	1.00
1 log waggon	G.W. Gossett	50.00
1 log chain	James Bobbitt	2.00
(p 367)		
1 double tree	G.M. Perdue	1.00
1 plow	W.B. Hooper	.10
1 lot plows	W.B. Hooper	.10
1 no 8 plow	Widow	8.00
1 no 8 plow	Widow	4.50
1 lot old plows	W.B. Hooper	.10
1 lot old plows	W.B. Hooper	.10
1 Ox Cart	W.B. Hooper	4.10
1 Ox Cart	J.D. Tucker	5.50
1 Ox Cart	J.D. Tucker	55.05
1 ring and steeple	J.D. Tucker	.25
1 culling knife	Widow	3.50
1 culling knife	W.B. Hooper	1.50
4 1st choice sheep	Widow	12.25
4 - 2nd choice sheep	W.A. Eatherly	6.00
1 pided cow	G.M. Perdue	13.00
1 red heifer	Widow	14.00
1 white heifer	L.J. Perdue	12.00
1 sorrel colt	G.W. Gupton	75.00
1 gray mule	Widow	102.00
1 bay colt	Willey Bell	82.00
1 black sow	W.T. Bell	4.00
1 black sow	W.T. Bell	4.00

1 white sow	J.W. Gupton	3.10
5 - 1st choice shoats	Widow	21.00
5 - 2nd choice shaots	J. Gupton	16.25
5 - 3rd choice shoats	J. Gupton	10.00
5 4th choice shoats	J. Gupton	4.10
4 Remainder	J. Gupton	3.00
1 sow outside	J.D. Tucker	2.00
8 shaots	J.W. Tucker	14.00
1 lot boxes & bbls	J.D. Tucker	.75
4 cow hides	W.H. Stuart	5.60
1 saddle	Widow	6.25
5 hhd. bundles oats	David Sanders at 2/34	13.75
5 " " "	Widow @ 2 7/8	14.37½
5 " " "	James Wadkins	12.50
5 " " "	James Wadkins	13.75
1 loom	Widow	1.00
1 fan mill	A.H. Stuart	3.25
Horse Collars	W.H. Gent	.25
1 scalding tub	Bob Stewart	1.00
Boxes and barrels	J.D. Tucker	.25
1 bbl vinegar	J.W. Gupton	2.50
1 bbl. vinegar	J.D. Tucker	2.00
(p 368)		
L BBL. VINEGAR	J.W. Gupton	3.25
1 keg	W.B. Hooper	.25
5 hhd lbs bacon by lb.	Jack Stack @ 14½cts	72.00
5 " " "	J.W. Gupton @ 15	75.00
Remainder		18.00
50 lbs lard by the lb.	E. Harris @ 14¾	6.65
Remainder	J.C. Shivers	7.67
Tin lard stand	Widow	2.00
Salt Tray	J.D. Tucker	.10
1 kettle	W.B. Hooper	.15
1 kettle	Widow	2.00
1 Pail	Widow	.25
1 Piggin	Widow	.25
1 Tub	Widow	.50
1 Table	Mary Hunter	1.20
2 tin buckets	J?C? Shivers	.30
1 cup and strainer	J.C. Shivers	.10
1 Blow horn	JohnnSanders	.40
2 stone jars	Cyntha Gupton	.40
2 stone jars	Mary Hunter	.20
1 stone jar	Mary Hunter	.15
2 stone jars	Widow	.60
1 stone jar	Widow	.80
1 stone jar	Widow	.35
1 churn	J.D. Tucker	.05
1 lot ware	Geo. Bell	.10
1 demmey John	J.D. Tucker	.80
1 " "	J.D. Tucker	1.15
1 keg	J.D. Tucker	.60
1 jug	M.M. Chambliss	.30
1 jug	Widow	.25
1 lot vinegar	Hooper	.25
6 plates and a dish	J.D. Tucker	4.00
1 lot sundries	J.W. Smith	.10
4 plates &C	Rebeca Hooper	1.25

6 plates , 1 cup	Widow	0.25
1 glass	Billy Bell	.10
1 set cups and saucers	Mary Hunter	.15
5 glasses	Mary Hunter	.35
5 plates	Willis Hunter	.25
1 dish &C	J.D. Tucker	.65
1 bottle and contents	J.D. Tucker	.40
candle moles 7 dipper	Willis H nt	.50
Tea pitcher and cream pot	Mary Hunter	.30
1 pitcher	J.D. Tucker	.10
1 mug	Mrs.Hooper	.10
(p 369)		
2 dishes	Cynthia Hooper	.40
per dish		.10
1 lot bottles	V. Stewart	.20
1 pitcher & Pan	Thos. Gupton	.10
1 bowl and dish	Thos. Council	.30
1 dish	G.W. Maxey	.10
1 Tablw	J.D. Tucker	.25
1 cupboard	Widow	2.00
1 gritter	E.T. Harris	.15
1 clock	W. Gent	.50
1 watch	J.D. Tucker	16.50
1 chest	Rob Stuart	4.00
1 cupboard	Widow	2.00
1 chest	W. Gent	.25
1 basket	Widow	.60
1 wash stand &C	Widow	1.50
2 pr cards	Widow	.25
1 trunk	Widow	1.00
1 basket	Widow	.25
1 lot knives and forks	Widow	1.15
1 candle stick	J.D. Tucker	.20
1 Hammer	W. Gent	.10
1 Basket	J.D. Tucker	.90
1 bed and contents	Henry Bell	10.00
1 bed and contents	Widow	41.00
1 Bed and contents	Mrs. Gupton	30.00
1 sugar chest	Mrs. Gupton	8.00
1 gun	Rob Stewart	1.00
1 shot pouch	W.B. Hooper	7.00
1 rifle gun	James Stewart	.25
1 counterpin	V. STewart	.25
1 counterpin	Widow	2.25
1 Bed quilt	Mrs. Hooper	2.25
1 Bed quilt	Widow	1.25
1 bed quilt	Widow	.50
1 bed quilt	Widow	.50
1 bed qilt	Widow	.25
2 butcher knives	Widow	.10
1 night mug	W. Gent	.10
1 night mug	Widow	.50
1 lot books	Widow	.50
1 candle stand	Widow	1.00
1 Bible	Widow	1.00
1 lot books	W. White	.10
1 umbrella	Mary Hooper	.50
(p 370)		
Sleighs	Widow	.25

1 Box	Widow	.25
1 looking glass	W. Gent	.15
1 looking glass	Mrs. Gupton	.75
10 chairs	Widow	3.00
2 chairs	Widow	.25
1 Trunk	Widow	.25
1 Flat Basket	Widow	.25
1 looking glass	J.D. Tucker	/20
1 goad powder	Thos. Council	.40
1 pr.scissots	J.D. Tucker	.10
2 razors and straps	W. White	.55
Buck Shot	E.T. Herron	.25
Ammunition	J.D. Tucker	.30
Ammunition	J.D. Tucker	.30
Brush and Box	W. White	.20
1 Beaureau	Widow	3.00
1 basket and contents	W. White	.55
1 Bottle	W. White	.25
Iron rest	Widow	.05
1 qt. pot &C	W. Gent	.25
1 lot tallow	Widow	.20
10 chickens	Widow	.50
10 chickens	Widow	.55
10 chickens	Mrs. Hooper	1.00
1 skimmer	Widow	.10
Broiling Iron	Tom Knox	.10
Dye kettle	Widow	.50
Ouben	Widow	.50

Alist of notes and apos.

1 note on J.H. Walker for		115.00
1 note on L.J. Perdue		150.00
1 note on	L.J. Perdue	32.00
1 note on L.J. Perdue cr. by	100.00	125.00
1 note on	L.J. Perdue	40.00
1 note on L.J. Perdue		85.00
1 note on	L.J. Perdue	125.00
1 note on	L.J. Perdue	22.00
1 note on G.M. Perdue		150.00
1 note on	L.J. Perdue for	170.00
1 note on	John W. Gupton	22.28
1 note on	Thos. Bell Jr.	35.00
1 note Insolvent G.W. Wilson & D. Cames Decd. (Carnes)		56.35
1 note on J.A. Dodson decd. cr. 43.50		59.36
1 note on Thos. Bell Jr.		8.75
(P 371)		
1 due Bill	W.B. Hooper	23.13
1 note on Abner Gupton		3.07
1 note on Abner Gupton		12.00
1 note on J.T. Hooper		15.00
1 note on L.J. Perdue		100.00
1 note on Robert Weakley		100.00
1 note on	R.T. Gupton decd. cr. 17.00	90.90
1 acct. on	Abner Hunter	1.05
1 " "	Abner Hunter	18.17
1 noteon	J.T. Hooper	16.10
1 note on	John W. Gupton	25.00
1 act. on B.J. Barnes Doubtful		12.00

1 note on	W.H. Stuart	34.15
1 note on	Thos. Bell Sr	90.00
1 noteon T.J. Miles doubtful		50.00
1 note on A.F. Carney		94.00
1 cost receipt	G.E. Harris decd.	31.00
1 apc on Abner Hunter	James W. Smith	22.06
1 " " "	James W. Smith	2.03
1 order from	A.W. Stewart, doubtful	15.00
1 due bill on	H.A. Folks, doubtful	16.15

Amount of money found	
Green backs	531.50
Silver	256.25
State Bank Tennessee	4.00
Gold	5.00
Silver more found	33.00

Second day Sale and renting omited.

1 coffee mill	W. Gent	.15
2 Augers	W.B. Hooper	.60
1 mortar	Martha Knox	.15
1 lot wheet	Mary Hunter 8 bu @ 1.65	13.20
1 lot boards	G.W. Harris	1.00
1 lot boards	G.W. Harris	1.00
1 sugar kegs	W.B. Hooper	.10
1 sugar bowl	G.W. Harris	.05
1 flat iron	Mara Knox	.35
1 flat iron	Mara Knox	.45
1 fly broom	W.B. Hooper	.05
1 coverlid	Mary Hunter	.05
1 sheet	Mary Hunter	.35
1 muskeeter bar	Mary Hooper	.40
2 Baskets	G.W. Harris	.10
1 Field for grain	Widow	100.00
(p 372)		
One field for grain	Widow	5.00
1 field for corn	Widow	13.00
1 Pasteore		5.00
1 bread tray		.45
1 grub Hoe		.05

We, Thomas Bell and J.T. Hooper do hereby certify that this a true and correct inventory of all the effects that come into out hands of the estate of Thos. Bell dec. this 6th day of May 1867.

Thos. Bell
J.T. Hooper

Sworn to before me May the 6th 1867.

G.W. McQuary, Clj.

Settlement of John J. Bradley admr. of J.B. Moore decd.

To amt of sales Sept. 14th 1861	423.71
To amt. notes due Jas. B. Moore decd.	24.85
To amt. act against Smith	.70
To amt. Interest	57.43
To amt. cash paid by Jordan Special Com.	16.00
	522.69

Contra Cr.

By Hawkins for coffin	13.00

By O. Edwards for coffin	.75
By A.J. Bright act	8.80
By W.H. Stuart Receipt	3.00
By J.J. Lenox Receipt	1.00
By A.J. Bright apc for coffdn	7.50
By James A? Shearon apc.	1.00
By B.H. Bradley apc	1.00
By Cynthia Moore	11.20
Tax Receipt for 1861	2.88
Mary Moore Receipt	1.75
To Elizabeth Moore	1.25
To Benj. Moore	2.25
To Julia Moore	2.00
To H.F. White	2.50
To J.J. Bradley	13.80
To A.J. Bright Rect. for cost	262.10
To J.R. Binkley Tax R"ceipt	1.35
To J.J. Lenox File bill to sell land	10.00
To Shaw and Bros. apc	13.92
To Cost Littleton Perry	1.10

(p 373)

Amount Dr. forwarded		522.69
Allowance to Administrator		25.00
Cost for bond recording inventory &C		7.25
To Clerk for settlement 1.25	404.81	1.25
To balance due by admr	117.88	

The above settlement is in both words and figures confirmed by the court May Term 1967.

Settlement of W.G. and Lucy Smith, Exrs. of James H. Smith Dec.
To amt. due the heirs on sale of land $2006.50 $2006.50

Contra Cr.

By allowance to Exr.	61.00
By surveying fees by J.M. Joslin	15.00
By attorneys fees M.M. Brient	25.00
By allowance to heirs to make them equal in furniture	230.00
By Clerk for settlement	1.50
	232.50
Amount due heirs	$1674.00
Amt. due each heir	167.40

The above settlement is in both words and figures confirmed by the court May Term 1867.

Inventory of the personal Estate of WM. Ellison Dec.

One note on hand on Joseph Kreighter for due 24th day of Dec. 1862	227.00
One note on Joseph Kreighter for due 24th December 1863	227.00
Cash Collected on Judge ment from W.W. Hutton	52.50
	506.50

I, James M. Dunn administratorof William Ellison hereby certify that the above five hundred and six dollars and 50 cents is all of the effects that has come into my hands as administrator of Wm. Ellison dec. this June 18th

1867.
Sworn to before me day and date above.
James M. Dunn, Admr.
G.W. McQuary Clerk

(374) JOHN P. PEGRAMS WILL.
I, John P. Pegram do on the 25th April eighteen hundred and sixty seven (1867) being of sound mind and memory do make this my last will& Testament. My will is that my funeral expencis be paid then all just debts that may come against my estate to be paid by my executor.

I will to my wife Pernina Emily Pegram all the land lying South of a line to begin on the River Bank running with the cross fence that divides the Kellum field from the Well field E to R. Pegrams line then with my line South to the beginning. To have and to hold during her life time or widowhood in case she should marry the above mentioned land is to belong to my son, John Jaes Pegram , his life time and at his death to his heirs.

I will to my son John James Pegram a lot of land lying on the North side of the line just mentioned. Beginning at Pernina E. Pegrams corner running up theriver with the second cross fence at the foot of the hill or road then with the road at gate the foor of the hill thence East with the fence on the back of the hill to Rogers Pegrams line thence with Rogers Pegrams line South to Pernina E. Pegrams corner on said line thence with her line to the Beginning to him and his heirss forever.

I will to my son Martin Pegram and Lydia Ann Holt, my daughter a lot of land beginning at James Pegrams corner on R. Pegrams line runnung to the river thence down the River to James Pegrams corner thence with James Pegrams line to the begginning the above mentioned tract of land is to be equally divided between Waslin Pegram and LydiaAnn Holt, thecross fence is to be set on the line running between the two to them and their children forever.

I also give to my son Mastin Pegram the following described tract of land that he now livws on to wit.
Beginning on the North side of Harpeth River below the mouth of Turneys creek thence with the cross fence along the lane between R. Pegrams to Benjamin Woodards line thence west with the lane twell you get against the two oaks that Holt has his bars fastened to on the old lot fence, thence South to Kellums line, thence east to the bluff, thence up the river to the beginning. To have and to hold and his heirs forever.

I also give to my daughter Lydia Holt the land she now lives on, Beginning at Mastin Pegrams corner on Benjamin Woodwards line , thence with said line to Joseph Kellums line to Benjamin Woodwards line, thence with Woodwards line, to the beginning to her and her children forever. I also give to my daughter Elizabeth Walkup all the Barclift tract of land on which she now lives accotding to the Barclift deed to have and to hold as long as she lives and at her death to her children. I also give to my wife Pernina Emily the fout lots of land that I own in the town of Edgefield to have and to hold during her lifetime or widowhood and at her death or marriage to be sold and equally divided between my lawful heirs.

I have also two hundred and seventy (270) acres of land lying on the North (375) side of the N.W. Railroad adjoining the land of Benjamin Woodward, Roger Pegram and others that I want my executor to sell and divide equally between my lawful heirs with the exceptions of one hundred acres that I want run off of the west end of said tract of land that I give to my nephew Wm. James Pegram, son of Thomas Pegram Decd..

I also give to my daughter Walkup, four hundred dollars out of the proceeds of the store that she is now clerking in after the four hundred dollars is paid out of the store to Elizabeth Walkup and invoice is to be taken by my executor and the proceeds of the store to be equally divided between my lawful heirs by my executor, my son James Pegram is to havethe amount of stock, houhehold and kitchen furniture that I have to my older children out of mt estate.

I also give to my wife Pernina Emily Pegram all the stock household and kitchen furniture , all money anddues to the estate and all that belongs to the place where I now live and at her death all os to be sold and equally divided between my lawful heirs. I also appoint my wife Pernina E. Pegram and Mastin Pegram my executors.

John P. Pegram

Test
Mastin Ussery
W.C. Hutton.

Settlement of J.W. Hunt admr. of Jacob Jones Dec. made June 28th 1867.

To amount of Inventory		$249.65
	Contra Cr.	
By Jo Sparks	Attorneys fee	10.00
By J.W. Harris	proven acct	1.41
By H.J. Shaw	proven medical acct.	7.45
By Thomas Gupton	proven acct.	7.80
By E.N. Gupton	proven acct.	20.00
By T.H. Tractions	proven acct.	3.20
By Tax receipt for 1866		2.70
By James Jones	note	73.28
paid James Jones wife and Judah Majors		18.00
By John W. Hunt	proven acct.	25.59
By John W. Hunt	note	52.08
By Amount allowed administrator		12.48
By amount paid clerk for letters of adm.		3.00
By amt. to clerk for settlement		.75
		237.74
Amount due the heirs		11.91

The above settlement is in both words and figures confirmed by the court.

(p 376) A list of the property sold belonging to the estate of J.B. Felts Dec. June 21st 1867.

Names of purchasers	Articles sold	Amt.
William Ramer	one lot old plows	.25
William Ramer	One pr cart hubs	1.60
William Ramer	1 fan mill	.60
William Ramer	6 barrels old	.50
Widow Felts	One tub	.10
Widow Felts	3 half bushels	.10
Widow Felts	Grindstone	.12½
T.W. Morris	1 lot plows, harness etc.	.50
Widow Felts	1 lot barrels	.60
William Ramer	1 lot iron	.10
Widow Felts	1 shovel plow &C	.20
Widow Felts	3 Hoes	.10
Widow Felts	1 lot axes	.10
William Ramer	L board froe	.20
Widow Felts	1 bell	.30
William Ramer	1 bell	.15
Widow Felts	1 auger & Knife	.10
Widow Felts	1 saw and chisel	.10
Widow Felts	1 adz and jointer	.10
Mrs. Ramer	1 patrage net	.15
William Ramer	1 pr saddle bags	.10

William Ramer	1 lot shoe tools	.25
A.H. Felts	1 spinning wheel & Cards	1.30
Widow Felts	3 pr cards	.10
Widow Felts	1 safe and contents	1.50
Widow Bob Felts	1 jug	.25
Widow Felts	1 jug	.10
Widow Felts	1 jar	.10
Widow Felts	1 pr of --	.40
Widow Felts	1 trunk	.25
Widow Felts	1 chest	.50
Mrs. Ramer	1 lot pf 5 chairs	.50
Widow Felts	1 clock case	.20
Widow Felts	1 small table	.20
Widow Felts	1 lot books	.10
Widow Felts	1 lot books	.05
Mrs. Ramer	1 bed stead & Cord	1.60
Widow Felts	1 Desk	.50
Widow Felts	1 desk	.50
Widow Felts	1 bureau	5.00
Widow Felts	1 clock	1.00
Widow Felts	1 candle stand	.25
Widow Felts	1 bed stead and cord	.25
Widow Felts	1 bed stead and cord	.25
(p 377)		
Widow Felts	1 Table	.50
Widow Felts	1 flax wheel & Hackle	.25
Mrs. Carney	1 candlestick	.20
Widow Felts	1 candlestick	.05
Wm. Ramer	1 cross cut saw	4.50
Widow Felts	1 Table	.25
Widow Felts	1 lot tinware	.05
Widow Felts	1 churn &C	.10
Widow Felts	1 dye pot	.25
Widow Felts	1 Oven	.10
Widow Felts	1 skillet pot &C	.10
A.H. Felts	1st lot sheep 2 heads	3.00
Mrs. Ramer	2nd lot sheep 2 head	3.50
Mrs. Casey	4 head hogs	8.50
J.L. Felts	1 heifer yearling	7.00
William Ramer	100 ft. lumber	1.15
William Ramer	1 lot wheat gums	.15
		50.32

A list of notes and receipts and accounts Dec. 23rd 1829	
Receipt H.P. Felts & W.W. Felts	110.00
Jan. 15, 1845 on W.W. Felts	19.55
Receipt on W.W. Felts 1846	.50
Note on W.W. Felts July 2nd 1842	94.12
Receipt on State of Tenn. 1860	20.00
Acct on H. Dowlen Feb. & March 1858	1.65
Acct. on H. Dowlen	3.65
Acct. on W.W. Felts 1843	3.25
Acct on W. Bennett 1843	.75
Acct on W.W. Felts 1842	2.25
Acct. on W.E. Felts 1847	3.02½
Acct. J0hn Dowlen 1839-40-41	3.93
Acct. on W.W. Felts 1841	23.75
Acct. on John Dowlen 1836-37-38	
Adct. on W.W. Felts 1840	21.37
Acct. on W. Bennett 1864	9.50

Cash in hand in Greenbacks 1.10
Cash in hand South Carolina 1.00

I return these claims as being doubtful wether I Can collect them or not, June the 30th 1867.

The above is a true and perfect Inventory od sale of the personal effects belong to the estate of J.B. Felts Dec. Sold by C.R. Felts admr. on the 21st day of June 1867.
C.R. Felts & admr.
G.W. McQuary Clk.

(p 378) Inventory of all the personal estate that has come into my hands as Executor of John Walker decd.

1 note on Isaac Eatherly due 2nd April 1860	200.00
Credit $15.18 June 10th 1861,for48.80 Feb. 2nd 1864	48.80
1 note on Henry H nter due 20th Feb. 1862 for	186.00
Cr. $10 July 12th"1862 also cr. 10th Oct. 1863 for	170.00
1 note on G.W. Harris and N. Harris due 25th Dec. 1859	60.00
Cr. $80.23c Nov. 1861 Cr. $10 with no date Cr. 31.05 Feb25th 1862	
1 note on J. Teasley due the 1st Nov. 1860	5.00
1 note on Uriah Murff & R.J. Mallory due 24th Dec. 1859 for	50.00
Cr. 25.00 26th March 1863	
1 note on Josueva Walker due 26th March 1862 for	25.00
due Jan 1st 1865 for	20.00
1 note on Josueva H.A. Pool andJ.T. Batts due 17th Sept. 1865 for	10.00
Paid in repairs	
1 note on Moarning Stewart due 1st Jan. 1863 for	24.00
1 note on J.T. Batts & G.W. Williams due 1st Jan. 1866 for	43.15
1 note on S.P. Knox due 1st Jan. 1864 for	35.00
1 note on Eliza Prichett and Gid Nicholson due 17th Feb. 1865 for	21.00
1 note on John Perdue & D. Council due 17th Sept. 1865 for	71.50
1 note on T.W. Williams & D Council due 17th Se pt. 1865	110.75
Collected	60.80
1 note on James Nicholson E.G. Williams for	699.00
1 note on Thomas Pool, J.T. Batts, Wm. Pool J.W. Webber and James Hunt	236.00

The above is a true and correct account or statement of all the effects of John Walker Dec. that have come into my hands this Sept. 28th 1865.
Henry Hunter Executor

Sworn to before me 6th Nov. 1865.
Warren Jordan Clk.

An Inventory of the Real Estate belonging to the Estate of John Walker dec.

One tract of land of 106 acres soldf for $6 per acre	636.00
One tract of 174 acres sold for $4 per acre	699.00
	1335.00

State of Tennessee
Cheatham County

Personall appeared before me Henry Hunter Executor of John Walker Dec. and made oath in due form of law that the above is a true and perfect inventory of the real estate belonging to the estate of John Walker decd.
Henry Hunter Executor
Sworn to and suscribed to before me this 3rd Oct. 1866.
G.W. McQuary ClK.

www.ingramcontent.com/pod-product-compliance
Lightning Source LLC
Chambersburg PA
CBHW081430270326
41932CB00019B/3146

* 9 7 8 0 7 8 8 4 9 0 6 9 9 *